I'm sometimes asked, "Who's your favorite *Dragon Ball* character?" It'd probably be more interesting if I said someone like Oolong or Pilaf, but I can't lie to myself. My true favorite character is, of course, Son Goku!!

—**Toyotarou, 2016**

Toyotarou

Toyotarou created the manga adaptation for the *Dragon Ball Z* anime's 2015 film, *Dragon Ball Z: Resurrection F*. He is also the author of the spin-off series *Dragon Ball Heroes: Victory Mission*, which debuted in *V-Jump* in Japan in November 2012.

Akira Toriyama

Renowned worldwide for his playful, innovative storytelling and humorous, distinctive art style, Akira Toriyama burst onto the manga scene in 1980 with the wildly popular *Dr. Slump*. His hit series *Dragon Ball* (published in the U.S. as *Dragon Ball* and *Dragon Ball Z*) ran from 1984 to 1995 in Shueisha's *Weekly Shonen Jump* magazine. He is also known for his design work on video games such as *Dragon Quest*, *Chrono Trigger*, *Tobal No. 1* and *Blue Dragon*. His recent manga works include *COWA!*, *Kajika*, *Sand Land*, *Neko Majin*, *Jaco the Galactic Patrolman* and a children's book, *Toccio the Angel*. He lives with his family in Japan.

SHONEN JUMP Manga Edition

STORY BY **Akira Toriyama**
ART BY **Toyotarou**

TRANSLATION **Toshikazu Aizawa**
TOUCH-UP ART & LETTERING **Paolo Gattone and Chiara Antonelli**
DESIGN **Shawn Carrico**
EDITOR **Marlene First**

DRAGON BALL SUPER © 2015 BY BIRD STUDIO, Toyotarou
All rights reserved. First published in Japan in 2015 by SHUEISHA Inc., Tokyo.
English translation rights arranged by SHUEISHA Inc.

Printed in the U.S.A.

Published by VIZ Media, LLC
P.O. Box 77010
San Francisco, CA 94107

10 9 8 7 6 5 4 3
First printing, December 2017
Third printing, August 2019

viz.com

shonenjump.com

PARENTAL ADVISORY
DRAGON BALL SUPER is rated T for Teen
and is recommended for ages 13 and up.
This volume contains fantasy violence.

SHONEN JUMP MANGA

DRAGON BALL SUPER

THE WINNING UNIVERSE IS DECIDED!

STORY BY **Akira Toriyama**

ART BY **Toyotarou**

2

CAST OF CHARACTERS

UNIVERSE 7

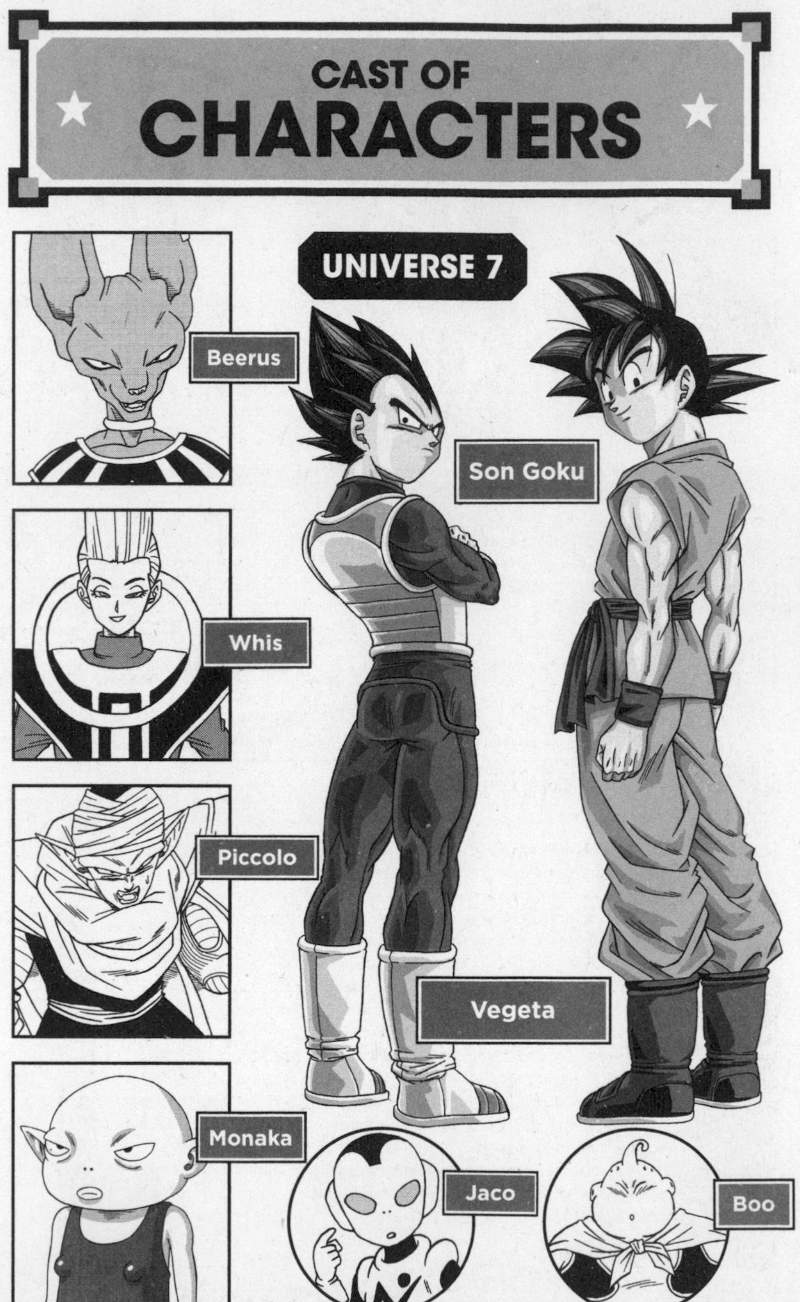
Beerus
Son Goku
Whis
Piccolo
Vegeta
Monaka
Jaco
Boo

UNIVERSE 6

Hit

Vados

Champa

Frost

Cabbe

Otta Magetta

STORY THUS FAR

A long, long time ago, Son Goku left on a journey in search of the legendary Dragon Balls—a set of seven balls that, when gathered, would summon the dragon Shenlong to grant any wish. After a great adventure, he collects them all. Later, he becomes the apprentice of Kame-Sen'nin, fights a number of vicious enemies, defeats the great Majin Boo and restores peace on Earth. Some time passes, and then Lord Beerus, the God of Destruction, suddenly awakens and sets out in search of the Super Saiyan God. Goku, by becoming that Super Saiyan God, manages to stop Beerus from destroying the Earth and starts training under him with Vegeta. One day, Champa, the God of Destruction from Universe 6, shows up and challenges Universe 7 to a match to gain control of the Earth and its food—whoever wins will get the Super Dragon Balls to make their wish come true! Goku wins his first match, but his next opponent is a man who is identical to Freeza, named Frost. He seems gentle enough, but how much is he really capable of?

DRAGON BALL SUPER 2

CONTENTS

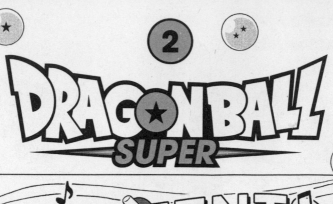

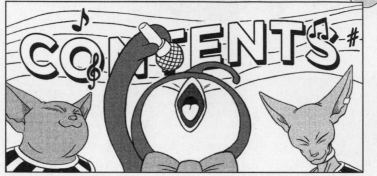

DRAGON BALL SUPER

CHAPTER 10: FROST'S TRUE FORM

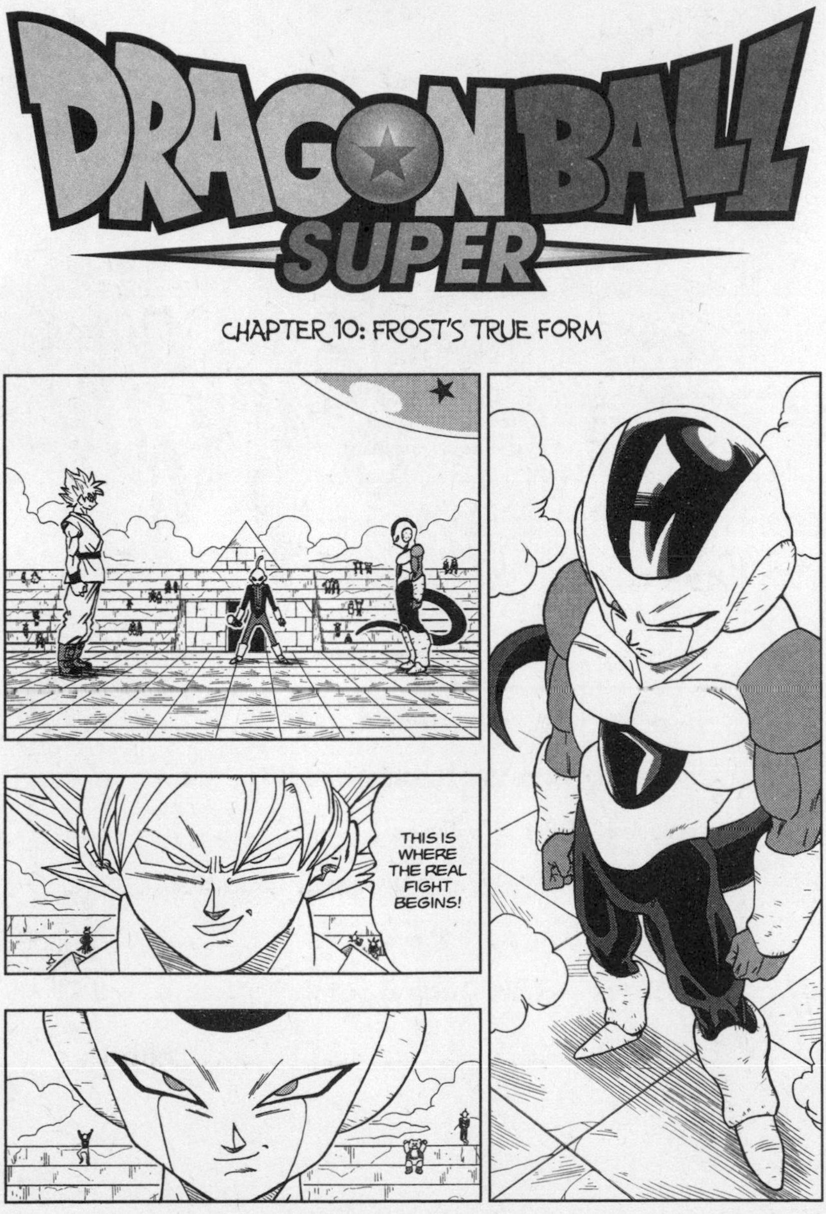
THIS IS WHERE THE REAL FIGHT BEGINS!

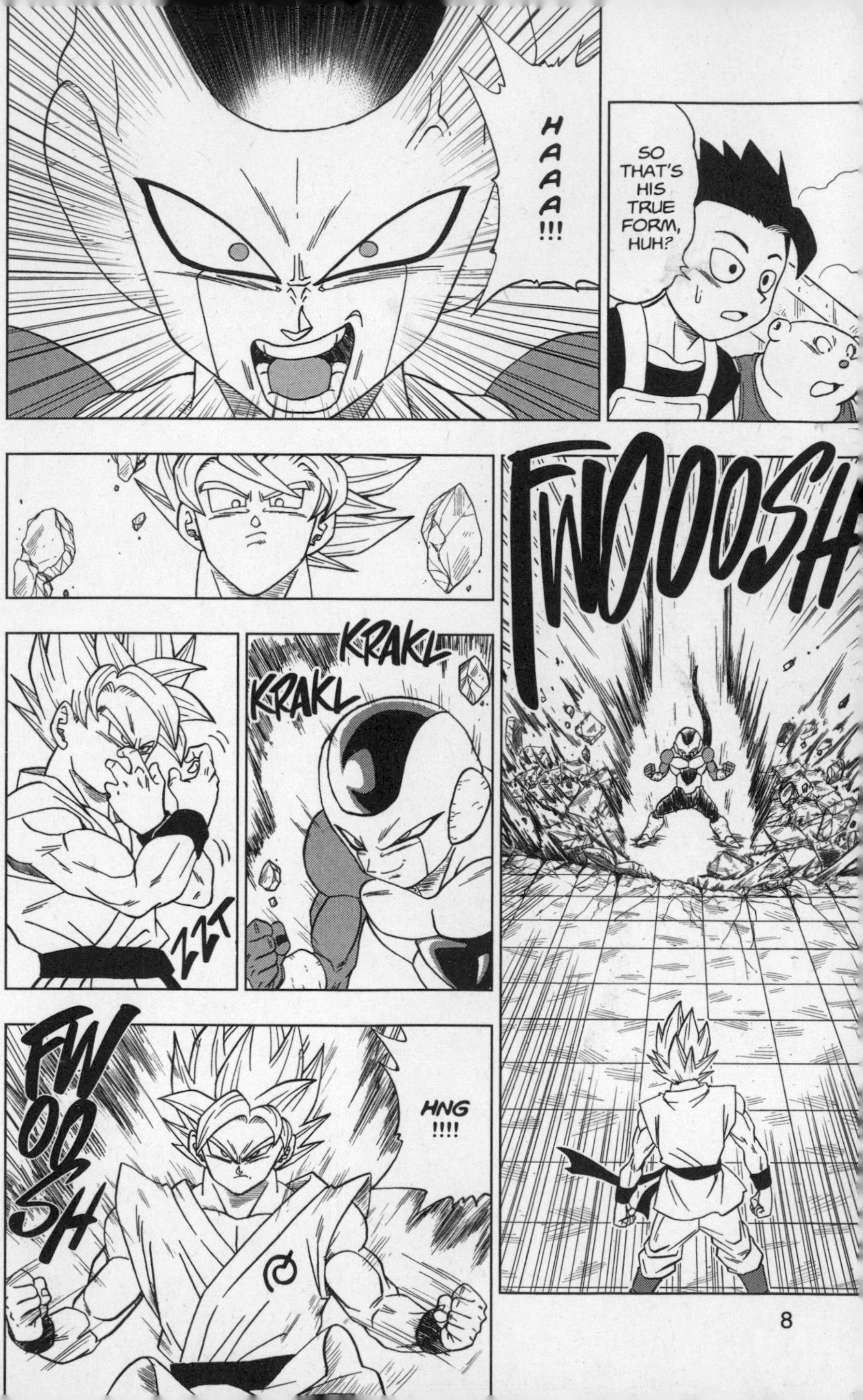
SO THAT'S HIS TRUE FORM, HUH?
HAAAA!!!
FWOOOSH
KRAKL
KRAKL
ZZZT
HNG!!!!
FWOOSH

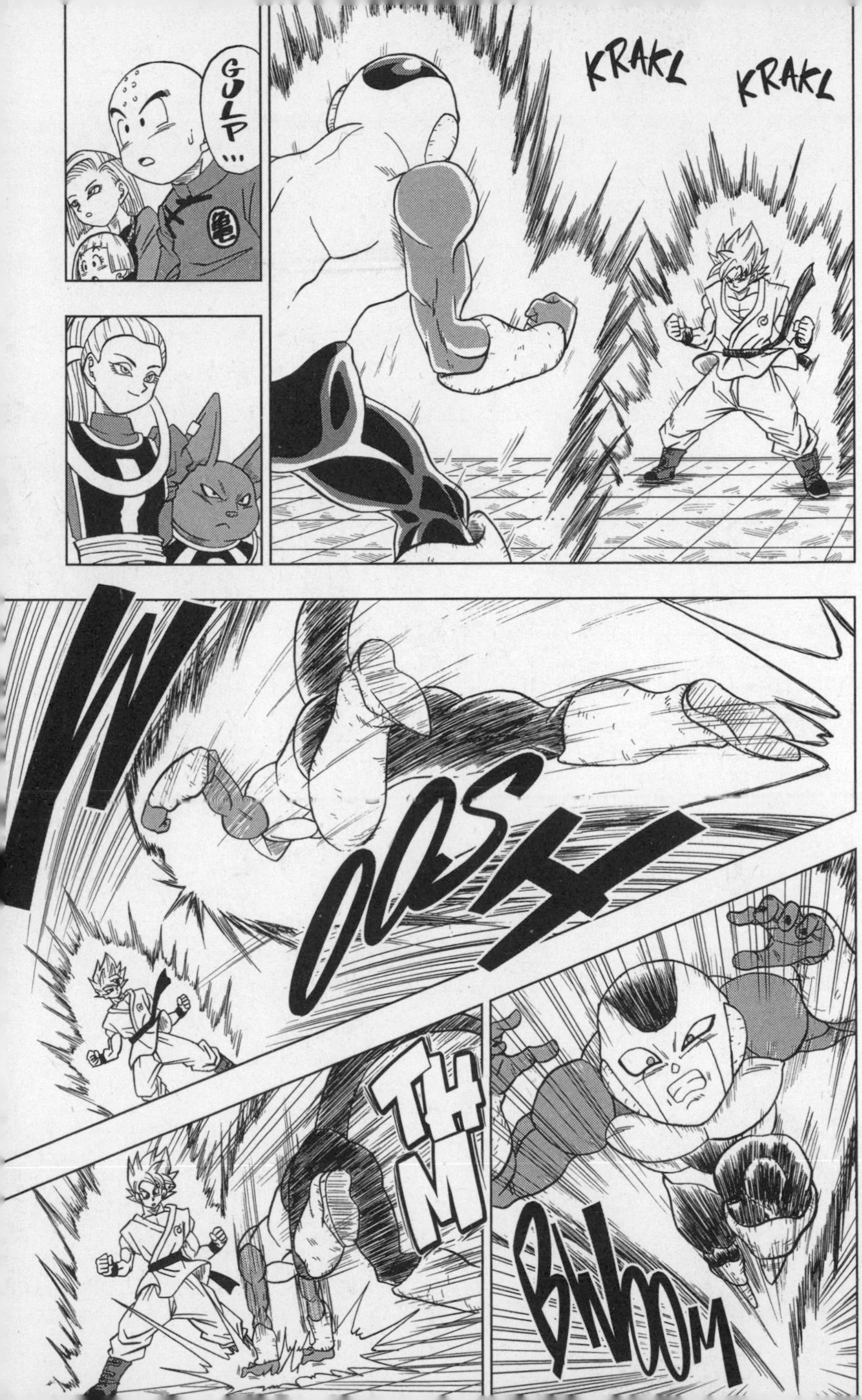
KRAKL
KRAKL
GULP...
WOOSH
BWOOM
THM

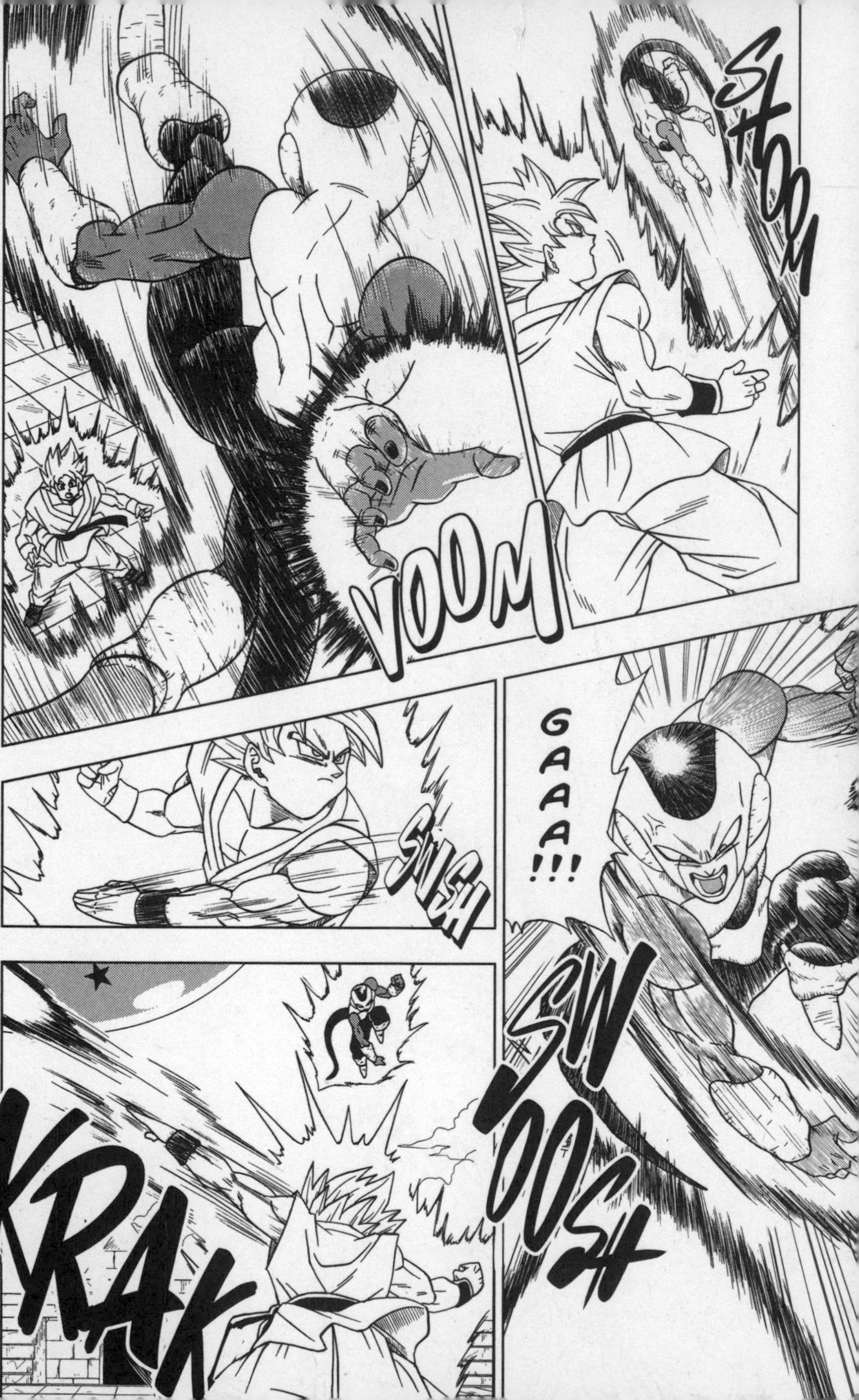
SHOOM
VOOM
GAAAA!!!
SWOOSH
SWISH
KRAK

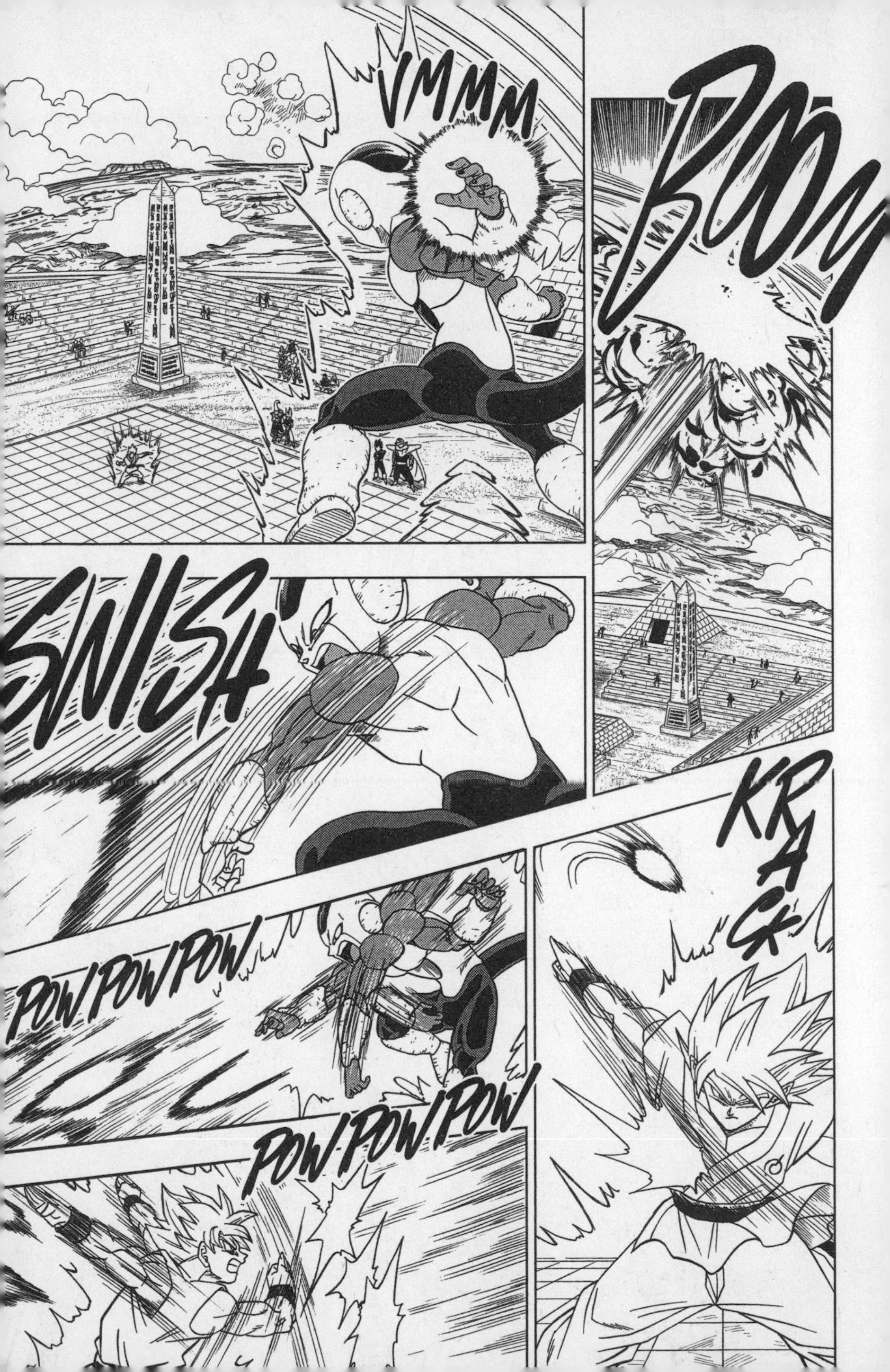
BOOM
VMMMM
SWISH
KRACK
POWPOWPOW
POWPOWPOW

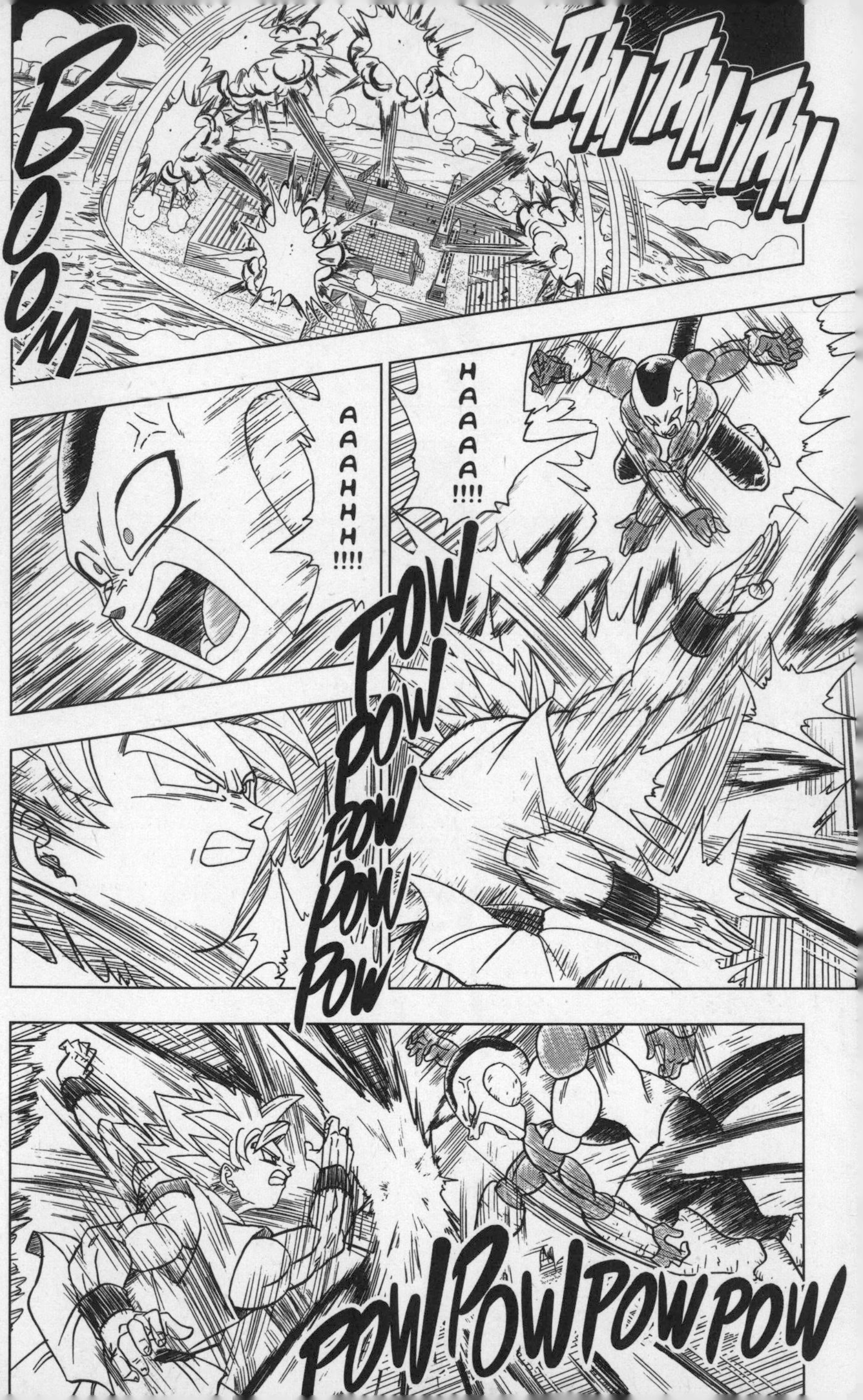
TAN TAN TAN
BOOM
HAAAAA!!!!
AAAHHH!!!!
POW POW POW POW POW POW
POW POW POW POW

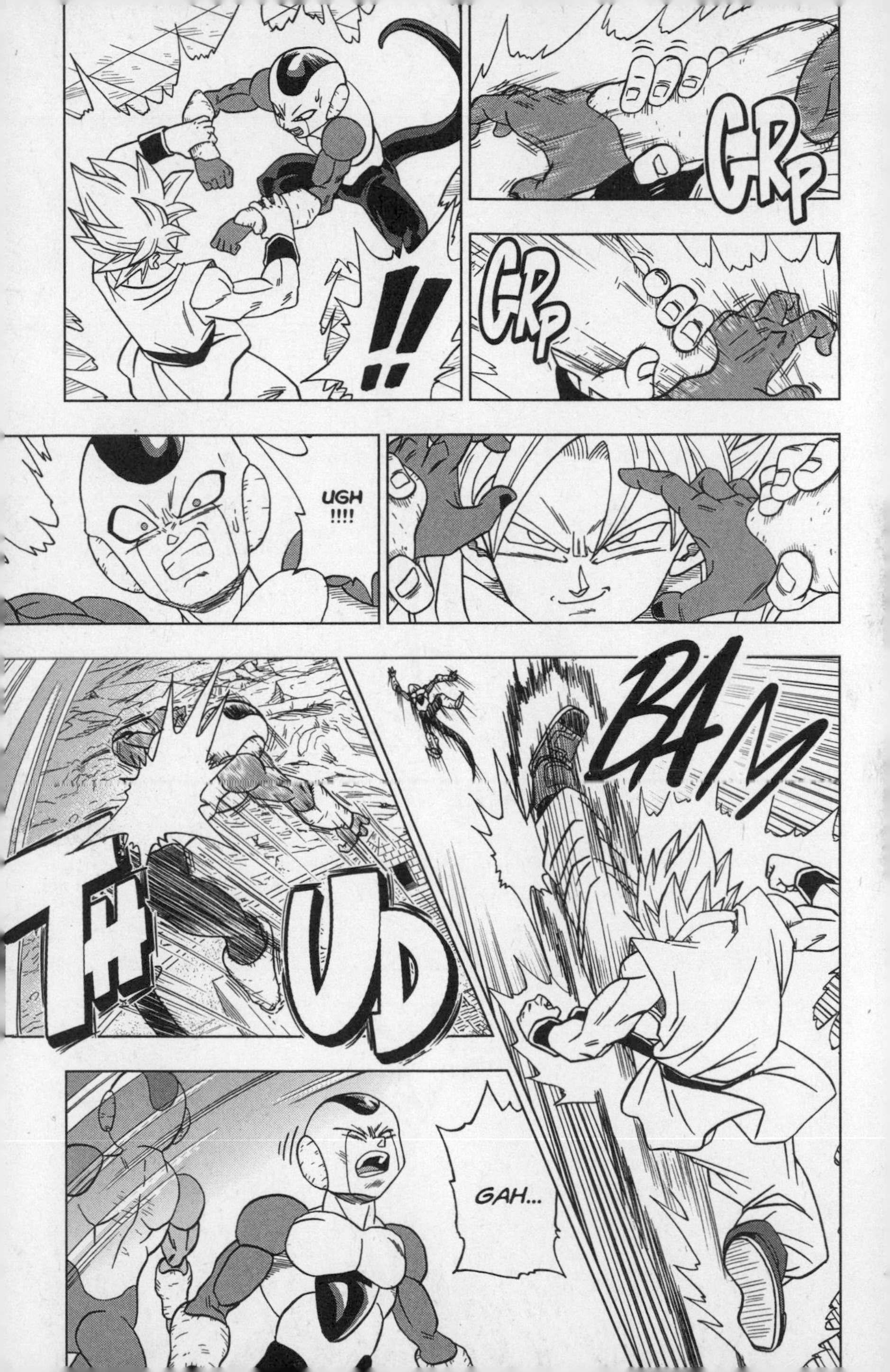
CRP
CRP
!!
UGH !!!!
BAM
THUD
GAH...

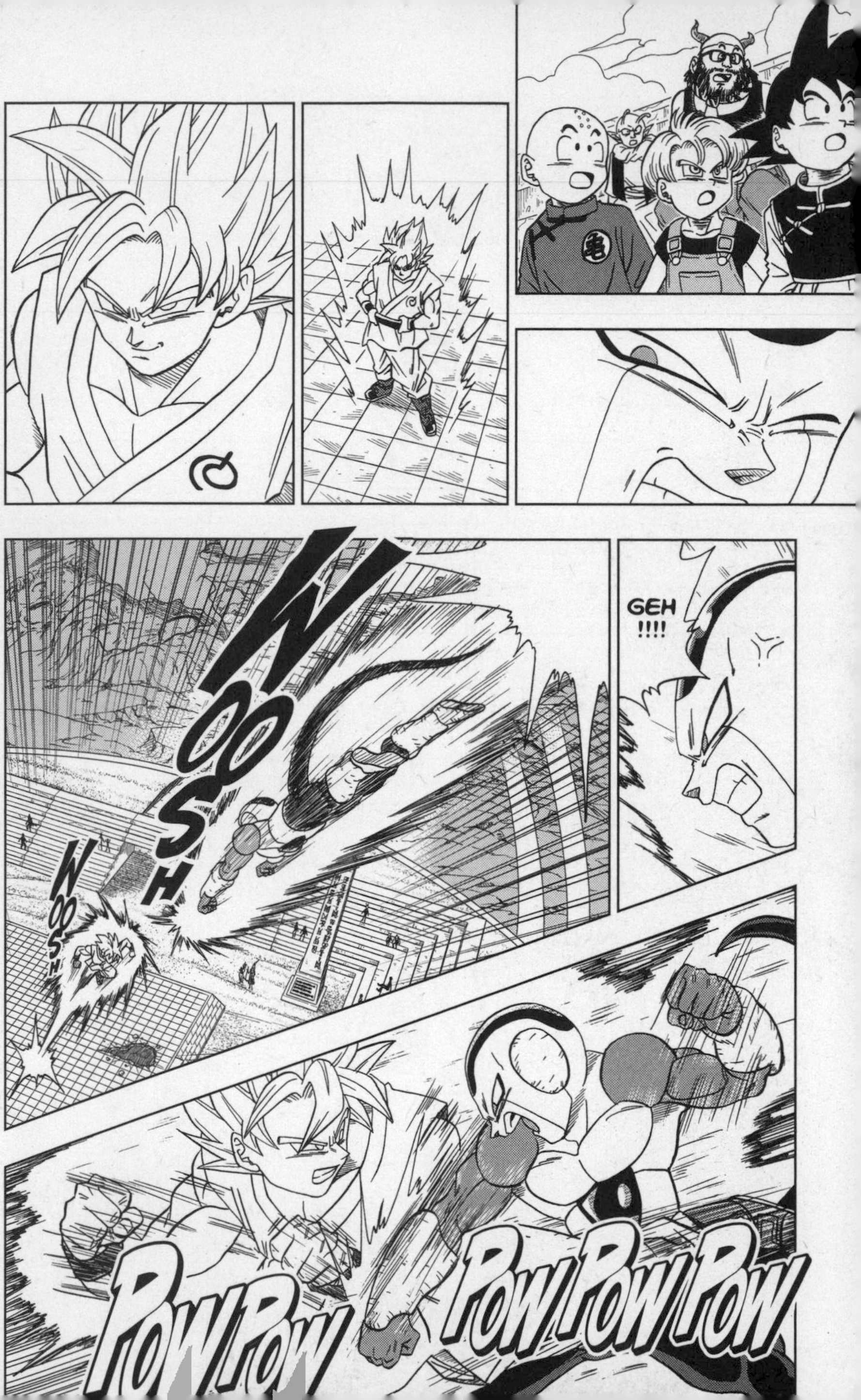
GEH !!!!
WOOSH
WOOSH
POW POW POW
POW POW

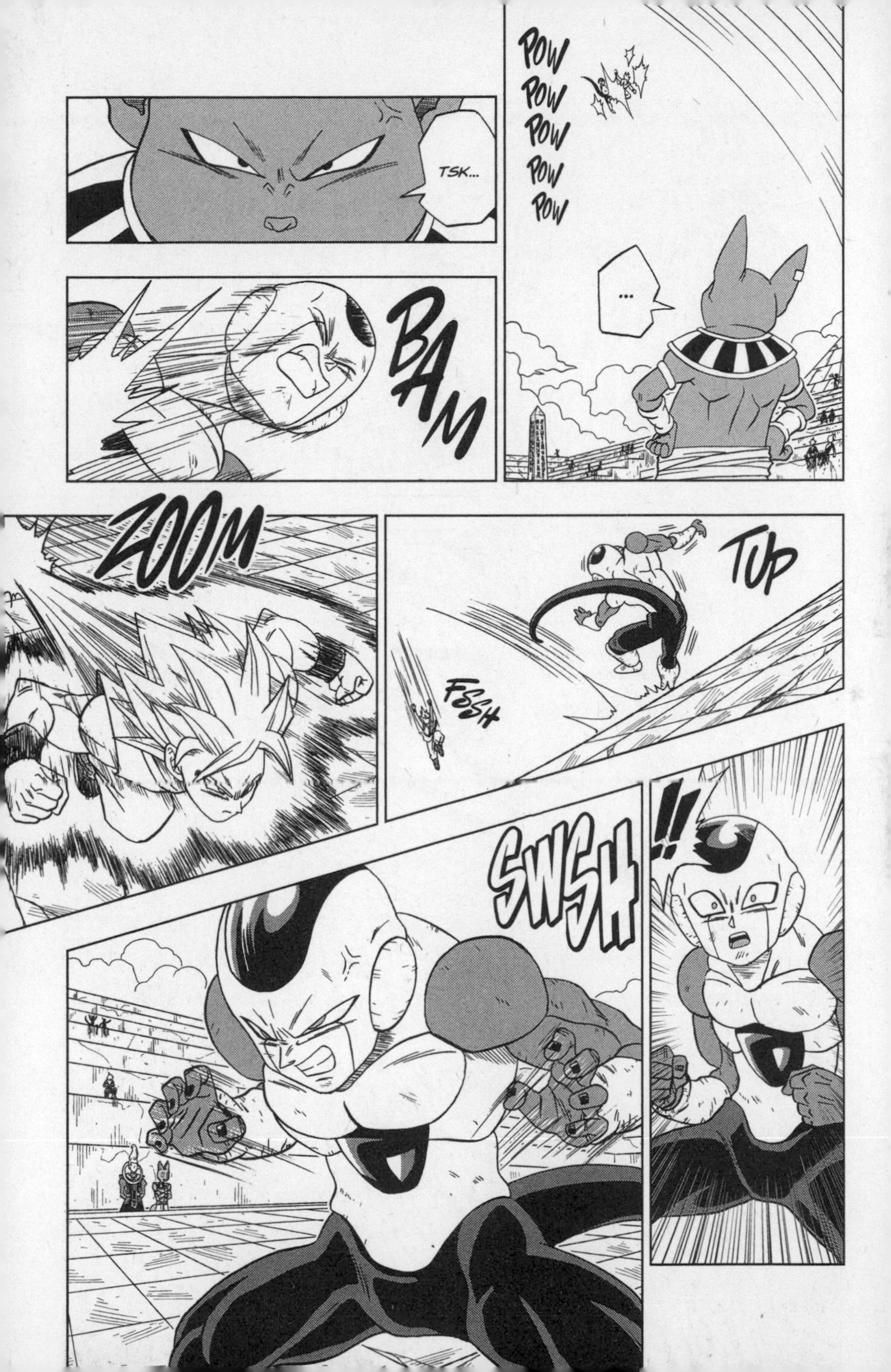
POW
POW
POW
POW
POW
...
TSK...
BAM
TUP
FSSH
ZOOM
!!
SWSH

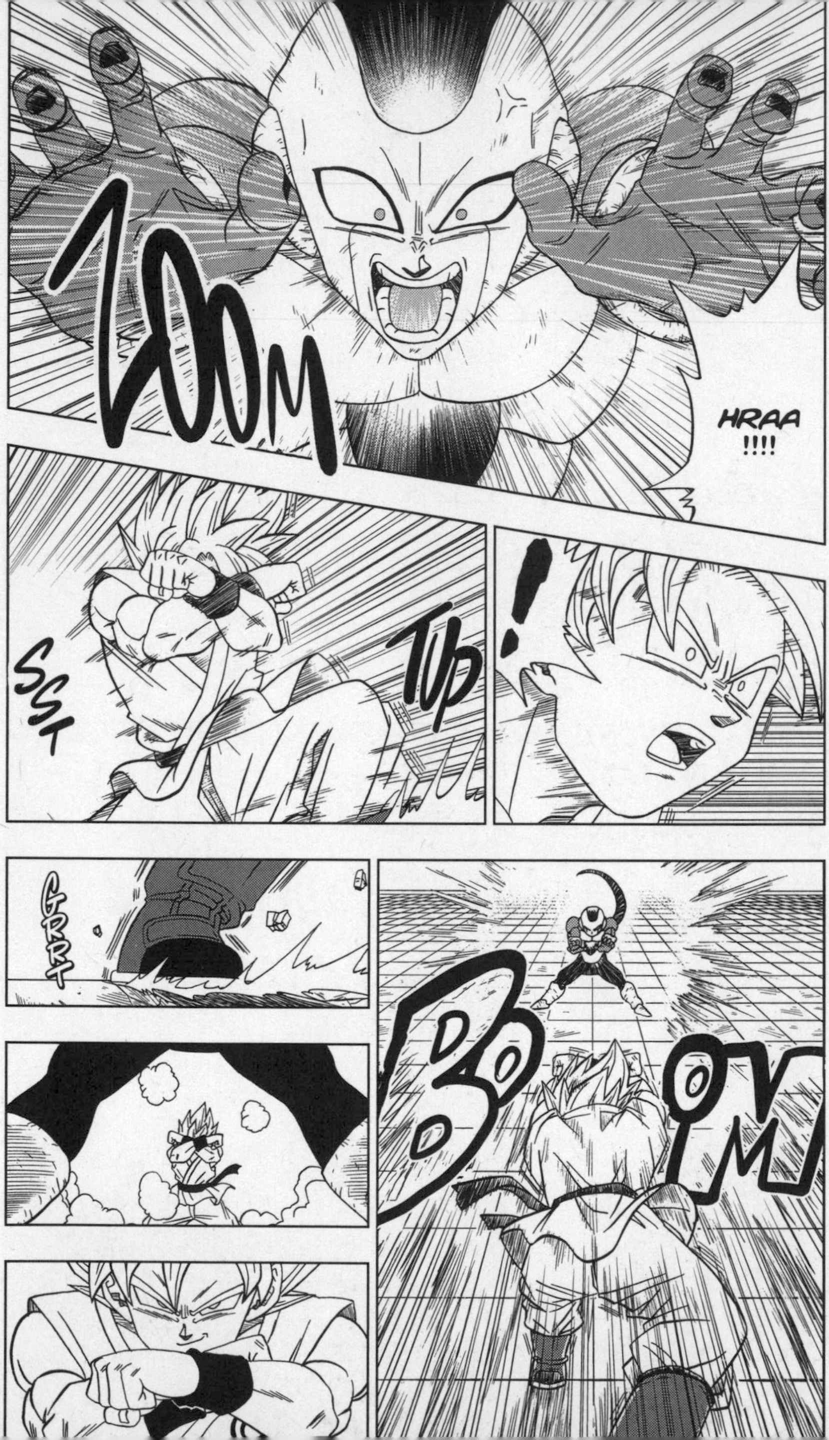
ZOOM
HRAA
!!!!
!
TUP
SSST
BOOM
GRRT

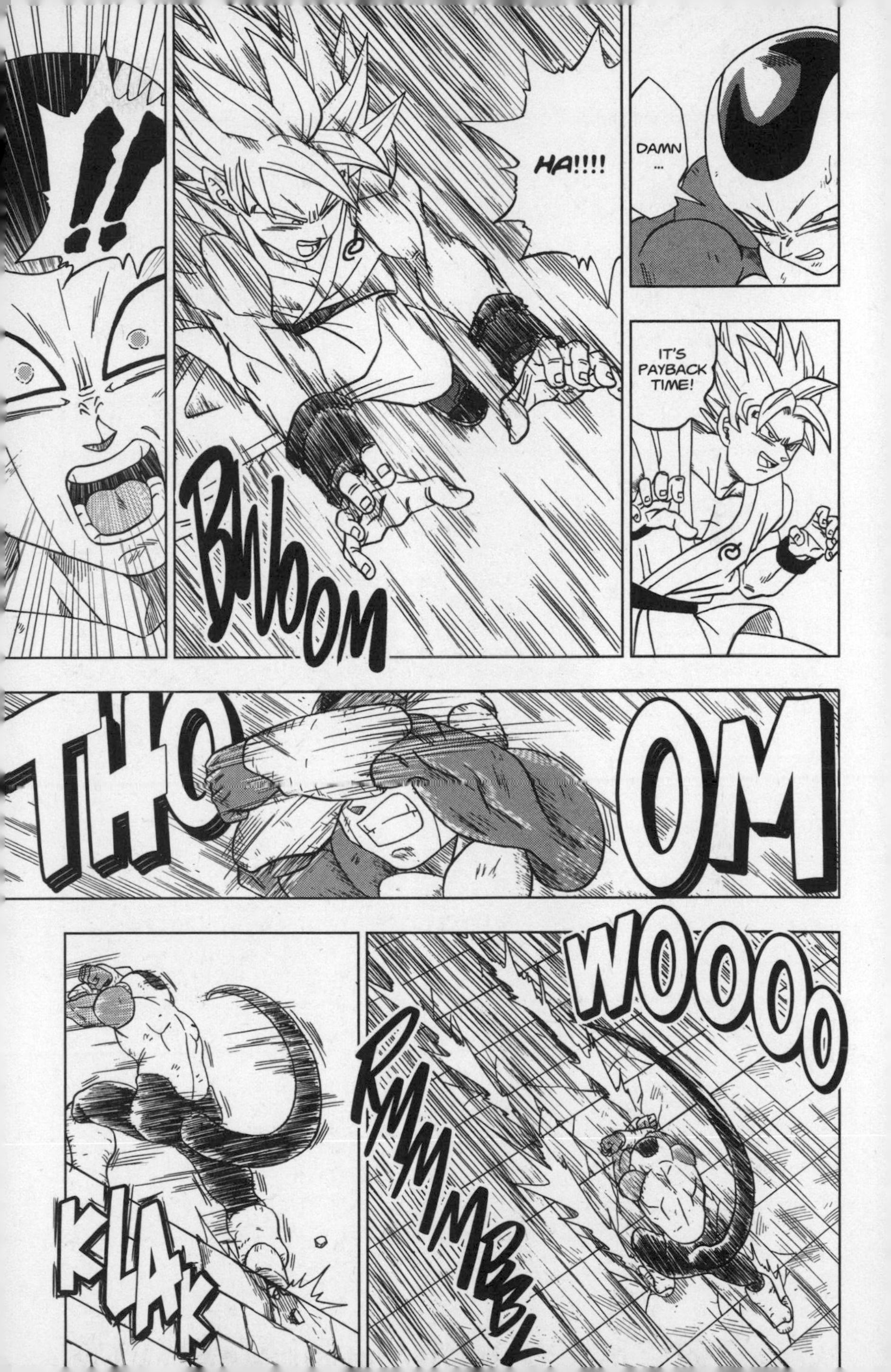
DAMN ...
IT'S PAYBACK TIME!
HA!!!!
BWOOM
!!
THO OM
WOOOO
KLAK

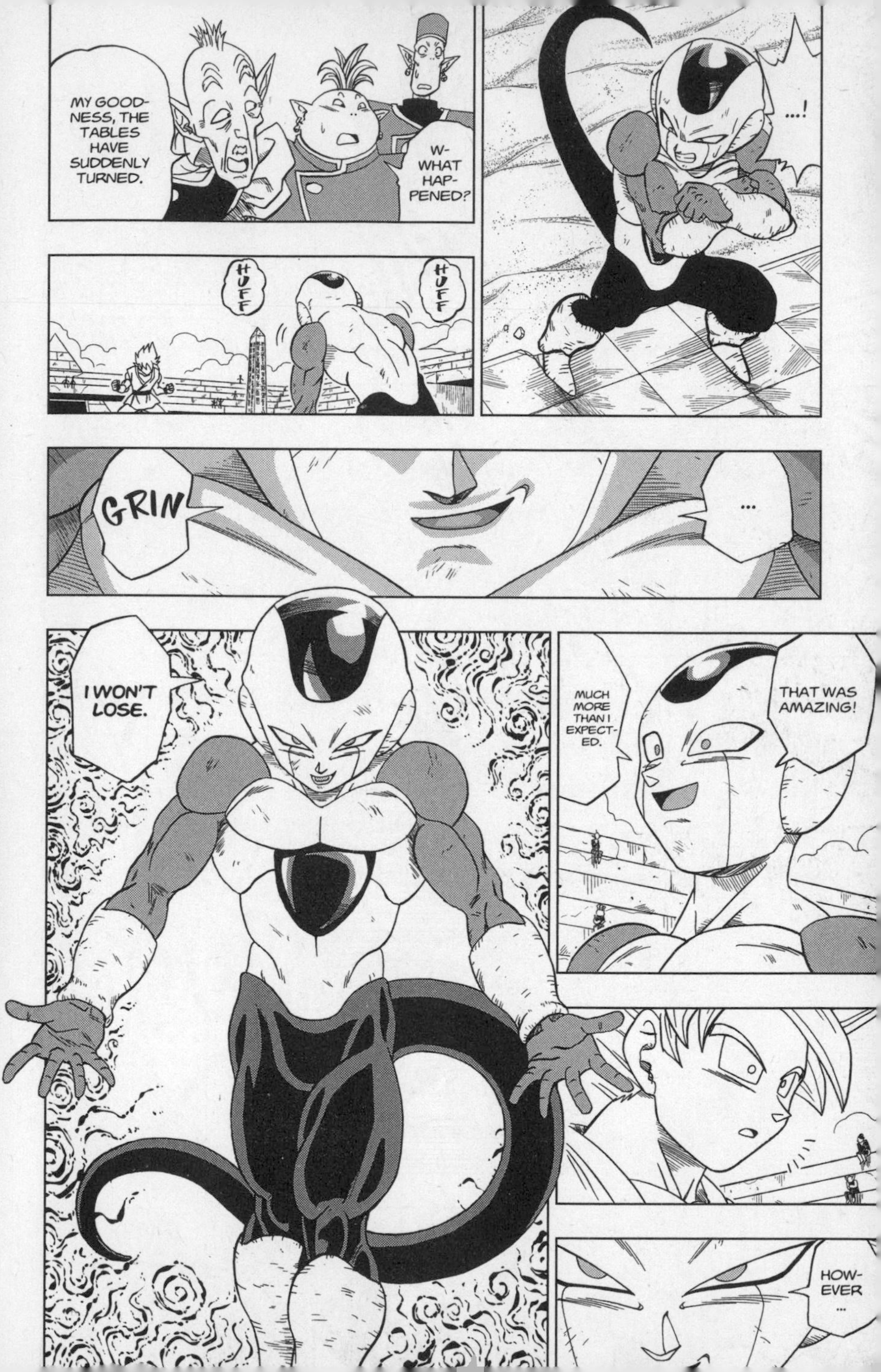

...!
W-WHAT HAPPENED?
MY GOODNESS, THE TABLES HAVE SUDDENLY TURNED.
HUFF
HUFF
...
GRIN
THAT WAS AMAZING!
MUCH MORE THAN I EXPECTED.
HOWEVER ...
I WON'T LOSE.

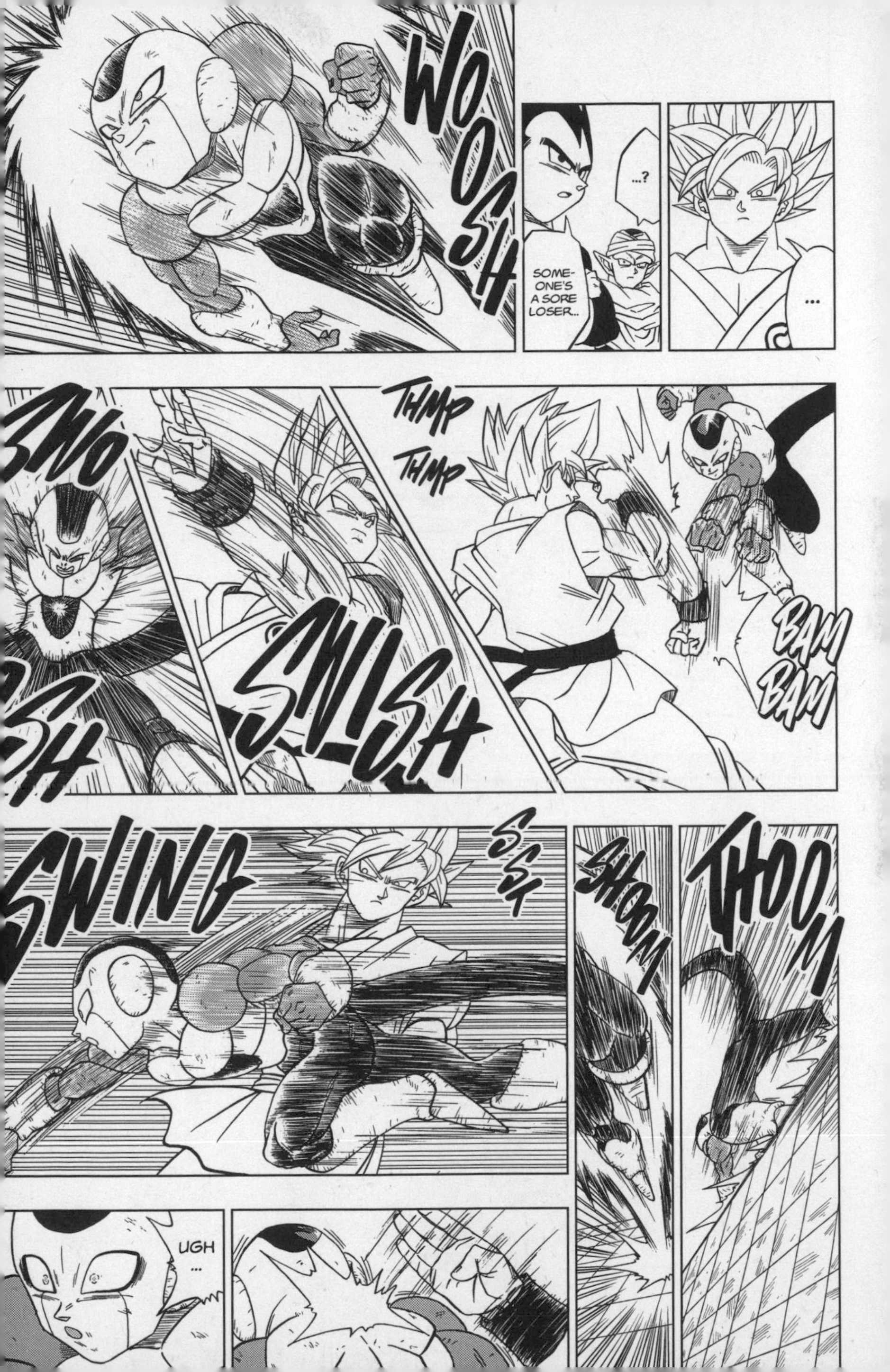
...
...?
SOME-ONE'S A SORE LOSER...
WOOOSH
THMP THMP
BAM BAM
SWISH
THOOM
SHOOM
S-SK
SWING
UGH ...

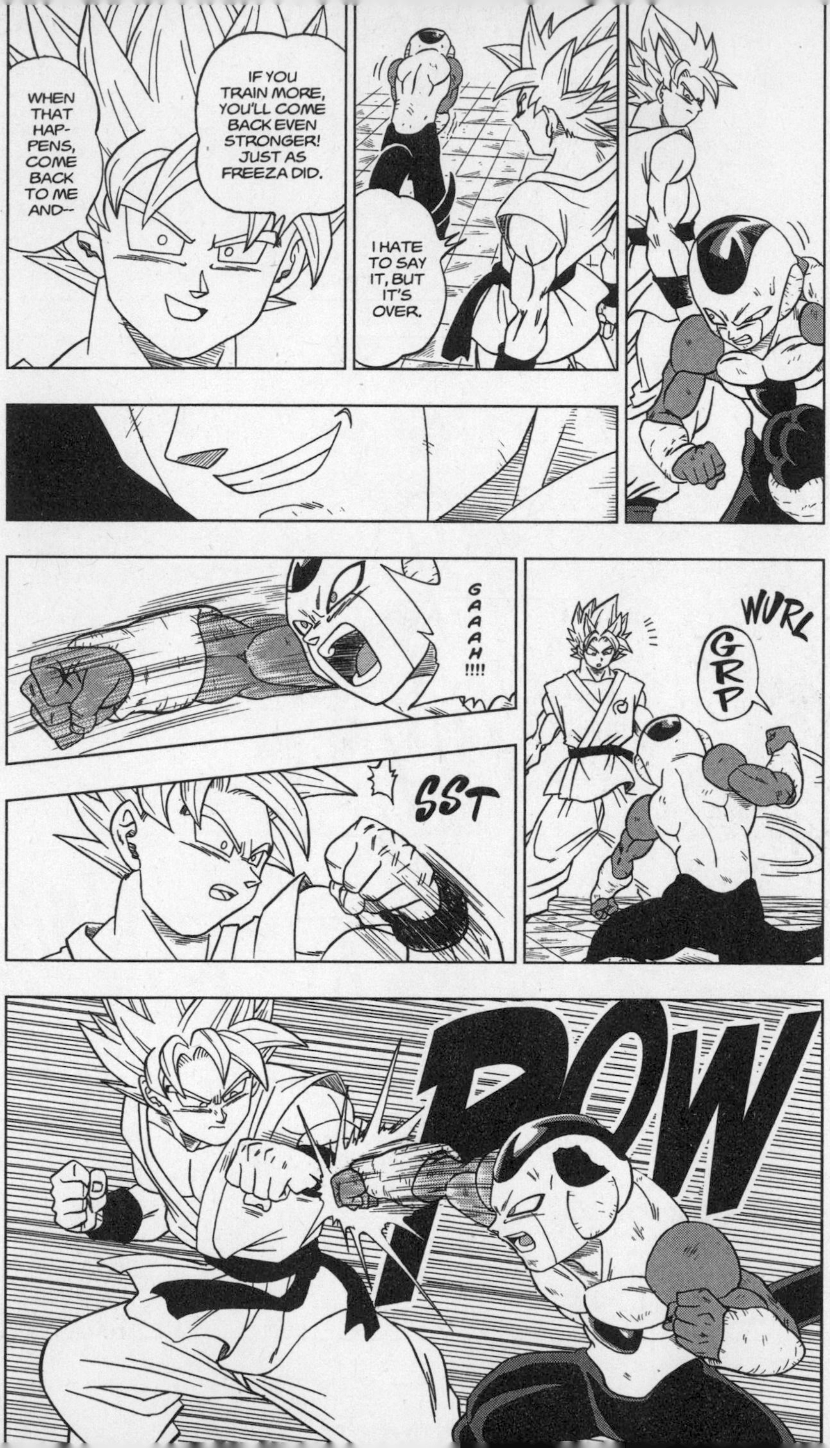
I HATE TO SAY IT, BUT IT'S OVER.
IF YOU TRAIN MORE, YOU'LL COME BACK EVEN STRONGER! JUST AS FREEZA DID.
WHEN THAT HAP-PENS, COME BACK TO ME AND--
WURL
GRP
GAAAAH!!!!
SST
POW

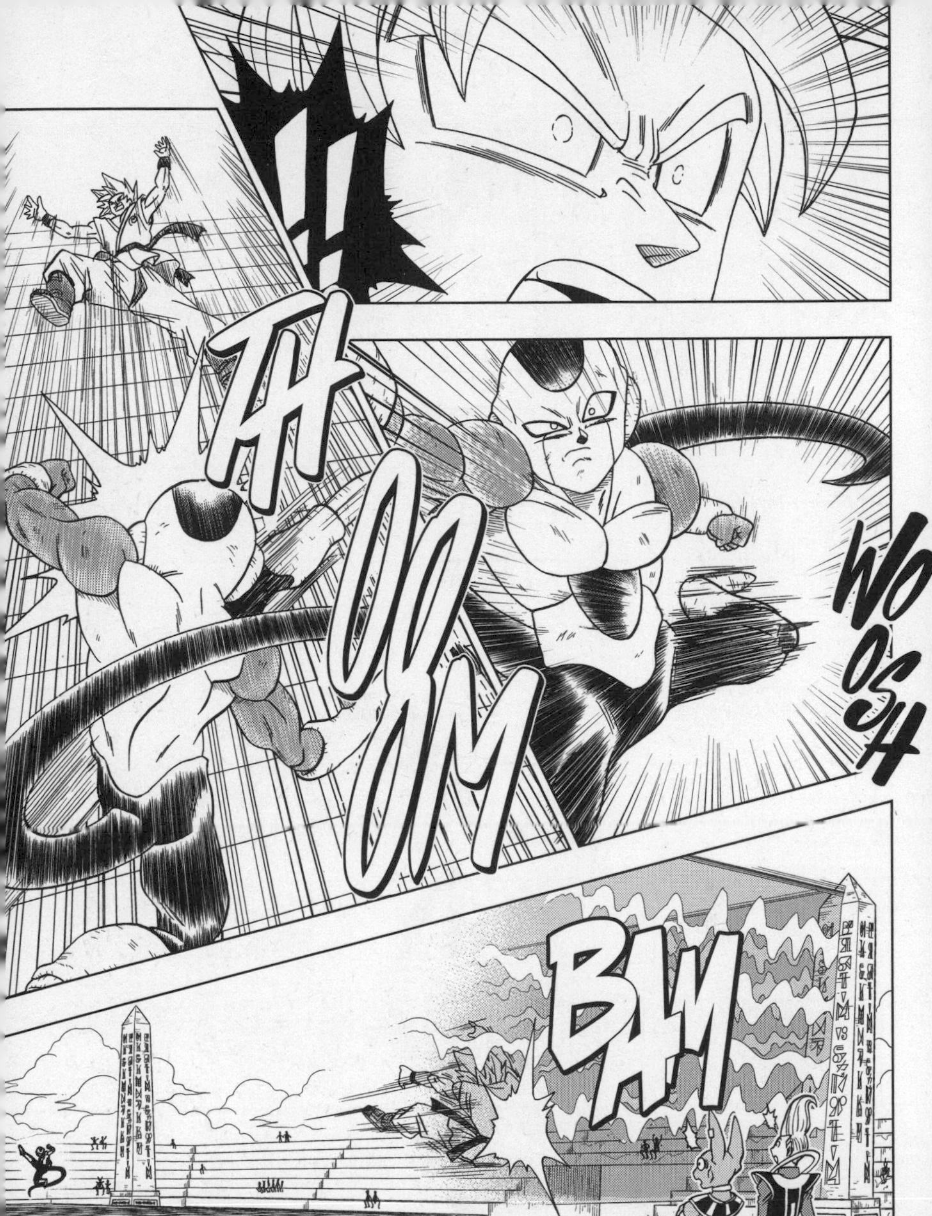
!!
WOOSH
THOOOM
BAM

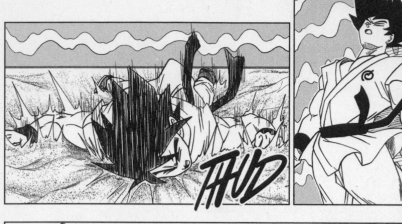

THUD

GRIN

TMP

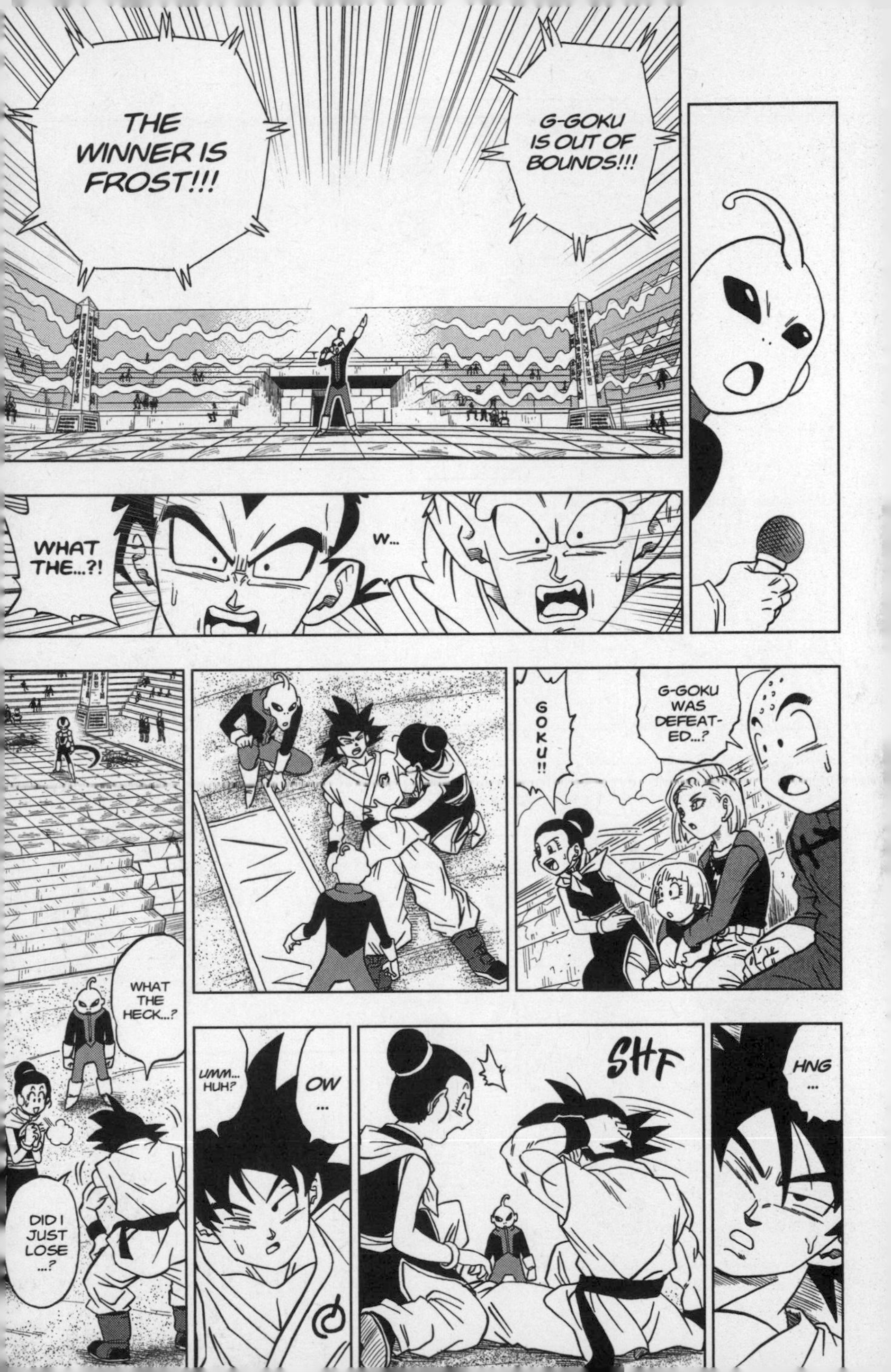
G-GOKU IS OUT OF BOUNDS!!!
THE WINNER IS FROST!!!
W...
WHAT THE...?!
G-GOKU WAS DEFEAT-ED...?
GOKU!!
HNG ...
SHF
OW ...
UMM... HUH?
WHAT THE HECK...?
DID I JUST LOSE ...?

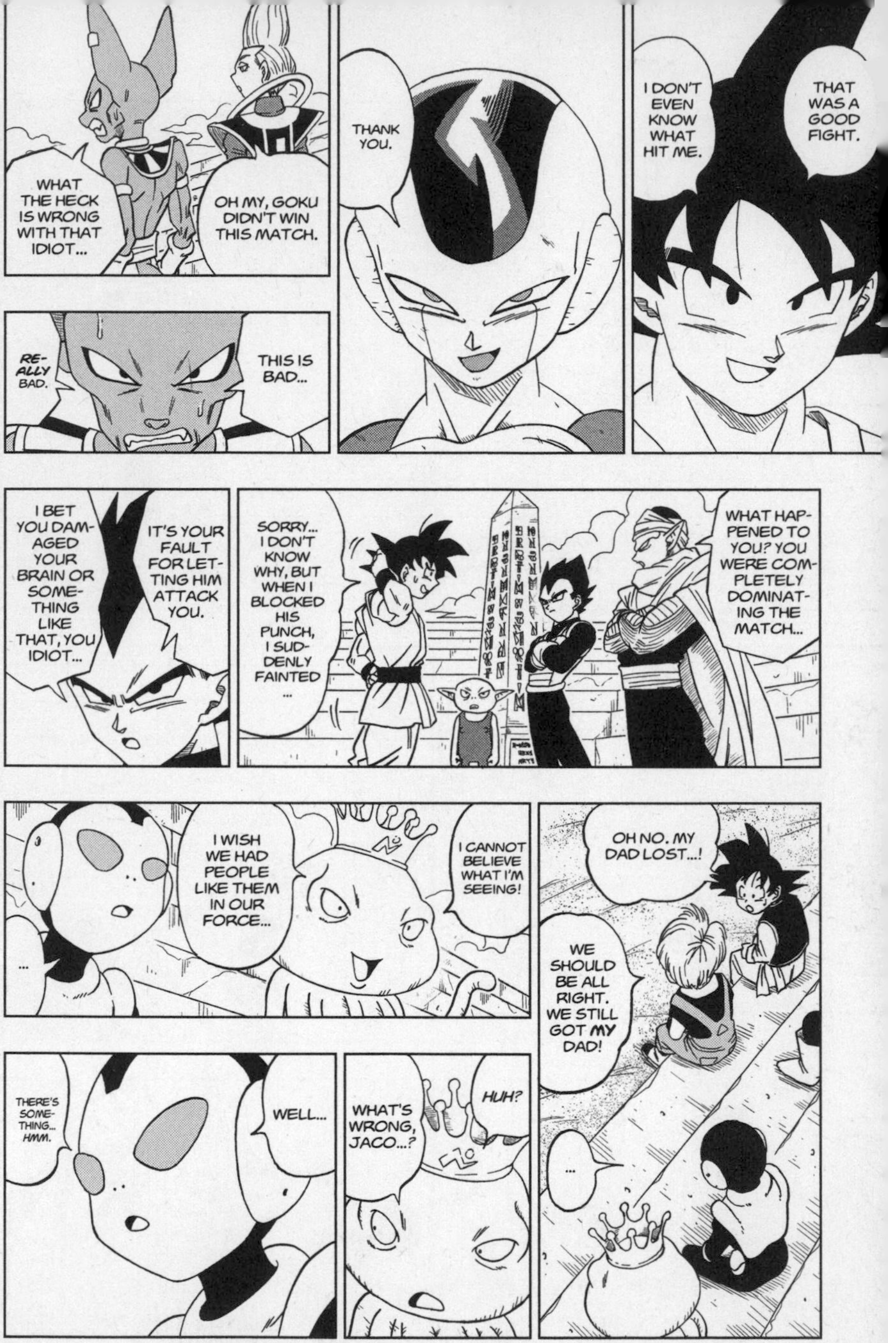
THAT WAS A GOOD FIGHT.
I DON'T EVEN KNOW WHAT HIT ME.
THANK YOU.
OH MY, GOKU DIDN'T WIN THIS MATCH.
WHAT THE HECK IS WRONG WITH THAT IDIOT...
THIS IS BAD...
RE-ALLY BAD.
WHAT HAP-PENED TO YOU? YOU WERE COM-PLETELY DOMINAT-ING THE MATCH...
SORRY... I DON'T KNOW WHY, BUT WHEN I BLOCKED HIS PUNCH, I SUD-DENLY FAINTED ...
IT'S YOUR FAULT FOR LET-TING HIM ATTACK YOU.
I BET YOU DAM-AGED YOUR BRAIN OR SOME-THING LIKE THAT, YOU IDIOT...
OH NO. MY DAD LOST...!
WE SHOULD BE ALL RIGHT. WE STILL GOT MY DAD!
...
I CANNOT BELIEVE WHAT I'M SEEING!
I WISH WE HAD PEOPLE LIKE THEM IN OUR FORCE...
...
HUH?
WHAT'S WRONG, JACO...?
WELL...
THERE'S SOME-THING... HMM.

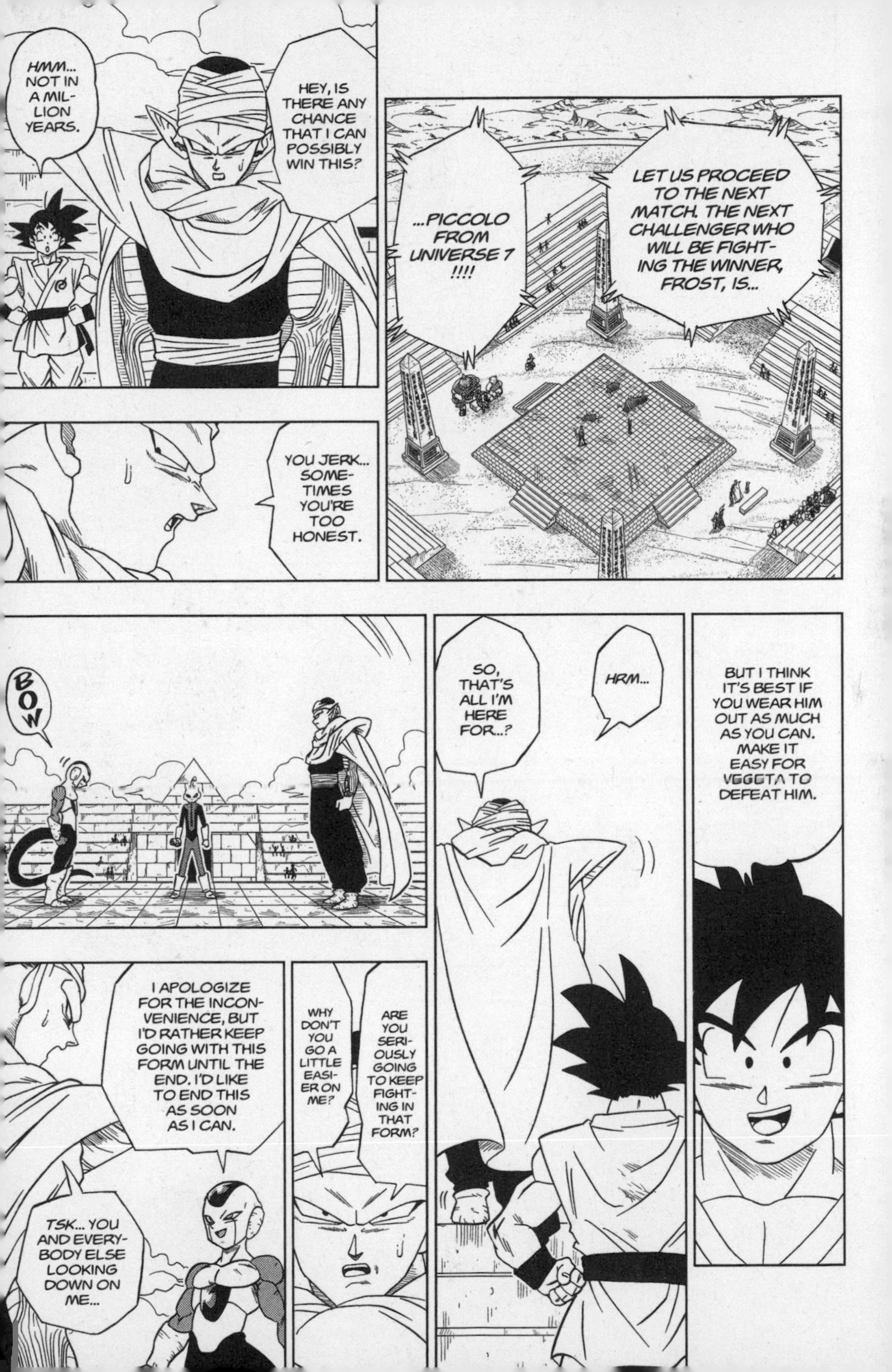
LET US PROCEED TO THE NEXT MATCH. THE NEXT CHALLENGER WHO WILL BE FIGHTING THE WINNER, FROST, IS...
...PICCOLO FROM UNIVERSE 7 !!!!
HEY, IS THERE ANY CHANCE THAT I CAN POSSIBLY WIN THIS?
HMM... NOT IN A MILLION YEARS.
YOU JERK... SOMETIMES YOU'RE TOO HONEST.
BUT I THINK IT'S BEST IF YOU WEAR HIM OUT AS MUCH AS YOU CAN. MAKE IT EASY FOR VEGETA TO DEFEAT HIM.
HRM...
SO, THAT'S ALL I'M HERE FOR...?
BOW
ARE YOU SERIOUSLY GOING TO KEEP FIGHTING IN THAT FORM?
WHY DON'T YOU GO A LITTLE EASIER ON ME?
I APOLOGIZE FOR THE INCONVENIENCE, BUT I'D RATHER KEEP GOING WITH THIS FORM UNTIL THE END. I'D LIKE TO END THIS AS SOON AS I CAN.
TSK... YOU AND EVERYBODY ELSE LOOKING DOWN ON ME...

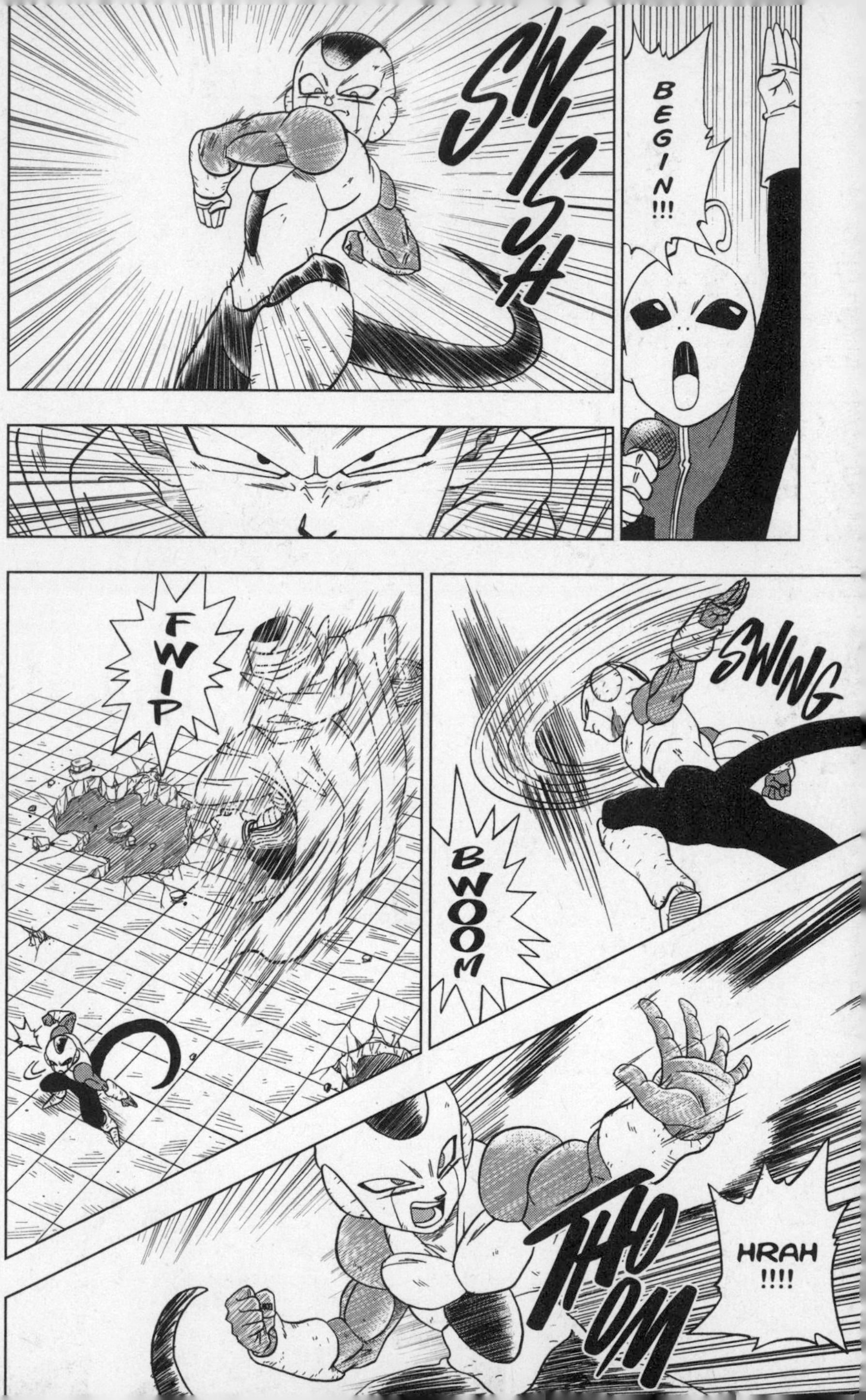
BEGIN!!!
SWISH
SWING
BWOOM
FWIP
HRAH!!!!
THOOM

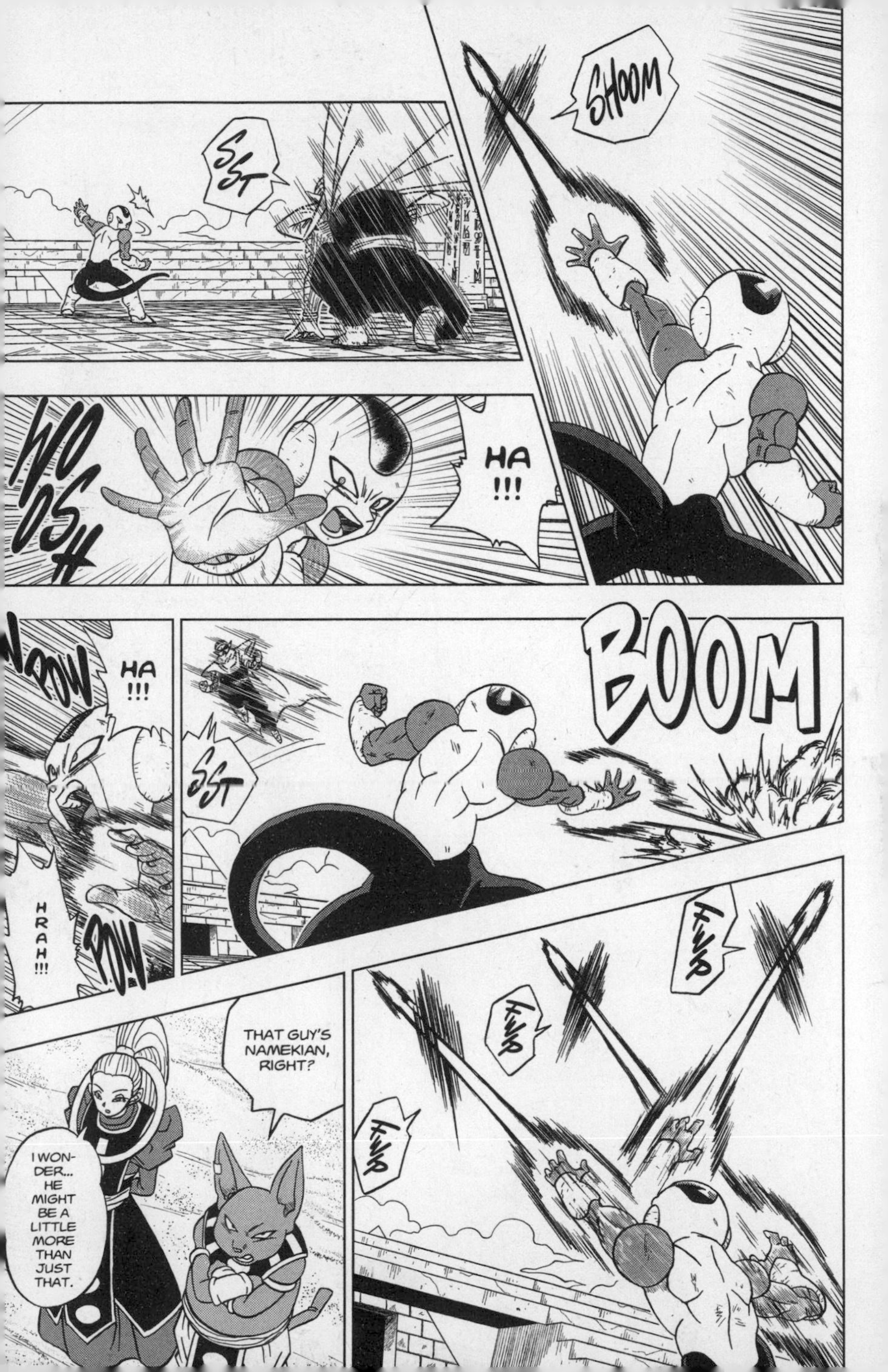
SHOOM
SST
HA!!!
WOOSH
BOOM
SST
HA!!!
POW
HRAH!!!
POW
FWIP
FWIP
FWIP
THAT GUY'S NAMEKIAN, RIGHT?
I WONDER... HE MIGHT BE A LITTLE MORE THAN JUST THAT.

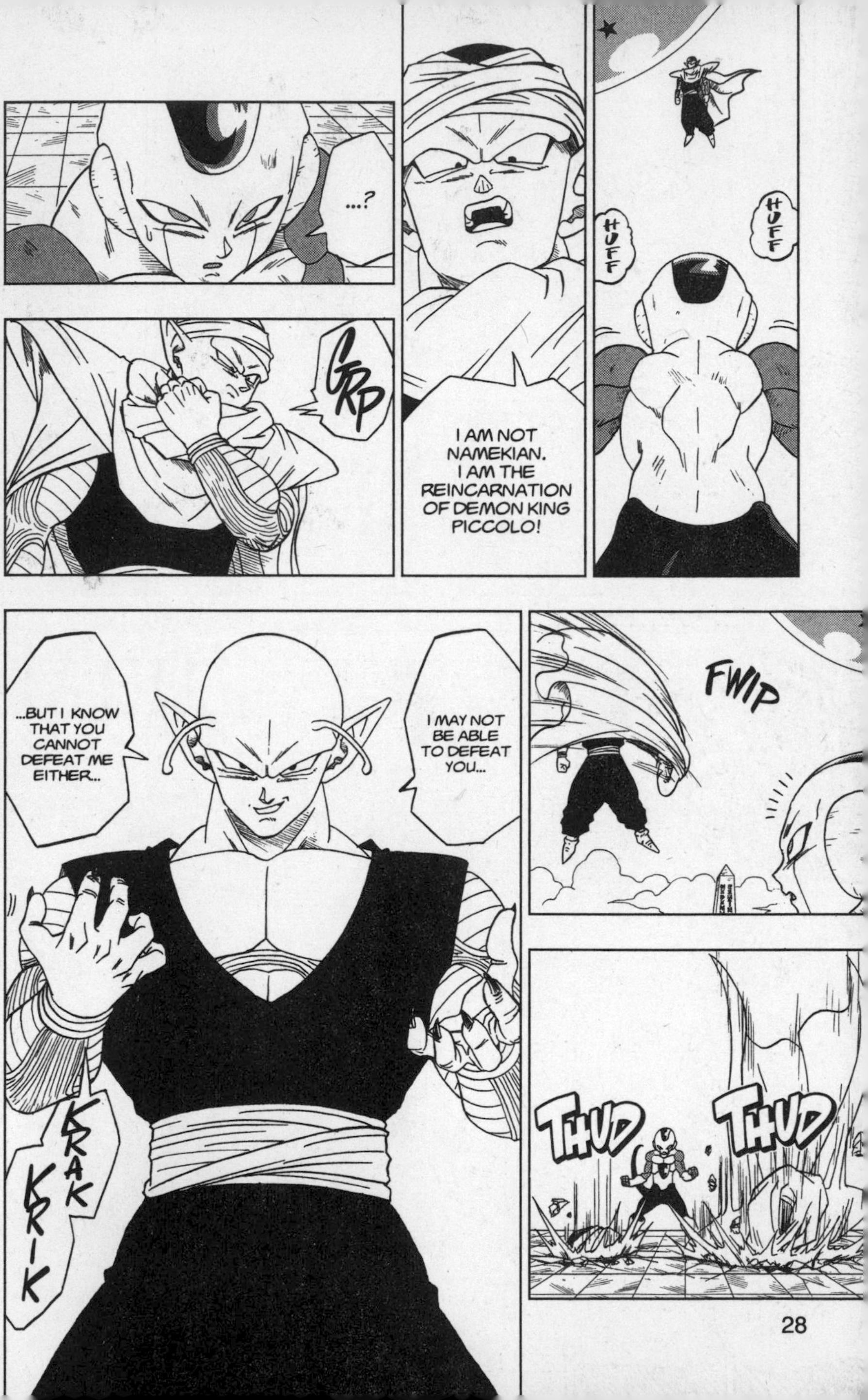
HUFF
HUFF
I AM NOT NAMEKIAN. I AM THE REINCARNATION OF DEMON KING PICCOLO!
...?
GRP
FWIP
THUD
THUD
I MAY NOT BE ABLE TO DEFEAT YOU...
...BUT I KNOW THAT YOU CANNOT DEFEAT ME EITHER...
KRAK
KRIK

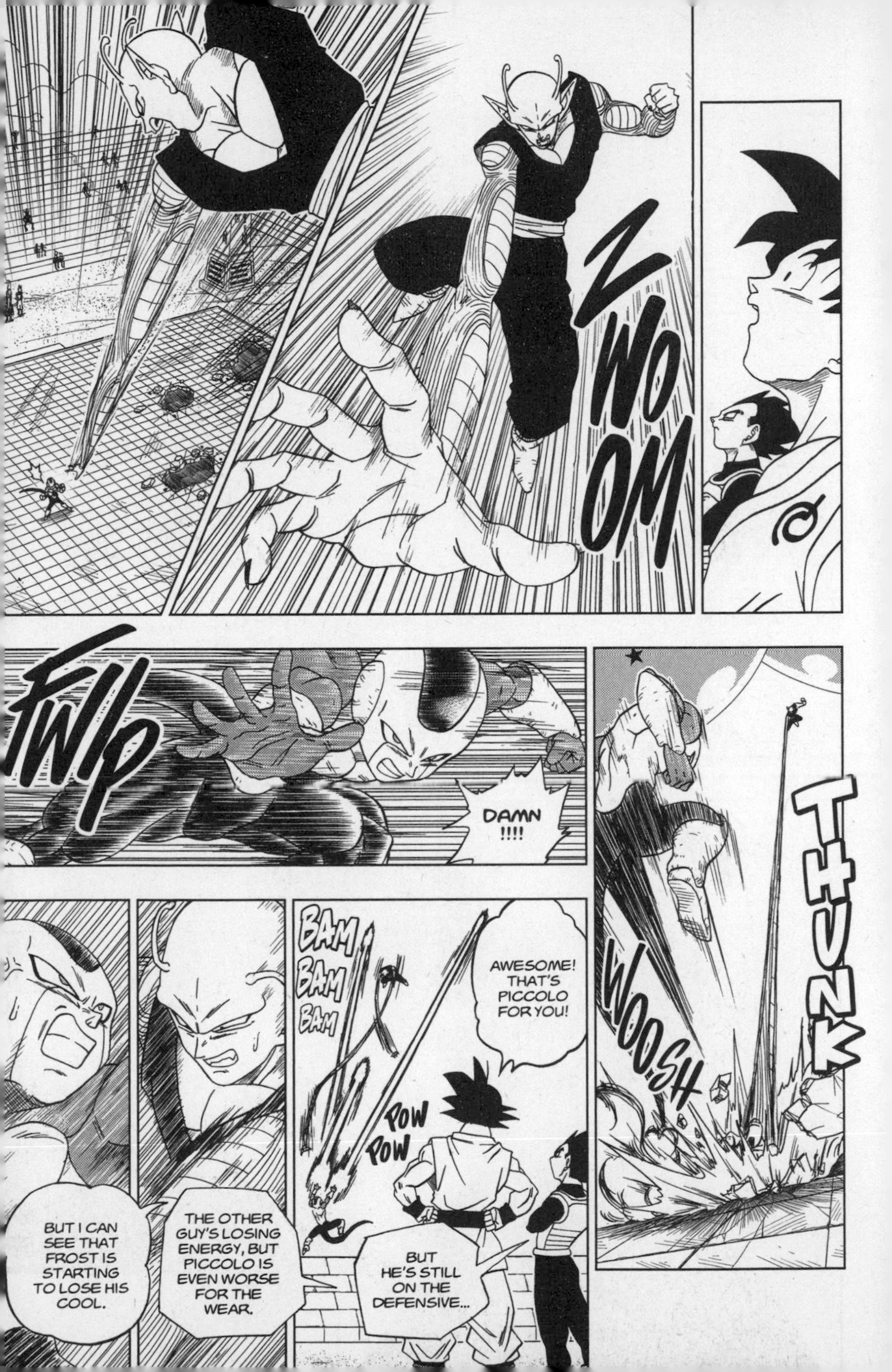
ZWOOM
THUNK
WOOSH
FWIP
DAMN !!!!
BAM BAM BAM
AWESOME! THAT'S PICCOLO FOR YOU!
POW POW
BUT HE'S STILL ON THE DEFENSIVE...
THE OTHER GUY'S LOSING ENERGY, BUT PICCOLO IS EVEN WORSE FOR THE WEAR.
BUT I CAN SEE THAT FROST IS STARTING TO LOSE HIS COOL.

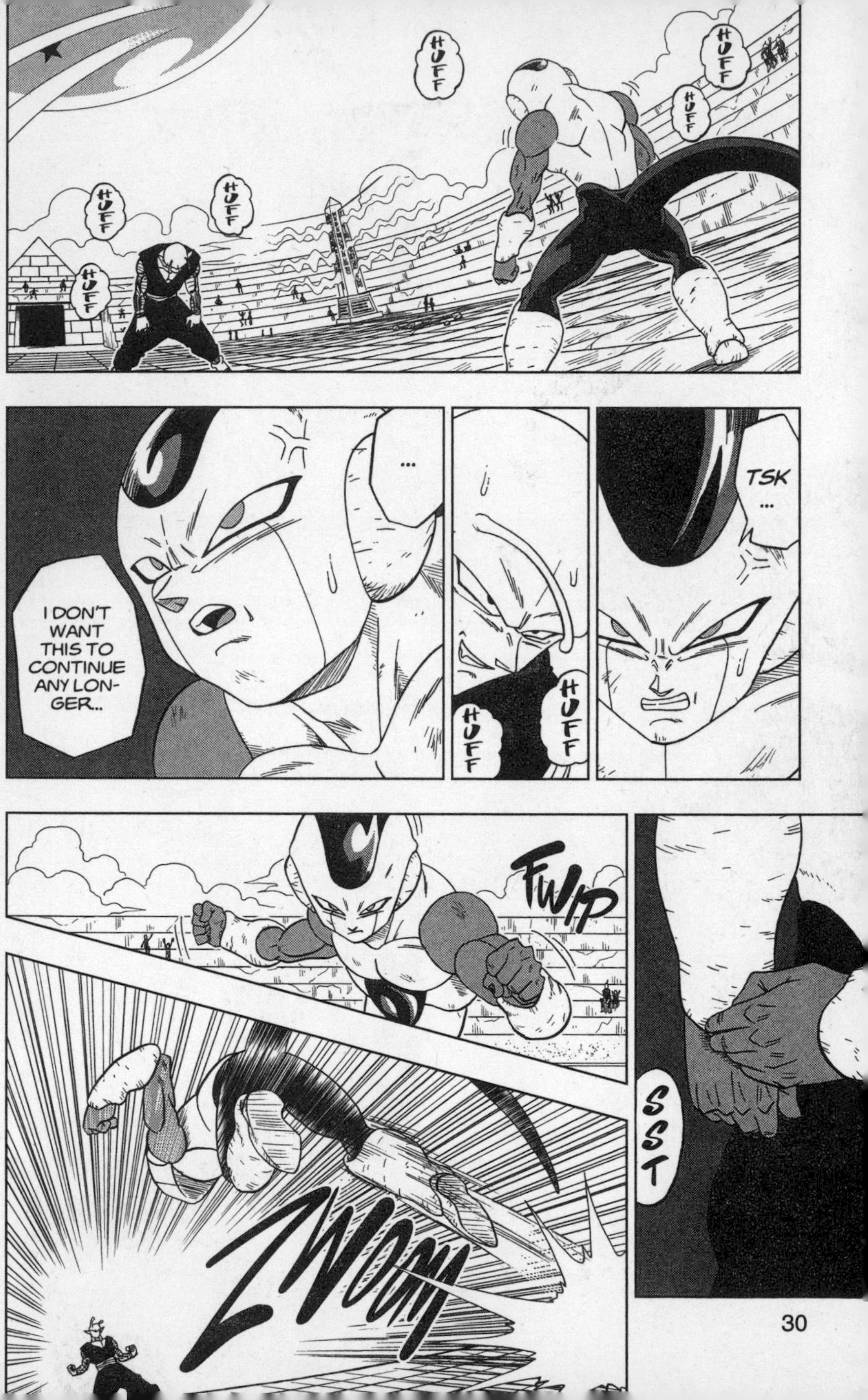
HUFF
HUFF
HUFF
HUFF
HUFF
TSK ...
...
HUFF
HUFF
I DON'T WANT THIS TO CONTINUE ANY LONGER...
SST
FWIP
ZWOOM

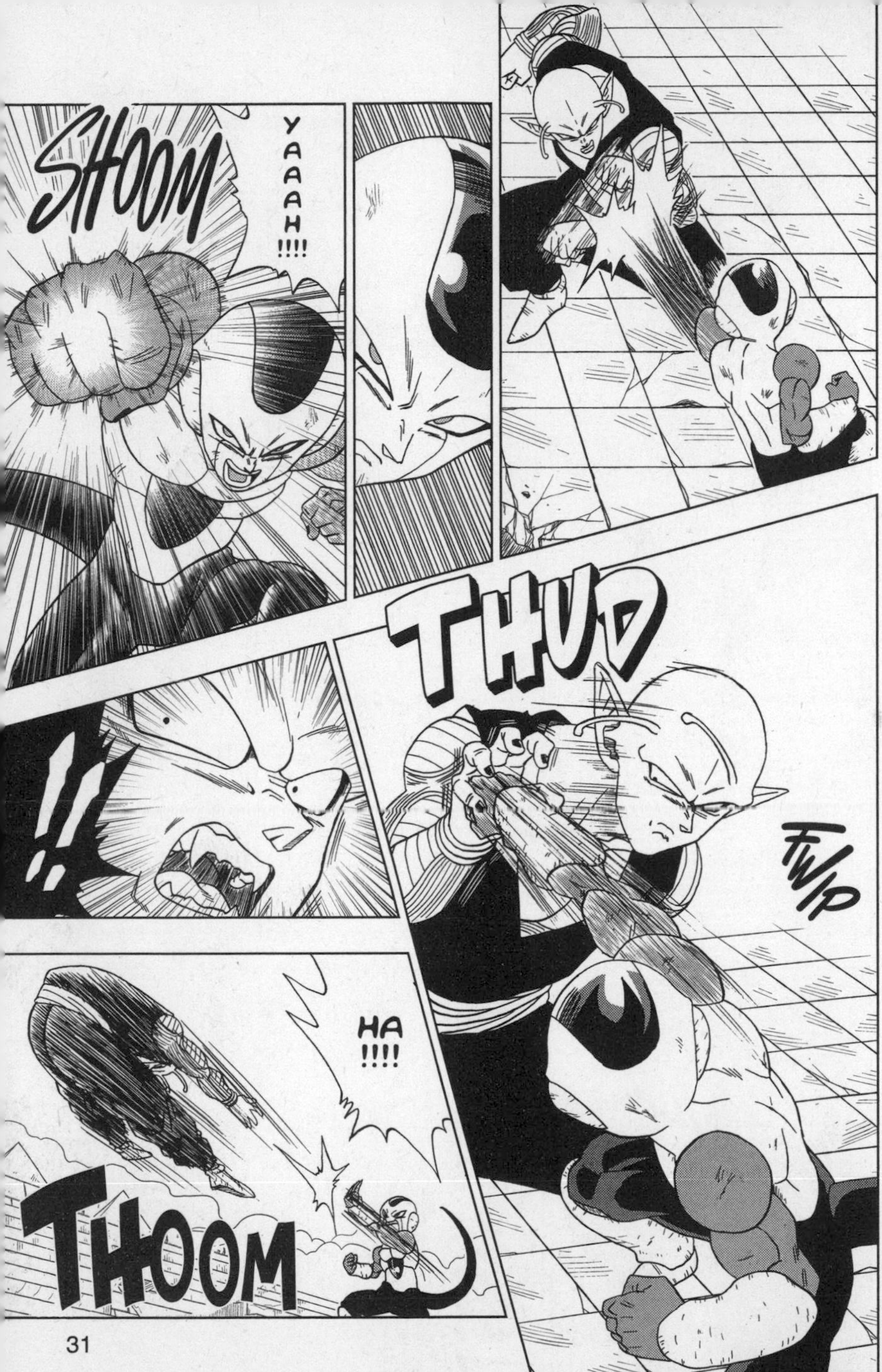
SHOOM
YAAAAH!!!!
THUD
FWIP
!!
HA!!!!
THOOM

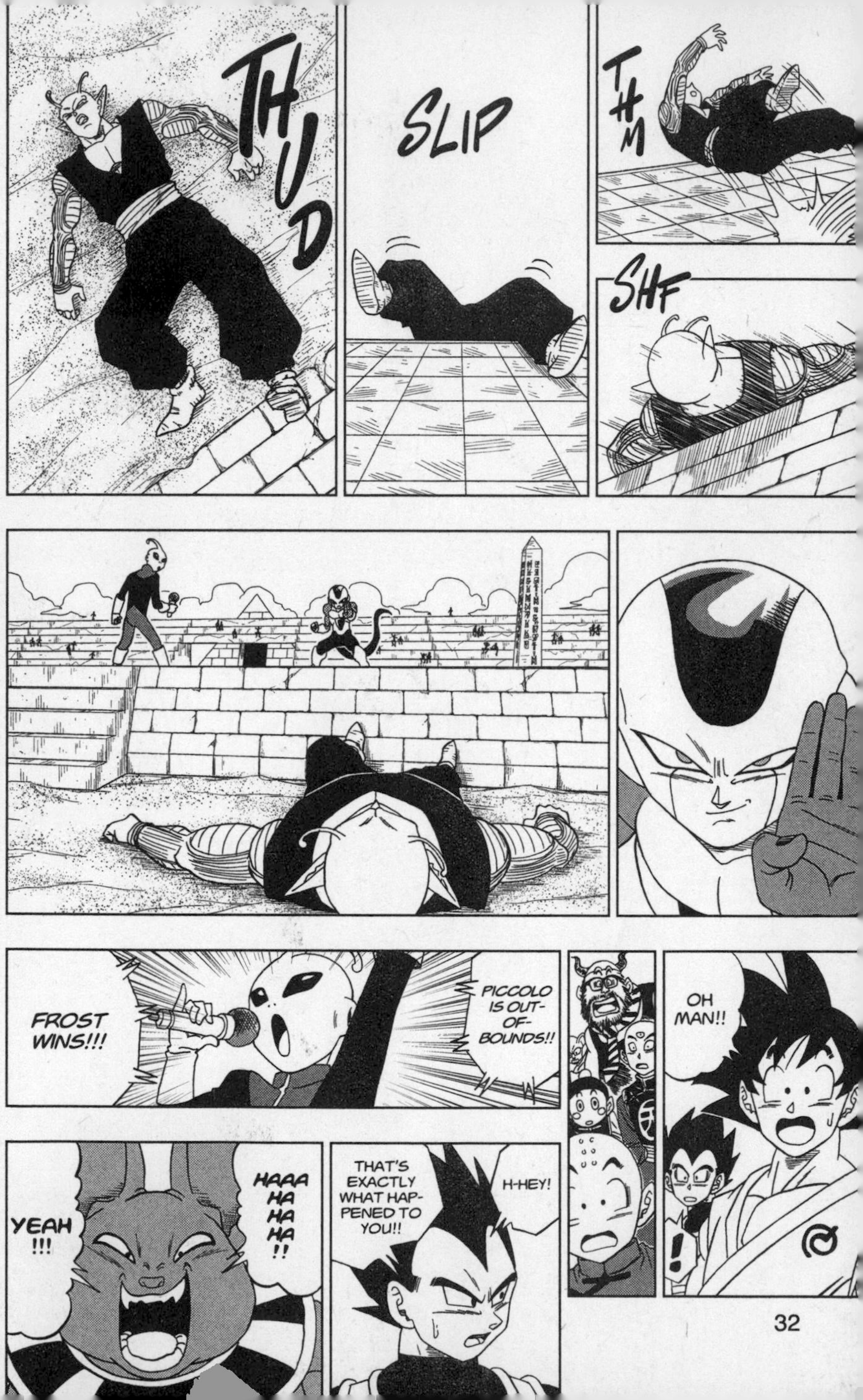
THM
SHF
SLIP
THUD
OH MAN!!
PICCOLO IS OUT-OF-BOUNDS!!
FROST WINS!!!
!
H-HEY!
THAT'S EXACTLY WHAT HAPPENED TO YOU!!
HAAAA HA HA HA!!
YEAH!!!

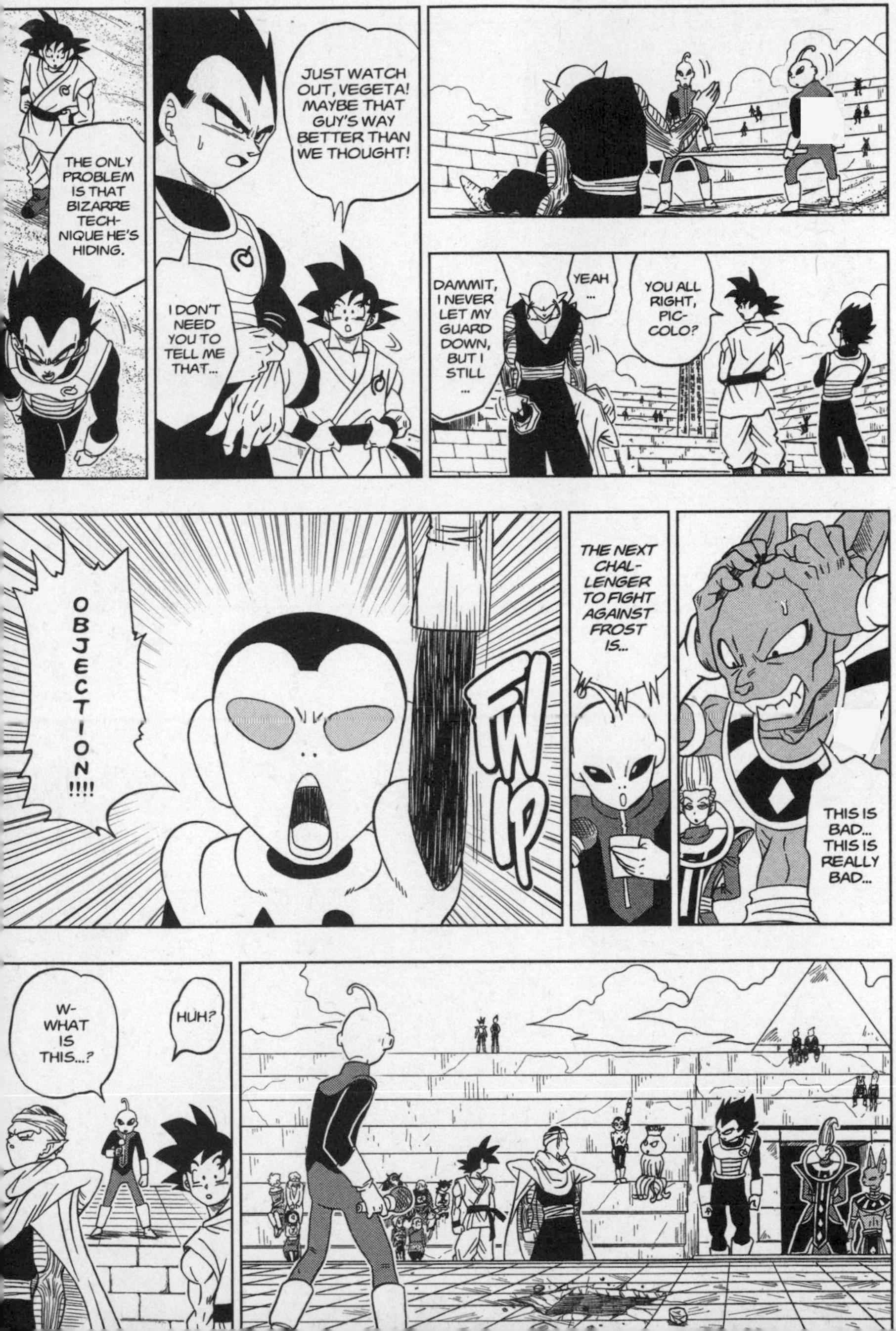
YOU ALL RIGHT, PICCOLO?
YEAH...
DAMMIT, I NEVER LET MY GUARD DOWN, BUT I STILL...
JUST WATCH OUT, VEGETA! MAYBE THAT GUY'S WAY BETTER THAN WE THOUGHT!
I DON'T NEED YOU TO TELL ME THAT...
THE ONLY PROBLEM IS THAT BIZARRE TECHNIQUE HE'S HIDING.
THIS IS BAD... THIS IS REALLY BAD...
THE NEXT CHALLENGER TO FIGHT AGAINST FROST IS...
FWIP
OBJECTION!!!!
HUH?
W-WHAT IS THIS...?

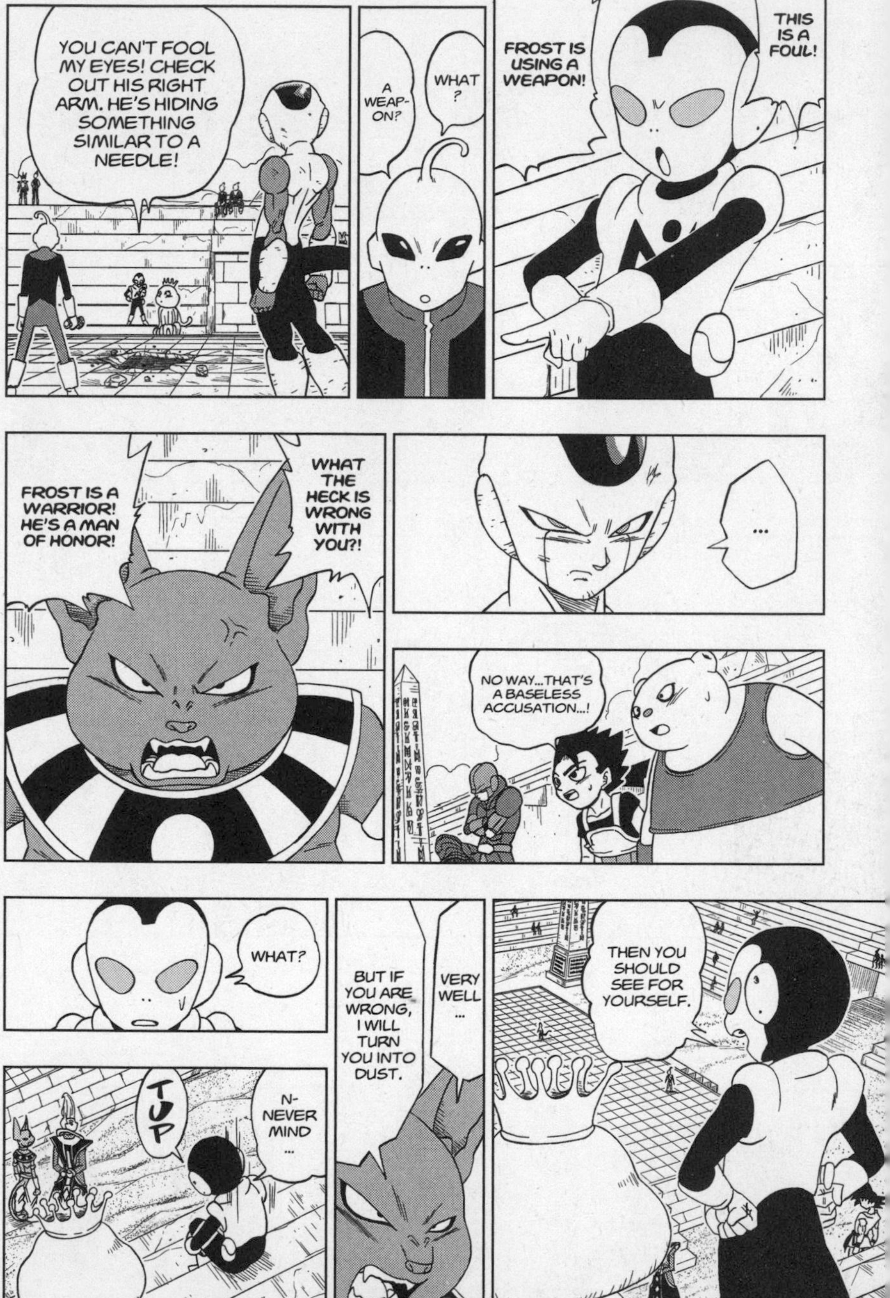
THIS IS A FOUL!
FROST IS USING A WEAPON!
WHAT?
A WEAPON?
YOU CAN'T FOOL MY EYES! CHECK OUT HIS RIGHT ARM. HE'S HIDING SOMETHING SIMILAR TO A NEEDLE!
...
NO WAY...THAT'S A BASELESS ACCUSATION...!
WHAT THE HECK IS WRONG WITH YOU?!
FROST IS A WARRIOR! HE'S A MAN OF HONOR!
THEN YOU SHOULD SEE FOR YOURSELF.
VERY WELL...
BUT IF YOU ARE WRONG, I WILL TURN YOU INTO DUST.
WHAT?
N-NEVER MIND...
TUP

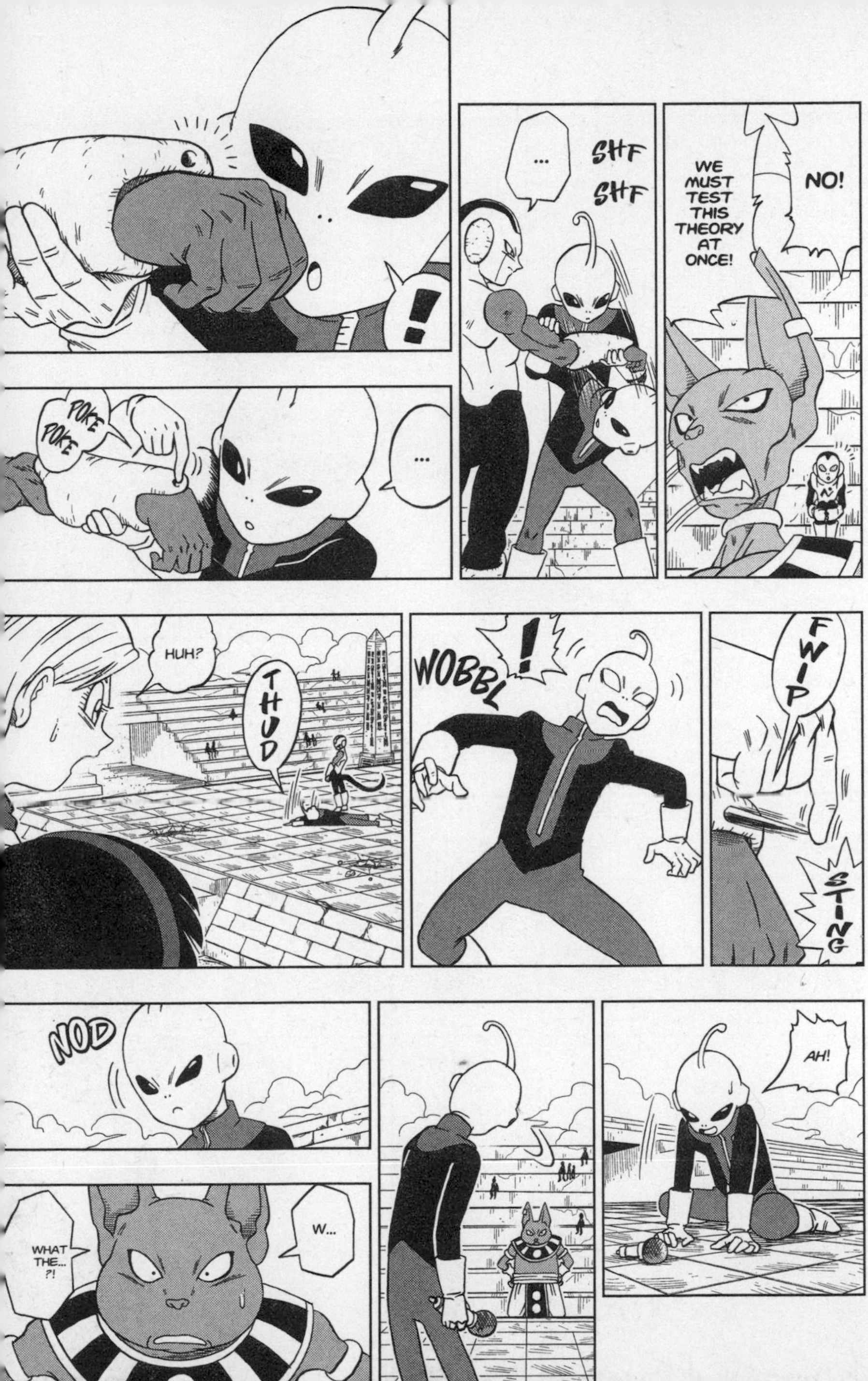
NO!
WE MUST TEST THIS THEORY AT ONCE!
...
SHF SHF
!
POKE POKE
...
FWIP
STING
!
WOBBL
HUH?
THUD
AH!
NOD
W...
WHAT THE... ?!

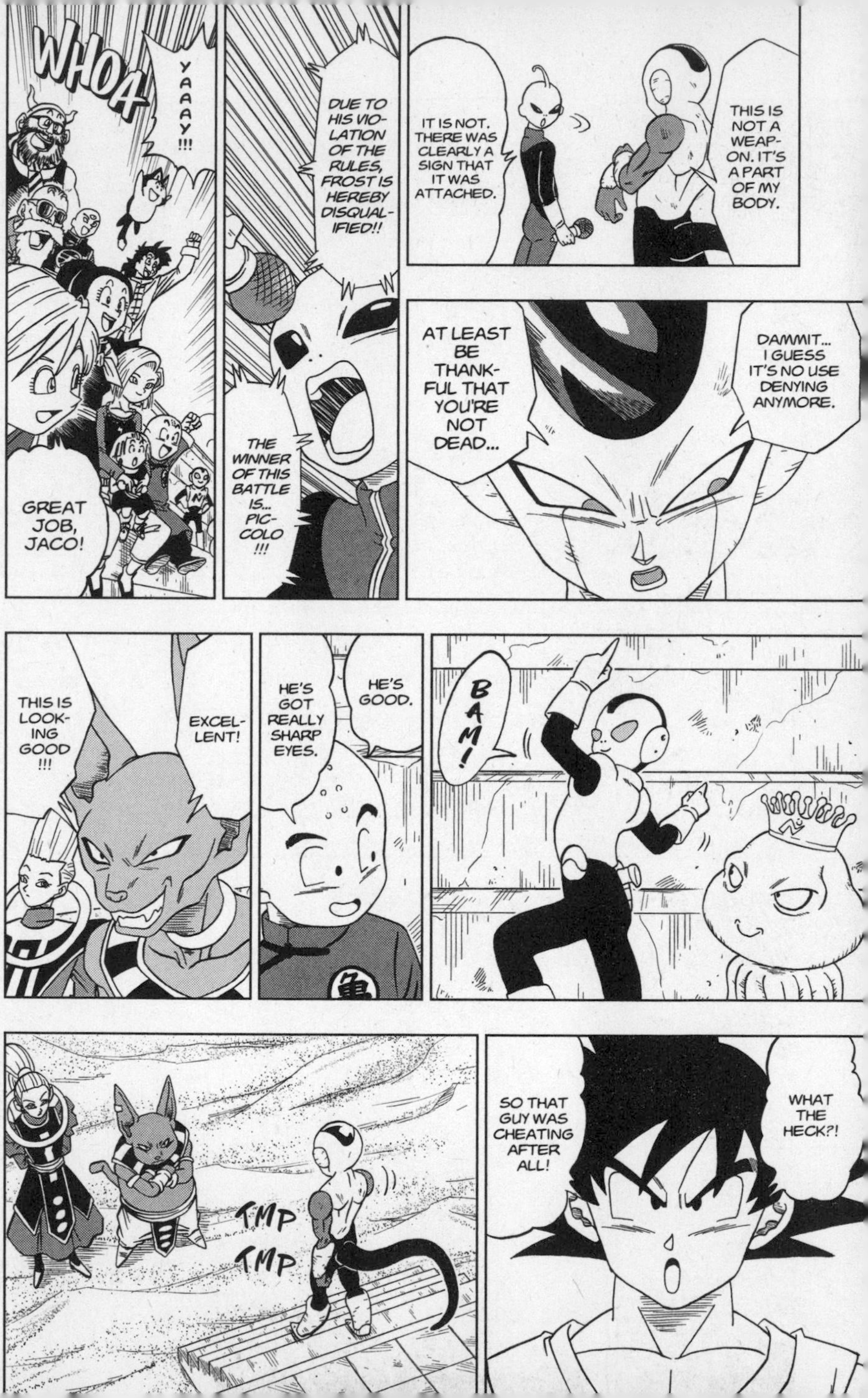
THIS IS NOT A WEAPON. IT'S A PART OF MY BODY.
IT IS NOT. THERE WAS CLEARLY A SIGN THAT IT WAS ATTACHED.
DAMMIT... I GUESS IT'S NO USE DENYING ANYMORE.
AT LEAST BE THANKFUL THAT YOU'RE NOT DEAD...
DUE TO HIS VIOLATION OF THE RULES, FROST IS HEREBY DISQUALIFIED!!
THE WINNER OF THIS BATTLE IS... PICCOLO!!!
WHOA
YAAAAY!!!
GREAT JOB, JACO!
BAM!
HE'S GOOD.
HE'S GOT REALLY SHARP EYES.
EXCELLENT!
THIS IS LOOKING GOOD!!!
WHAT THE HECK?!
SO THAT GUY WAS CHEATING AFTER ALL!
TMP
TMP

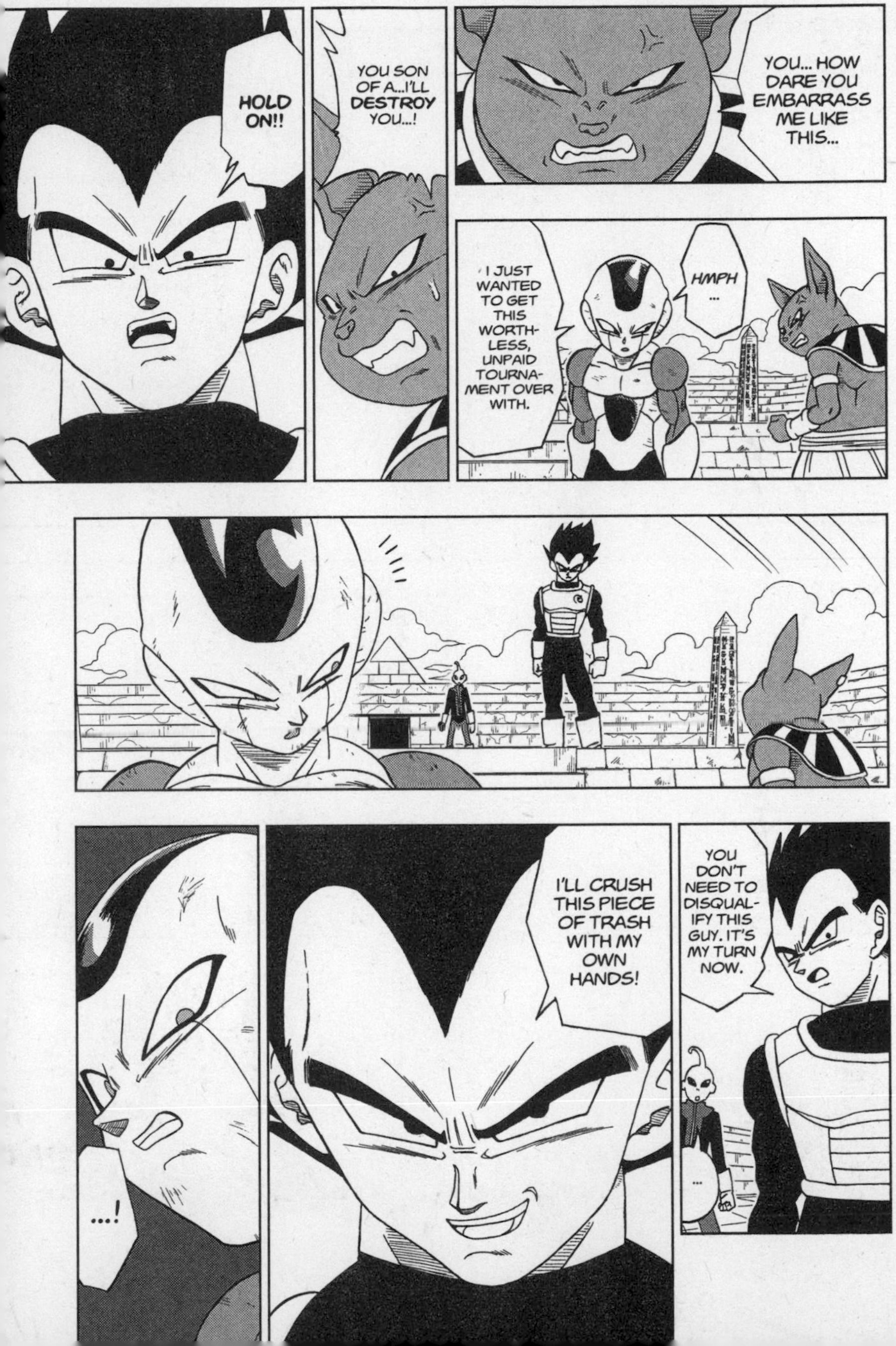
YOU... HOW DARE YOU EMBARRASS ME LIKE THIS...
HMPH ...
I JUST WANTED TO GET THIS WORTH-LESS, UNPAID TOURNA-MENT OVER WITH.
YOU SON OF A...I'LL DESTROY YOU...!
HOLD ON!!
YOU DON'T NEED TO DISQUAL-IFY THIS GUY. IT'S MY TURN NOW.
...
I'LL CRUSH THIS PIECE OF TRASH WITH MY OWN HANDS!
...!

CHAPTER 11: VEGETA'S TURN!!

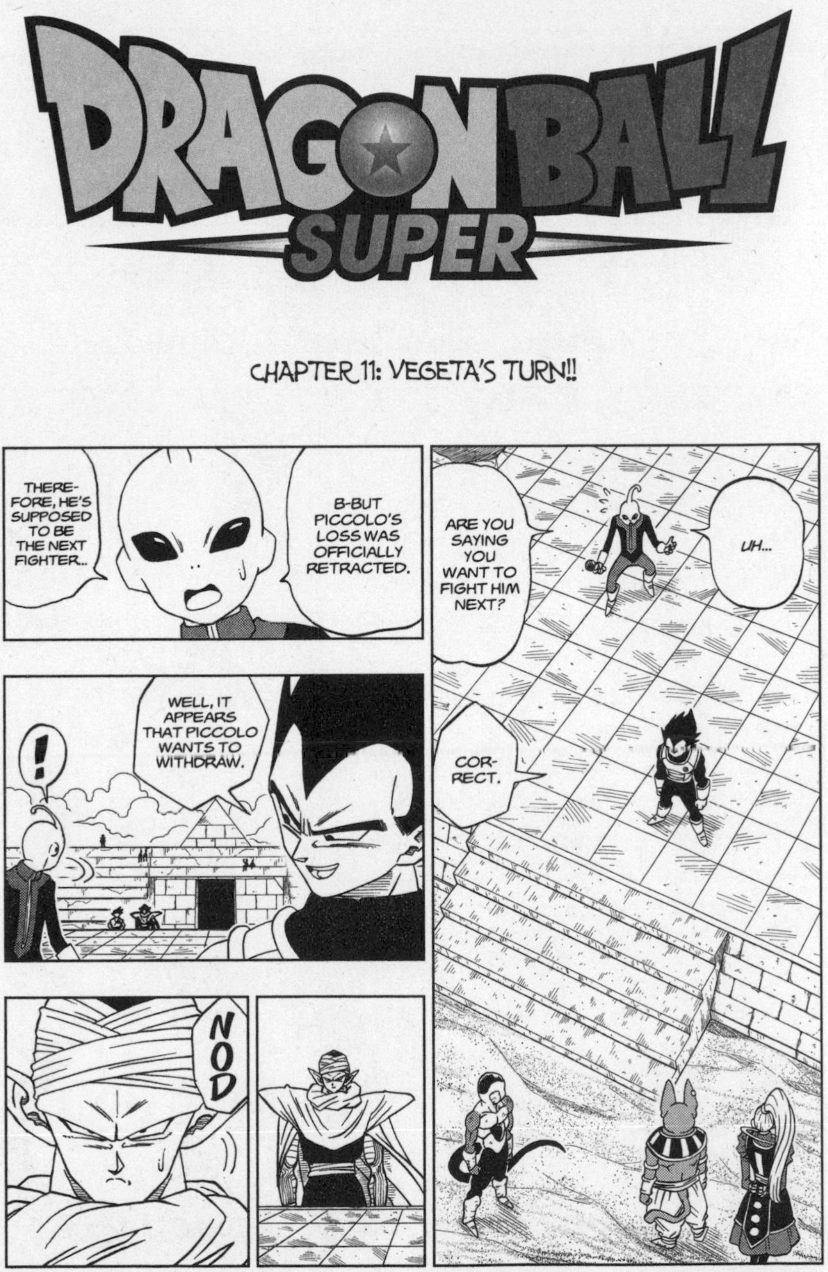
UH...
ARE YOU SAYING YOU WANT TO FIGHT HIM NEXT?
CORRECT.
B-BUT PICCOLO'S LOSS WAS OFFICIALLY RETRACTED.
THEREFORE, HE'S SUPPOSED TO BE THE NEXT FIGHTER...
WELL, IT APPEARS THAT PICCOLO WANTS TO WITHDRAW.
!
NOD

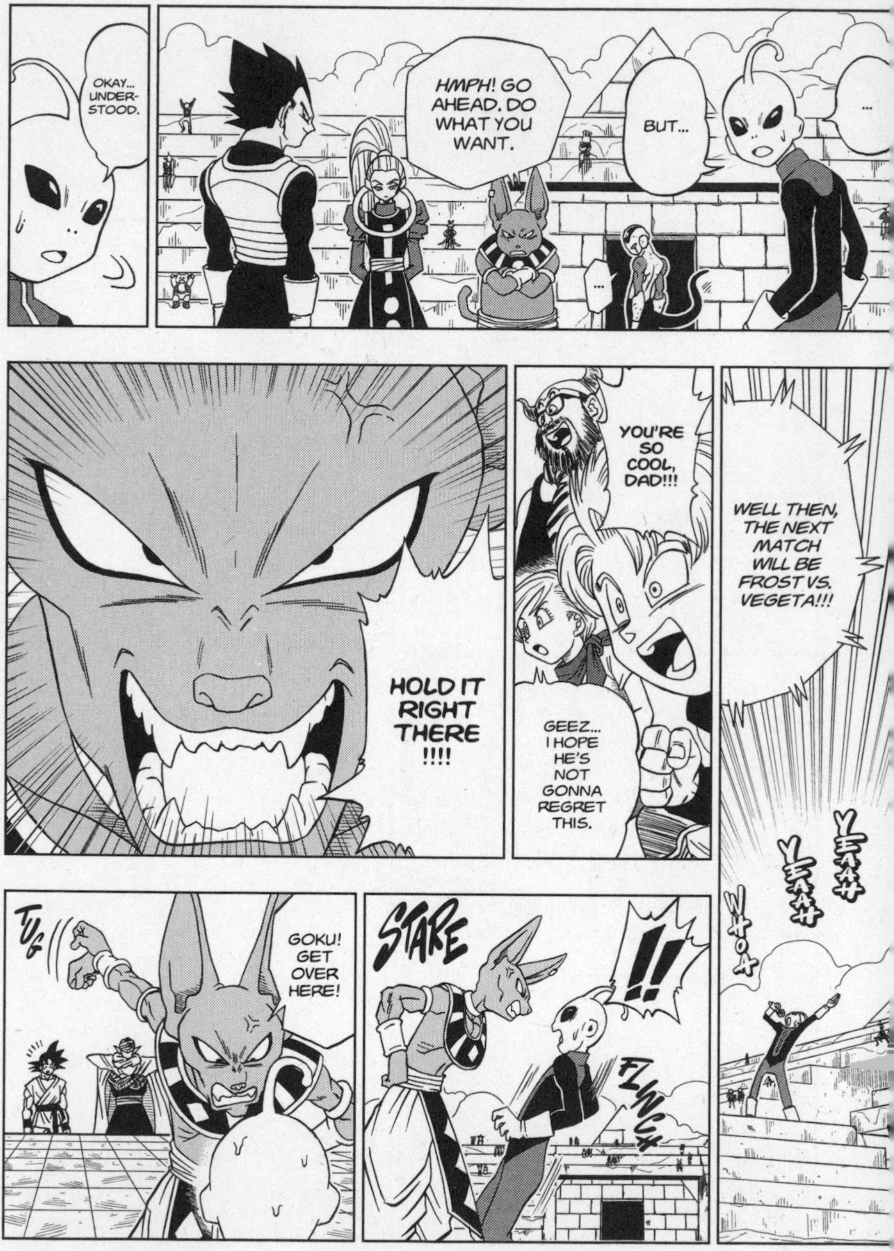
...
BUT...
HMPH! GO AHEAD. DO WHAT YOU WANT.
...
OKAY... UNDER-STOOD.
WELL THEN, THE NEXT MATCH WILL BE FROST VS. VEGETA!!!
YEAH
YEAH
WHOA
YOU'RE SO COOL, DAD!!!
GEEZ... I HOPE HE'S NOT GONNA REGRET THIS.
HOLD IT RIGHT THERE!!!!
!!
STARE
FLINCH
GOKU! GET OVER HERE!
TUG

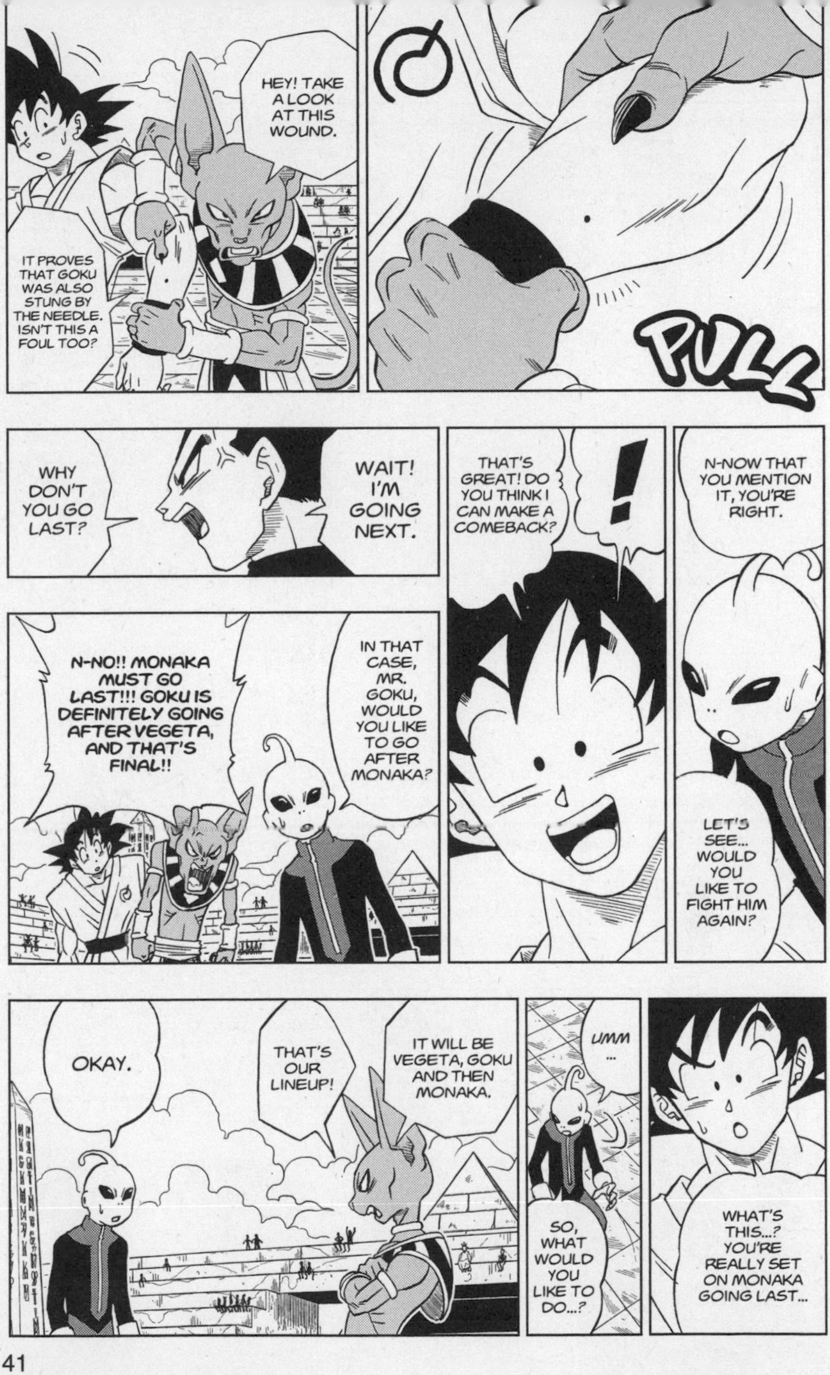
PULL
HEY! TAKE A LOOK AT THIS WOUND.
IT PROVES THAT GOKU WAS ALSO STUNG BY THE NEEDLE. ISN'T THIS A FOUL TOO?
N-NOW THAT YOU MENTION IT, YOU'RE RIGHT.
LET'S SEE... WOULD YOU LIKE TO FIGHT HIM AGAIN?
!
THAT'S GREAT! DO YOU THINK I CAN MAKE A COMEBACK?
WAIT! I'M GOING NEXT.
WHY DON'T YOU GO LAST?
IN THAT CASE, MR. GOKU, WOULD YOU LIKE TO GO AFTER MONAKA?
N-NO!! MONAKA MUST GO LAST!!! GOKU IS DEFINITELY GOING AFTER VEGETA, AND THAT'S FINAL!!
WHAT'S THIS...? YOU'RE REALLY SET ON MONAKA GOING LAST...
UMM ...
SO, WHAT WOULD YOU LIKE TO DO...?
IT WILL BE VEGETA, GOKU AND THEN MONAKA.
THAT'S OUR LINEUP!
OKAY.

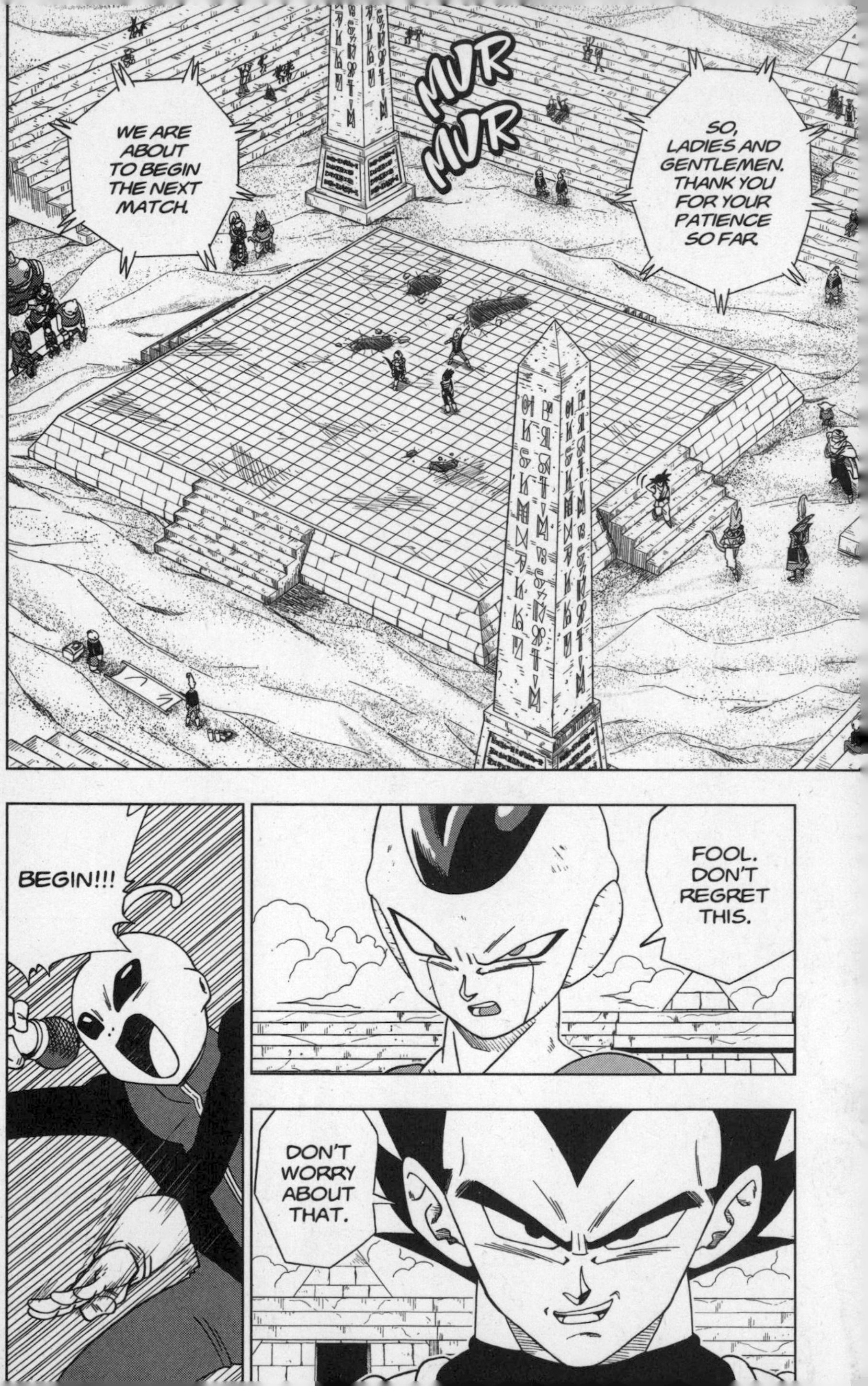
SO, LADIES AND GENTLEMEN. THANK YOU FOR YOUR PATIENCE SO FAR.
MUR MUR
WE ARE ABOUT TO BEGIN THE NEXT MATCH.
FOOL. DON'T REGRET THIS.
DON'T WORRY ABOUT THAT.
BEGIN!!!

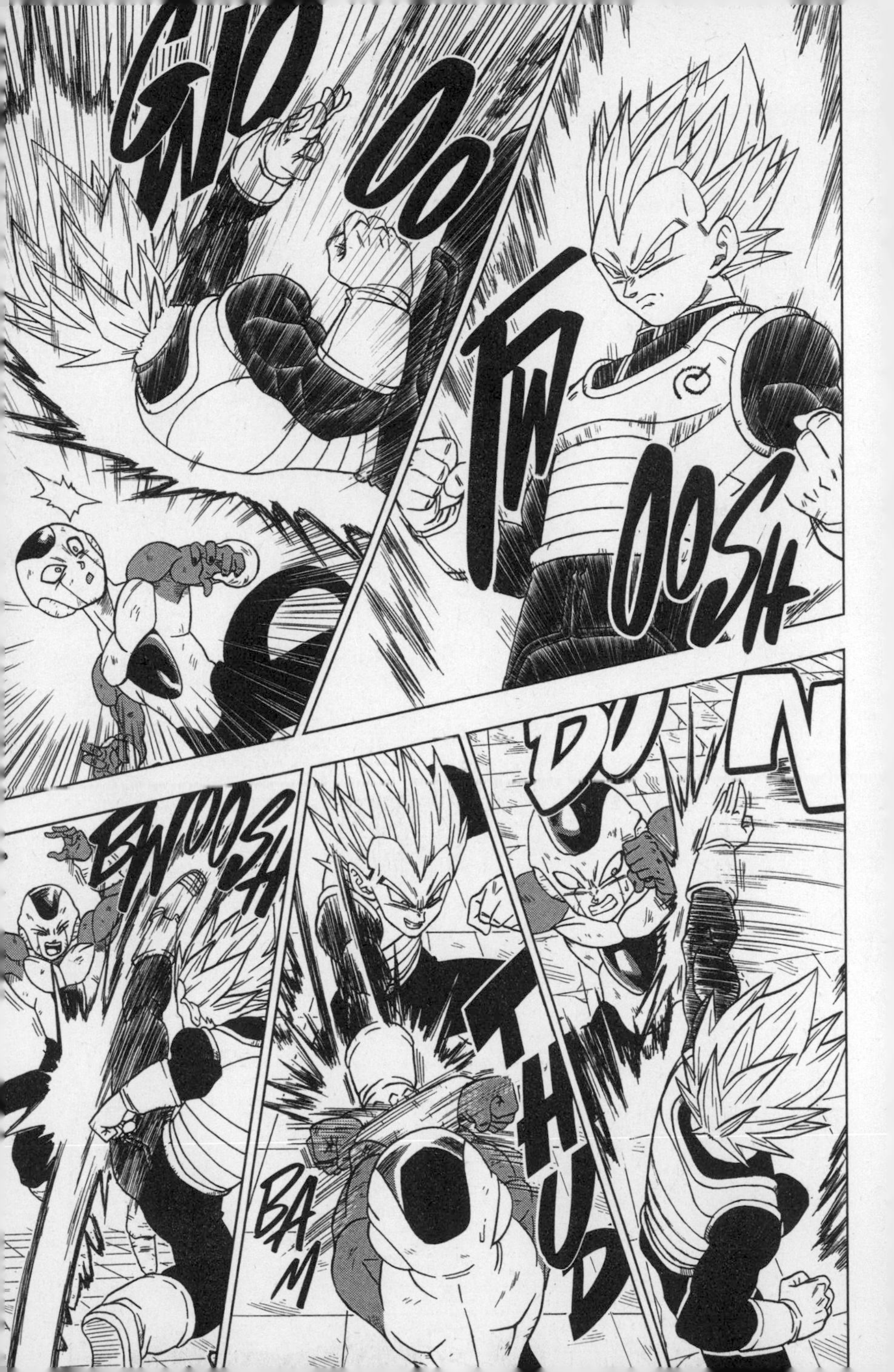
TWOOSH
GWOOO
DUN
THUD
BAM
BWOOSH

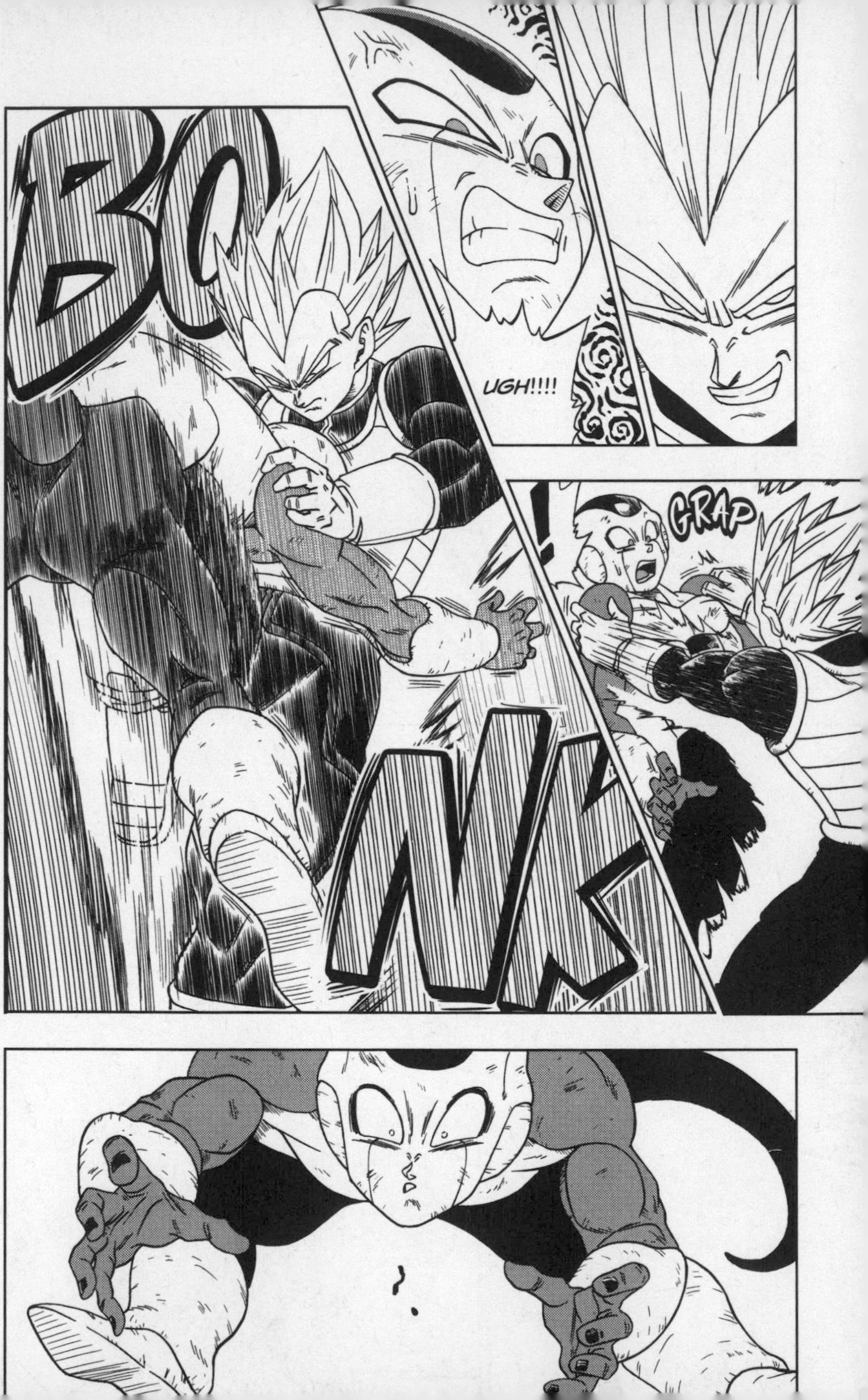
UGH!!!!
GRAP
BOM

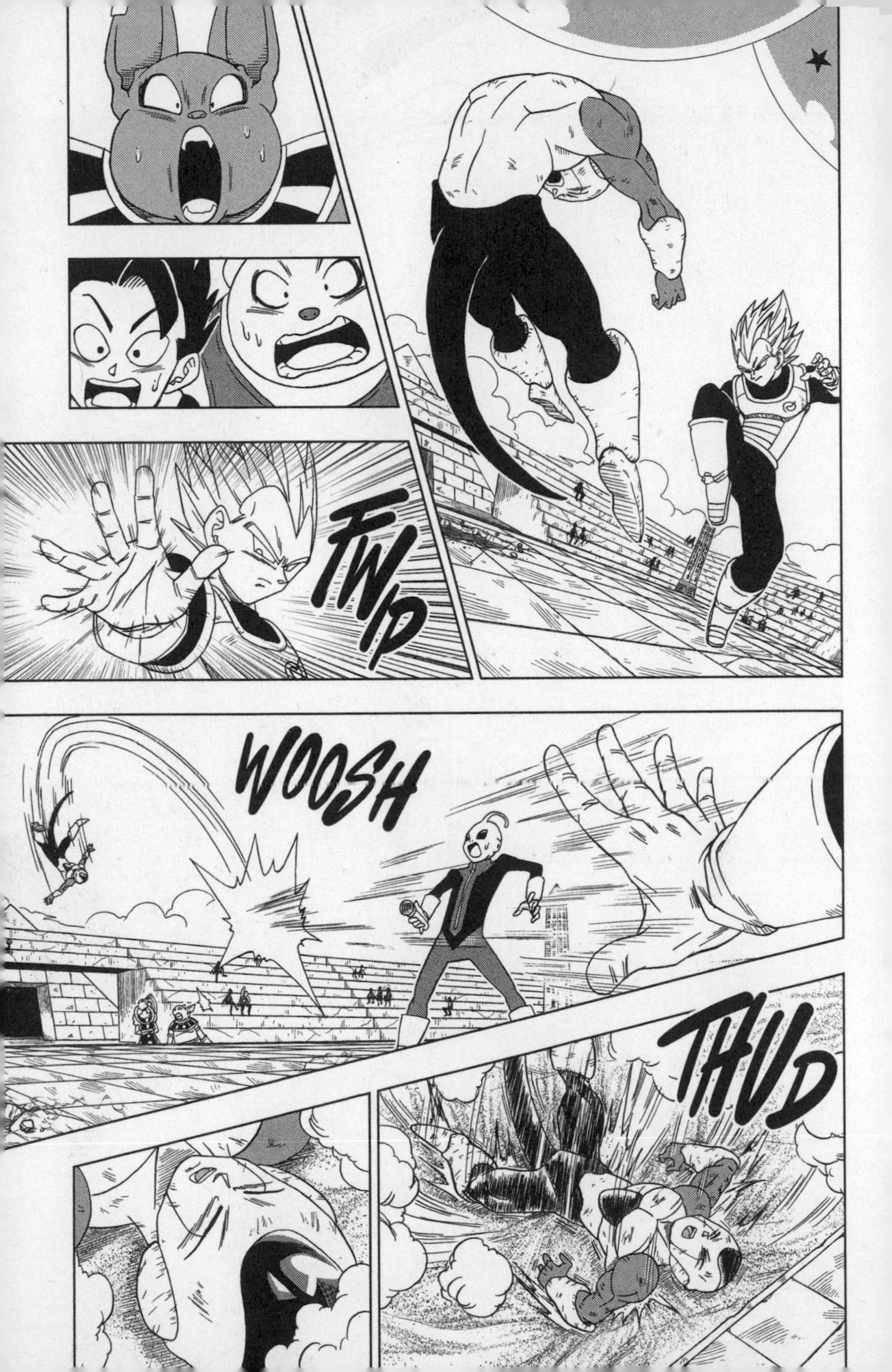
FWIP
WOOSH
THUD

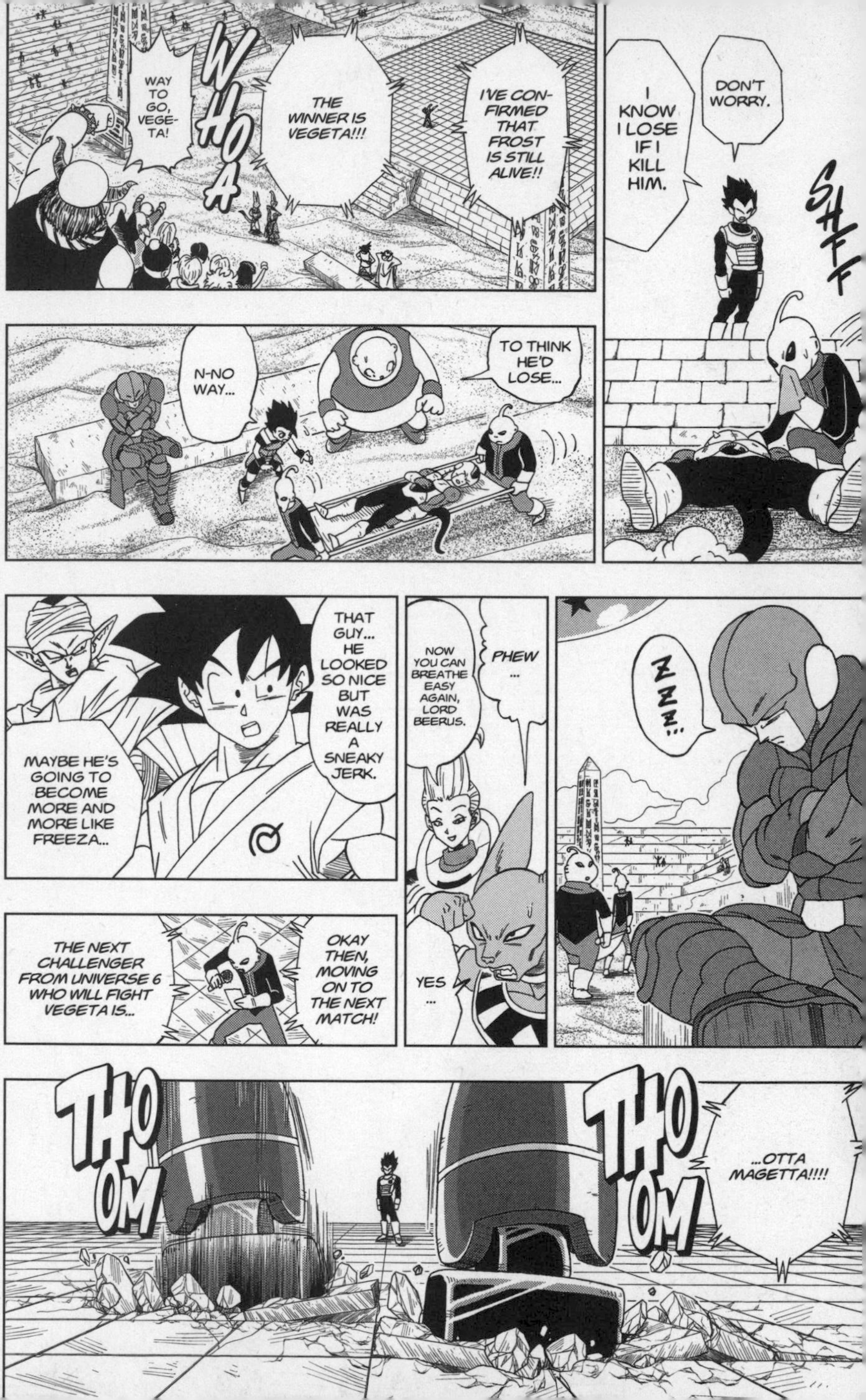
DON'T WORRY.
I KNOW I LOSE IF I KILL HIM.
SHFF
I'VE CONFIRMED THAT FROST IS STILL ALIVE!!
THE WINNER IS VEGETA!!!
WHOA
WAY TO GO, VEGETA!
TO THINK HE'D LOSE...
N-NO WAY...
ZZZ...
PHEW ...
NOW YOU CAN BREATHE EASY AGAIN, LORD BEERUS.
YES ...
THAT GUY... HE LOOKED SO NICE BUT WAS REALLY A SNEAKY JERK.
MAYBE HE'S GOING TO BECOME MORE AND MORE LIKE FREEZA...
OKAY THEN, MOVING ON TO THE NEXT MATCH!
THE NEXT CHALLENGER FROM UNIVERSE 6 WHO WILL FIGHT VEGETA IS...
...OTTA MAGETTA!!!!
THOOM
THOOM

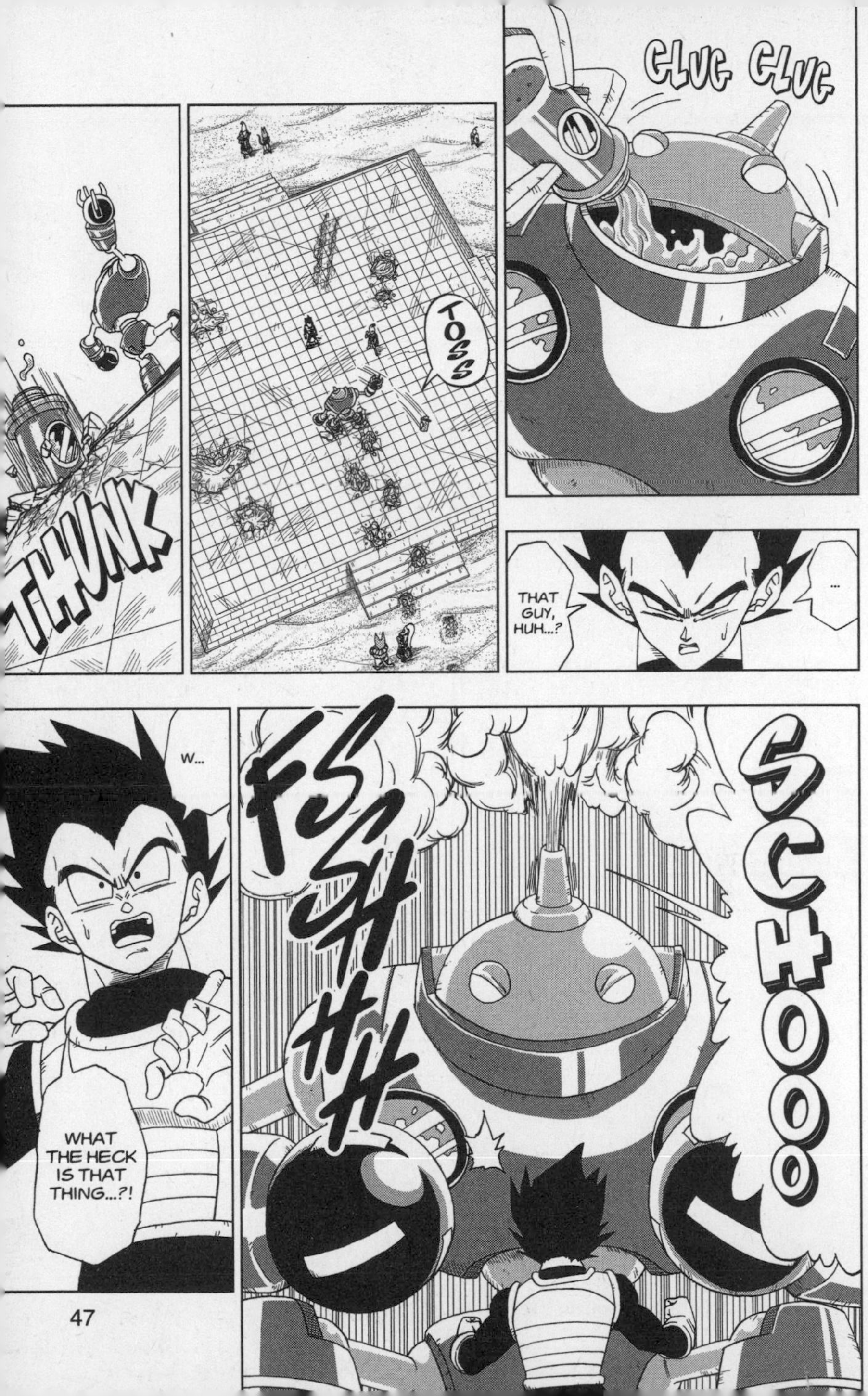
GLUG GLUG
...
THAT GUY, HUH...?
TOSS
THUNK
SCHOOO
FSSHHH
W...
WHAT THE HECK IS THAT THING...?!

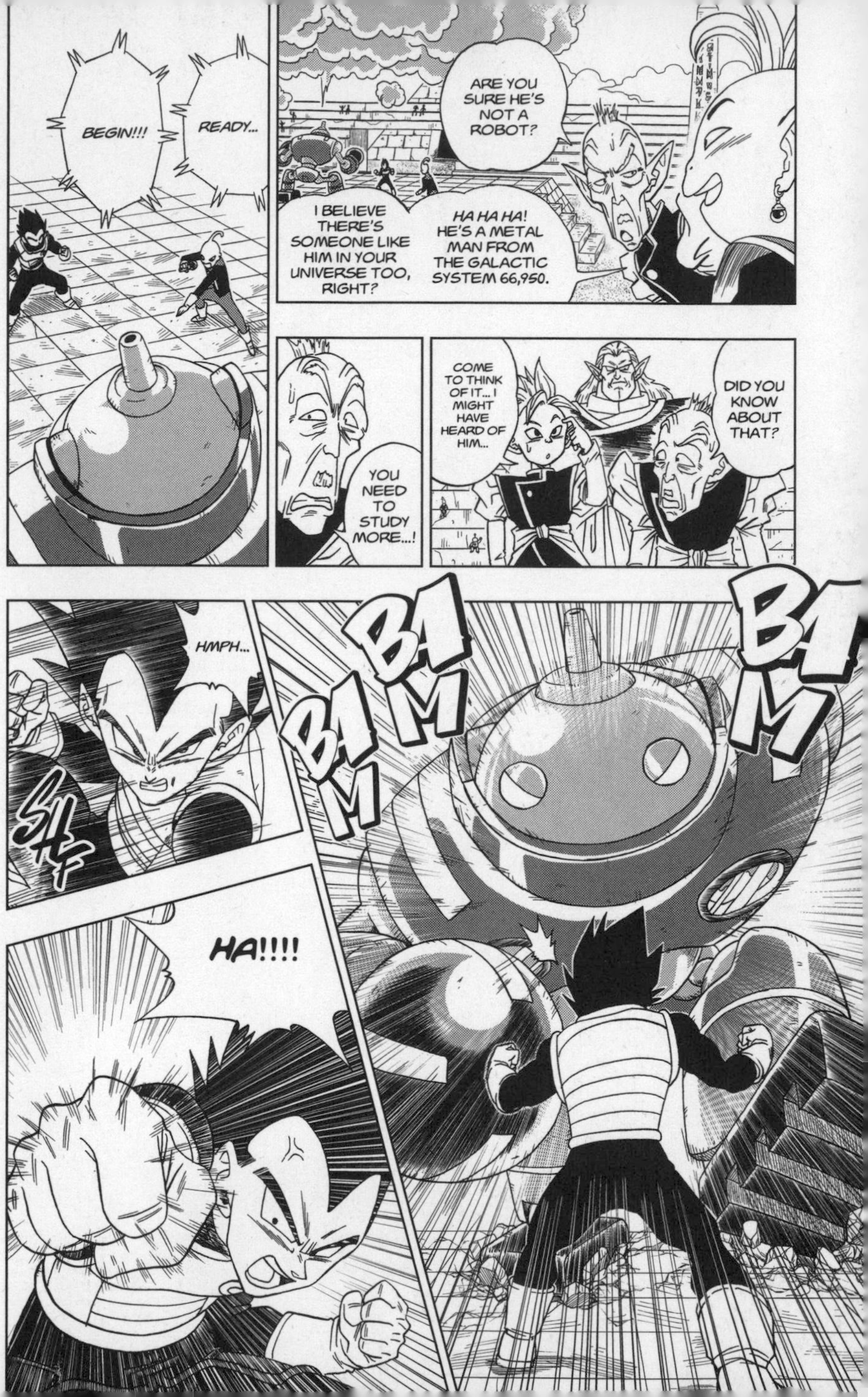
ARE YOU SURE HE'S NOT A ROBOT?
HA HA HA! HE'S A METAL MAN FROM THE GALACTIC SYSTEM 66,950.
I BELIEVE THERE'S SOMEONE LIKE HIM IN YOUR UNIVERSE TOO, RIGHT?
DID YOU KNOW ABOUT THAT?
COME TO THINK OF IT... I MIGHT HAVE HEARD OF HIM...
YOU NEED TO STUDY MORE...!
READY...
BEGIN!!!
BAM
BAM
BAM
HMPH...
SHF
HA!!!!

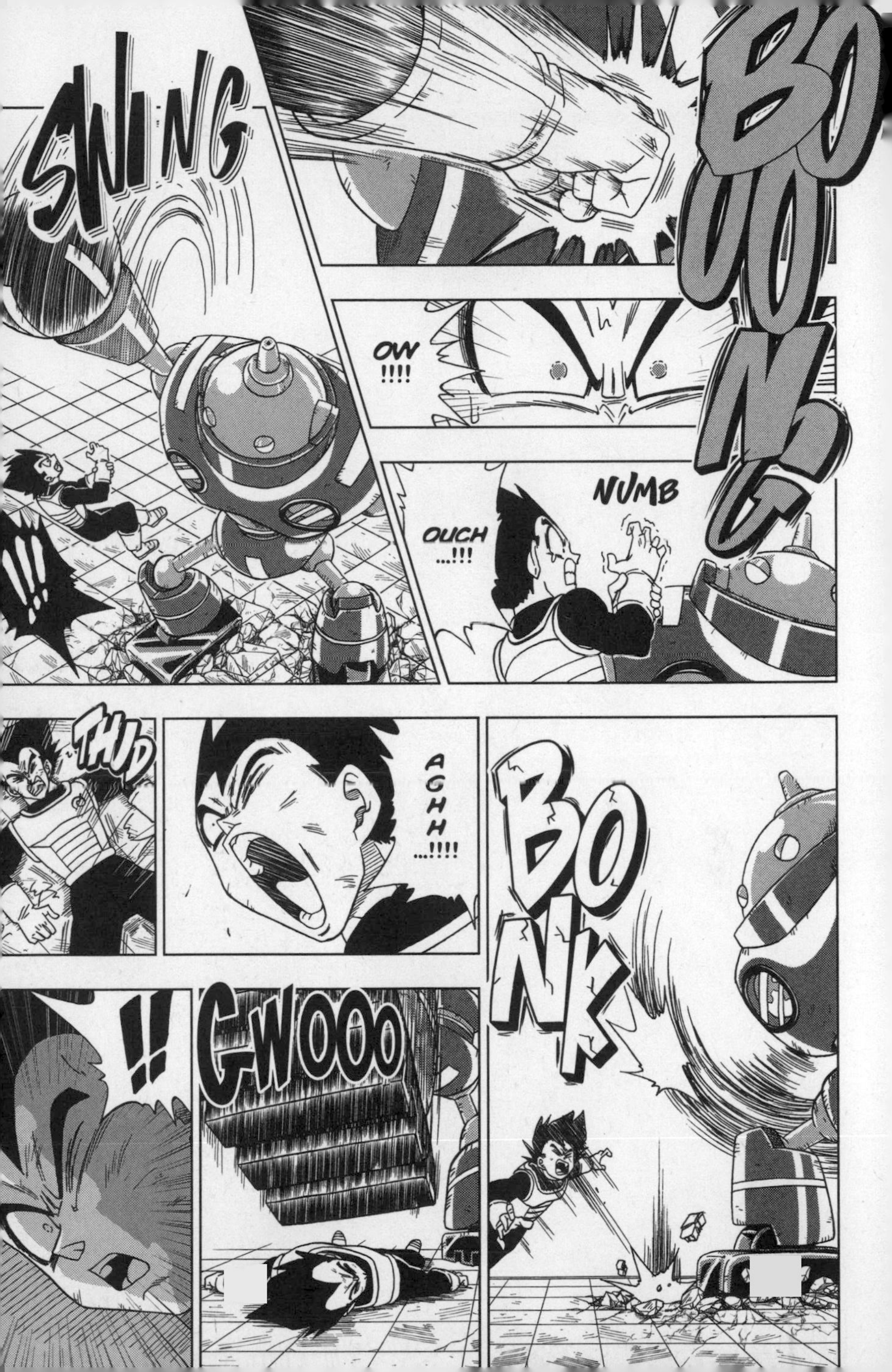

BOOOONG
OW !!!!
NUMB
OUCH ...!!!
SWING
!!!
BONK
AGHH ...!!!!
THUD
GWOOO
!!

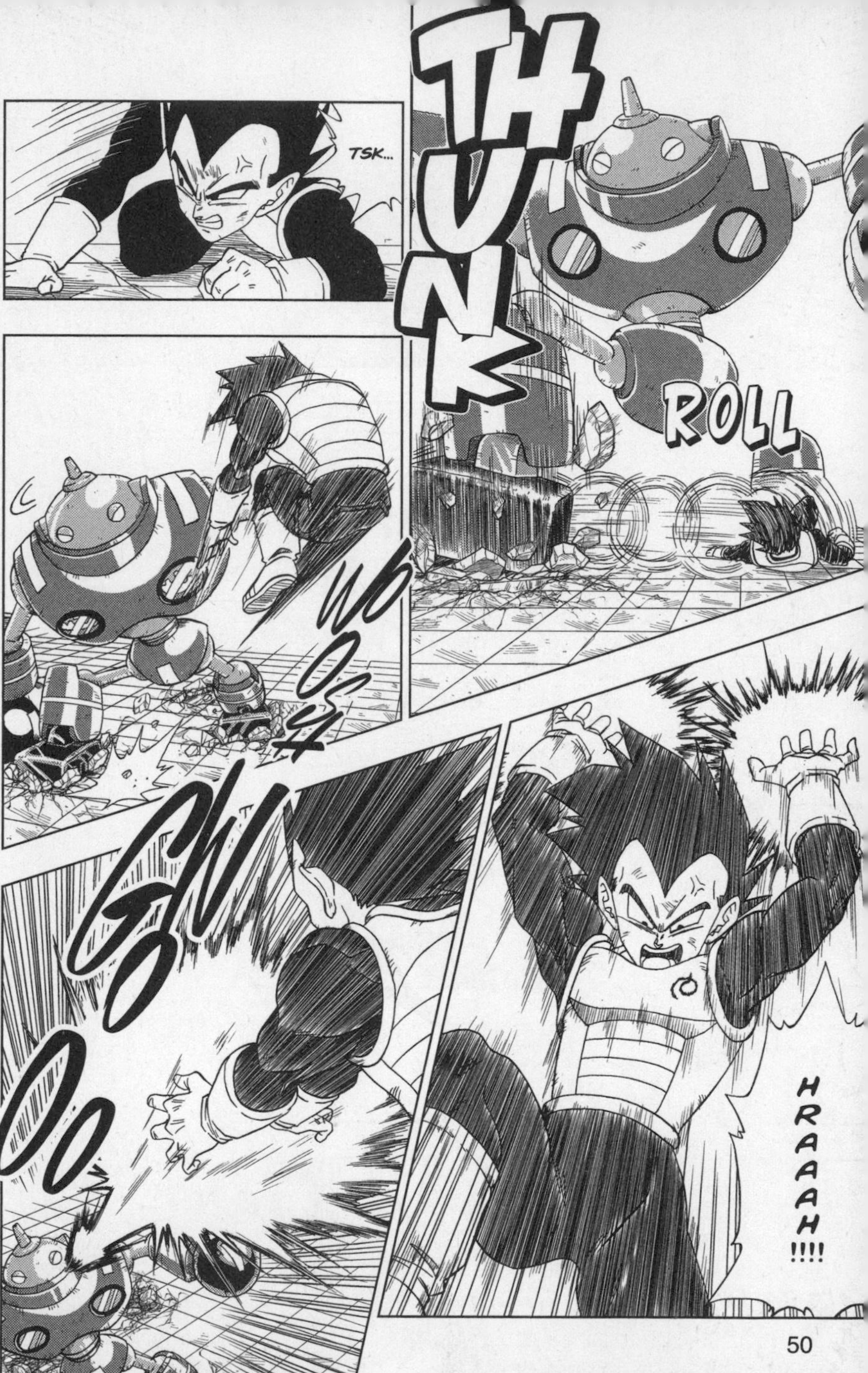
THUNK
ROLL
TSK...
WOOSH
HRAAAH!!!!

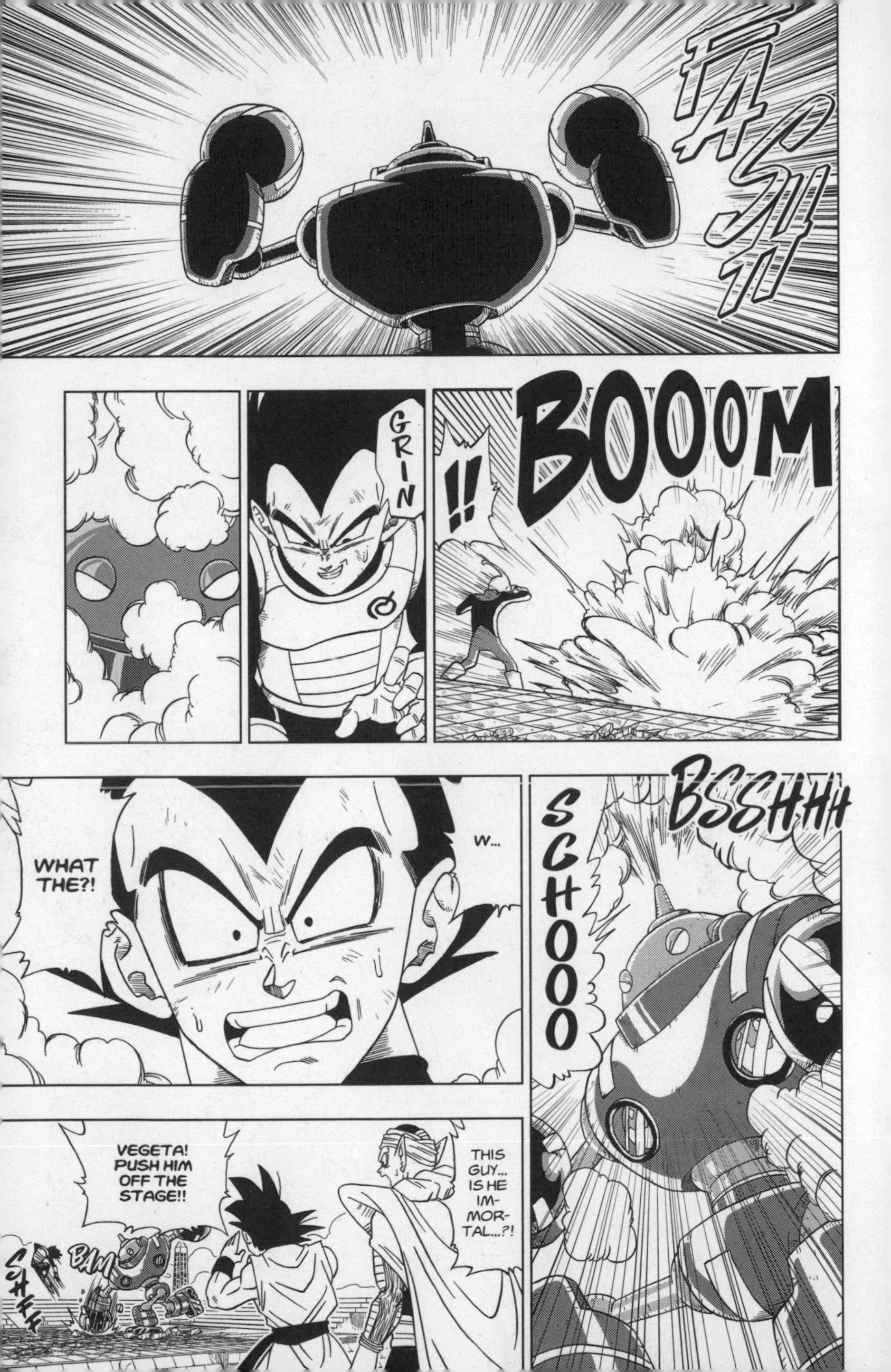

FASH
BOOOM
!!
GRIN
BSSHHH
SCHOOOO
W...
WHAT THE?!
THIS GUY... IS HE IM-MOR-TAL...?!
VEGETA! PUSH HIM OFF THE STAGE!!
BAM
SHFF

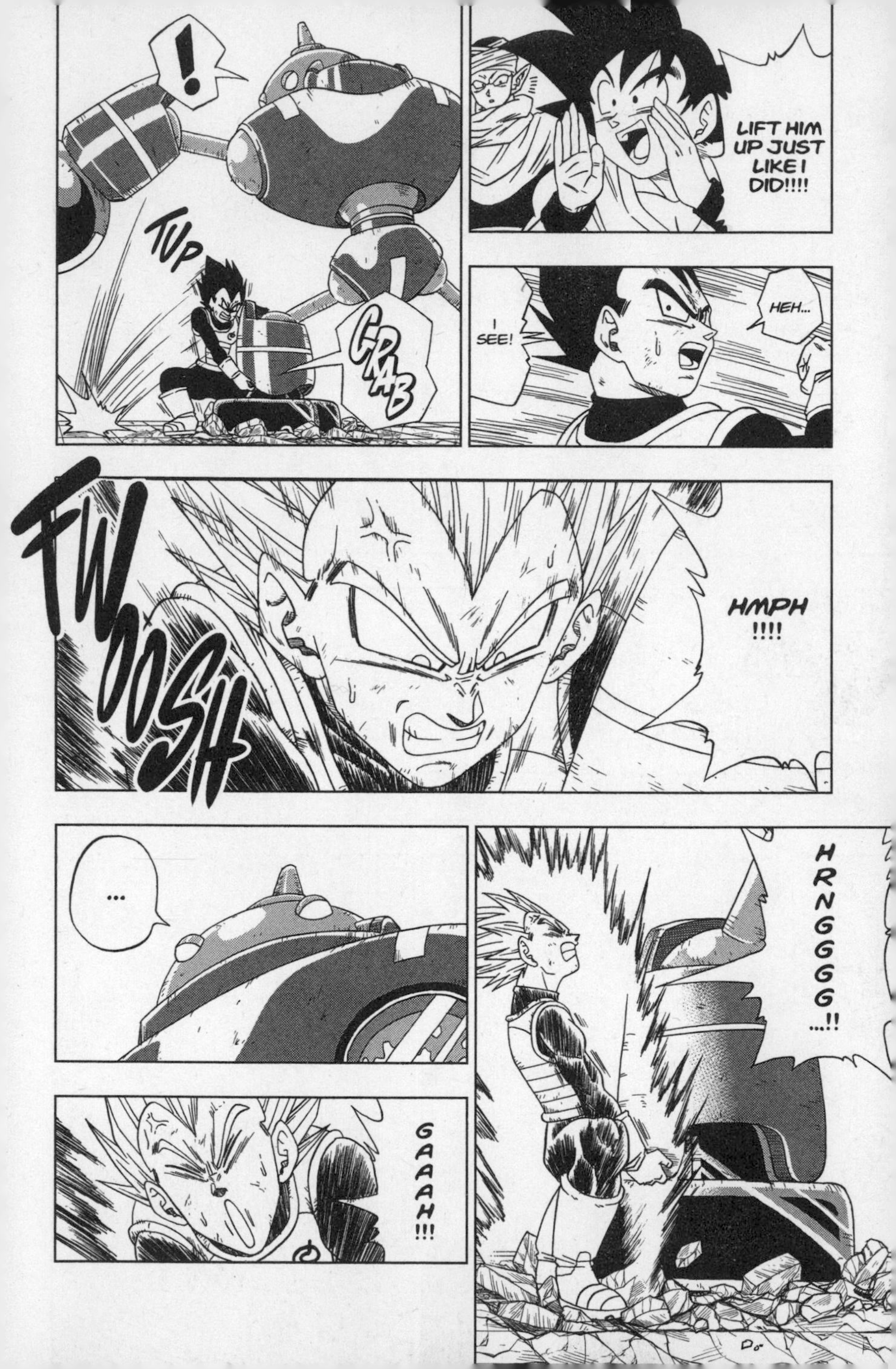
LIFT HIM UP JUST LIKE I DID!!!!
HEH...
I SEE!
!
TUP
GRAB
HMPH !!!!
FWOOSH
HRNGGGG...!!
...
GAAAH!!!

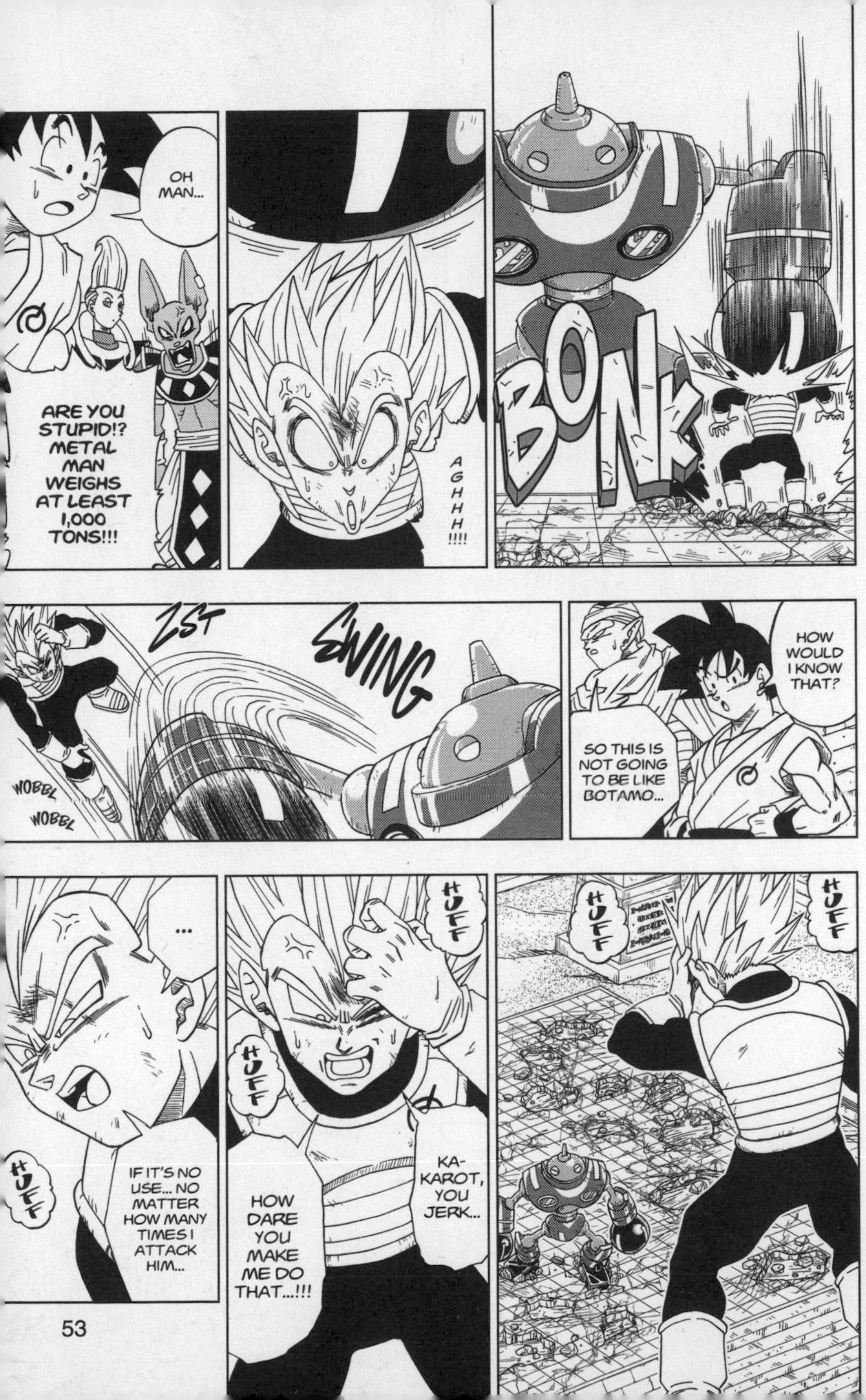
BONK
AGHHH!!!!
OH MAN...
ARE YOU STUPID!? METAL MAN WEIGHS AT LEAST 1,000 TONS!!!
HOW WOULD I KNOW THAT?
SO THIS IS NOT GOING TO BE LIKE BOTAMO...
SWING
ZST
WOBBL
WOBBL
HUFF
HUFF
HUFF
KA-KAROT, YOU JERK...
HOW DARE YOU MAKE ME DO THAT...!!!
...
IF IT'S NO USE... NO MATTER HOW MANY TIMES I ATTACK HIM...
HUFF

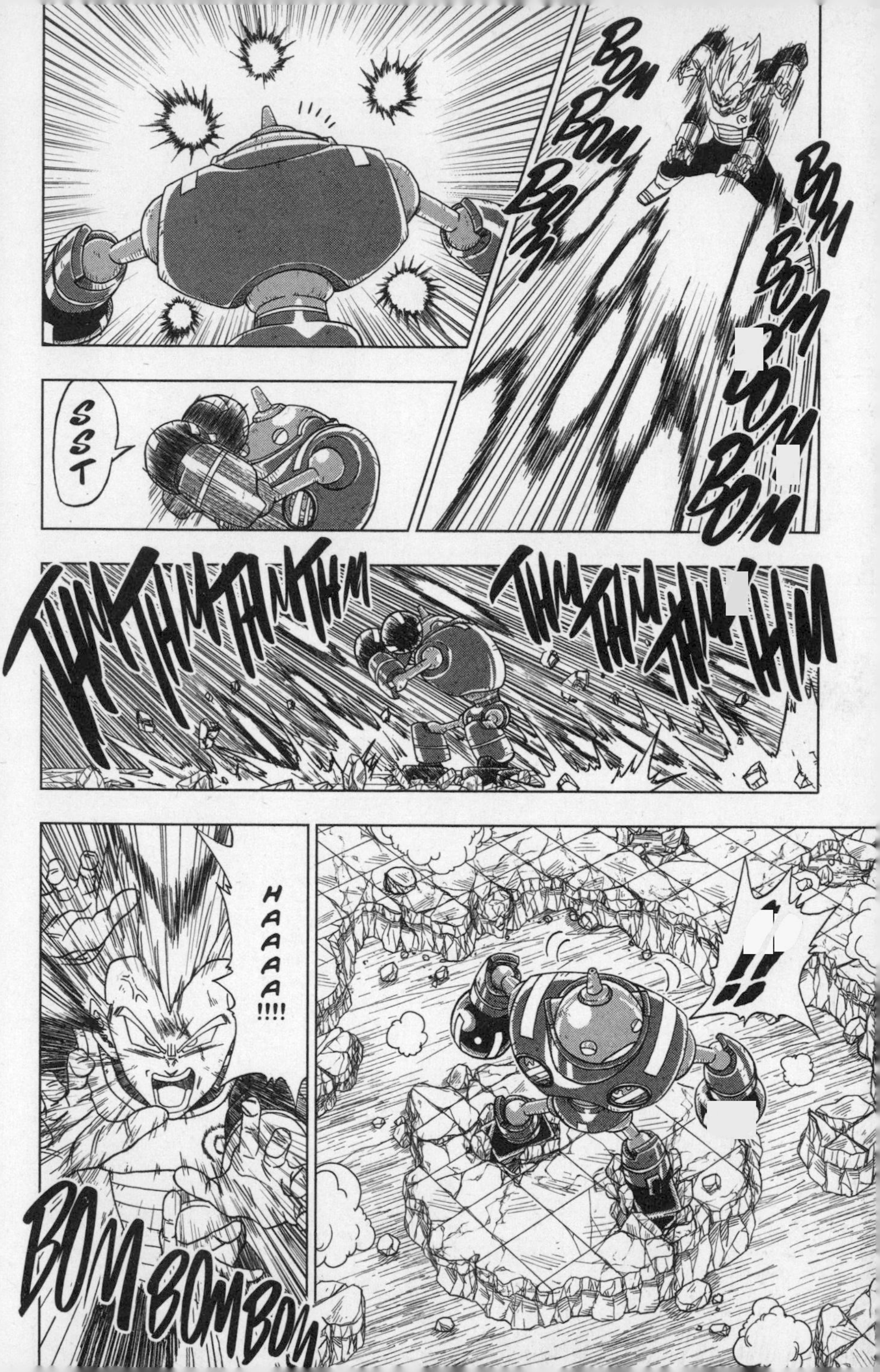
BOM BOM BOM
BOM BOM BOM BOM BOM
SST
THM THM THM THM THM THM THM THM
!!
HAAAAA!!!!
BOM BOMBOM

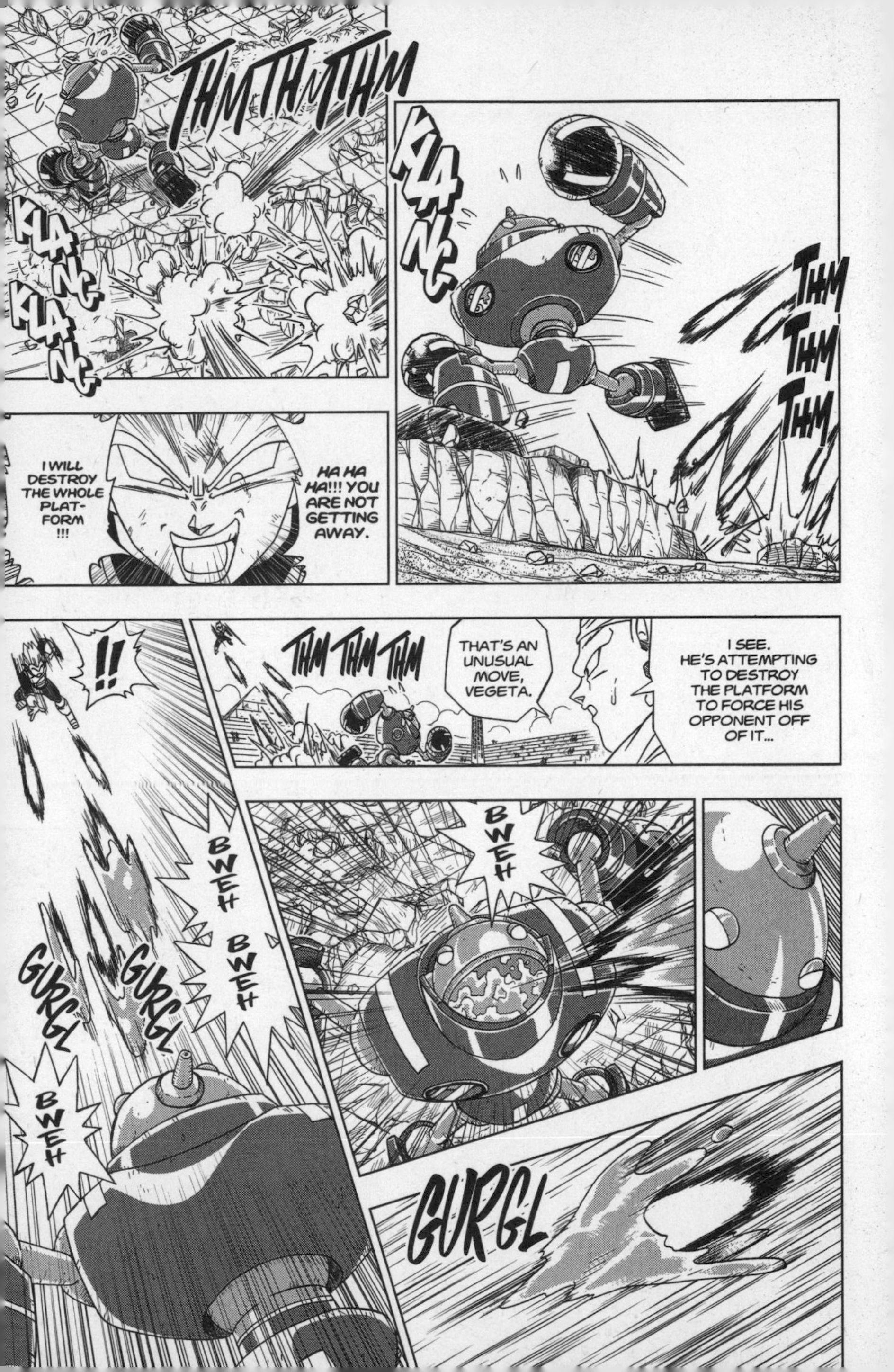
KLANG
THM THM THM
THMTHMTHM
KLANG KLANG
HA HA HA!!! YOU ARE NOT GETTING AWAY.
I WILL DESTROY THE WHOLE PLATFORM !!!
I SEE. HE'S ATTEMPTING TO DESTROY THE PLATFORM TO FORCE HIS OPPONENT OFF OF IT...
THAT'S AN UNUSUAL MOVE, VEGETA.
THM THM THM
!!
BWEH
BWEH BWEH
GURGL GURGL
BWEH BWEH
GURGL

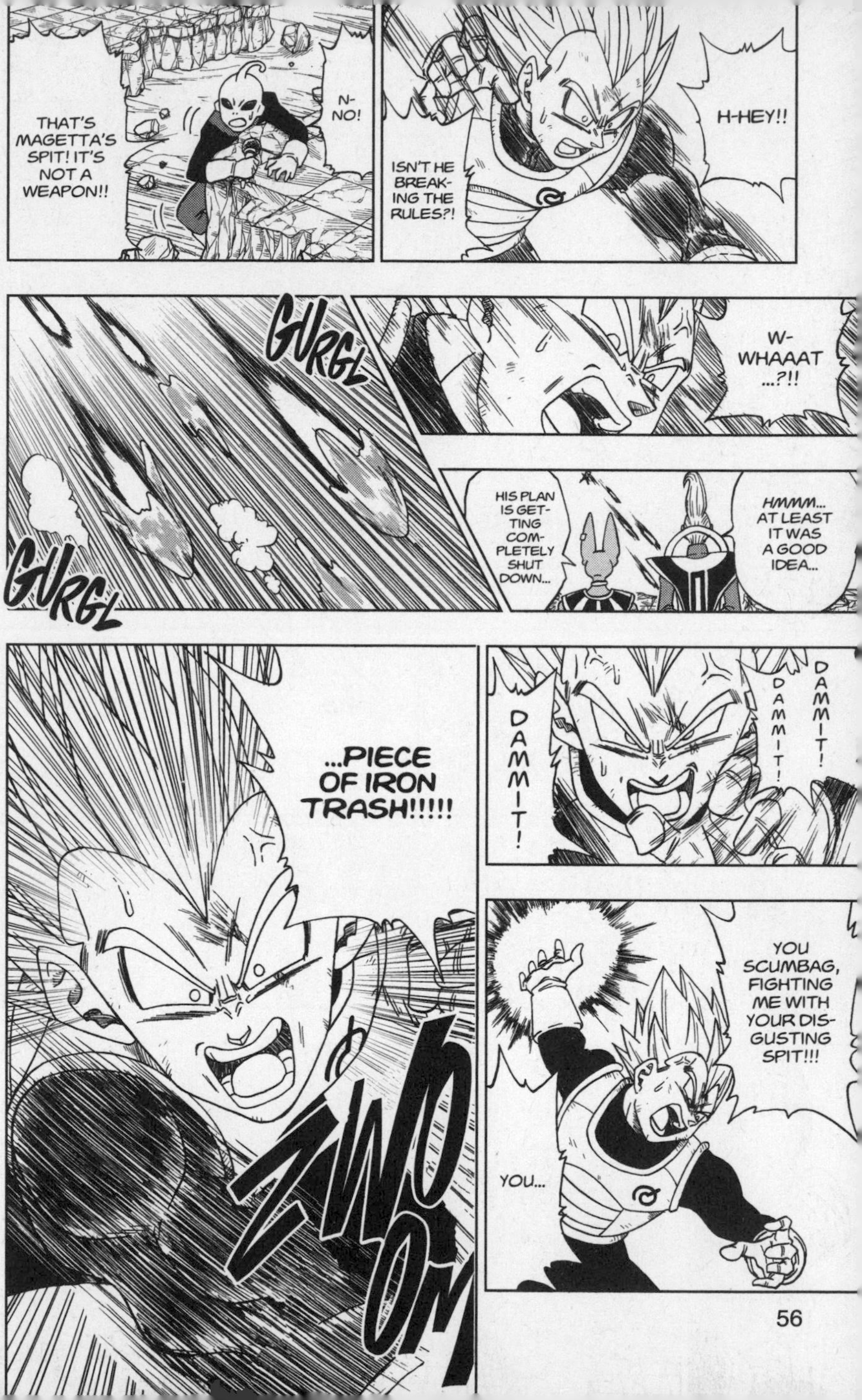
H-HEY!!
ISN'T HE BREAKING THE RULES?!
N-NO!
THAT'S MAGETTA'S SPIT! IT'S NOT A WEAPON!!
GURGL
W-WHAAAT...?!!
HMMM... AT LEAST IT WAS A GOOD IDEA...
HIS PLAN IS GETTING COMPLETELY SHUT DOWN...
GURGL
DAMMIT!
DAMMIT!
DAMMIT!
YOU SCUMBAG, FIGHTING ME WITH YOUR DISGUSTING SPIT!!!
YOU...
...PIECE OF IRON TRASH!!!!!

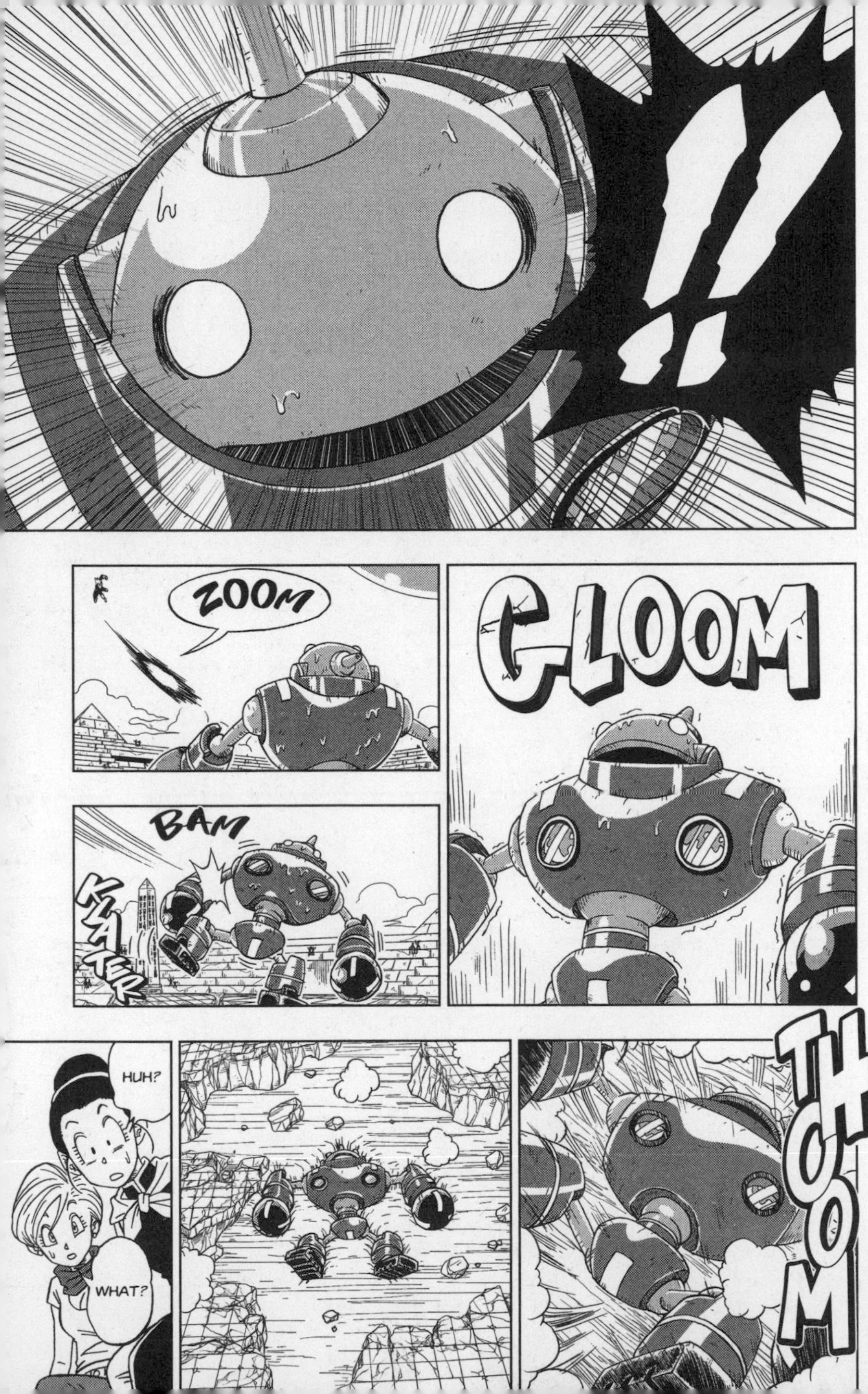
GLOOM
ZOOM
BAM
KLATTER
THOOM
HUH?
WHAT?

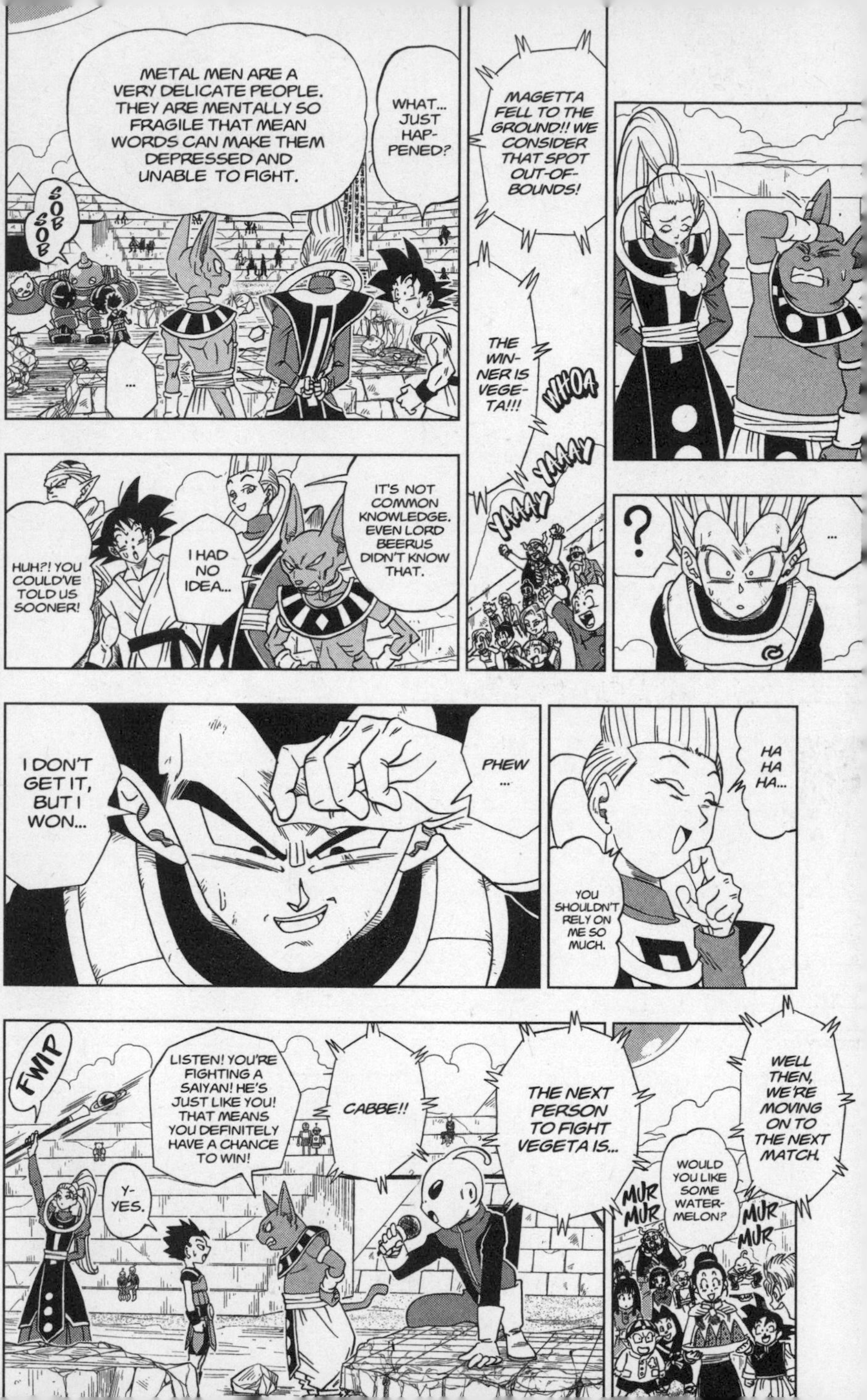
?
...
MAGETTA FELL TO THE GROUND!! WE CONSIDER THAT SPOT OUT-OF-BOUNDS!
THE WINNER IS VEGETA!!!
WHOA
YAAAAY
YAAAAY
WHAT... JUST HAPPENED?
METAL MEN ARE A VERY DELICATE PEOPLE. THEY ARE MENTALLY SO FRAGILE THAT MEAN WORDS CAN MAKE THEM DEPRESSED AND UNABLE TO FIGHT.
SOB SOB SOB
...
IT'S NOT COMMON KNOWLEDGE. EVEN LORD BEERUS DIDN'T KNOW THAT.
I HAD NO IDEA...
HUH?! YOU COULD'VE TOLD US SOONER!
HA HA HA...
YOU SHOULDN'T RELY ON ME SO MUCH.
PHEW...
I DON'T GET IT, BUT I WON...
WELL THEN, WE'RE MOVING ON TO THE NEXT MATCH.
MUR MUR
WOULD YOU LIKE SOME WATER-MELON?
MUR MUR
THE NEXT PERSON TO FIGHT VEGETA IS...
CABBE!!
LISTEN! YOU'RE FIGHTING A SAIYAN! HE'S JUST LIKE YOU! THAT MEANS YOU DEFINITELY HAVE A CHANCE TO WIN!
Y-YES.
FWIP

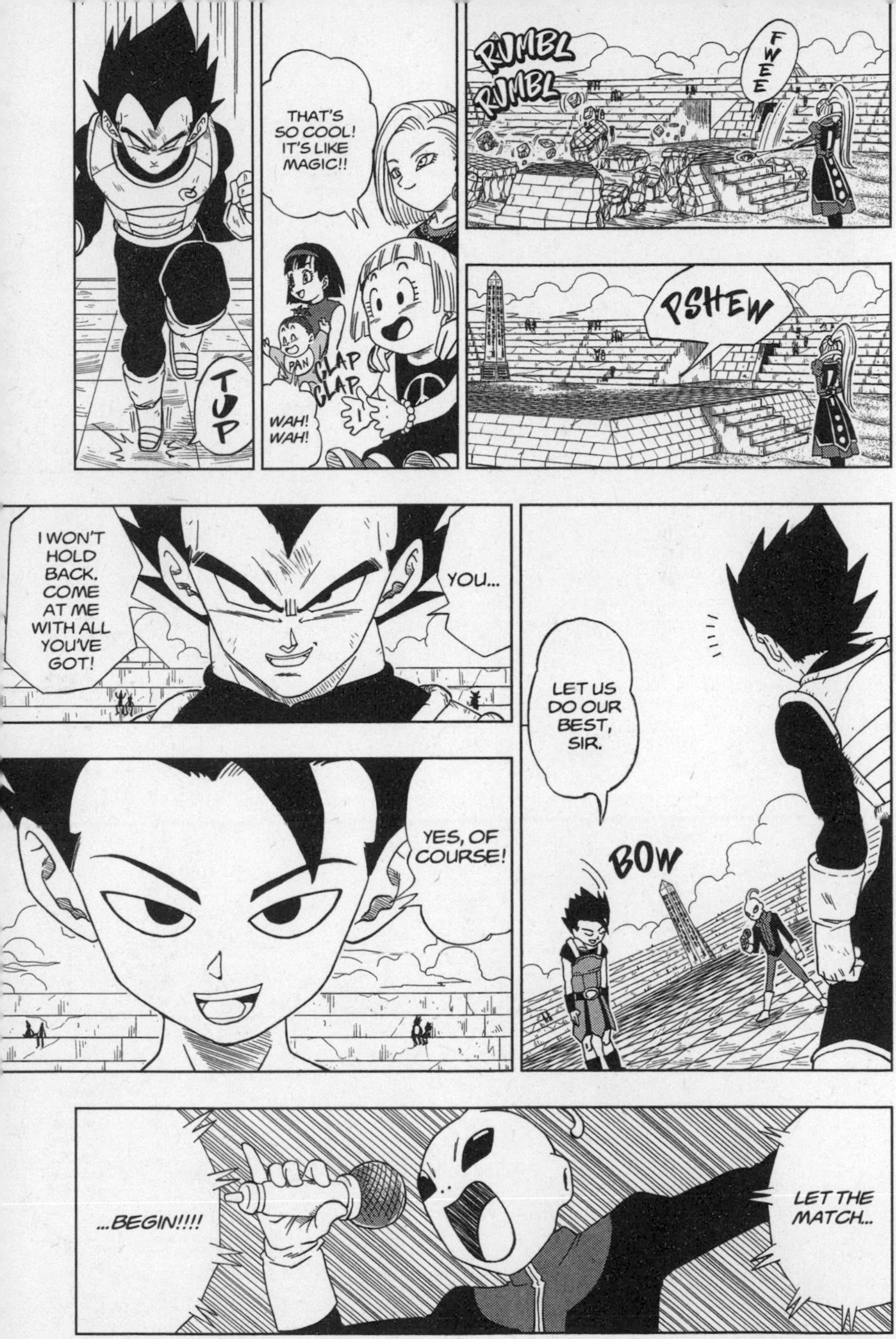
RUMBL
RUMBL
FWEE
PSHEW
THAT'S SO COOL! IT'S LIKE MAGIC!!
CLAP CLAP
WAH! WAH!
TUP
LET US DO OUR BEST, SIR.
BOW
YOU...
I WON'T HOLD BACK. COME AT ME WITH ALL YOU'VE GOT!
YES, OF COURSE!
LET THE MATCH...
...BEGIN!!!!

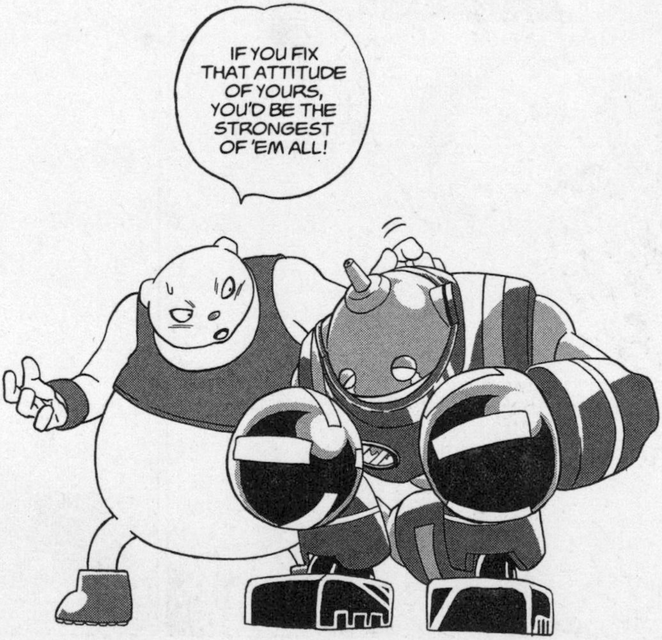
IF YOU FIX THAT ATTITUDE OF YOURS, YOU'D BE THE STRONGEST OF 'EM ALL!

DRAGON BALL SUPER

CHAPTER 12: SAIYAN'S PRIDE

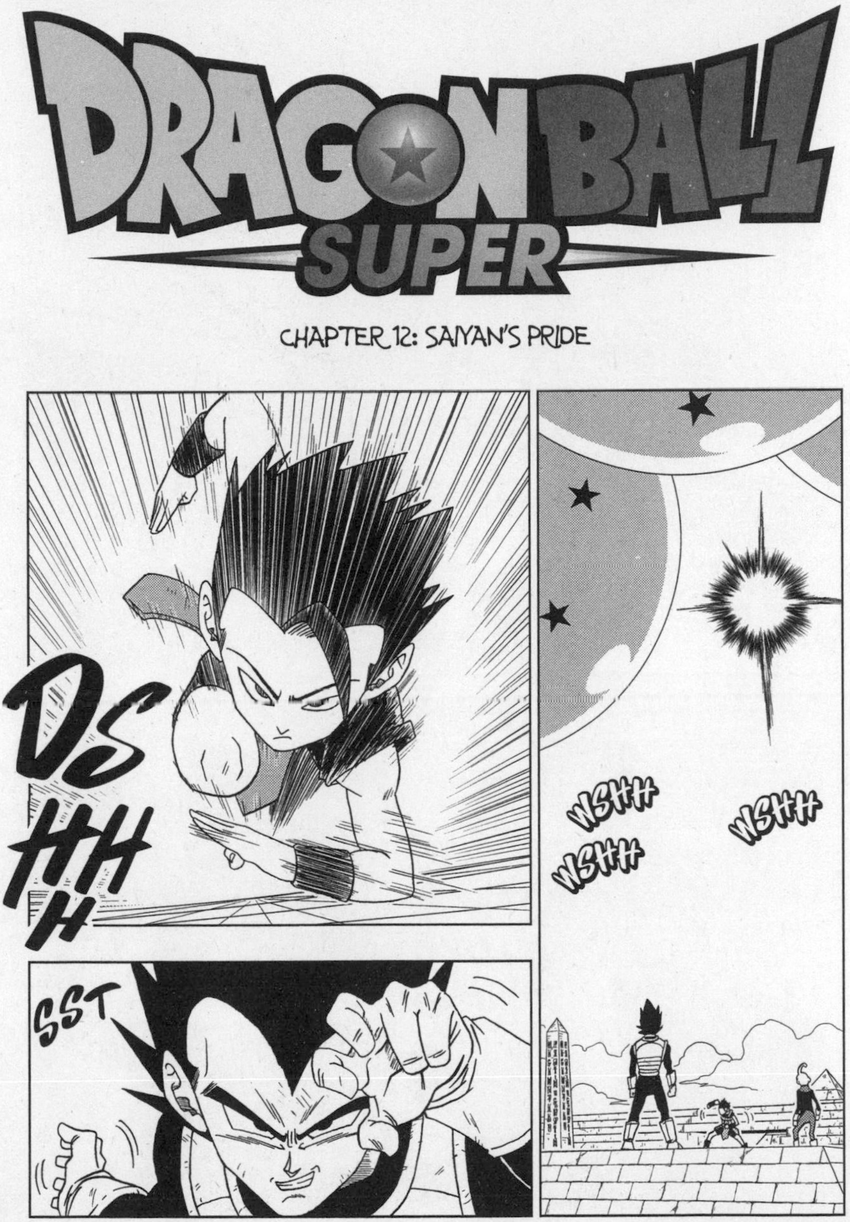
WSHH
WSHH
WSHH
DSHHHH
SST

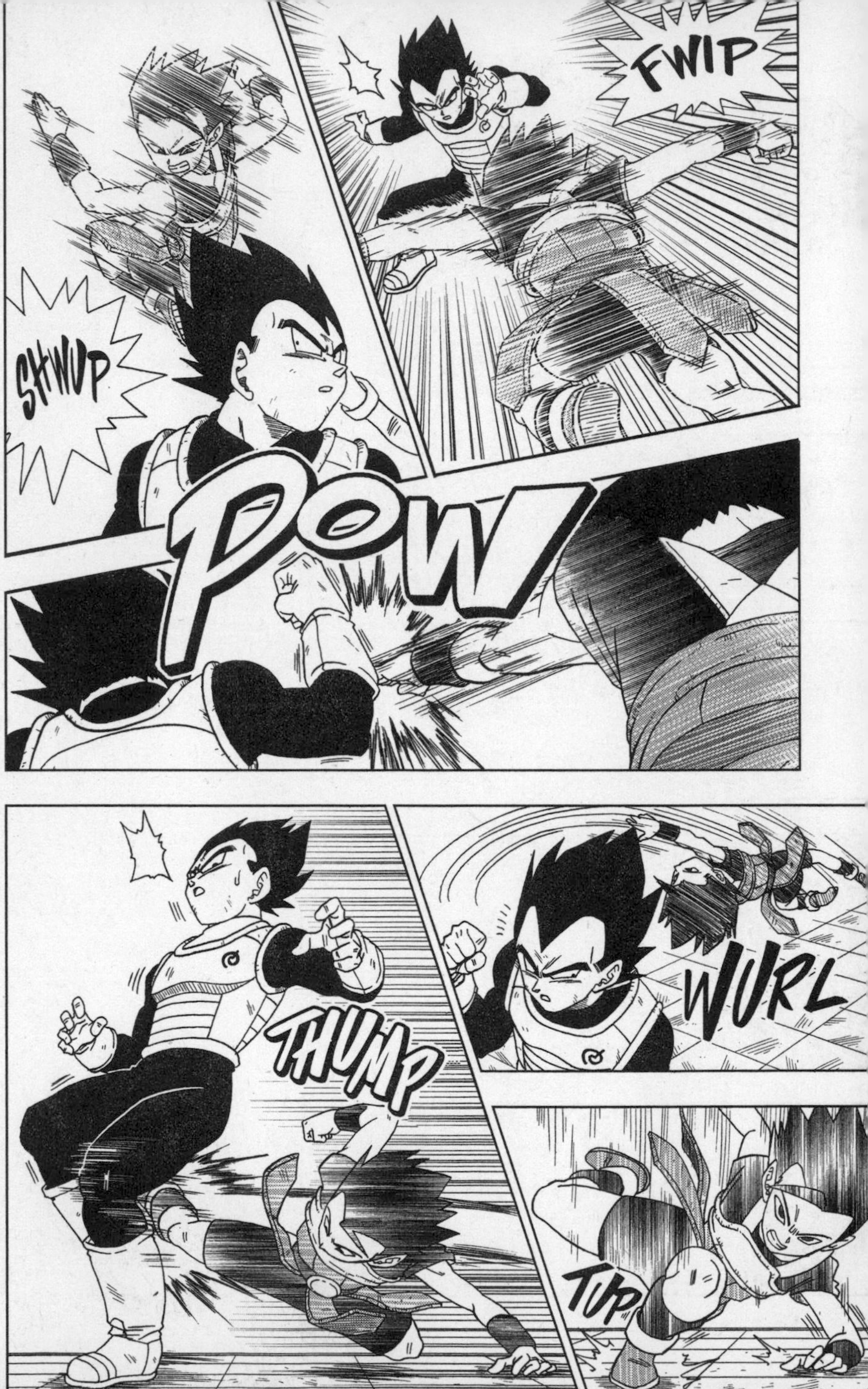
FWIP
SHWUP
POW
WURL
TUP
THUMP

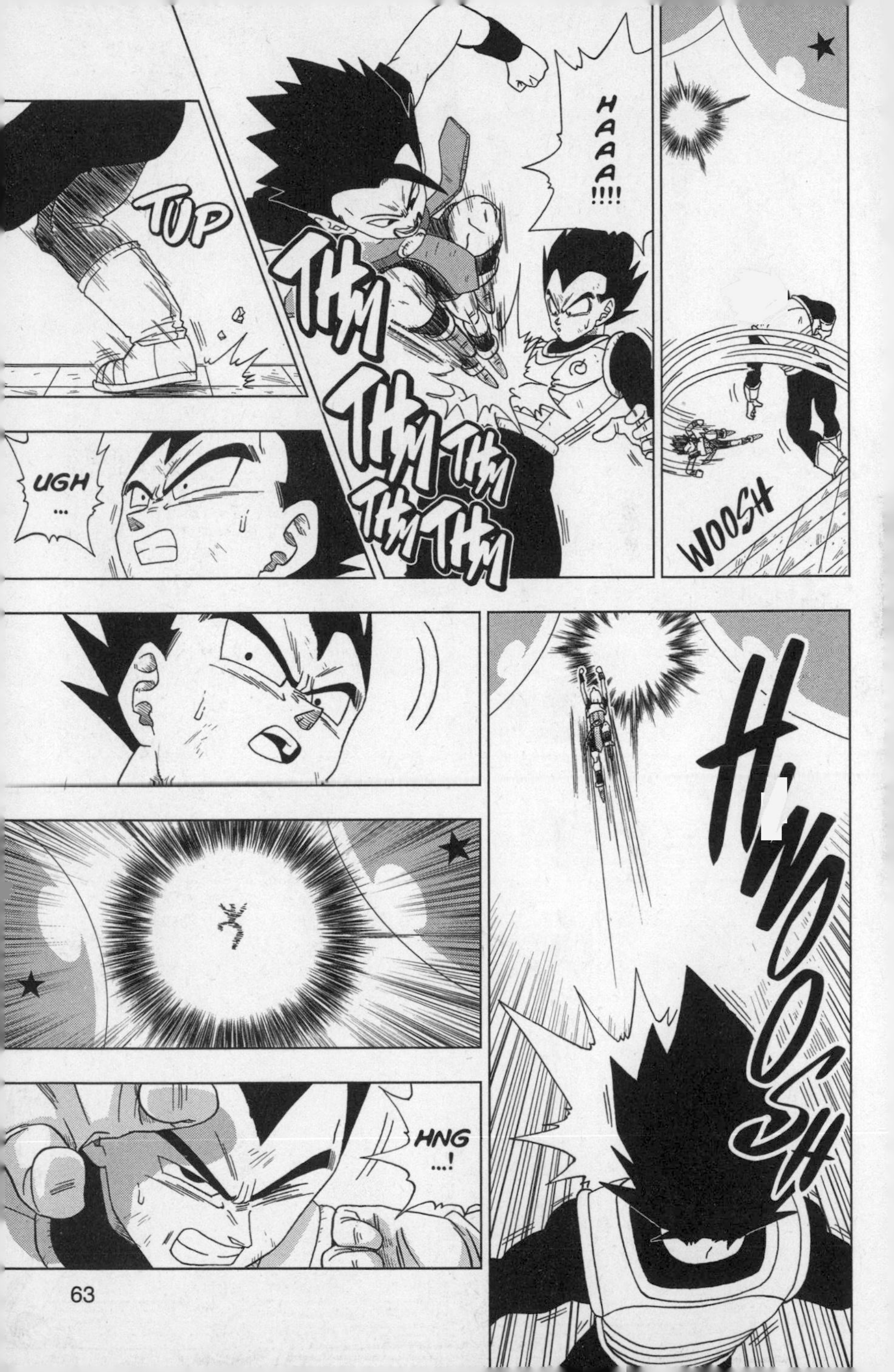

WOOSH
HAAAA!!!!
THM THM THM THM THM THM
TUP
UGH...
HWOOSH
HNG...!

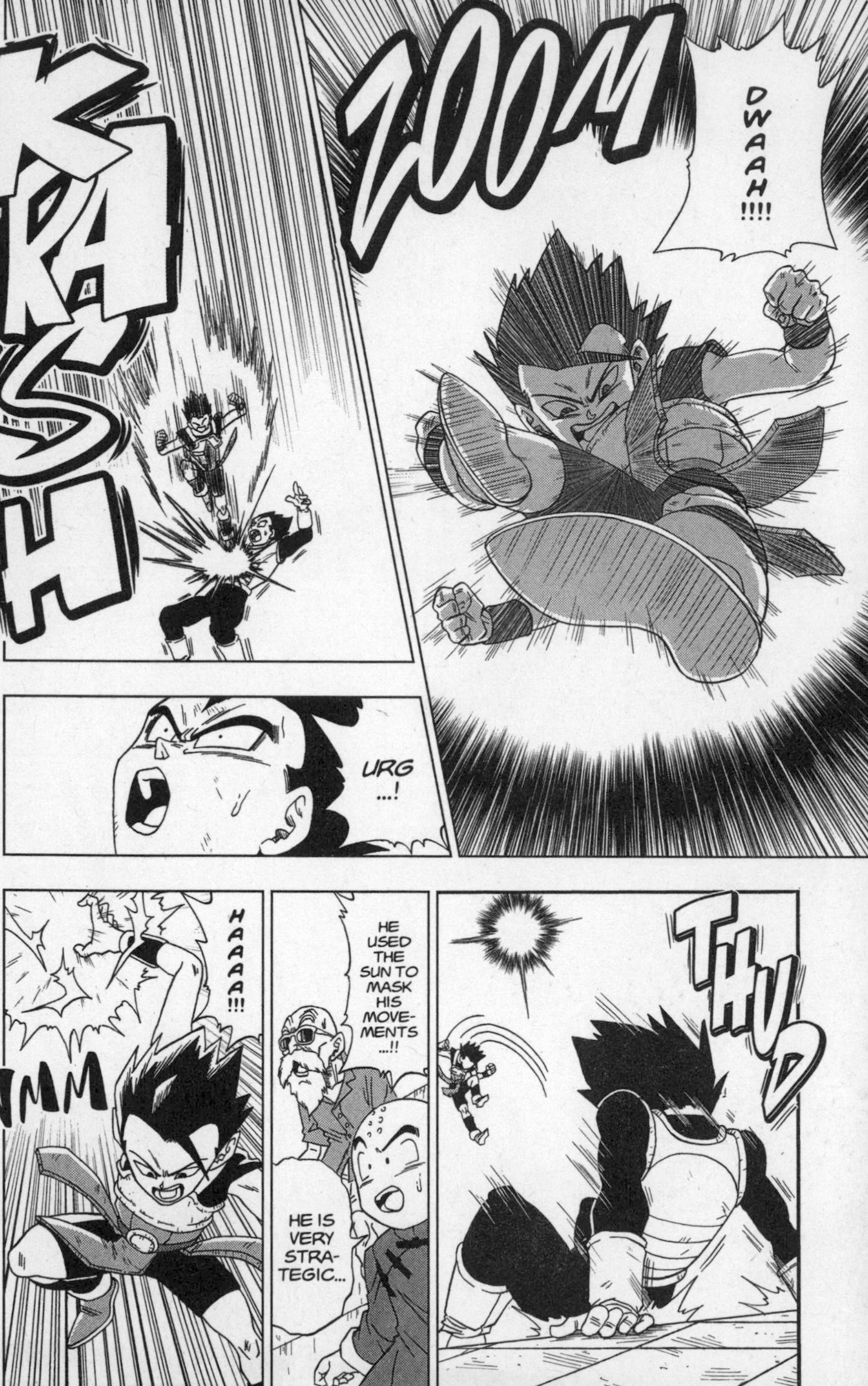
ZOOM
DWAAAH!!!!
KRASH
URG ...!
THUD
HE USED THE SUN TO MASK HIS MOVEMENTS ...!!
HE IS VERY STRATEGIC...
HAAAAA!!!
VMM

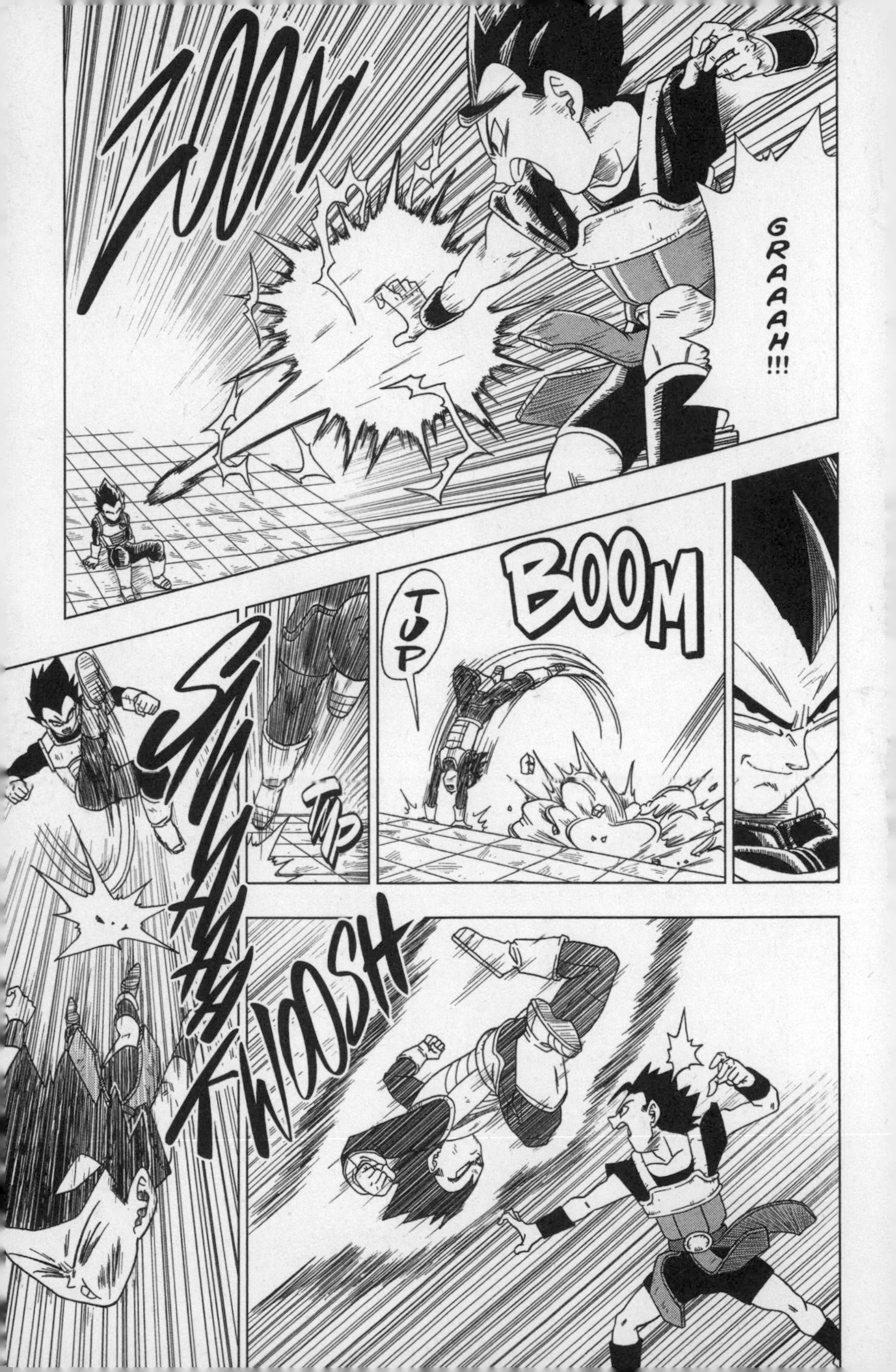
GRAAAAH!!!
BOOM
TUP
TAP
FWOOSH

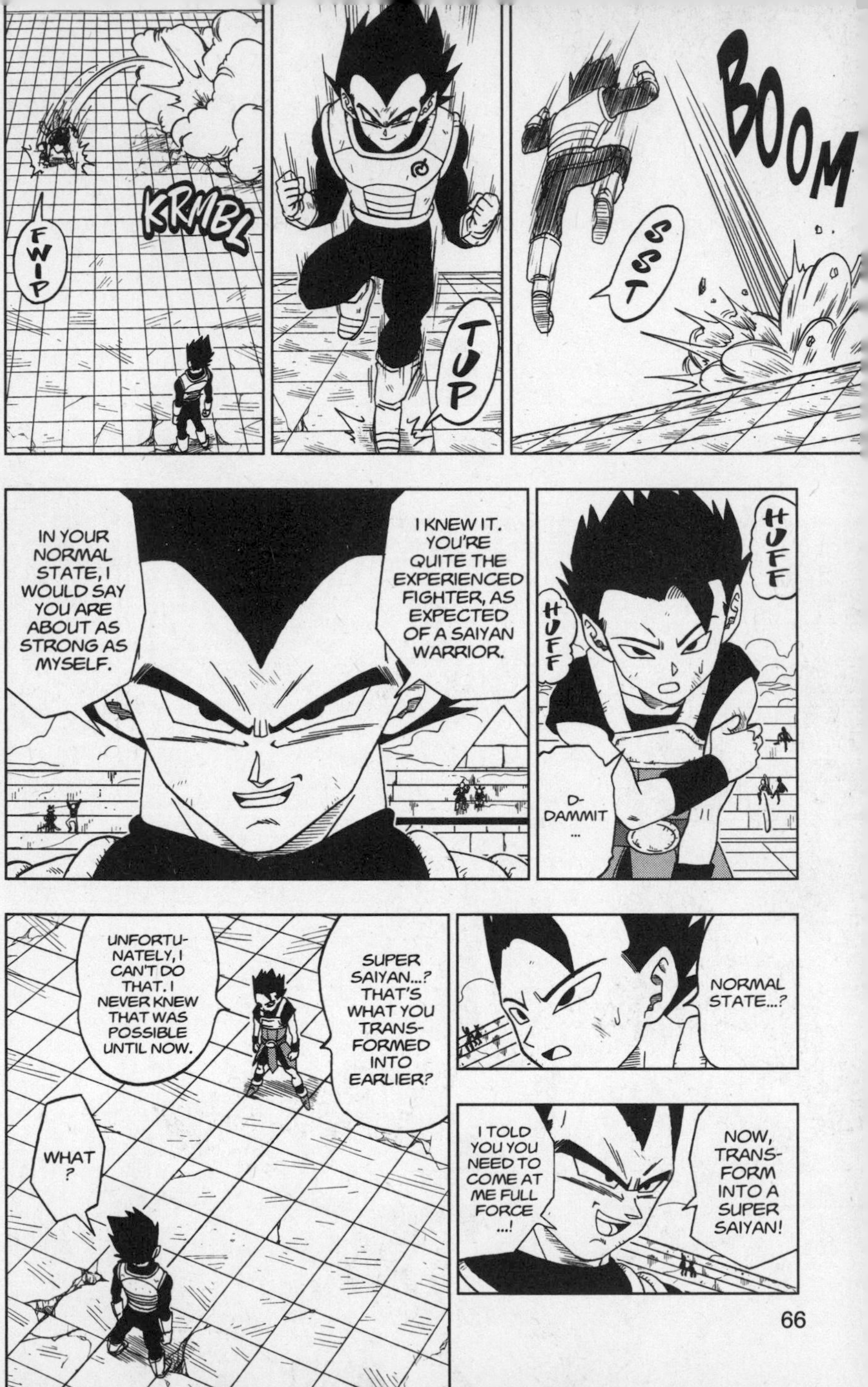
BOOM
SST
TUP
KRMBL
FWIP
HUFF
HUFF
D-DAMMIT ...
I KNEW IT. YOU'RE QUITE THE EXPERIENCED FIGHTER, AS EXPECTED OF A SAIYAN WARRIOR.
IN YOUR NORMAL STATE, I WOULD SAY YOU ARE ABOUT AS STRONG AS MYSELF.
NORMAL STATE...?
NOW, TRANS-FORM INTO A SUPER SAIYAN!
I TOLD YOU YOU NEED TO COME AT ME FULL FORCE ...!
SUPER SAIYAN...? THAT'S WHAT YOU TRANS-FORMED INTO EARLIER?
UNFORTU-NATELY, I CAN'T DO THAT. I NEVER KNEW THAT WAS POSSIBLE UNTIL NOW.
WHAT ?

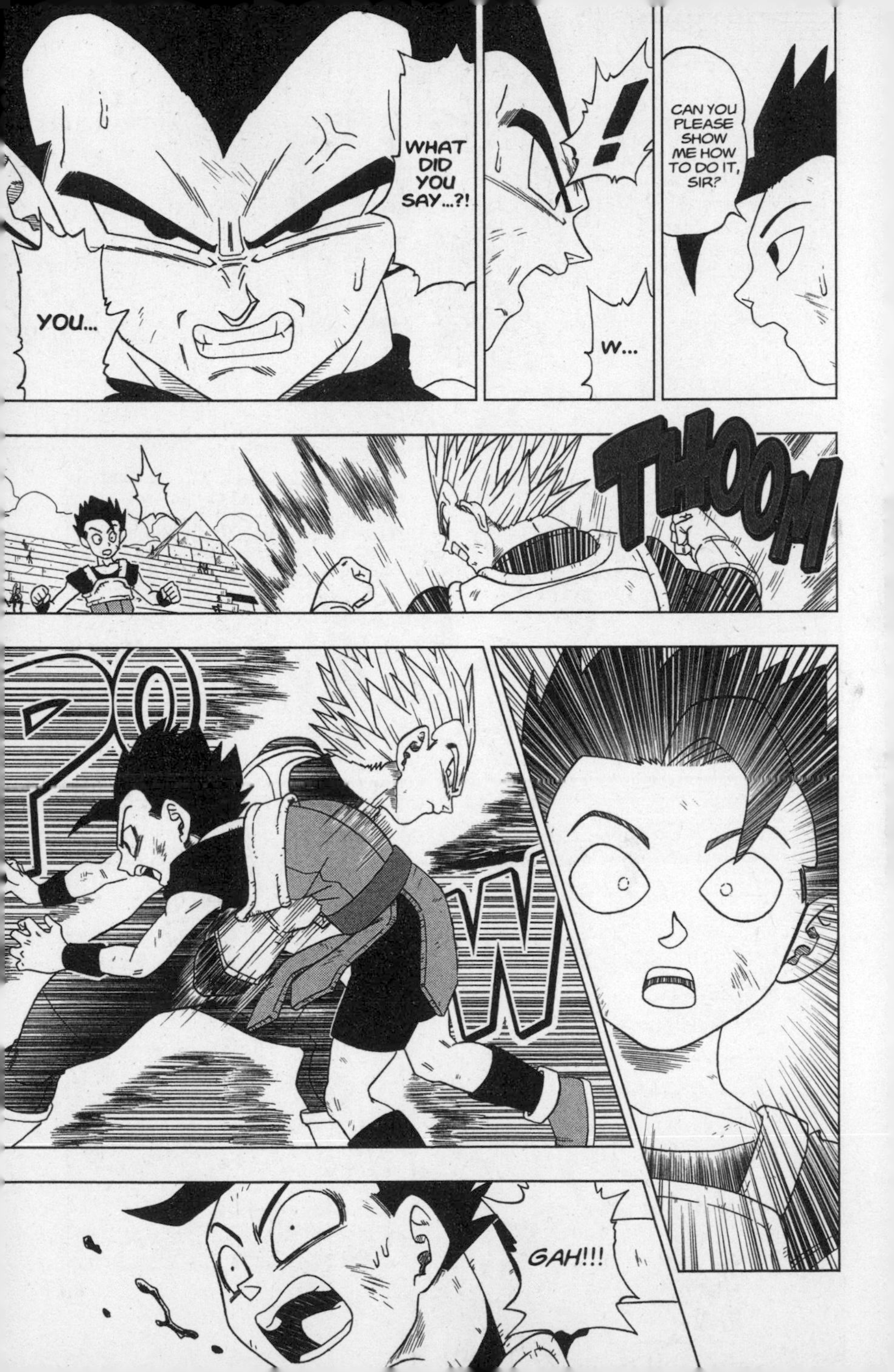

CAN YOU PLEASE SHOW ME HOW TO DO IT, SIR?
!
W...
WHAT DID YOU SAY...?!
YOU...
THOOM
POW
GAH!!!

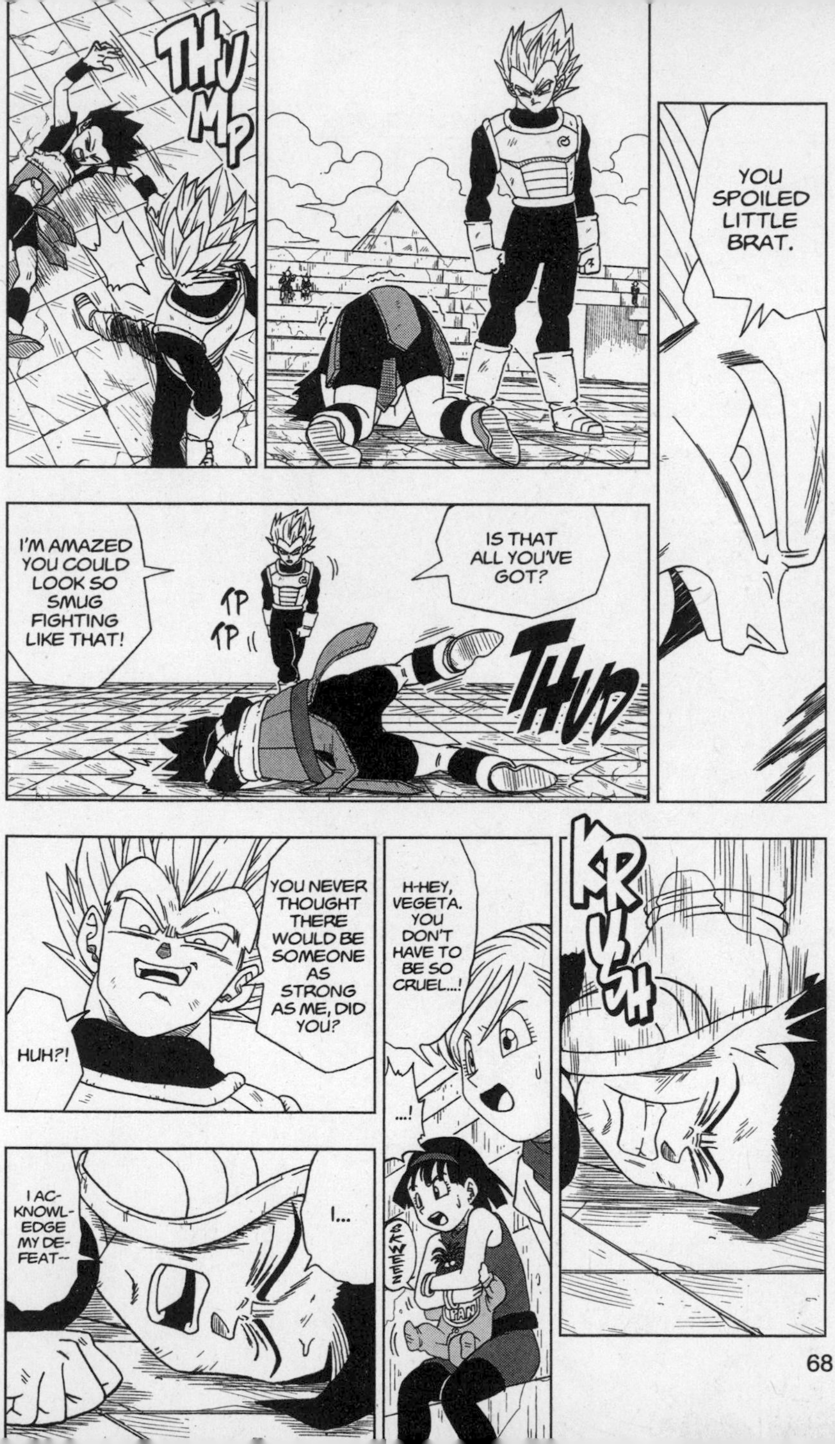
YOU SPOILED LITTLE BRAT.
THUMP
IS THAT ALL YOU'VE GOT?
THUD
TP TP
I'M AMAZED YOU COULD LOOK SO SMUG FIGHTING LIKE THAT!
KRUSH
H-HEY, VEGETA. YOU DON'T HAVE TO BE SO CRUEL...!
YOU NEVER THOUGHT THERE WOULD BE SOMEONE AS STRONG AS ME, DID YOU?
HUH?!
...!
SKWEEZ
I...
I AC-KNOWL-EDGE MY DE-FEAT--

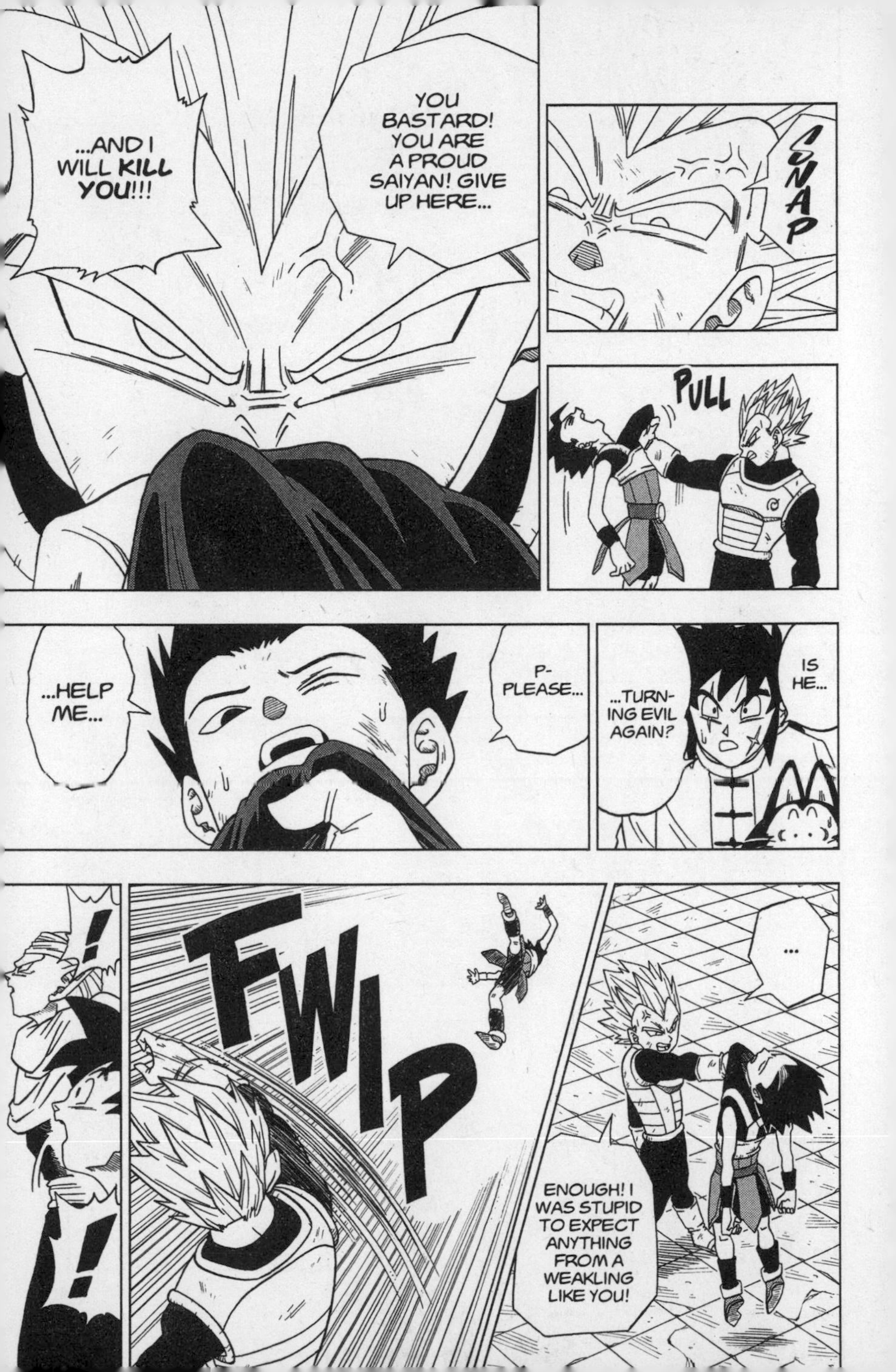
SNAP
PULL
YOU BASTARD! YOU ARE A PROUD SAIYAN! GIVE UP HERE...
...AND I WILL **KILL** YOU!!!
IS HE...
...TURNING EVIL AGAIN?
P- PLEASE...
...HELP ME...
...
ENOUGH! I WAS STUPID TO EXPECT ANYTHING FROM A WEAKLING LIKE YOU!
FWIP
!
!

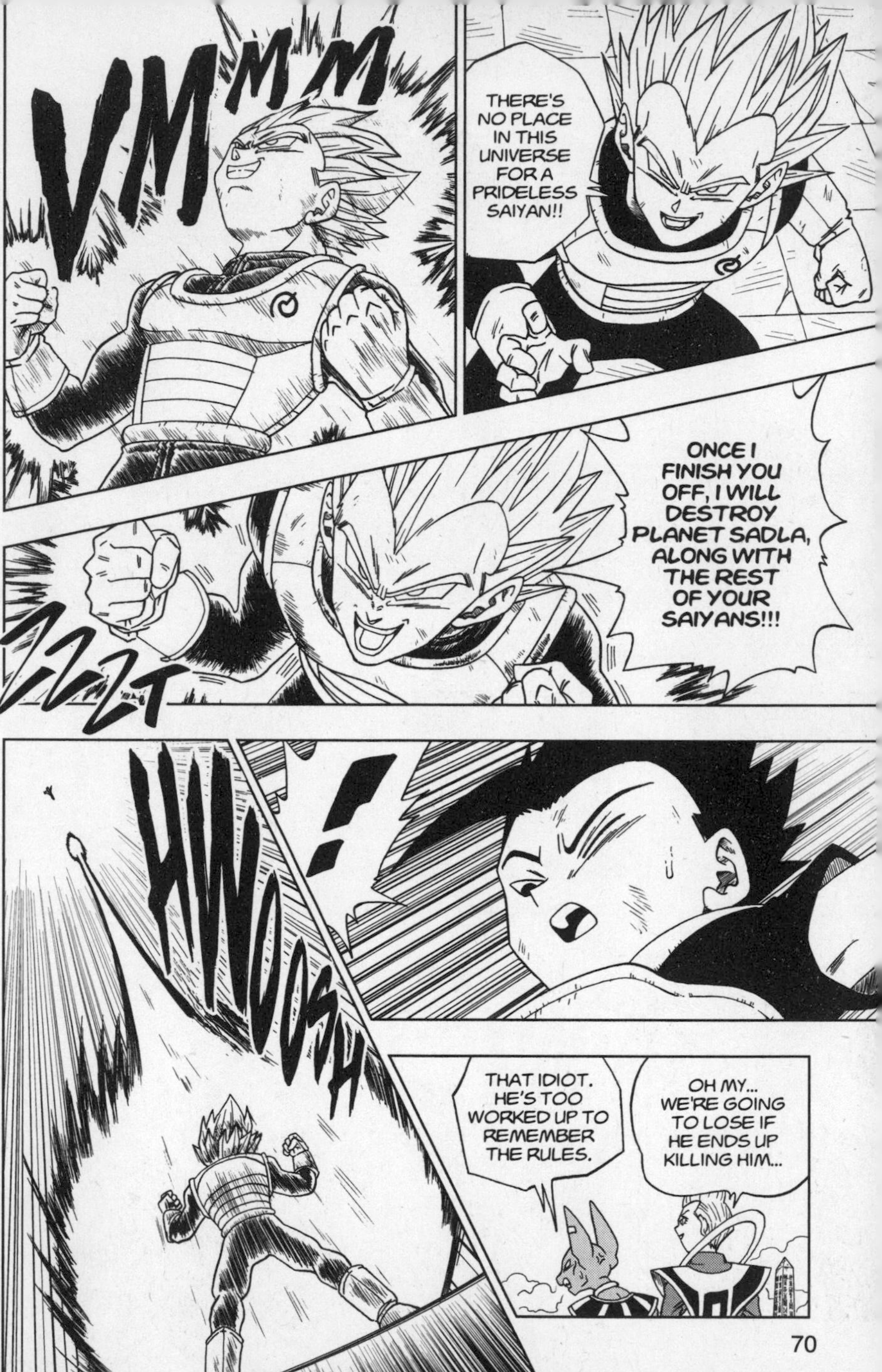
THERE'S NO PLACE IN THIS UNIVERSE FOR A PRIDELESS SAIYAN!!
VMMM
ONCE I FINISH YOU OFF, I WILL DESTROY PLANET SADLA, ALONG WITH THE REST OF YOUR SAIYANS!!!
ZZZT
!
OH MY... WE'RE GOING TO LOSE IF HE ENDS UP KILLING HIM...
THAT IDIOT. HE'S TOO WORKED UP TO REMEMBER THE RULES.
HWOOSH

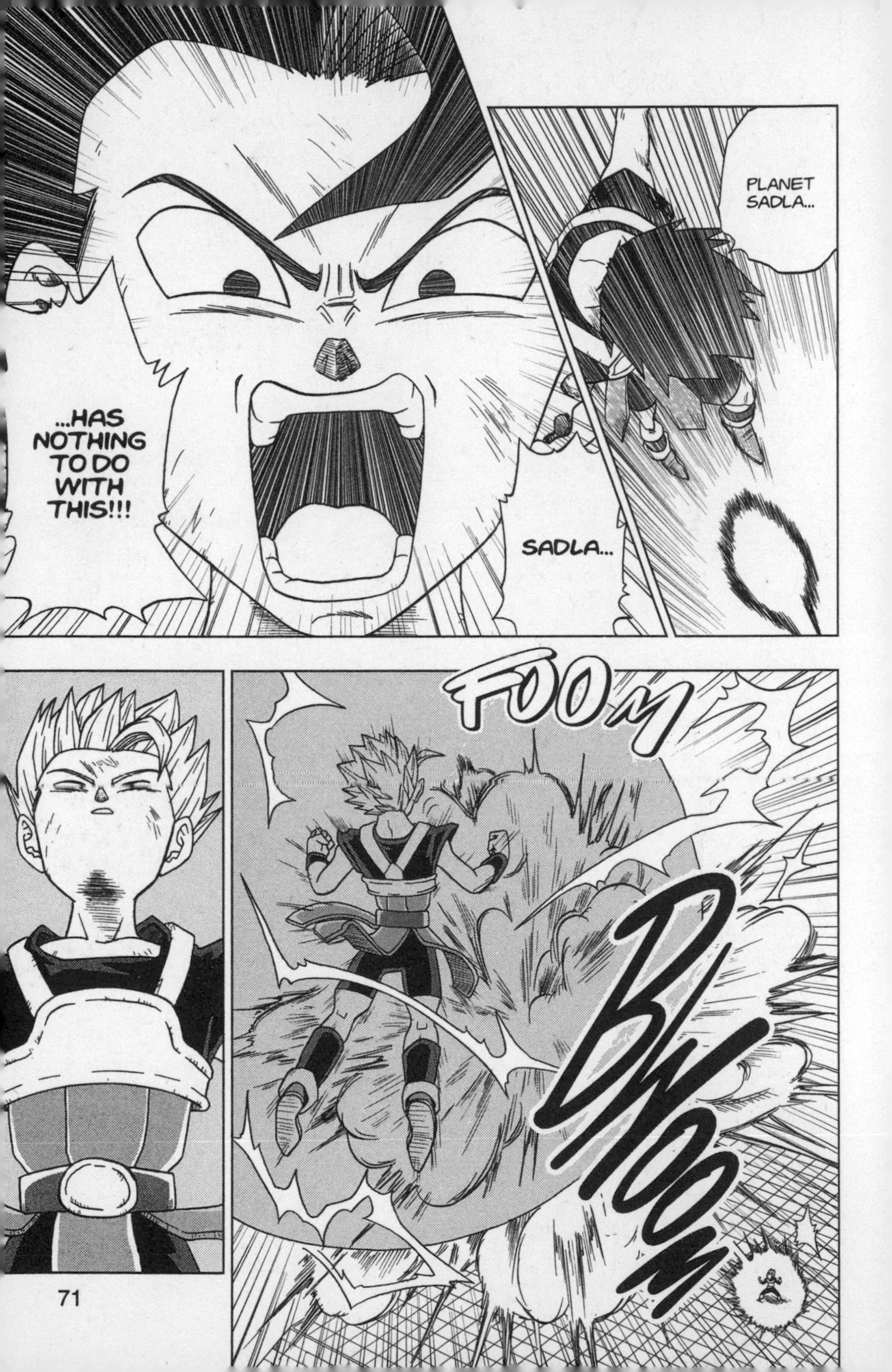
PLANET SADLA...
SADLA...
...HAS NOTHING TO DO WITH THIS!!!
FOOM
BWOOM

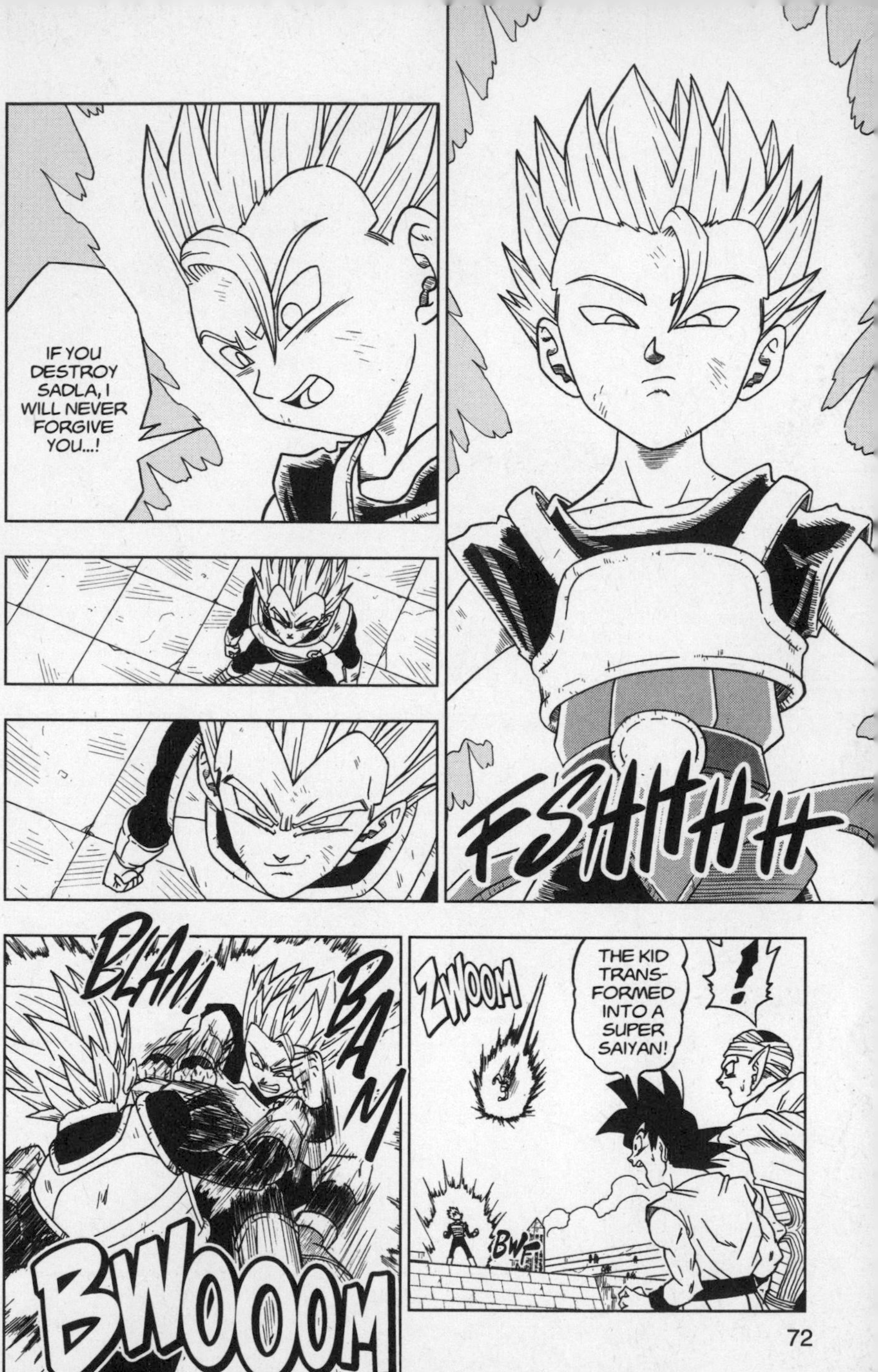
FSHHHH
IF YOU DESTROY SADLA, I WILL NEVER FORGIVE YOU...!
THE KID TRANS-FORMED INTO A SUPER SAIYAN!
!
ZWOOM
BWF
BAM
BLAM
BWOOOM

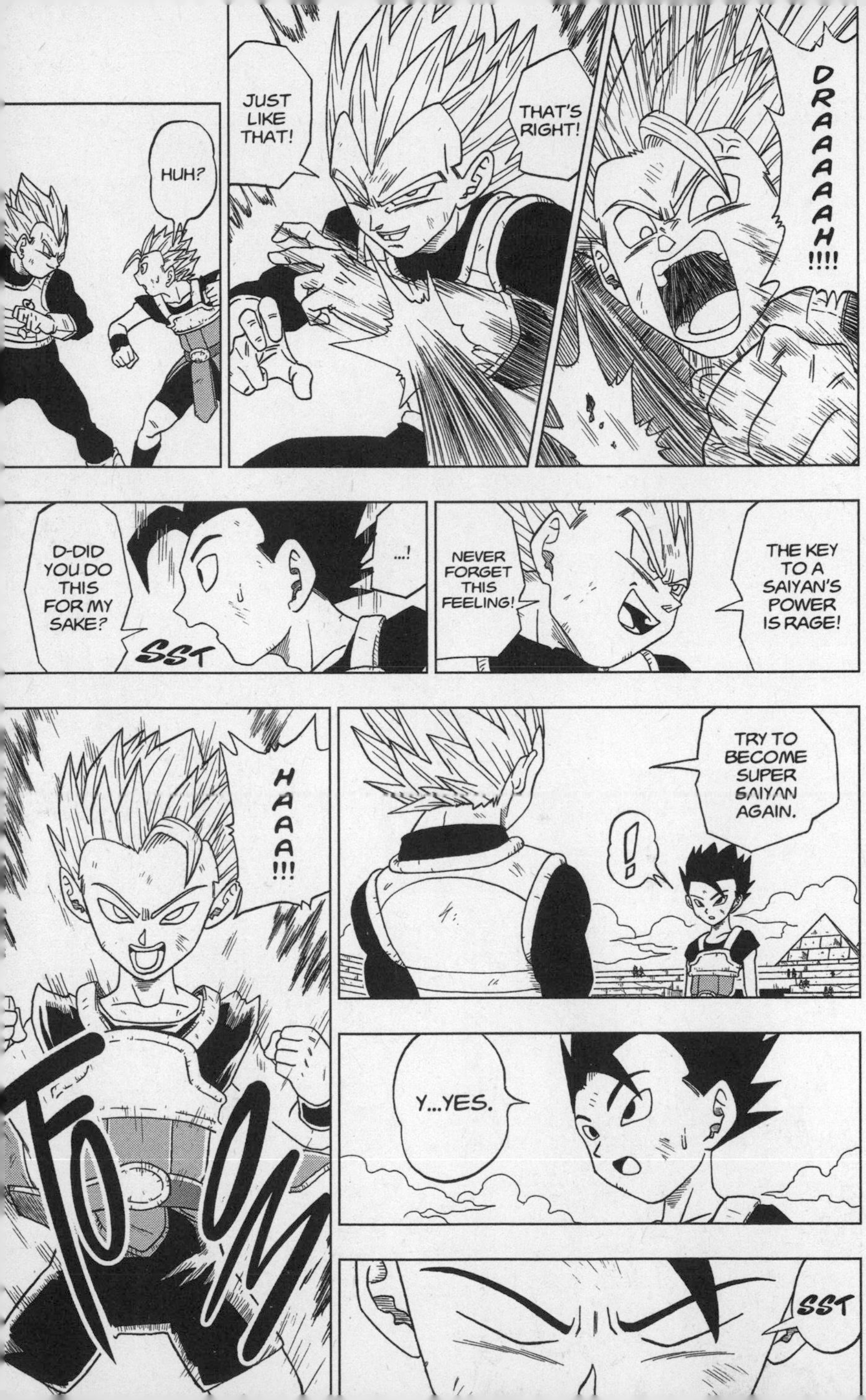
DRAAAAAAH!!!!
THAT'S RIGHT!
JUST LIKE THAT!
HUH?
THE KEY TO A SAIYAN'S POWER IS RAGE!
NEVER FORGET THIS FEELING!
...!
D-DID YOU DO THIS FOR MY SAKE?
SST
TRY TO BECOME SUPER SAIYAN AGAIN.
!
Y...YES.
SST
HAAAA!!!
FOOM

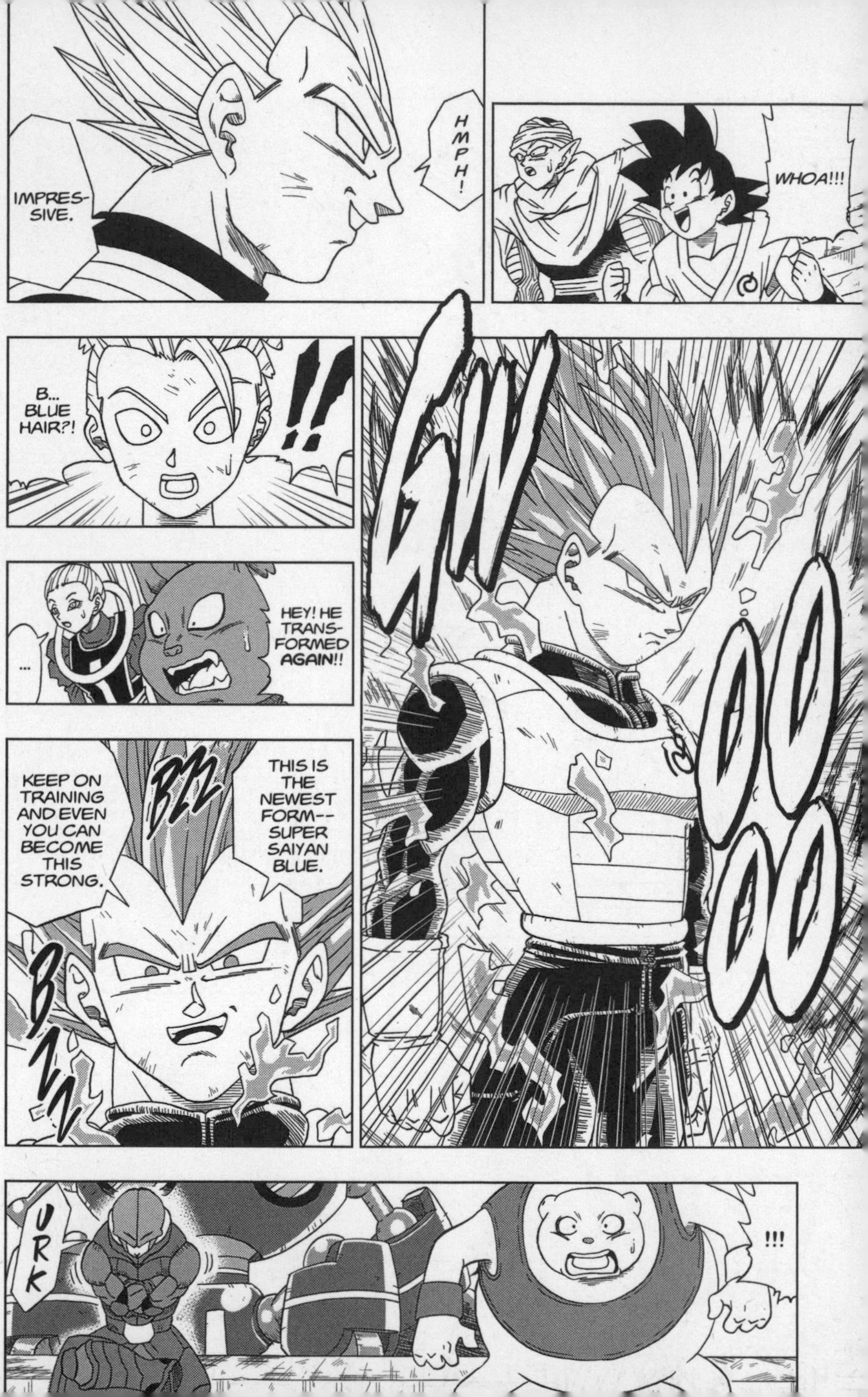

WHOA!!!
HMPH!
IMPRESSIVE.
B... BLUE HAIR?!
!!
HEY! HE TRANSFORMED AGAIN!!
...
THIS IS THE NEWEST FORM-- SUPER SAIYAN BLUE.
KEEP ON TRAINING AND EVEN YOU CAN BECOME THIS STRONG.
!!!
URK

BAM

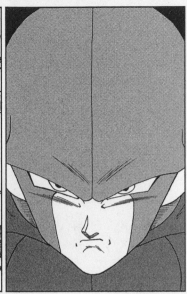

THUD

SO VEGETA WAS TEACHING HIM A LESSON AFTER ALL.

THAT'S COOL. I WONDER WHY, THOUGH...

HE WAS ONCE A PRINCE. I GUESS HE WAS NOSTALGIC SEEING ONE OF HIS OWN PEOPLE AGAIN.

I'M STILL HERE THOUGH...

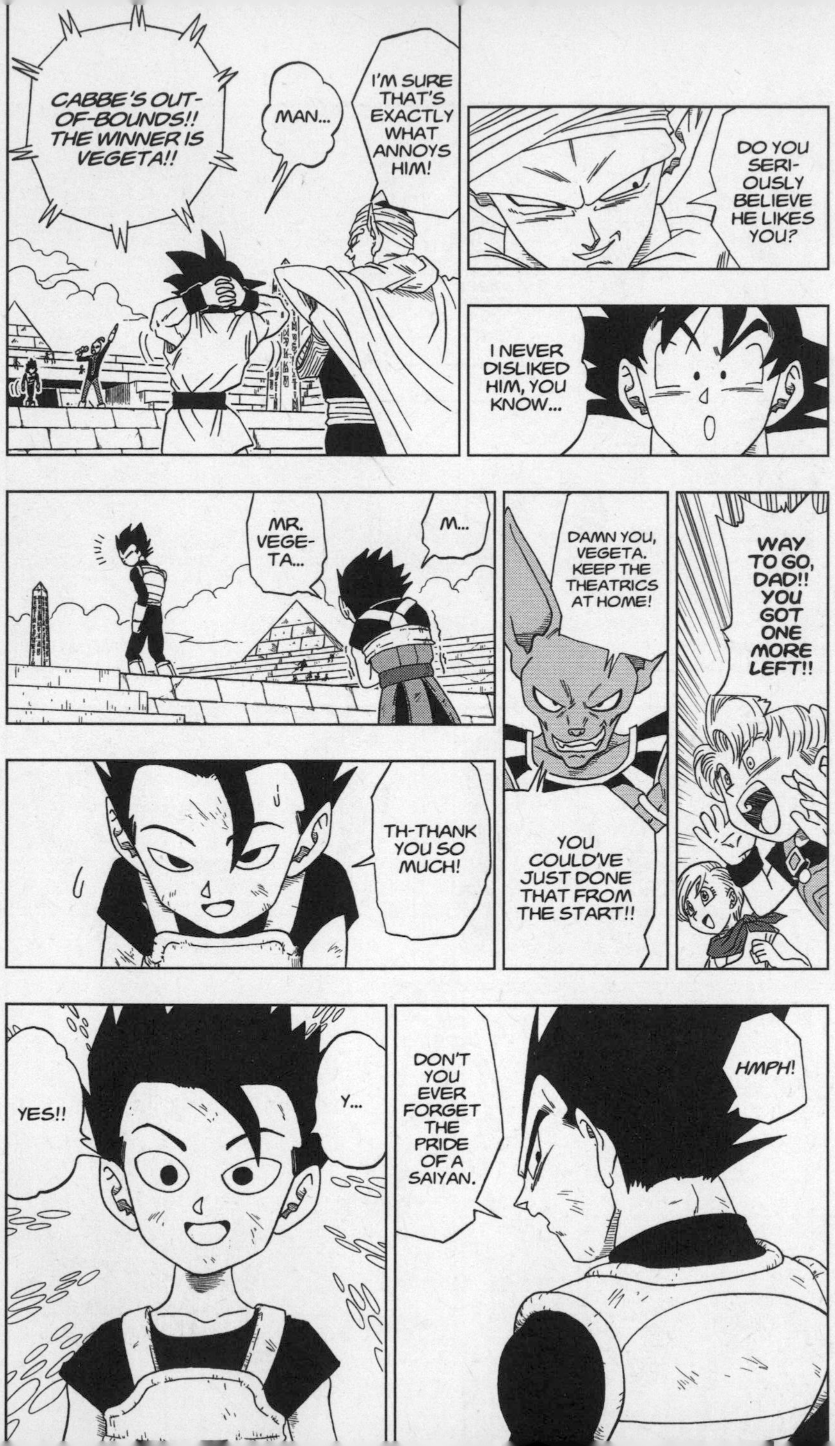
DO YOU SERI-OUSLY BELIEVE HE LIKES YOU?
I NEVER DISLIKED HIM, YOU KNOW...
I'M SURE THAT'S EXACTLY WHAT ANNOYS HIM!
MAN...
CABBE'S OUT-OF-BOUNDS!! THE WINNER IS VEGETA!!
WAY TO GO, DAD!! YOU GOT ONE MORE LEFT!!
DAMN YOU, VEGETA. KEEP THE THEATRICS AT HOME!
YOU COULD'VE JUST DONE THAT FROM THE START!!
M...
MR. VEGE-TA...
TH-THANK YOU SO MUCH!
HMPH!
DON'T YOU EVER FORGET THE PRIDE OF A SAIYAN.
Y...
YES!!

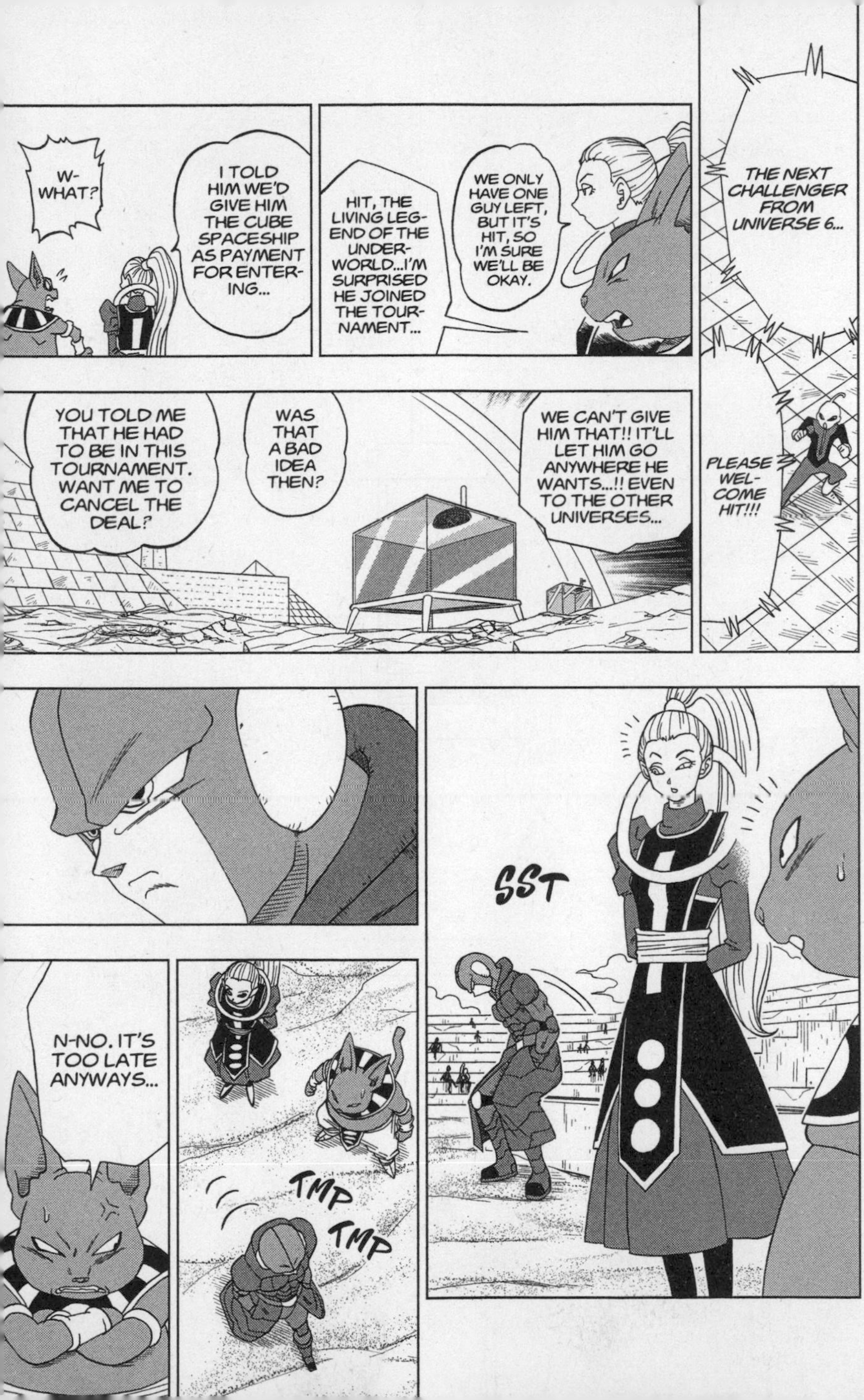
THE NEXT CHALLENGER FROM UNIVERSE 6...
PLEASE WEL-COME HIT!!!
WE ONLY HAVE ONE GUY LEFT, BUT IT'S HIT, SO I'M SURE WE'LL BE OKAY.
HIT, THE LIVING LEG-END OF THE UNDER-WORLD...I'M SURPRISED HE JOINED THE TOUR-NAMENT...
I TOLD HIM WE'D GIVE HIM THE CUBE SPACESHIP AS PAYMENT FOR ENTER-ING...
W-WHAT?
WE CAN'T GIVE HIM THAT!! IT'LL LET HIM GO ANYWHERE HE WANTS...!! EVEN TO THE OTHER UNIVERSES...
WAS THAT A BAD IDEA THEN?
YOU TOLD ME THAT HE HAD TO BE IN THIS TOURNAMENT. WANT ME TO CANCEL THE DEAL?
SST
TMP
TMP
N-NO. IT'S TOO LATE ANYWAYS...

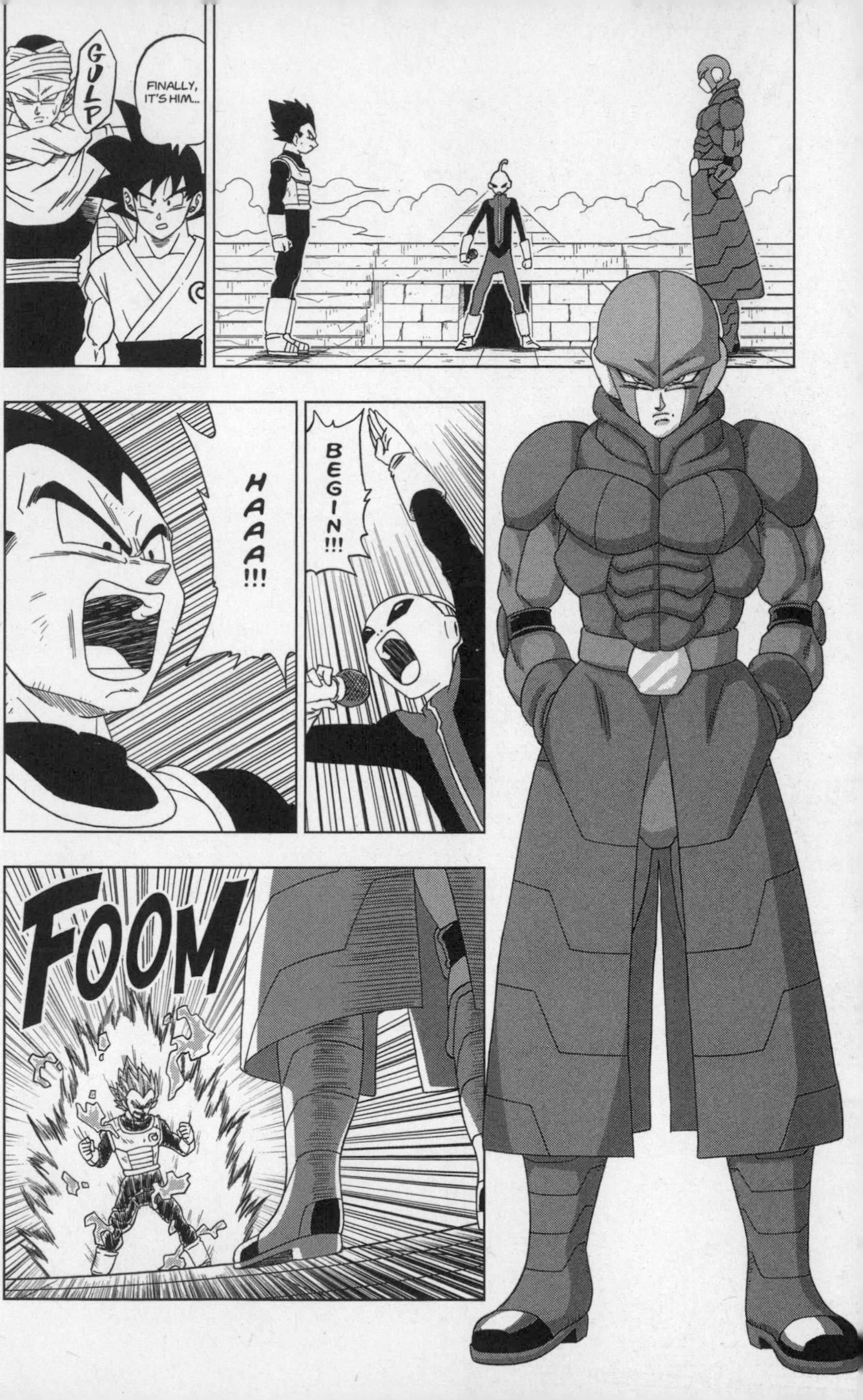
GULP
FINALLY, IT'S HIM...
BEGIN!!!
HAAAA!!!
FOOM

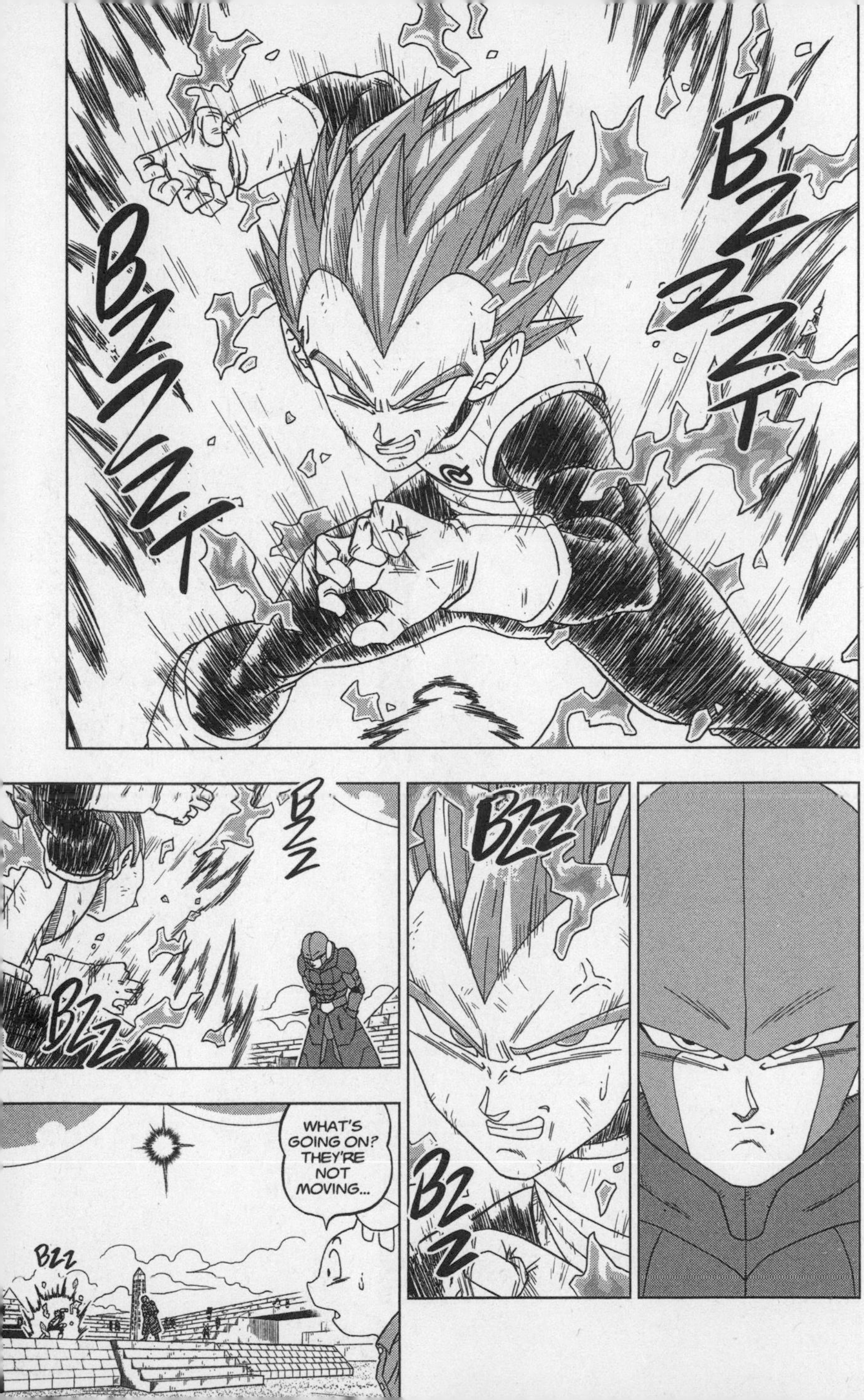
BZZZZT
BZZZZT
BZZ
BZZ
BZZ
BZZ
WHAT'S GOING ON? THEY'RE NOT MOVING...
BZZ

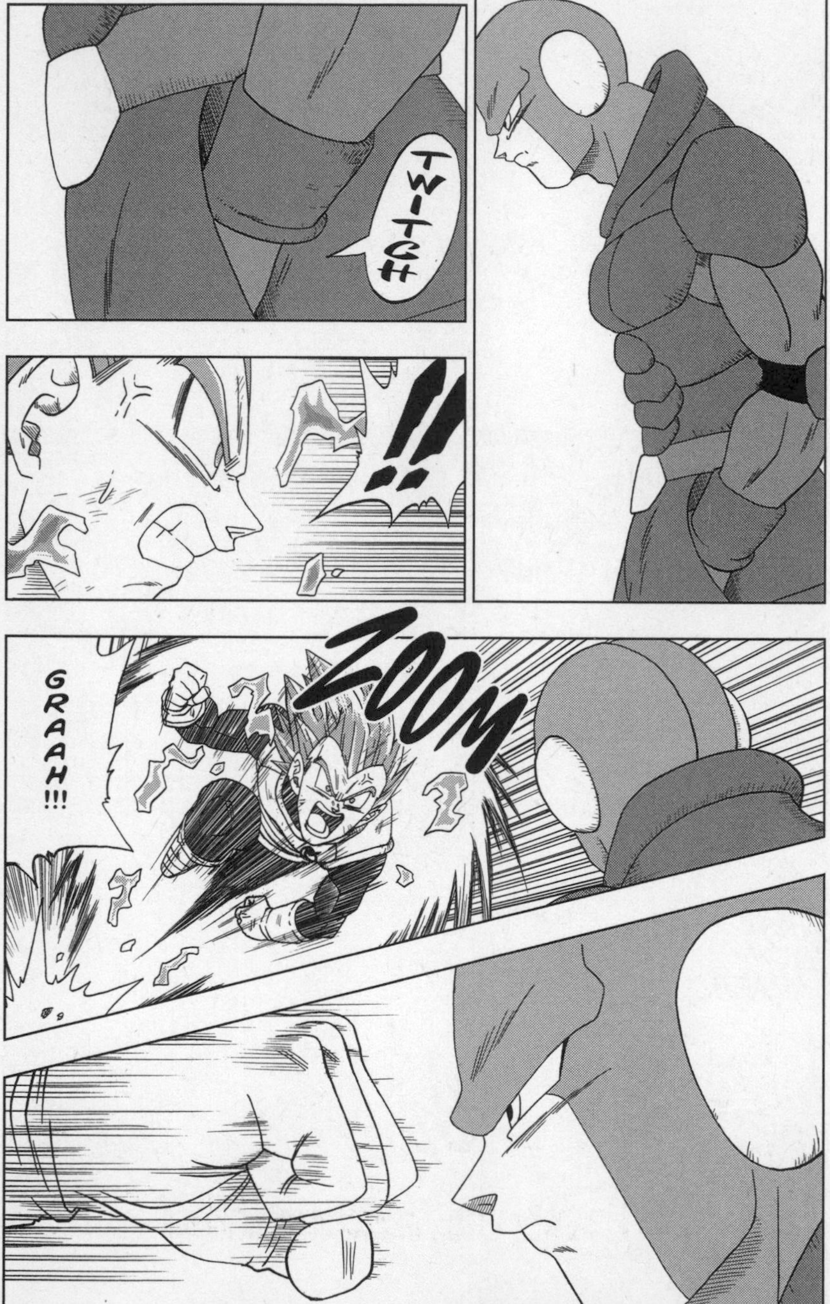
TWITCH
!!
ZOOM
GRAAAH!!!

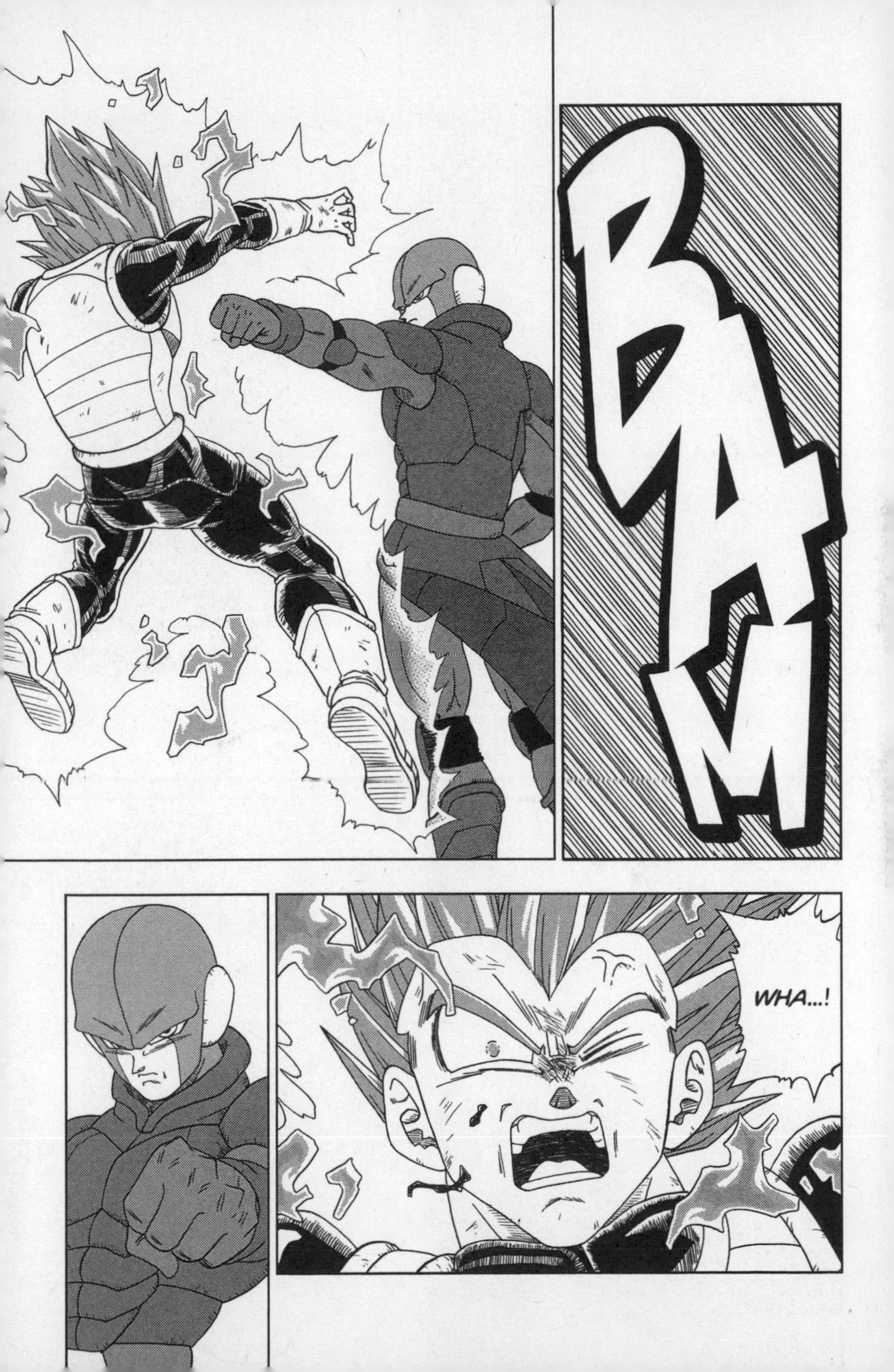
BAM
WHA...!

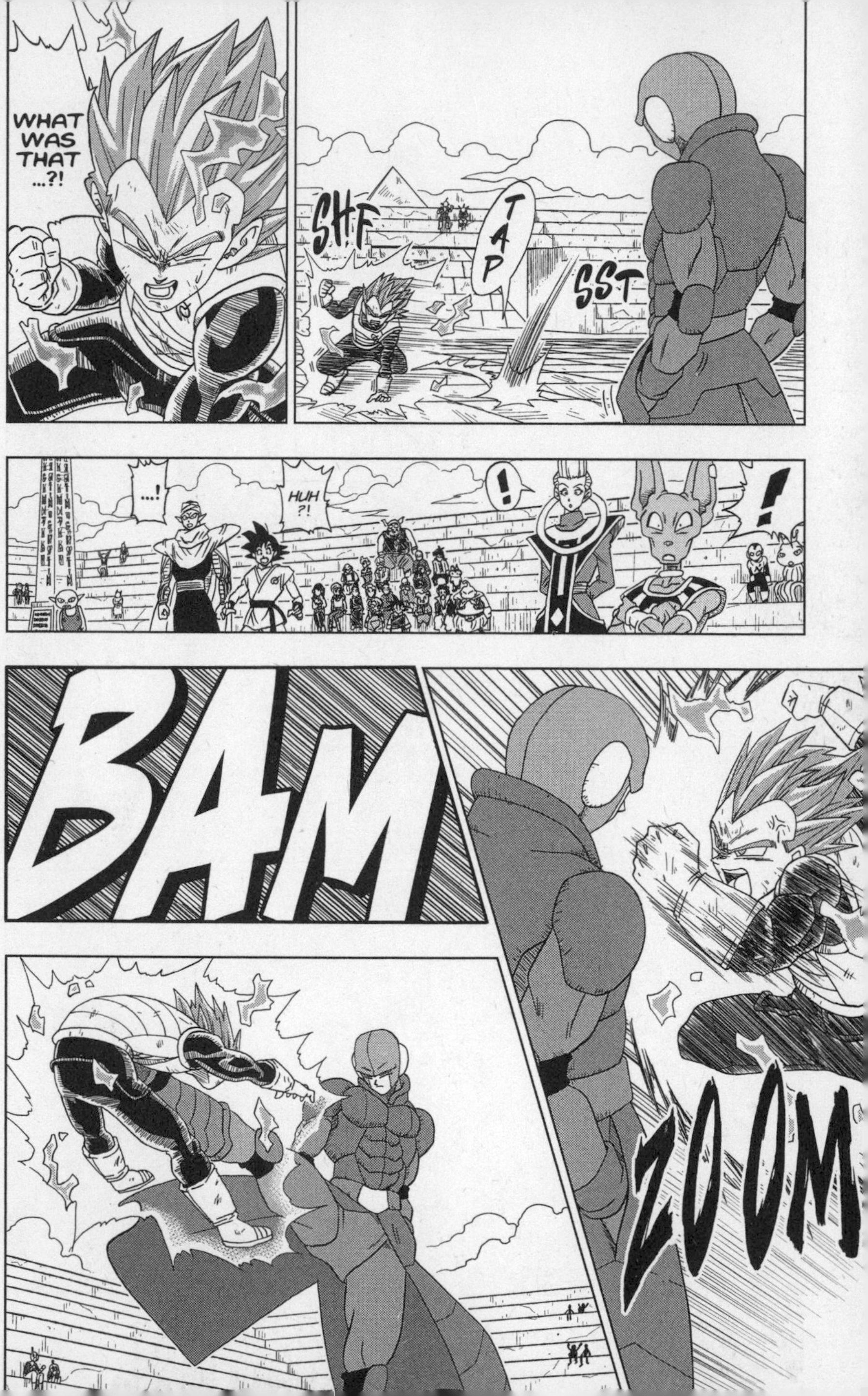
SST
TAP
SHF
WHAT WAS THAT ...?!
!
!
HUH ?!
...!
ZOOM
BAM

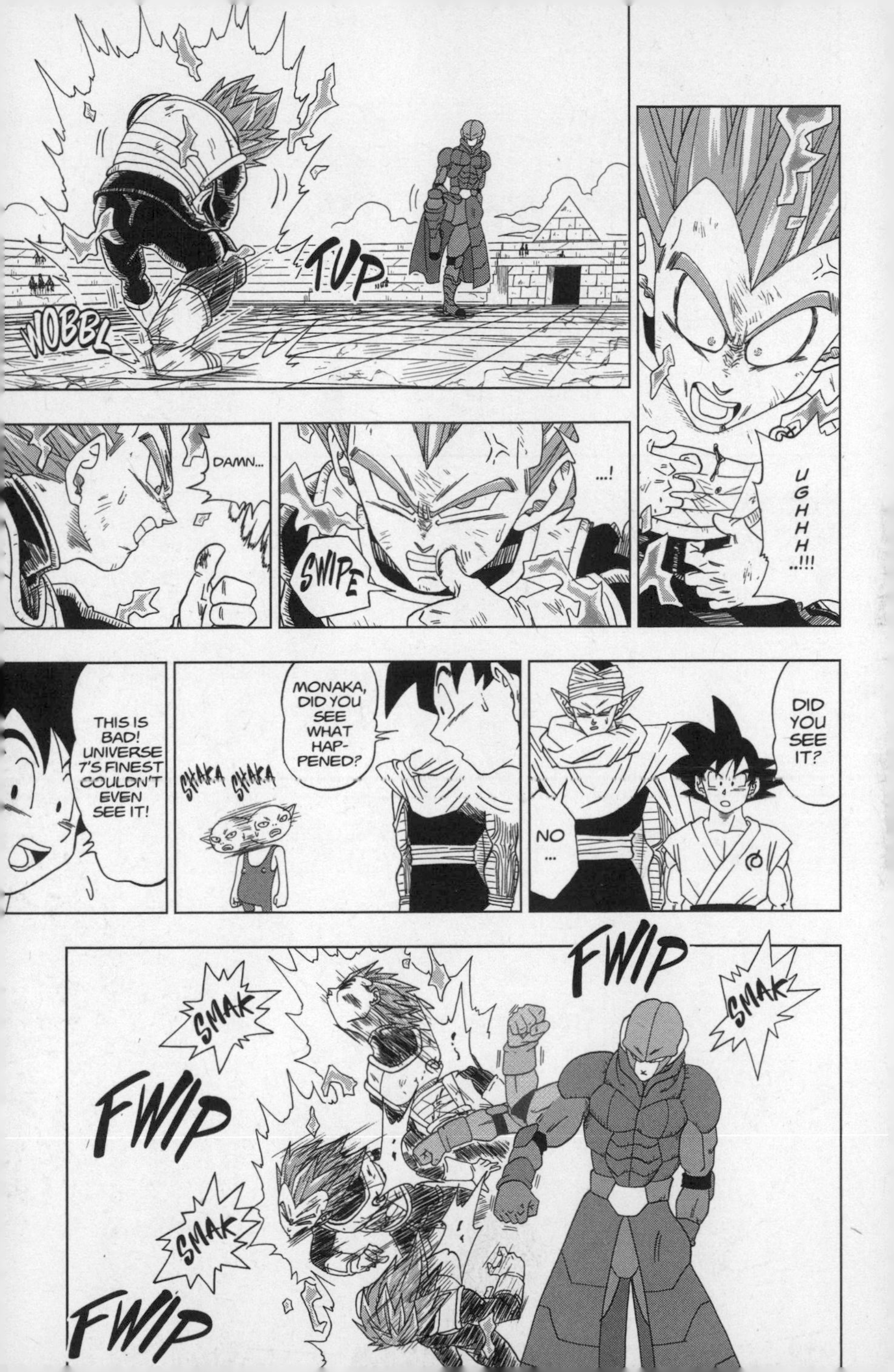
UGHHH...!!!
WOBBL
TUP...
...!
SWIPE
DAMN...
DID YOU SEE IT?
NO...
MONAKA, DID YOU SEE WHAT HAPPENED?
SHAKA SHAKA
THIS IS BAD! UNIVERSE 7'S FINEST COULDN'T EVEN SEE IT!
FWIP
SMAK
SMAK
FWIP
SMAK
FWIP

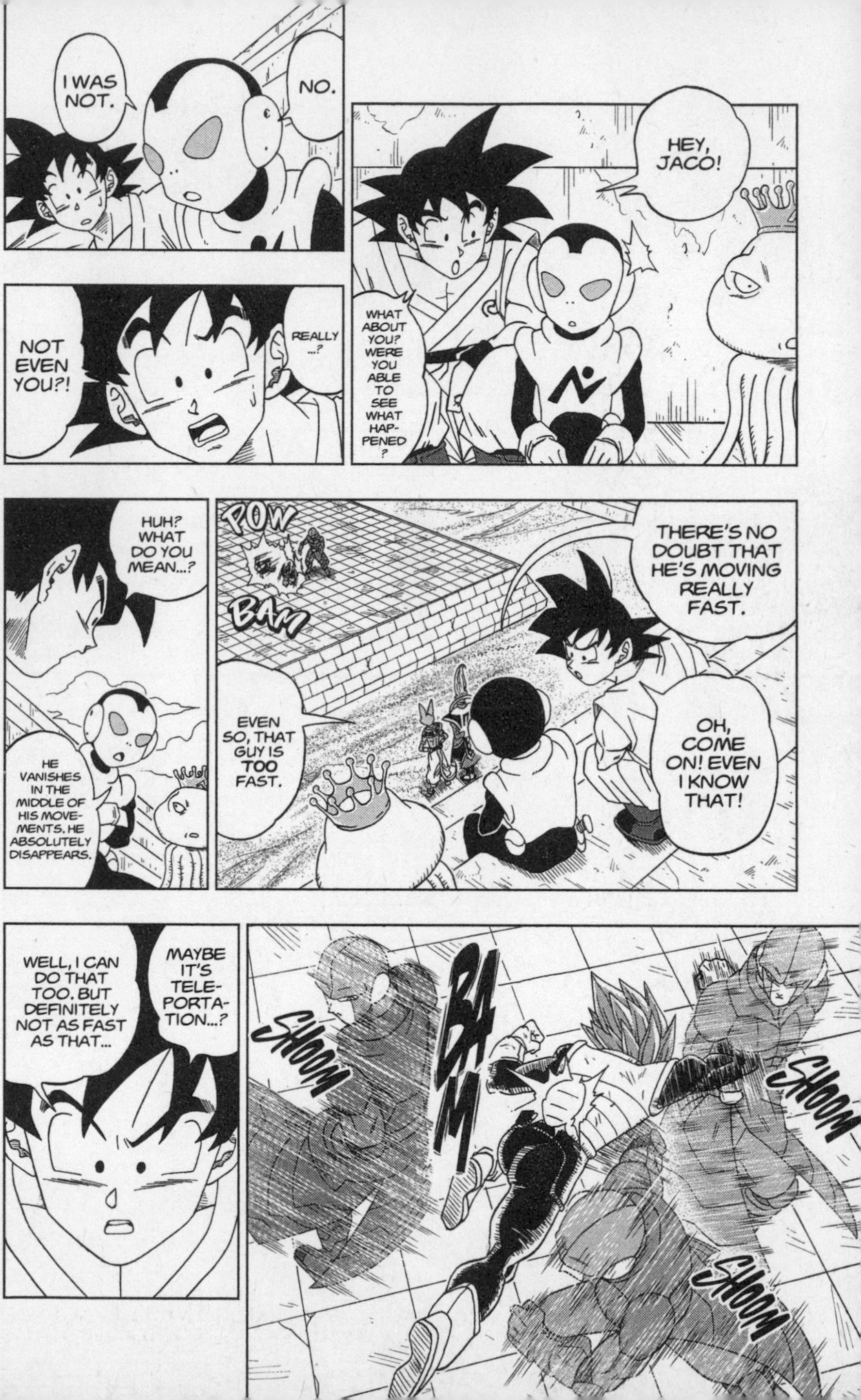
HEY, JACO!
WHAT ABOUT YOU? WERE YOU ABLE TO SEE WHAT HAP-PENED?
NO.
I WAS NOT.
REALLY ...?
NOT EVEN YOU?!
POW
BAM
THERE'S NO DOUBT THAT HE'S MOVING REALLY FAST.
OH, COME ON! EVEN I KNOW THAT!
EVEN SO, THAT GUY IS **TOO** FAST.
HUH? WHAT DO YOU MEAN...?
HE VANISHES IN THE MIDDLE OF HIS MOVE-MENTS. HE ABSOLUTELY DISAPPEARS.
SHOOM
SHOOM
SHOOM
BA DOM
SHOOM
MAYBE IT'S TELE-PORTA-TION...?
WELL, I CAN DO THAT TOO. BUT DEFINITELY NOT AS FAST AS THAT...

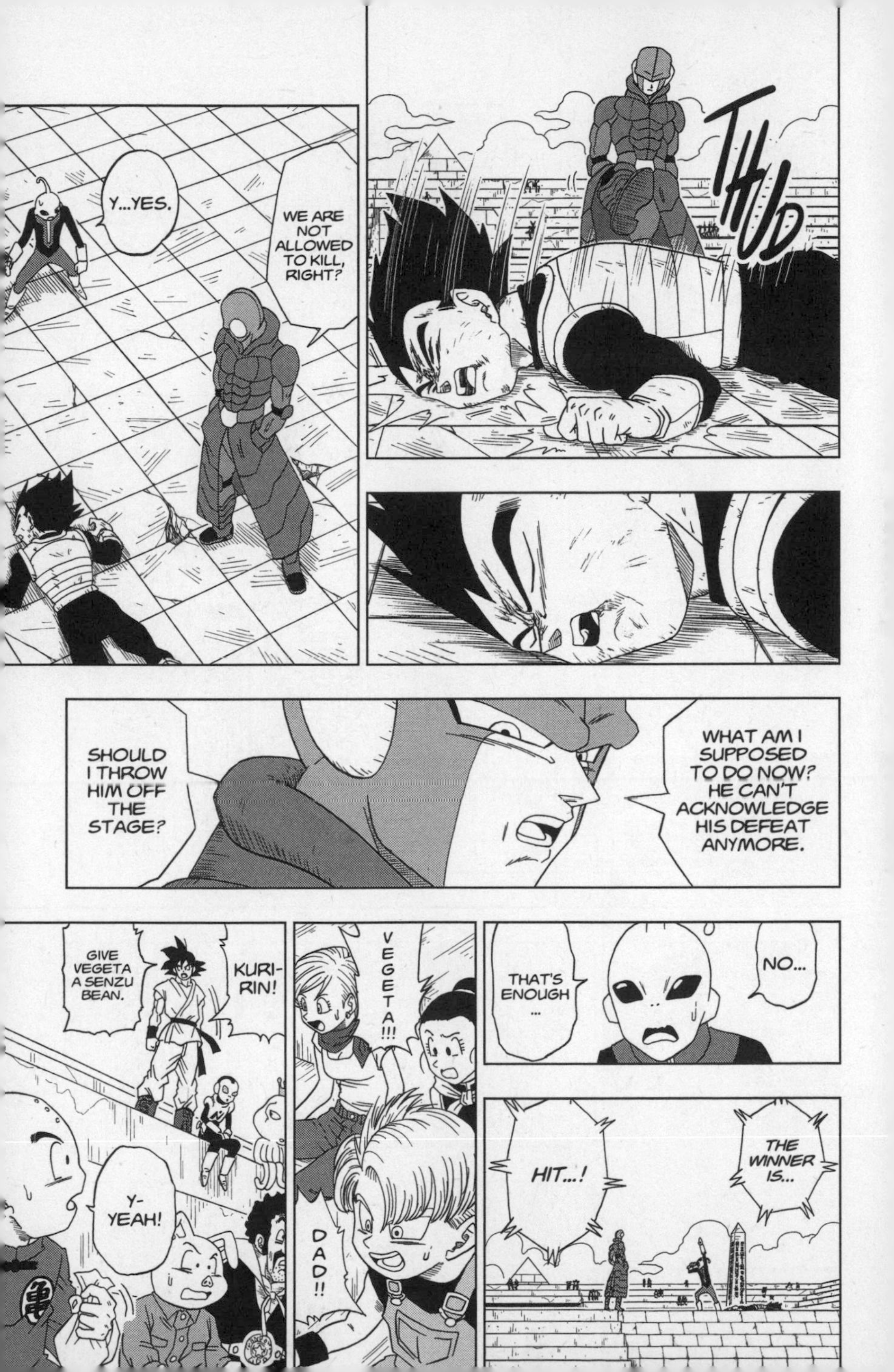
THUD
WE ARE NOT ALLOWED TO KILL, RIGHT?
Y...YES.
WHAT AM I SUPPOSED TO DO NOW? HE CAN'T ACKNOWLEDGE HIS DEFEAT ANYMORE.
SHOULD I THROW HIM OFF THE STAGE?
NO...
THAT'S ENOUGH ...
THE WINNER IS...
HIT...!
VEGETA!!!
DAD!!
KURI-RIN!
GIVE VEGETA A SENZU BEAN.
Y-YEAH!

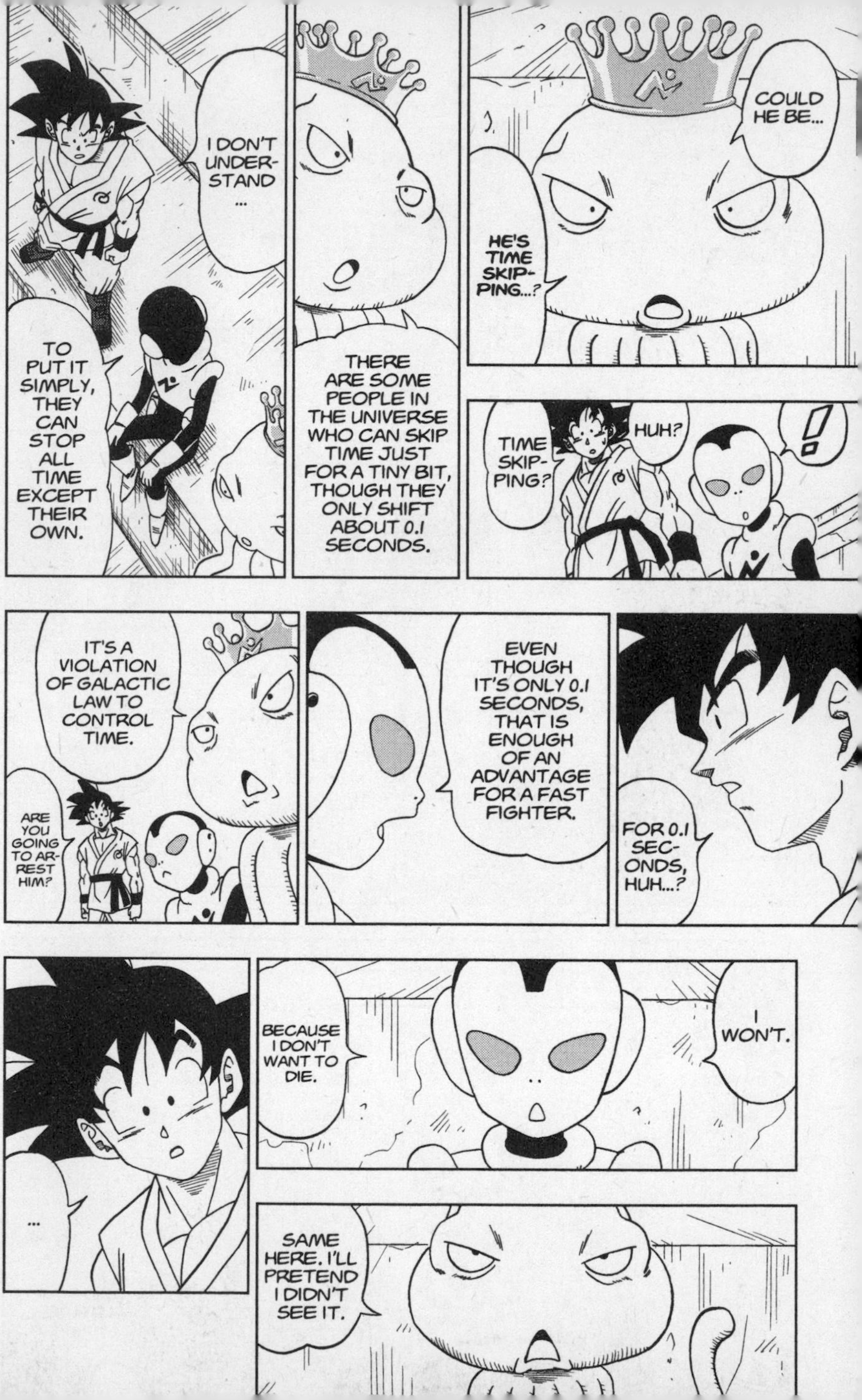
COULD HE BE...
HE'S TIME SKIP-PING...?
!
HUH?
TIME SKIP-PING?
THERE ARE SOME PEOPLE IN THE UNIVERSE WHO CAN SKIP TIME JUST FOR A TINY BIT, THOUGH THEY ONLY SHIFT ABOUT 0.1 SECONDS.
I DON'T UNDER-STAND ...
TO PUT IT SIMPLY, THEY CAN STOP ALL TIME EXCEPT THEIR OWN.
FOR 0.1 SEC-ONDS, HUH...?
EVEN THOUGH IT'S ONLY 0.1 SECONDS, THAT IS ENOUGH OF AN ADVANTAGE FOR A FAST FIGHTER.
IT'S A VIOLATION OF GALACTIC LAW TO CONTROL TIME.
ARE YOU GOING TO AR-REST HIM?
I WON'T.
BECAUSE I DON'T WANT TO DIE.
SAME HERE. I'LL PRETEND I DIDN'T SEE IT.
...

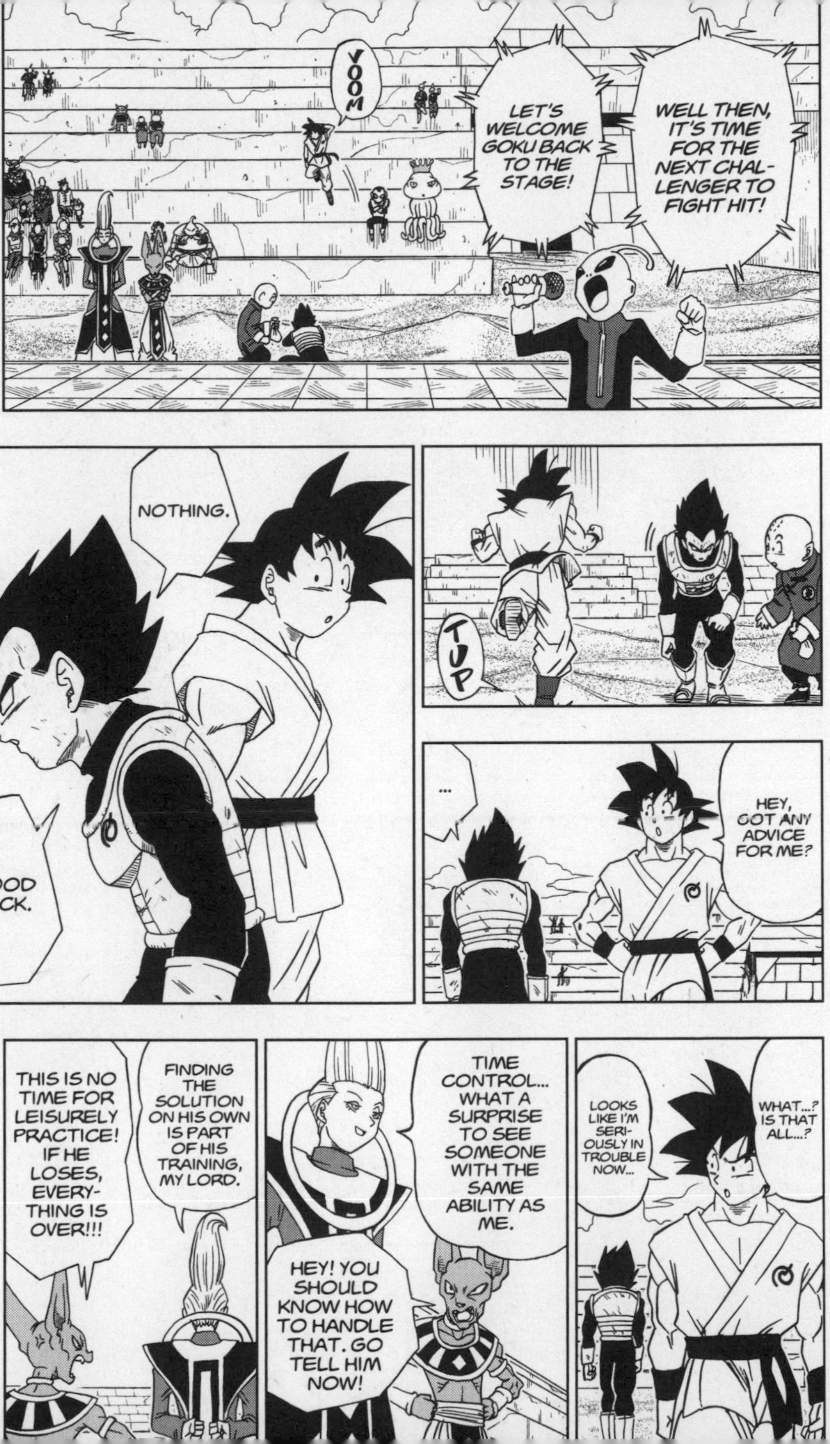

WELL THEN, IT'S TIME FOR THE NEXT CHALLENGER TO FIGHT HIT!
LET'S WELCOME GOKU BACK TO THE STAGE!
VOOM
TUP
HEY, GOT ANY ADVICE FOR ME?
...
NOTHING.
GOOD LUCK.
WHAT...? IS THAT ALL...?
LOOKS LIKE I'M SERIOUSLY IN TROUBLE NOW...
TIME CONTROL... WHAT A SURPRISE TO SEE SOMEONE WITH THE SAME ABILITY AS ME.
HEY! YOU SHOULD KNOW HOW TO HANDLE THAT. GO TELL HIM NOW!
FINDING THE SOLUTION ON HIS OWN IS PART OF HIS TRAINING, MY LORD.
THIS IS NO TIME FOR LEISURELY PRACTICE! IF HE LOSES, EVERYTHING IS OVER!!!

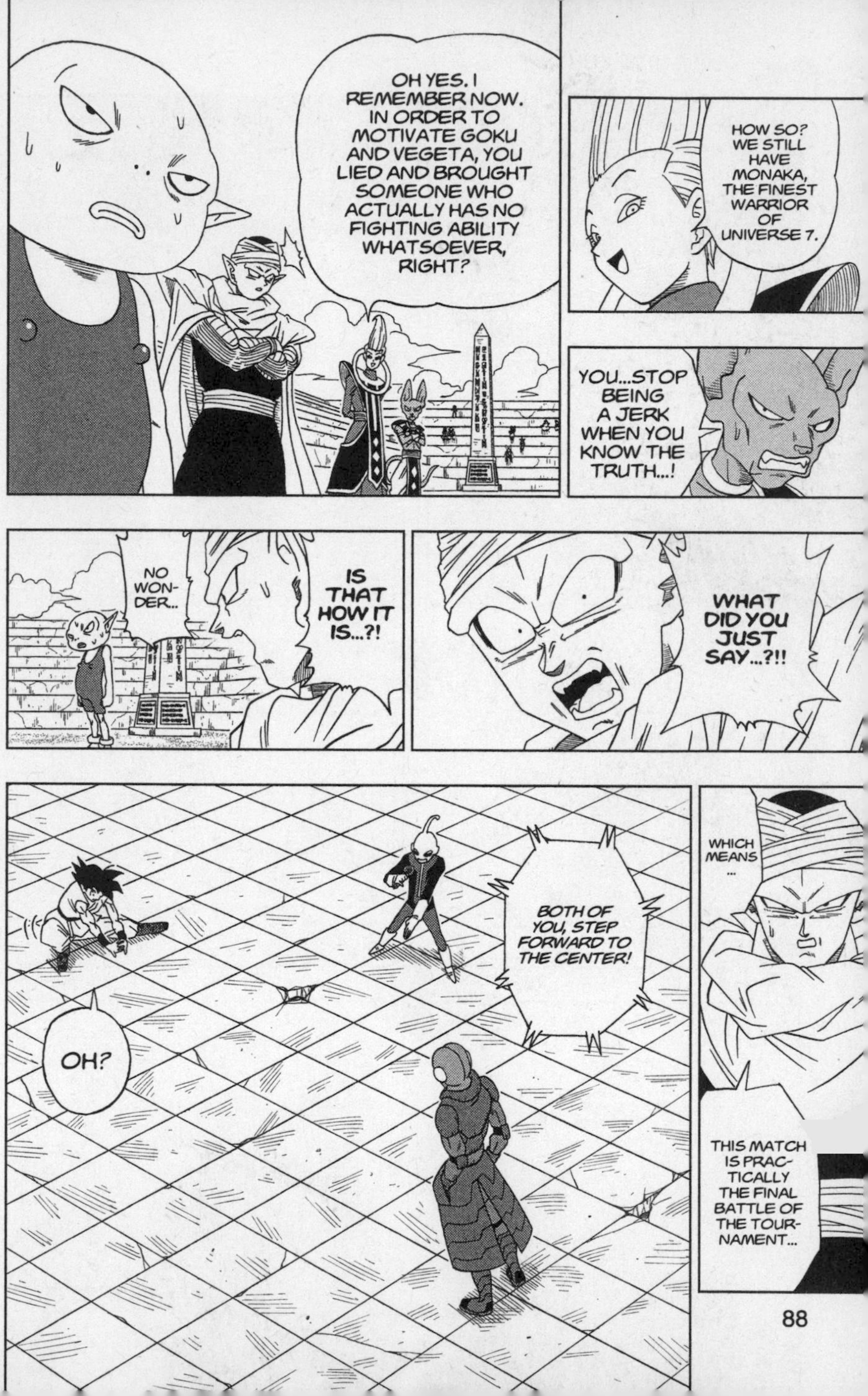
HOW SO? WE STILL HAVE MONAKA, THE FINEST WARRIOR OF UNIVERSE 7.
YOU...STOP BEING A JERK WHEN YOU KNOW THE TRUTH...!
OH YES. I REMEMBER NOW. IN ORDER TO MOTIVATE GOKU AND VEGETA, YOU LIED AND BROUGHT SOMEONE WHO ACTUALLY HAS NO FIGHTING ABILITY WHATSOEVER, RIGHT?
WHAT DID YOU JUST SAY...?!!
IS THAT HOW IT IS...?!
NO WONDER..
WHICH MEANS ...
THIS MATCH IS PRACTICALLY THE FINAL BATTLE OF THE TOURNAMENT...
BOTH OF YOU, STEP FORWARD TO THE CENTER!
OH?

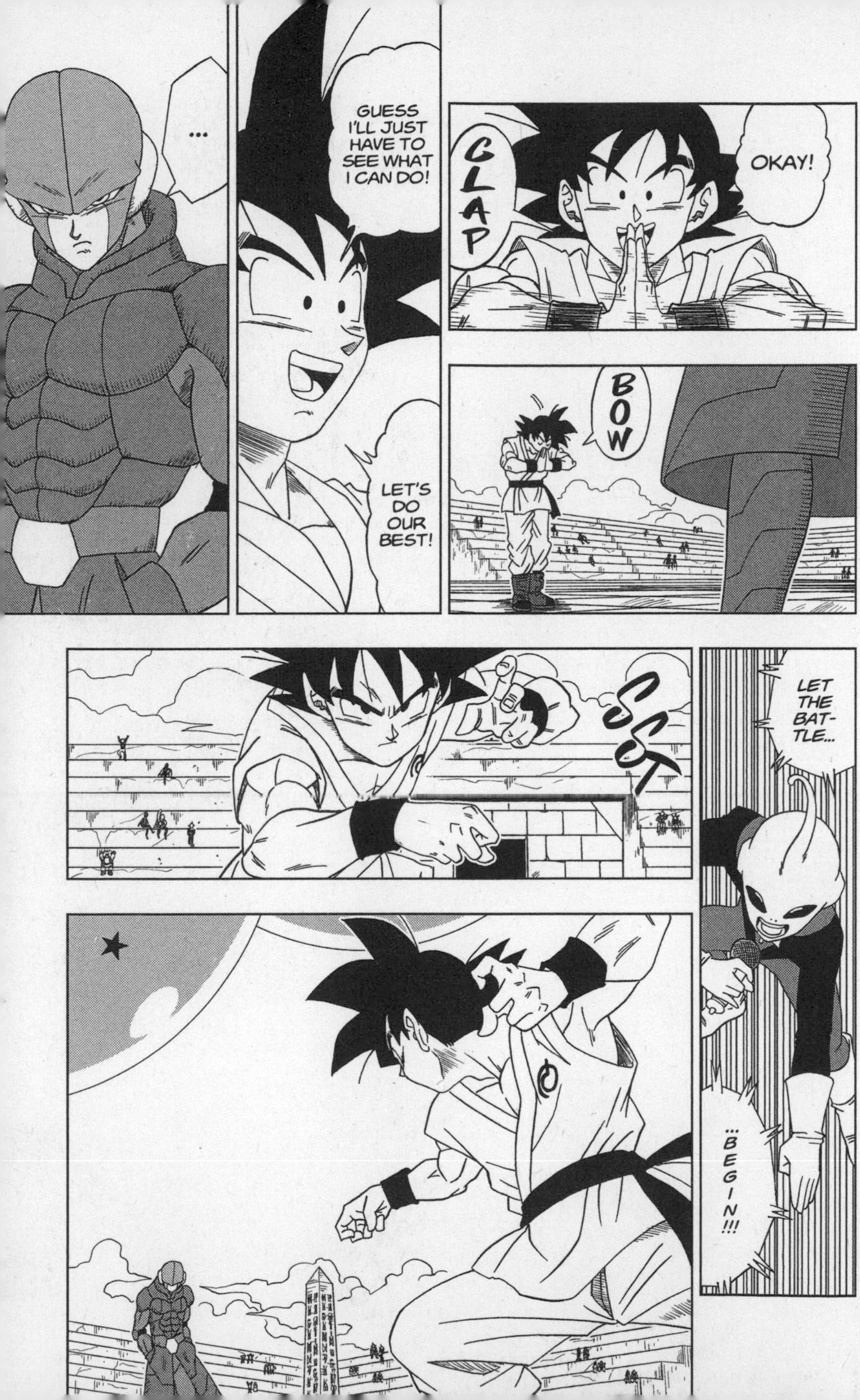
OKAY!
CLAP
BOW
GUESS I'LL JUST HAVE TO SEE WHAT I CAN DO!
LET'S DO OUR BEST!
...
LET THE BAT-TLE...
...BEGIN!!!
SST

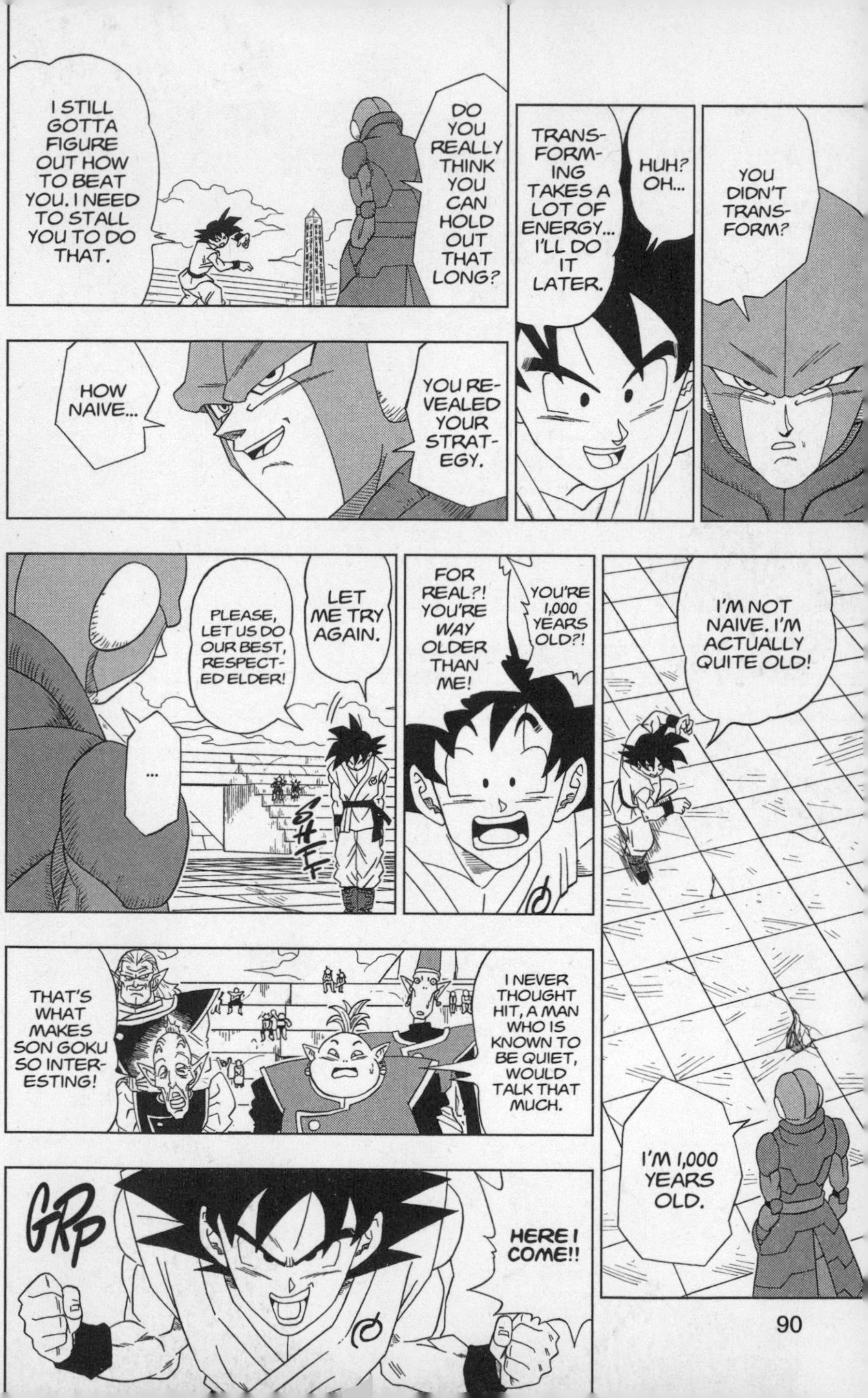
YOU DIDN'T TRANSFORM?
HUH? OH...
TRANSFORMING TAKES A LOT OF ENERGY... I'LL DO IT LATER.
DO YOU REALLY THINK YOU CAN HOLD OUT THAT LONG?
I STILL GOTTA FIGURE OUT HOW TO BEAT YOU. I NEED TO STALL YOU TO DO THAT.
YOU REVEALED YOUR STRATEGY.
HOW NAIVE...
I'M NOT NAIVE. I'M ACTUALLY QUITE OLD!
I'M 1,000 YEARS OLD.
YOU'RE 1,000 YEARS OLD?!
FOR REAL?! YOU'RE *WAY* OLDER THAN ME!
LET ME TRY AGAIN.
PLEASE, LET US DO OUR BEST, RESPECTED ELDER!
SHFF
...
I NEVER THOUGHT HIT, A MAN WHO IS KNOWN TO BE QUIET, WOULD TALK THAT MUCH.
THAT'S WHAT MAKES SON GOKU SO INTERESTING!
HERE I COME!!
GRP

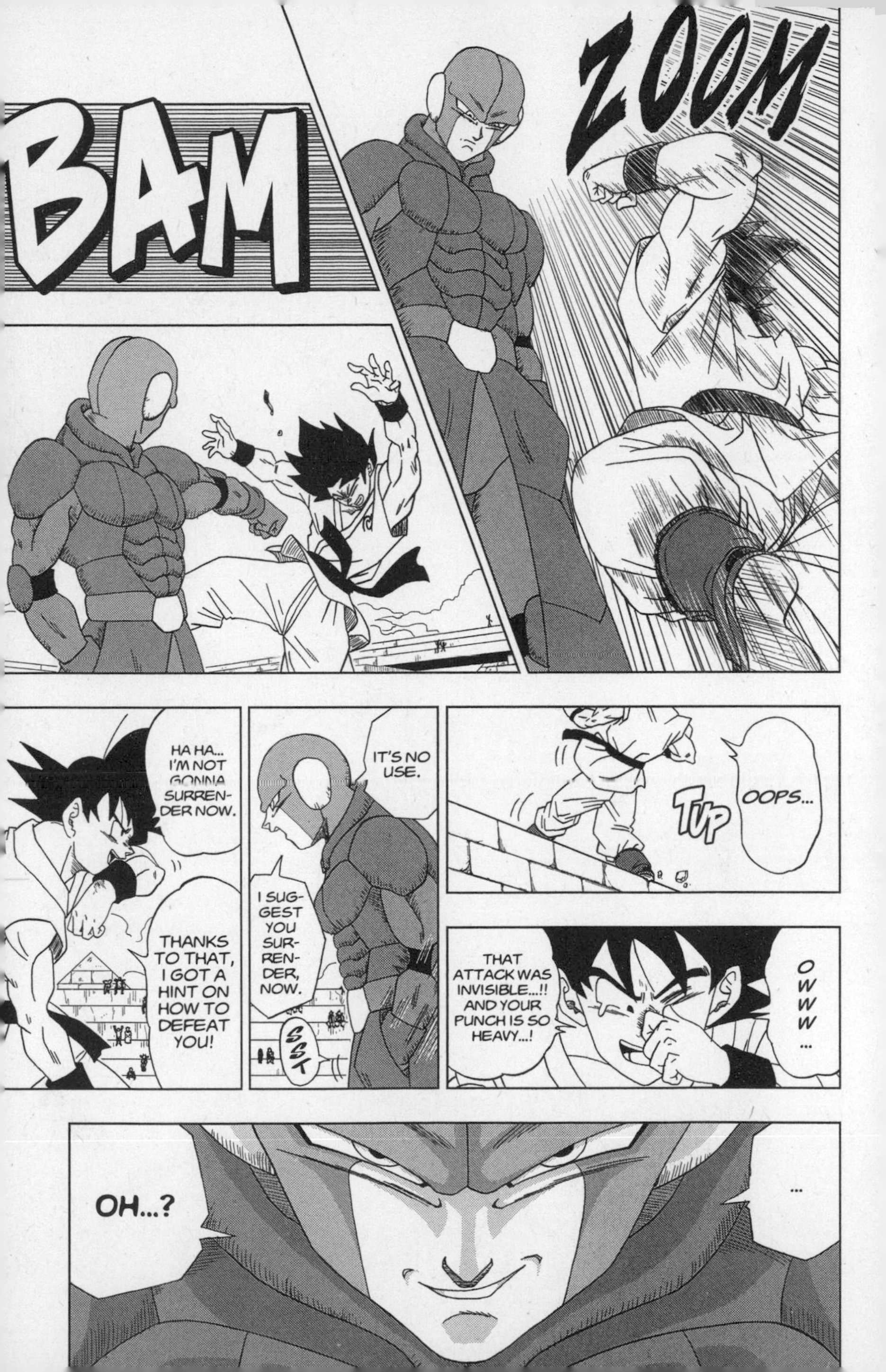
ZOOM
BAM
TUP
OOPS...
OWWW...
THAT ATTACK WAS INVISIBLE...!! AND YOUR PUNCH IS SO HEAVY...!
IT'S NO USE.
I SUGGEST YOU SURRENDER, NOW.
SST
HA HA... I'M NOT GONNA SURRENDER NOW.
THANKS TO THAT, I GOT A HINT ON HOW TO DEFEAT YOU!
...
OH...?

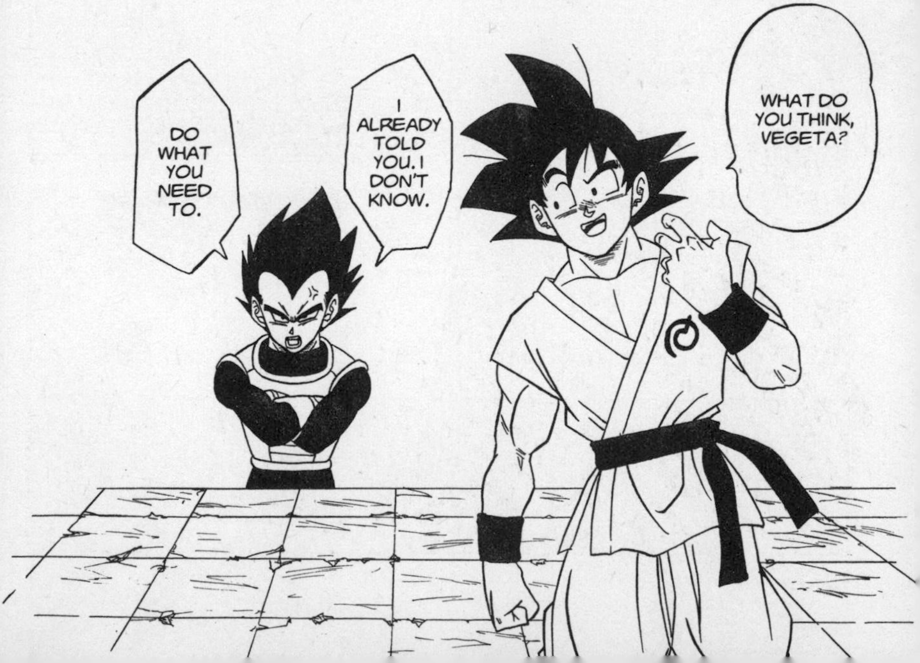
WHAT DO YOU THINK, VEGETA?
I ALREADY TOLD YOU. I DON'T KNOW.
DO WHAT YOU NEED TO.

DRAGON BALL SUPER

CHAPTER 13: THE WINNING UNIVERSE IS DECIDED!

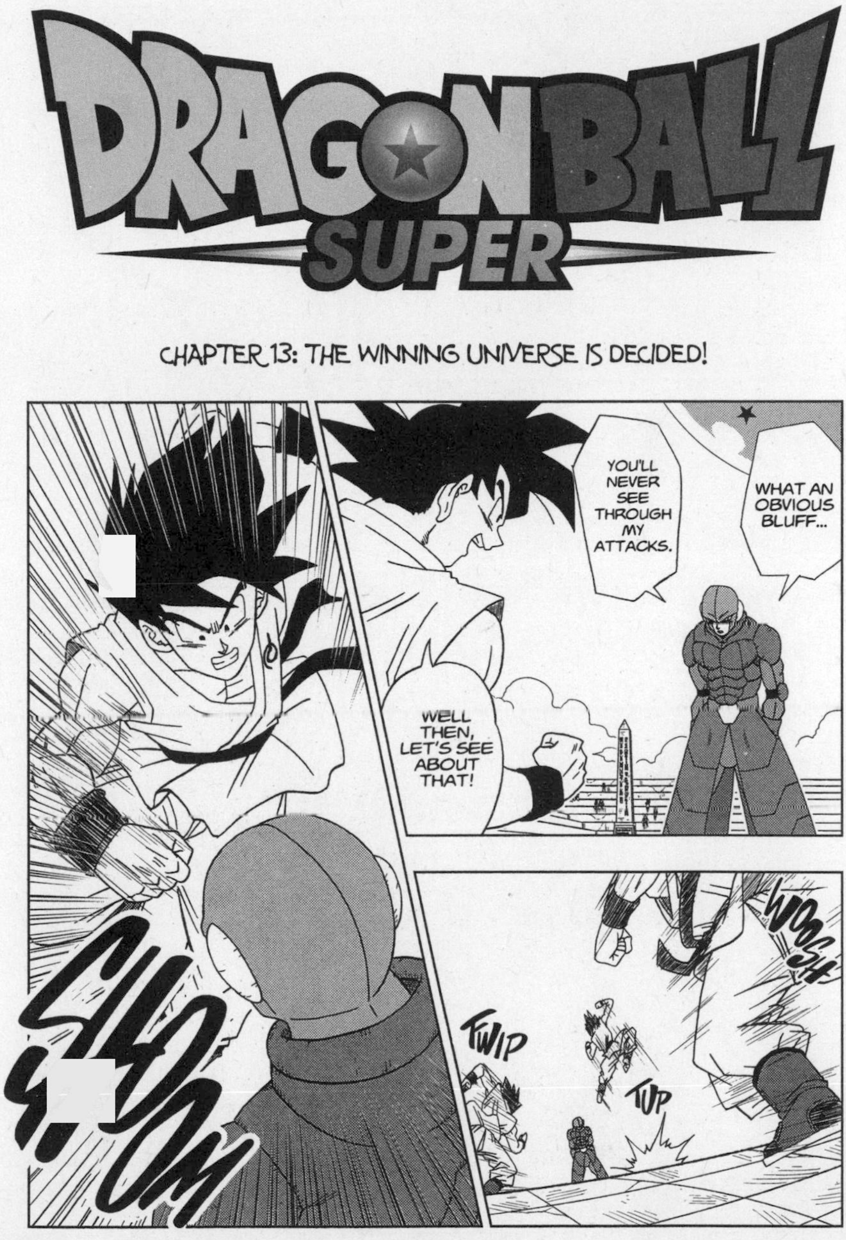
WHAT AN OBVIOUS BLUFF...
YOU'LL NEVER SEE THROUGH MY ATTACKS.
WELL THEN, LET'S SEE ABOUT THAT!
WOOSH
TUP
FWIP
CHOOM

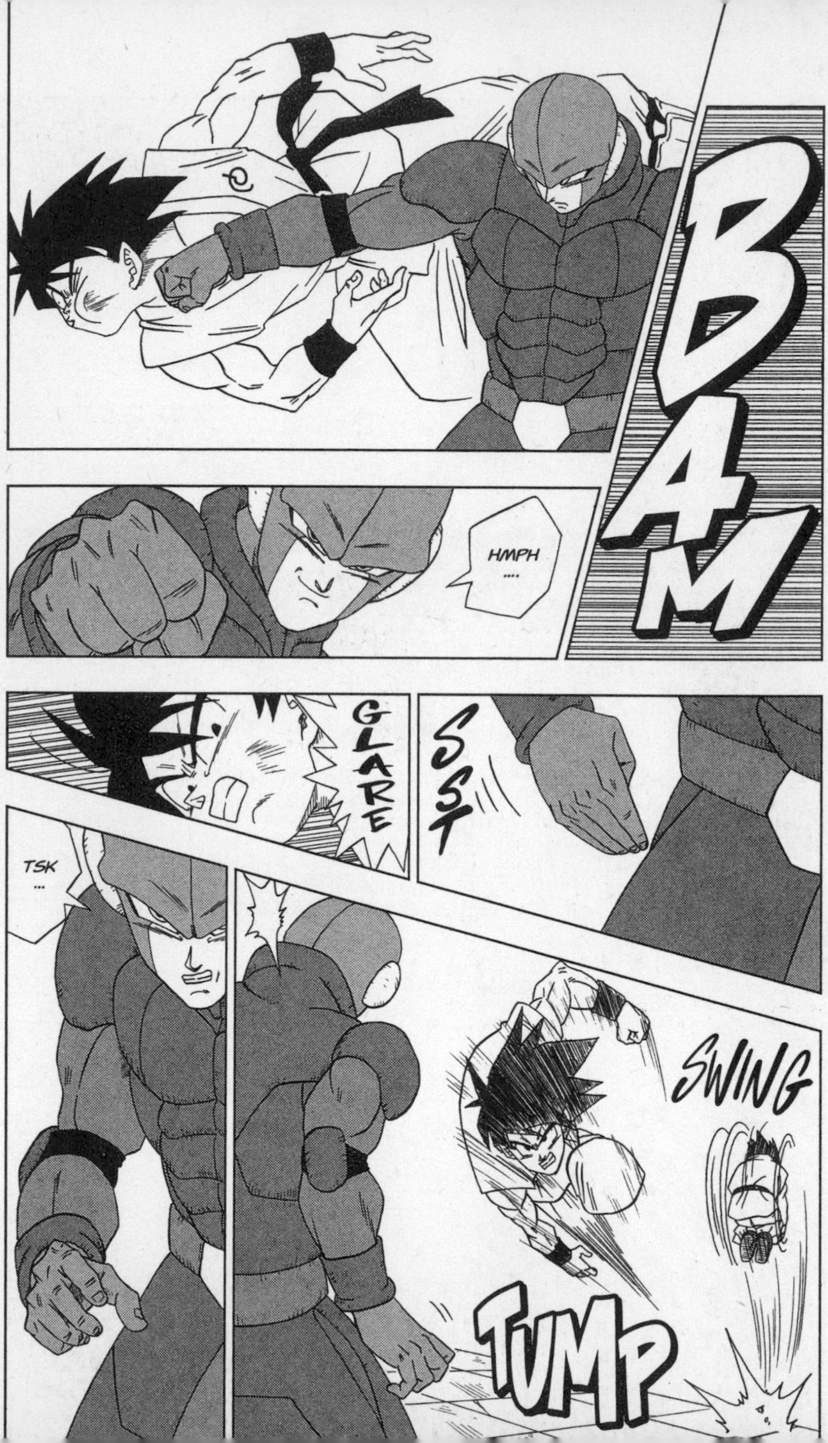
BAM
HMPH....
SST
GLARE
SWING
TUMP
TSK...

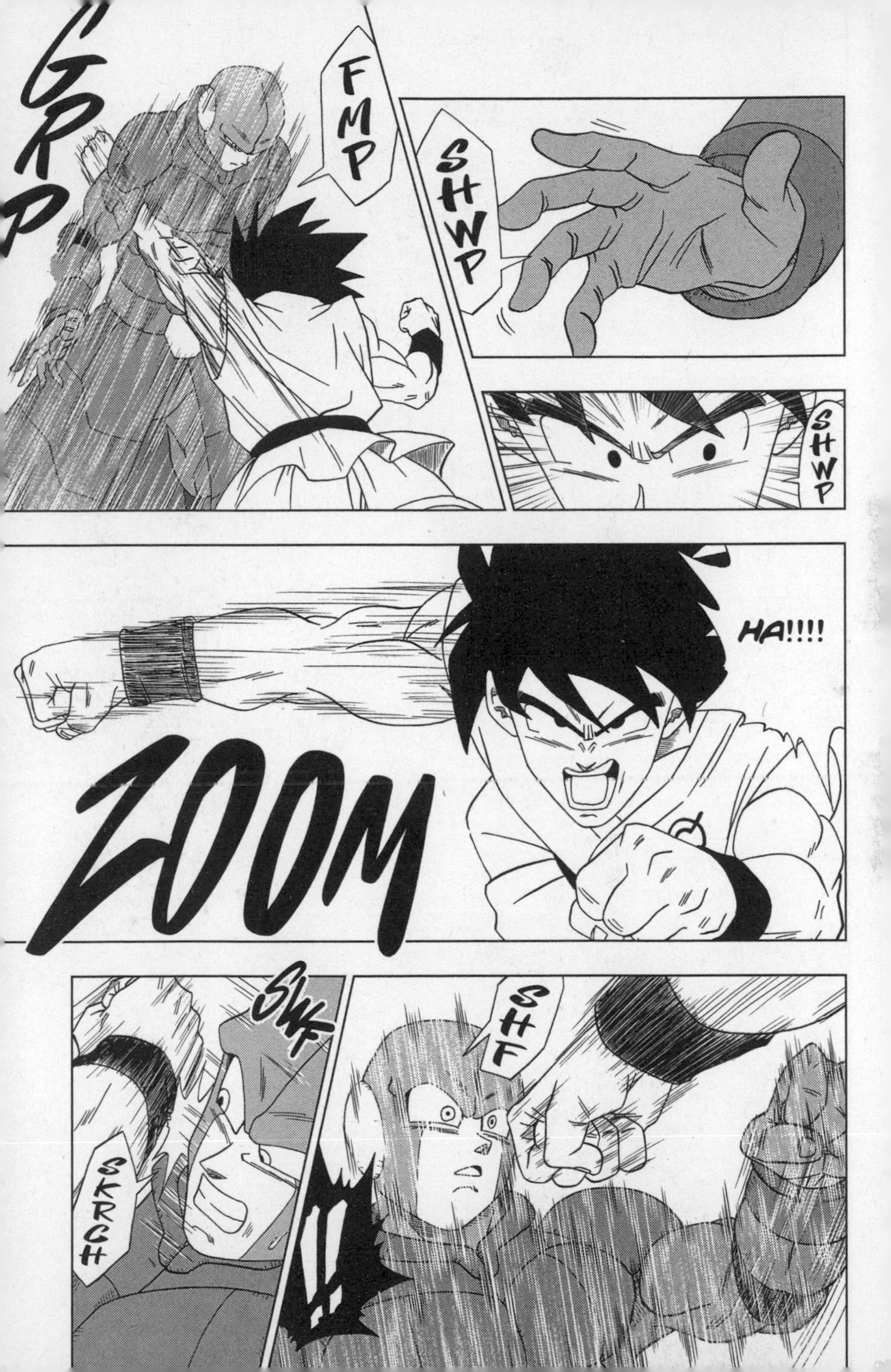

SHWP
SHWP
FMP
GRP
HA!!!!
ZOOM
SHF
SWF
SKRCH

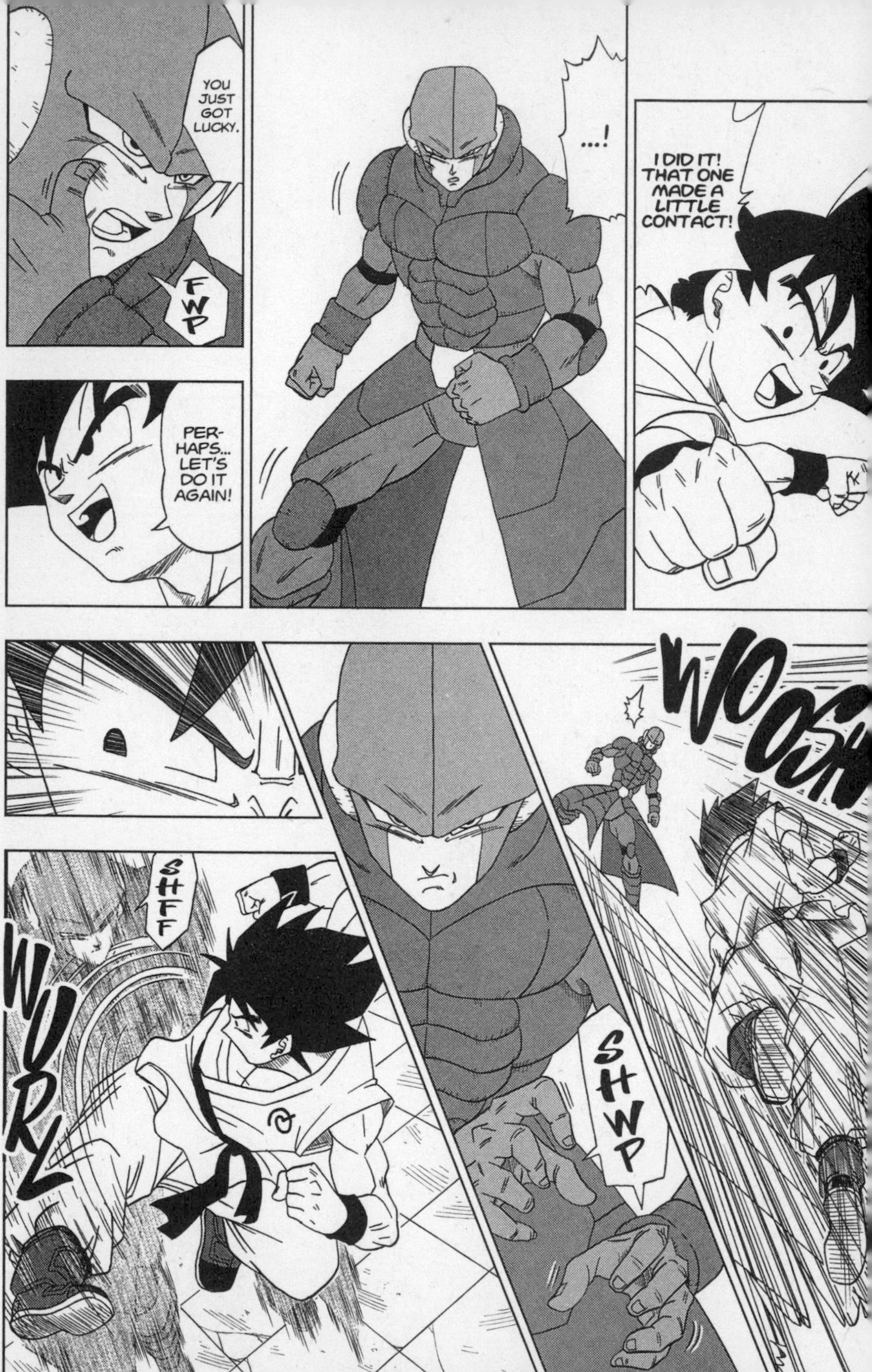
I DID IT! THAT ONE MADE A LITTLE CONTACT!
...!
YOU JUST GOT LUCKY.
FWP
PER-HAPS... LET'S DO IT AGAIN!
WOOSH
SHWP
SHFF
WURL

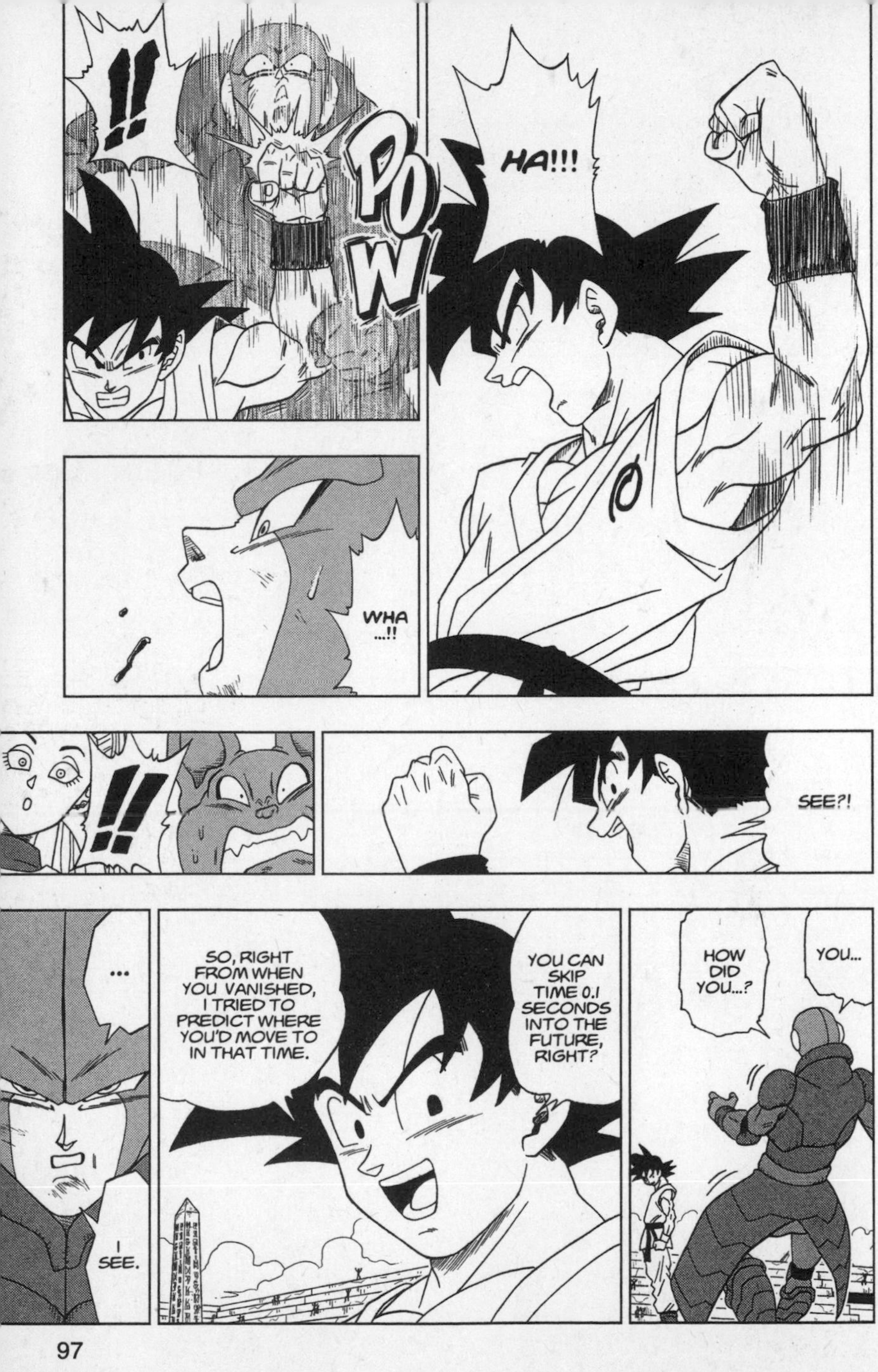
HA!!!
!!
POW
WHA...!!
SEE?!
!!
YOU...
HOW DID YOU...?
YOU CAN SKIP TIME 0.1 SECONDS INTO THE FUTURE, RIGHT?
SO, RIGHT FROM WHEN YOU VANISHED, I TRIED TO PREDICT WHERE YOU'D MOVE TO IN THAT TIME.
...
I SEE.

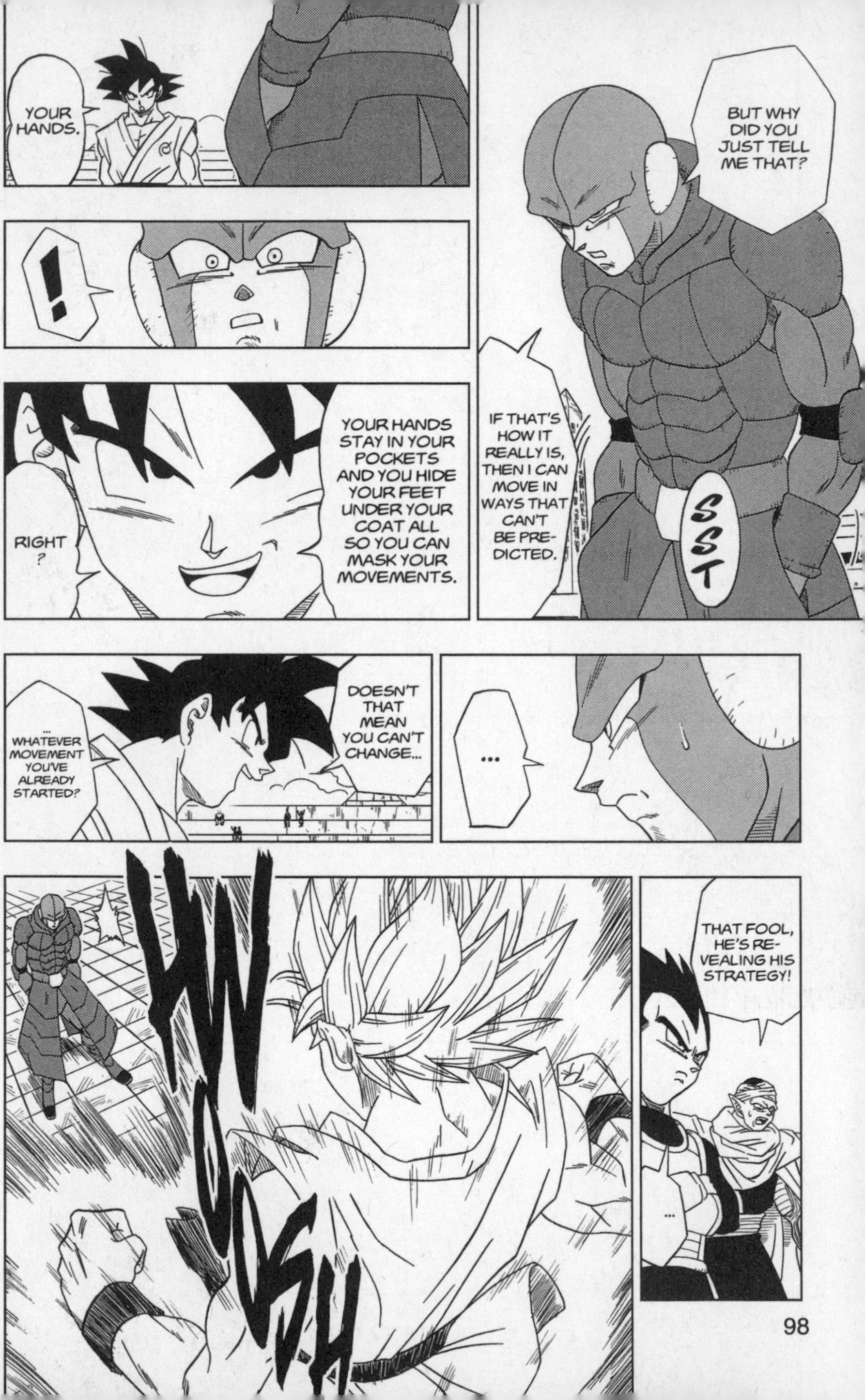
BUT WHY DID YOU JUST TELL ME THAT?
IF THAT'S HOW IT REALLY IS, THEN I CAN MOVE IN WAYS THAT CAN'T BE PRE-DICTED.
SST
YOUR HANDS.
!
YOUR HANDS STAY IN YOUR POCKETS AND YOU HIDE YOUR FEET UNDER YOUR COAT ALL SO YOU CAN MASK YOUR MOVEMENTS.
RIGHT?
...
DOESN'T THAT MEAN YOU CAN'T CHANGE...
...WHATEVER MOVEMENT YOU'VE ALREADY STARTED?
THAT FOOL, HE'S RE-VEALING HIS STRATEGY!
...
HWOOSH

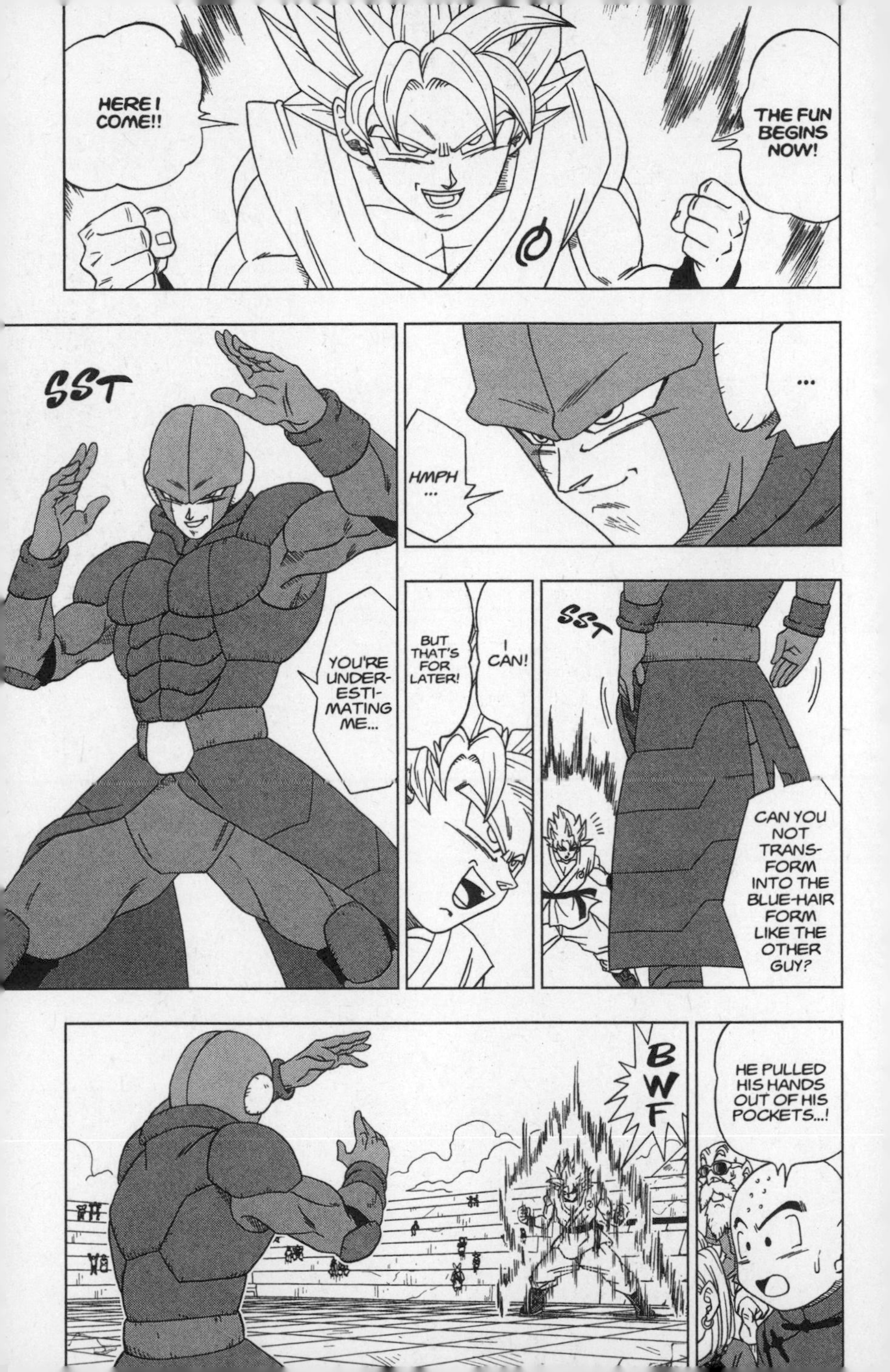
THE FUN BEGINS NOW!
HERE I COME!!
...
HMPH ...
SST
CAN YOU NOT TRANSFORM INTO THE BLUE-HAIR FORM LIKE THE OTHER GUY?
I CAN!
BUT THAT'S FOR LATER!
SST
YOU'RE UNDERESTIMATING ME...
HE PULLED HIS HANDS OUT OF HIS POCKETS...!
BWF

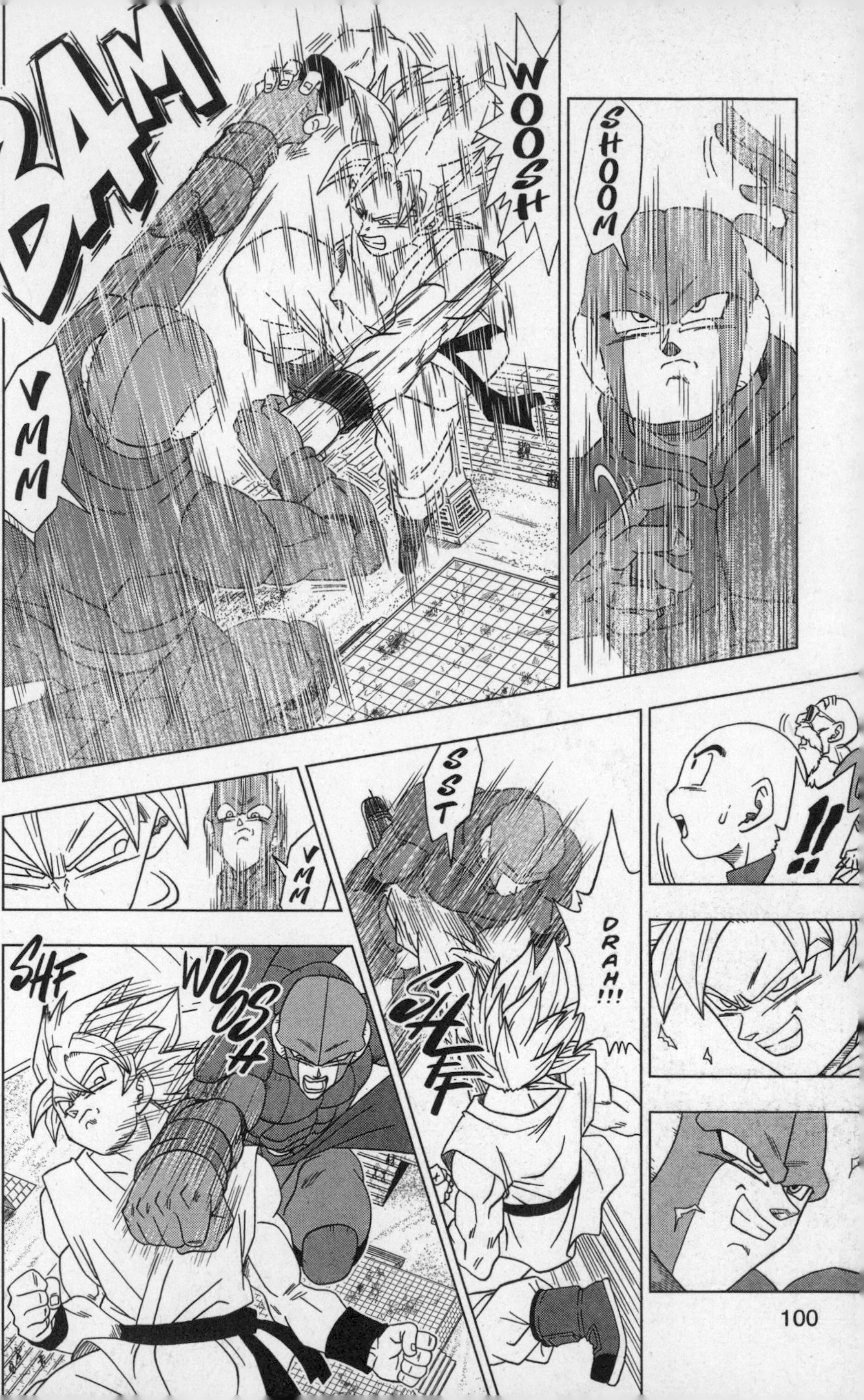
SHOOM
WOOSH
BAM
VMM
!!
SST
DRAH!!!
SHFF
VMM
WOOSH
SHF

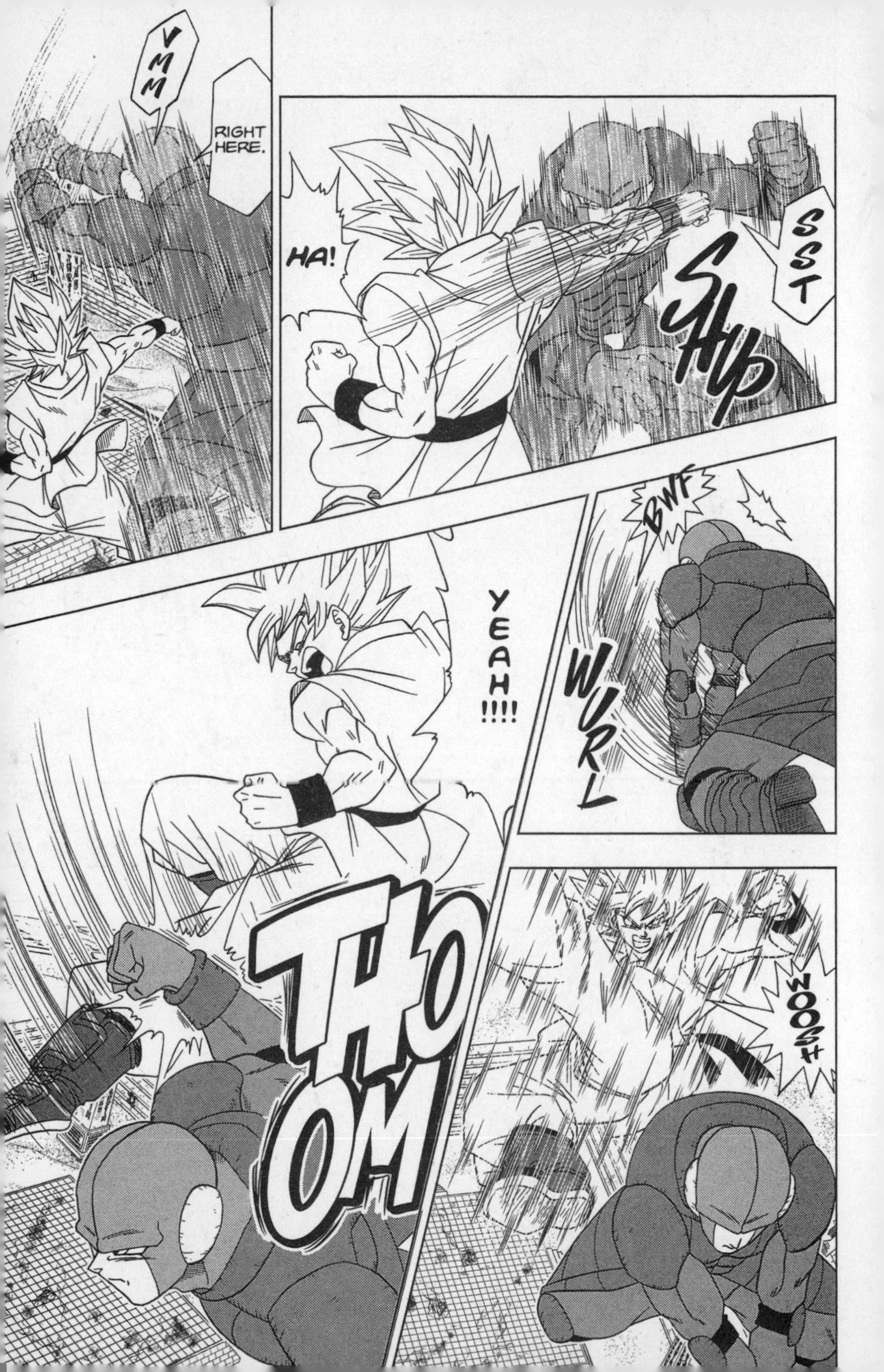
SSST
SHP
HA!
VMM
RIGHT HERE.
BWF
WURL
WOOSH
YEAH!!!!
THOOM

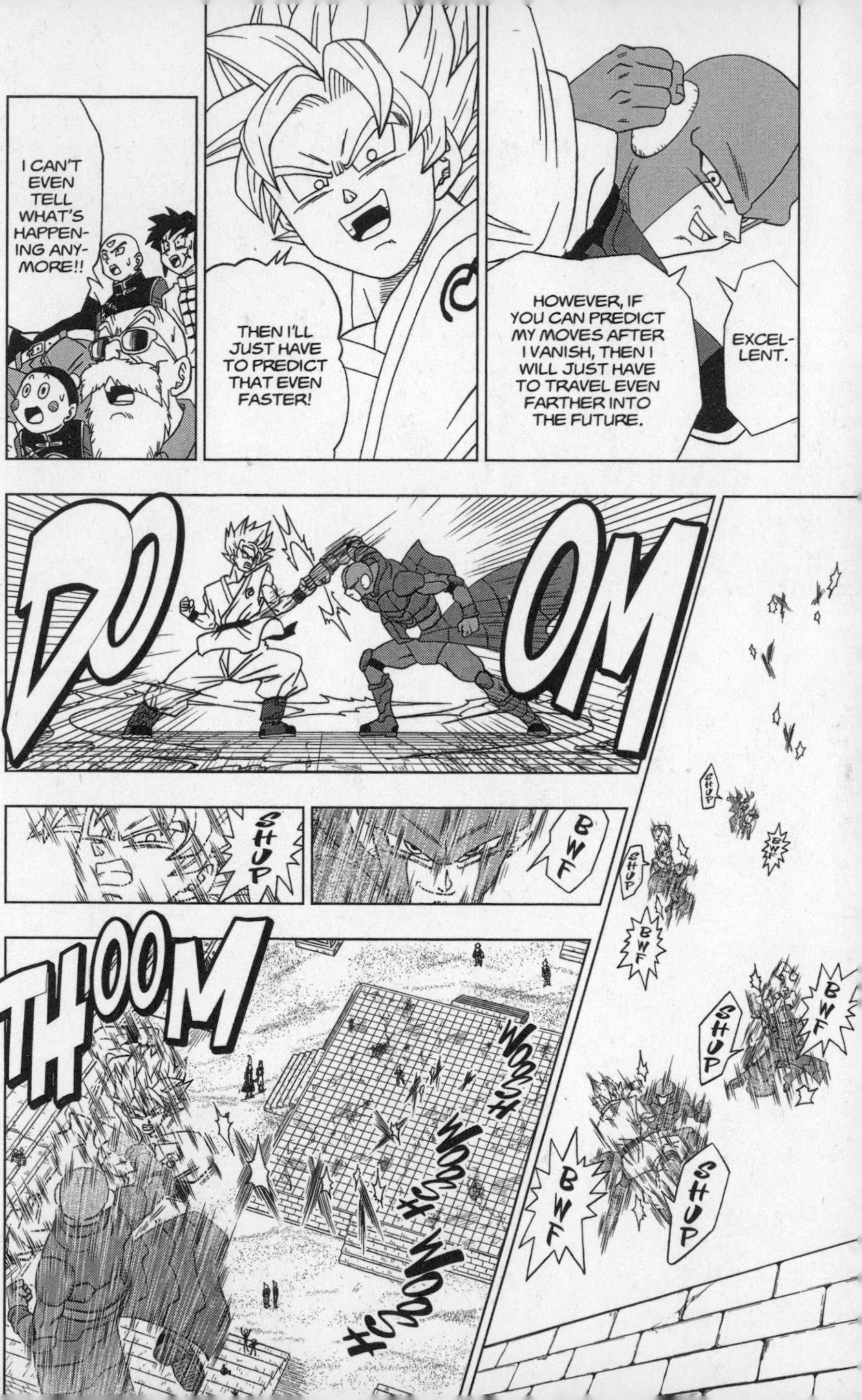
EXCEL-LENT.
HOWEVER, IF YOU CAN PREDICT MY MOVES AFTER I VANISH, THEN I WILL JUST HAVE TO TRAVEL EVEN FARTHER INTO THE FUTURE.
THEN I'LL JUST HAVE TO PREDICT THAT EVEN FASTER!
I CAN'T EVEN TELL WHAT'S HAPPENING ANY-MORE!!
SHUP
BWF
SHUP
BWF
BWF
SHUP
SHUP
BWF
DOOM
BWF
SHUP
THOOM
WOOSH
WOOSH
WOOSH

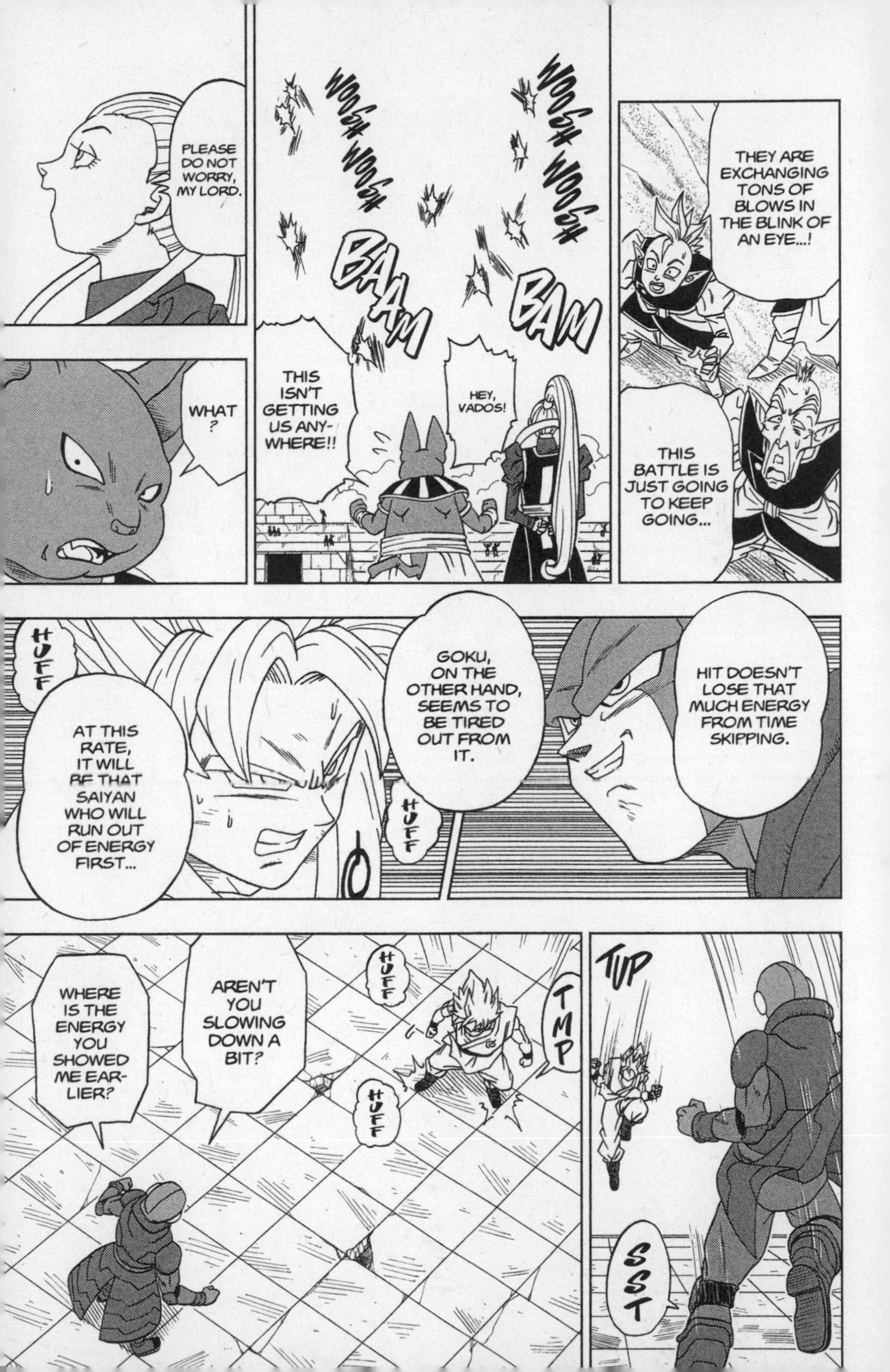
THEY ARE EXCHANGING TONS OF BLOWS IN THE BLINK OF AN EYE...!
THIS BATTLE IS JUST GOING TO KEEP GOING...
WOOSH WOOSH
WOOSH WOOSH
BAM
BAAM
HEY, VADOS!
THIS ISN'T GETTING US ANYWHERE!!
PLEASE DO NOT WORRY, MY LORD.
WHAT?
HIT DOESN'T LOSE THAT MUCH ENERGY FROM TIME SKIPPING.
GOKU, ON THE OTHER HAND, SEEMS TO BE TIRED OUT FROM IT.
HUFF
HUFF
AT THIS RATE, IT WILL BE THAT SAIYAN WHO WILL RUN OUT OF ENERGY FIRST...
TUP
TMP
SST
HUFF
HUFF
AREN'T YOU SLOWING DOWN A BIT?
WHERE IS THE ENERGY YOU SHOWED ME EARLIER?

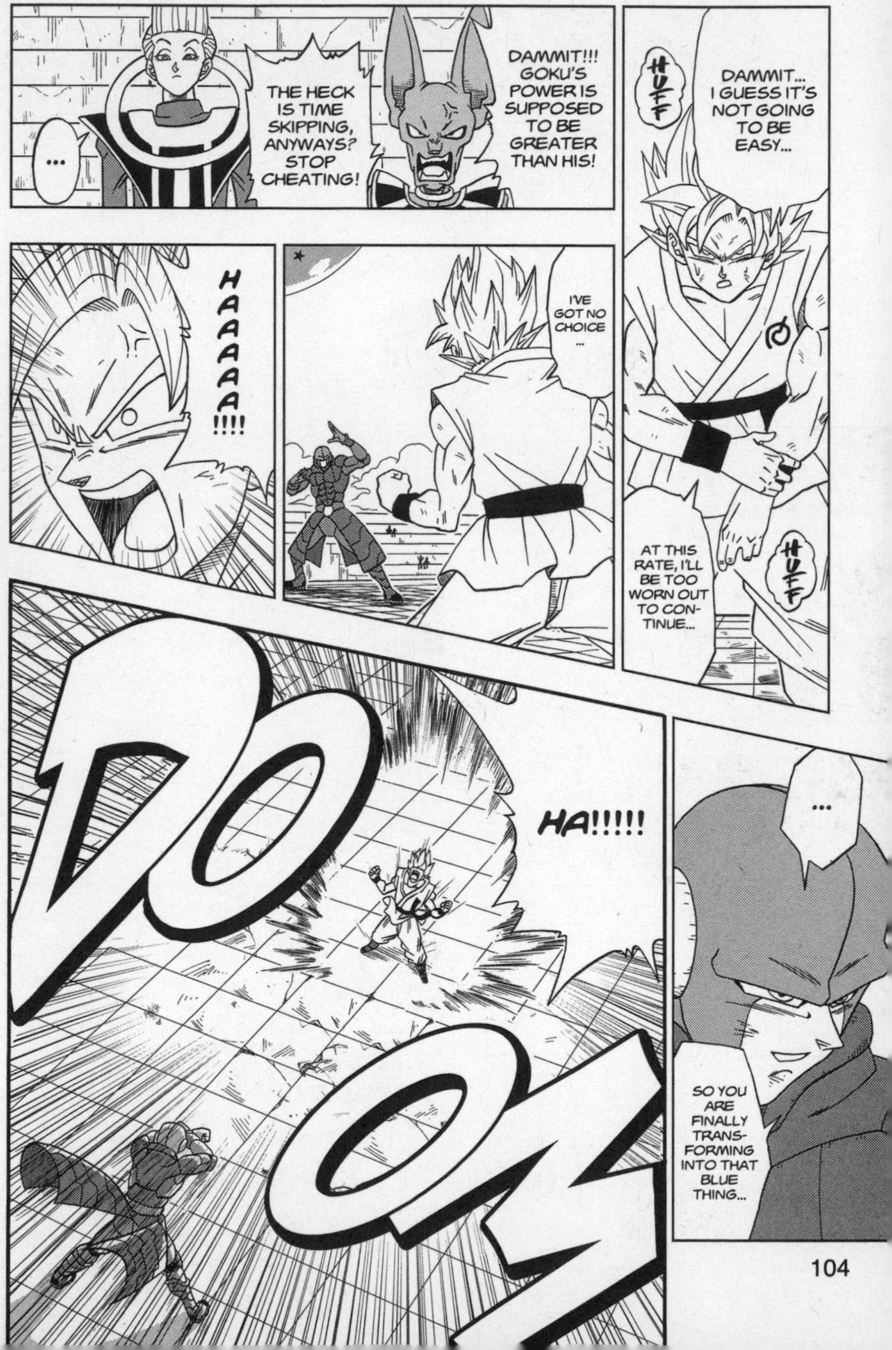
DAMMIT... I GUESS IT'S NOT GOING TO BE EASY...
HUFF
HUFF
AT THIS RATE, I'LL BE TOO WORN OUT TO CON-TINUE...
DAMMIT!!! GOKU'S POWER IS SUPPOSED TO BE GREATER THAN HIS!
THE HECK IS TIME SKIPPING, ANYWAYS? STOP CHEATING!
...
I'VE GOT NO CHOICE ...
HAAAAAA!!!!
...
SO YOU ARE FINALLY TRANS-FORMING INTO THAT BLUE THING...
HA!!!!!
DOOM

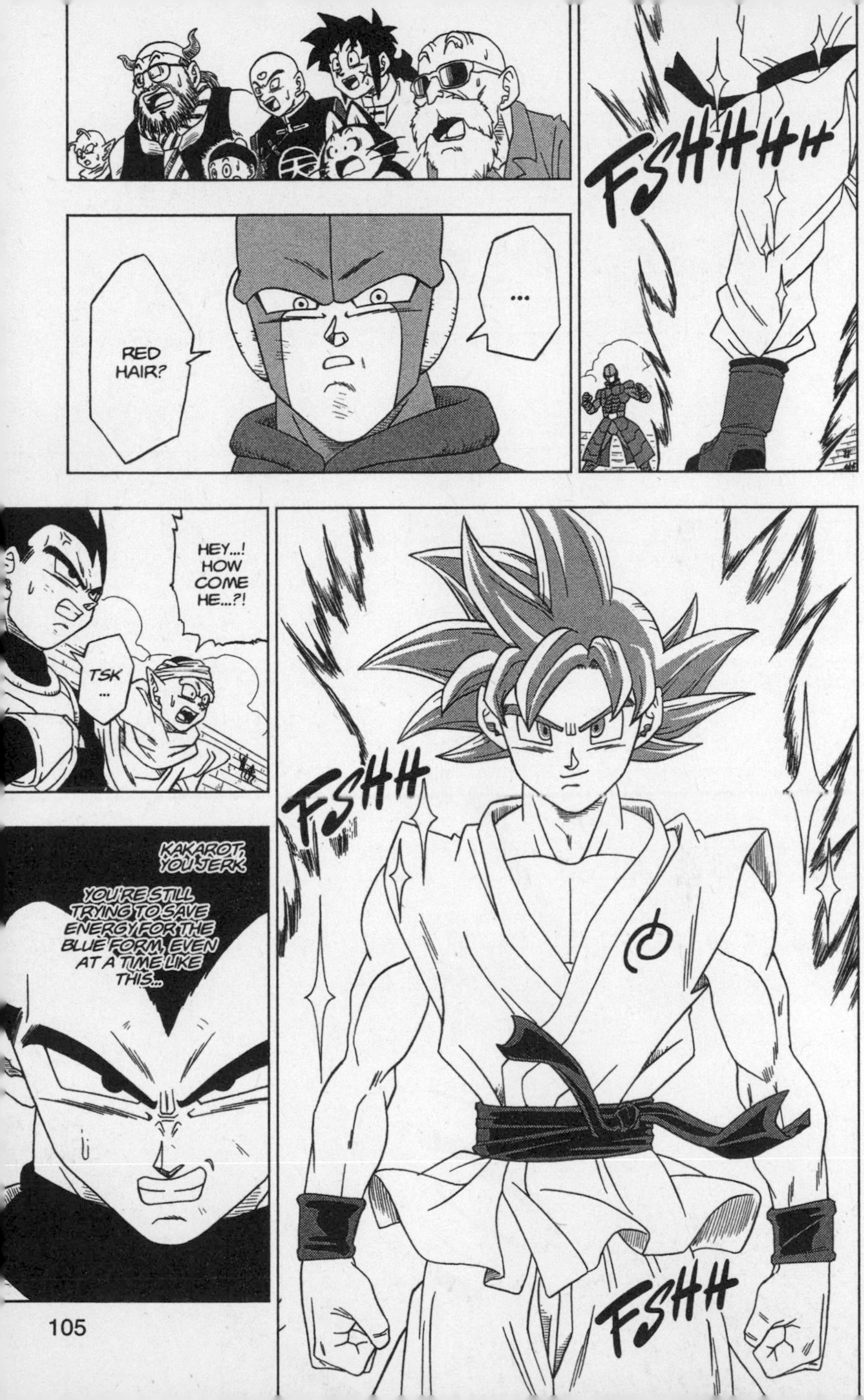
FSHHHHH
...
RED HAIR?
FSHH
FSHH
HEY...! HOW COME HE...?!
TSK ...
KAKAROT, YOU JERK
YOU'RE STILL TRYING TO SAVE ENERGY FOR THE BLUE FORM, EVEN AT A TIME LIKE THIS...

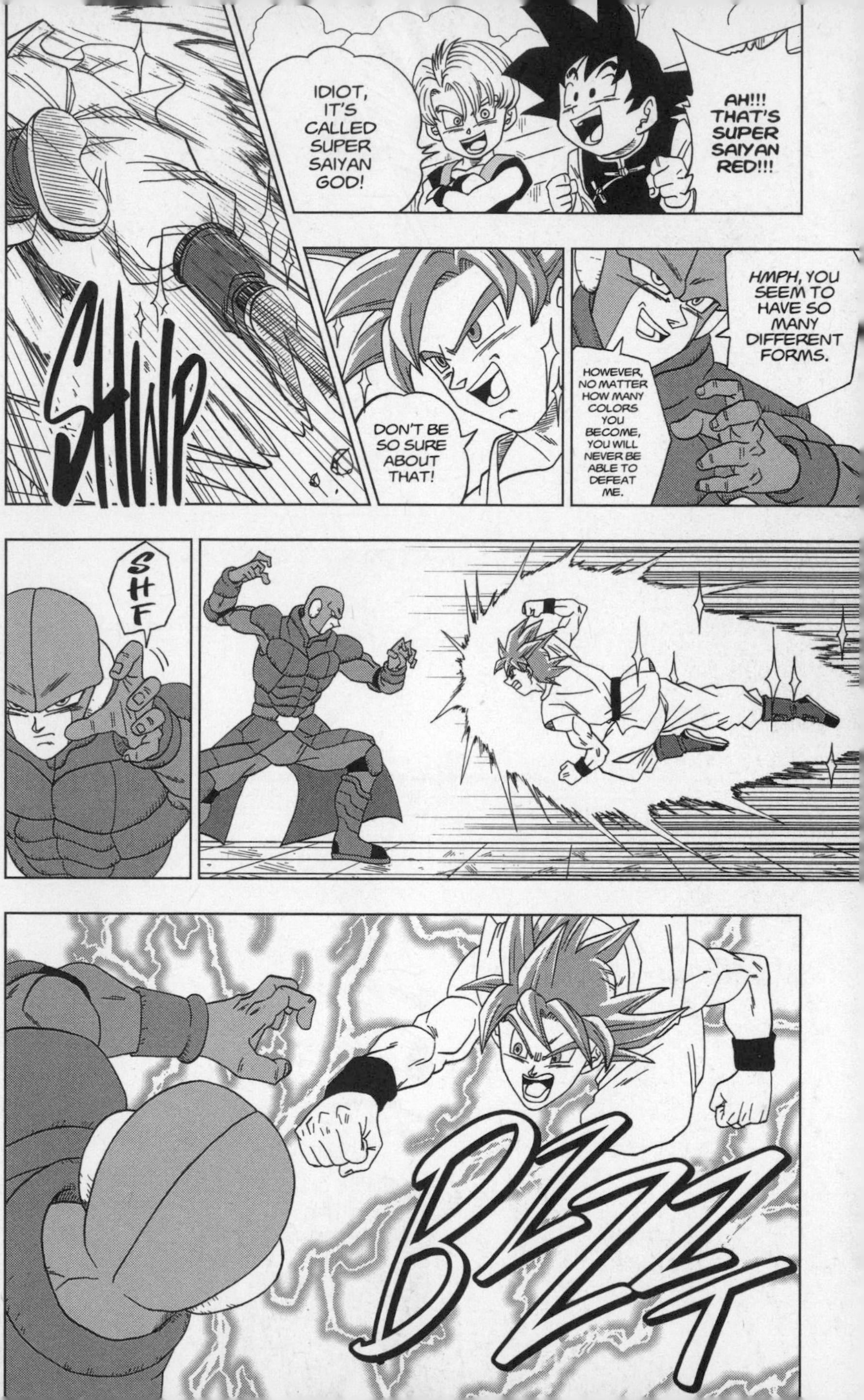
AH!!! THAT'S SUPER SAIYAN RED!!!
IDIOT, IT'S CALLED SUPER SAIYAN GOD!
HMPH, YOU SEEM TO HAVE SO MANY DIFFERENT FORMS.
HOWEVER, NO MATTER HOW MANY COLORS YOU BECOME, YOU WILL NEVER BE ABLE TO DEFEAT ME.
DON'T BE SO SURE ABOUT THAT!
SHWP
SHF
BZZZ

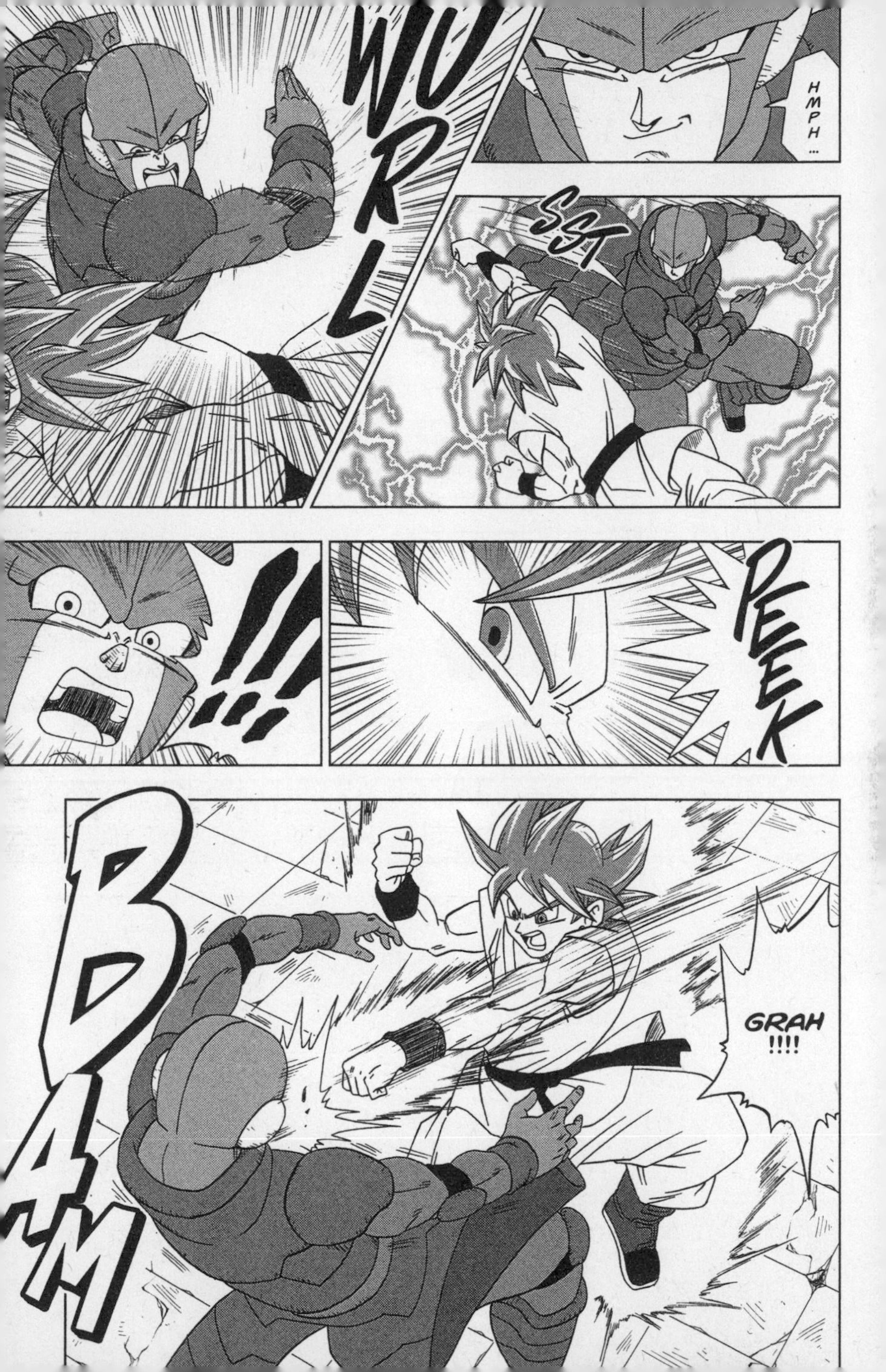

HMPH...
SST
WURL
PEEEK
!!!!
GRAH !!!!
BAM

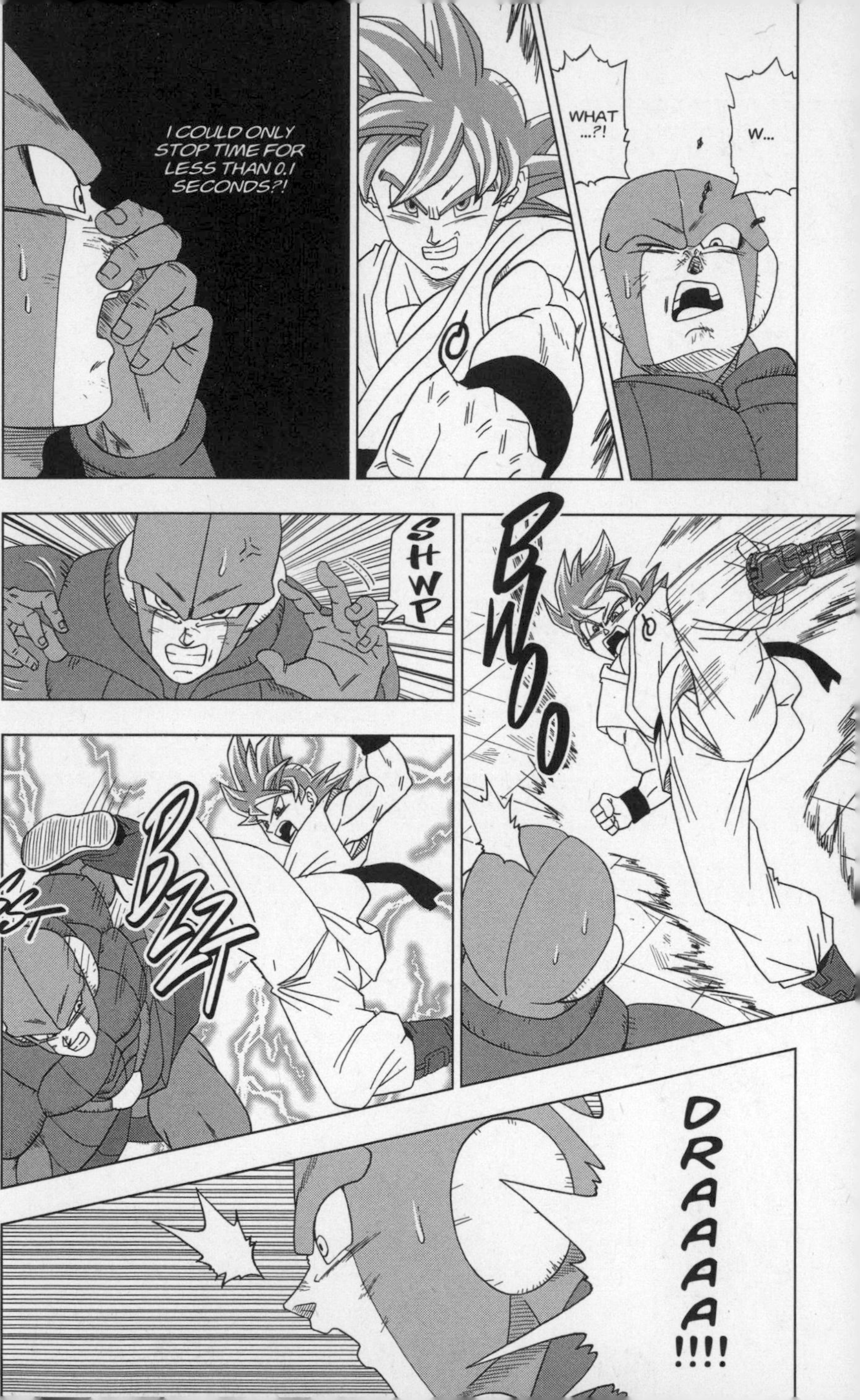
W...
WHAT ...?!
I COULD ONLY STOP TIME FOR LESS THAN 0.1 SECONDS?!
BWOOO
SHWP
BZZZT
DRAAAAA!!!!

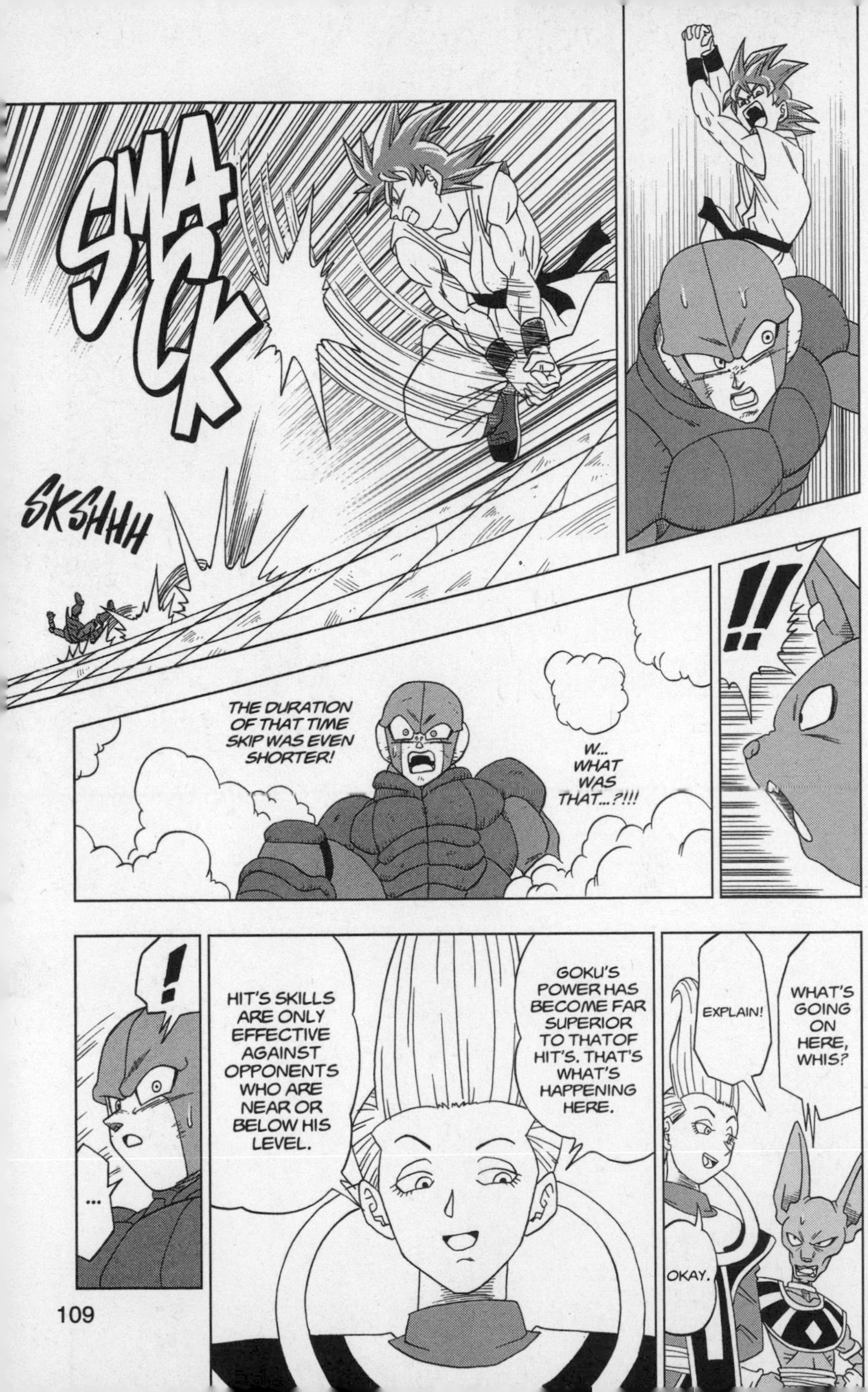

SMACK
SKSHHH
!!
W... WHAT WAS THAT...?!!!
THE DURATION OF THAT TIME SKIP WAS EVEN SHORTER!
WHAT'S GOING ON HERE, WHIS?
EXPLAIN!
OKAY.
GOKU'S POWER HAS BECOME FAR SUPERIOR TO THATOF HIT'S. THAT'S WHAT'S HAPPENING HERE.
HIT'S SKILLS ARE ONLY EFFECTIVE AGAINST OPPONENTS WHO ARE NEAR OR BELOW HIS LEVEL.
!
...

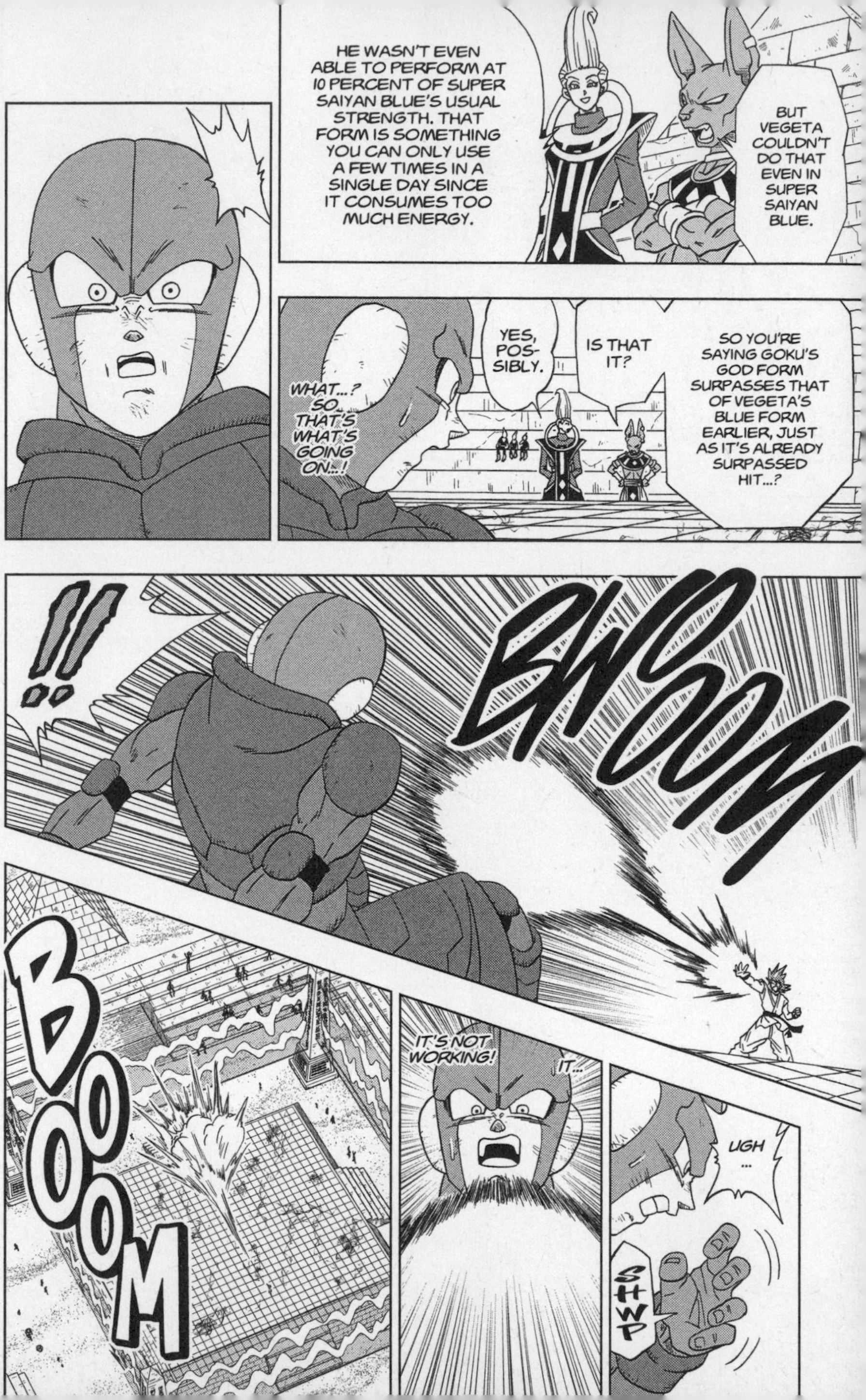
BUT VEGETA COULDN'T DO THAT EVEN IN SUPER SAIYAN BLUE.
HE WASN'T EVEN ABLE TO PERFORM AT 10 PERCENT OF SUPER SAIYAN BLUE'S USUAL STRENGTH. THAT FORM IS SOMETHING YOU CAN ONLY USE A FEW TIMES IN A SINGLE DAY SINCE IT CONSUMES TOO MUCH ENERGY.
SO YOU'RE SAYING GOKU'S GOD FORM SURPASSES THAT OF VEGETA'S BLUE FORM EARLIER, JUST AS IT'S ALREADY SURPASSED HIT...?
IS THAT IT?
YES, POSSIBLY.
WHAT...? SO... THAT'S WHAT'S GOING ON...!
BWOOM
!!
UGH ...
SHWP
IT...
IT'S NOT WORKING!
BOOOOM

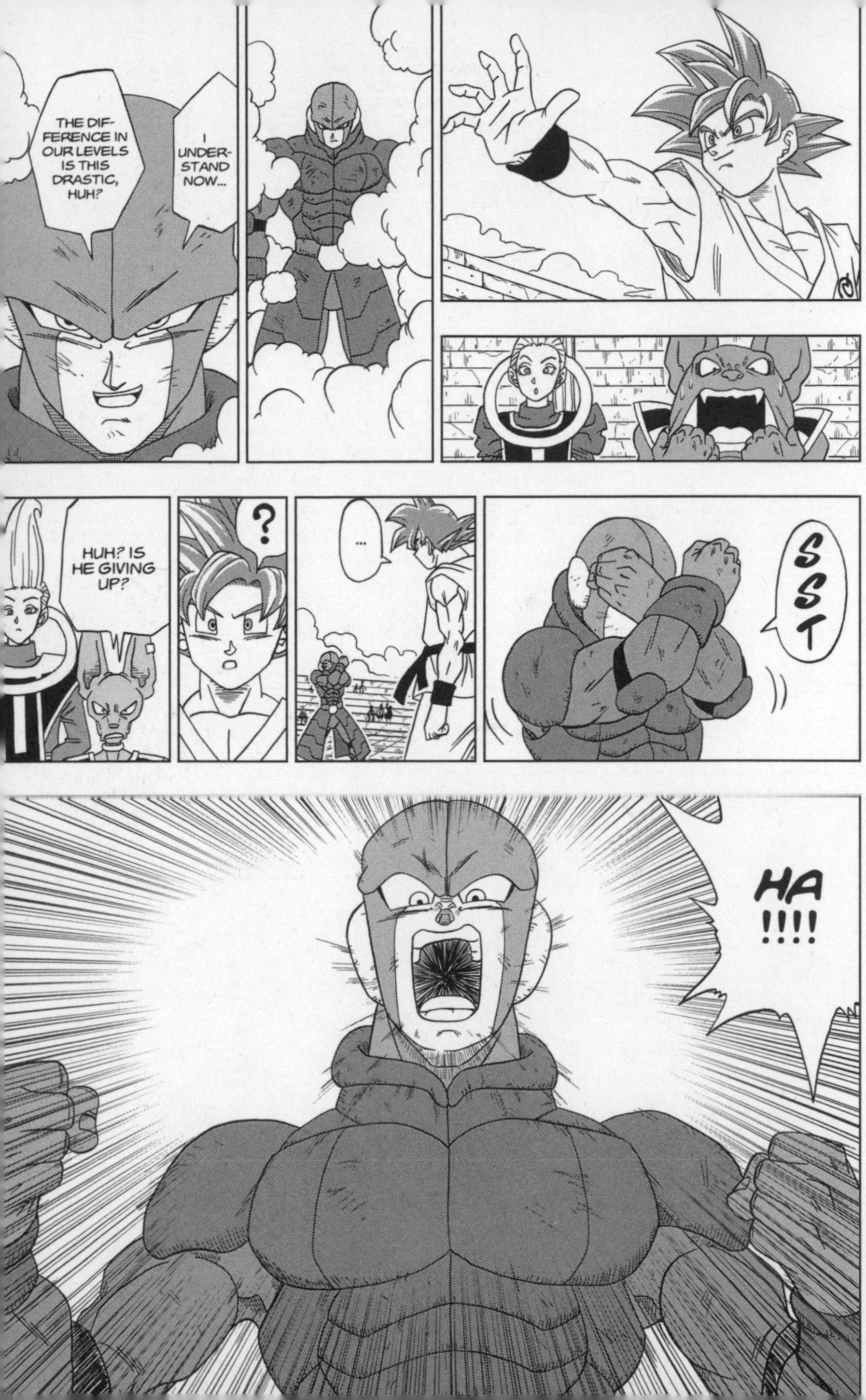
I UNDER-STAND NOW...
THE DIF-FERENCE IN OUR LEVELS IS THIS DRASTIC, HUH?
SST
...
?
HUH? IS HE GIVING UP?
HA!!!!

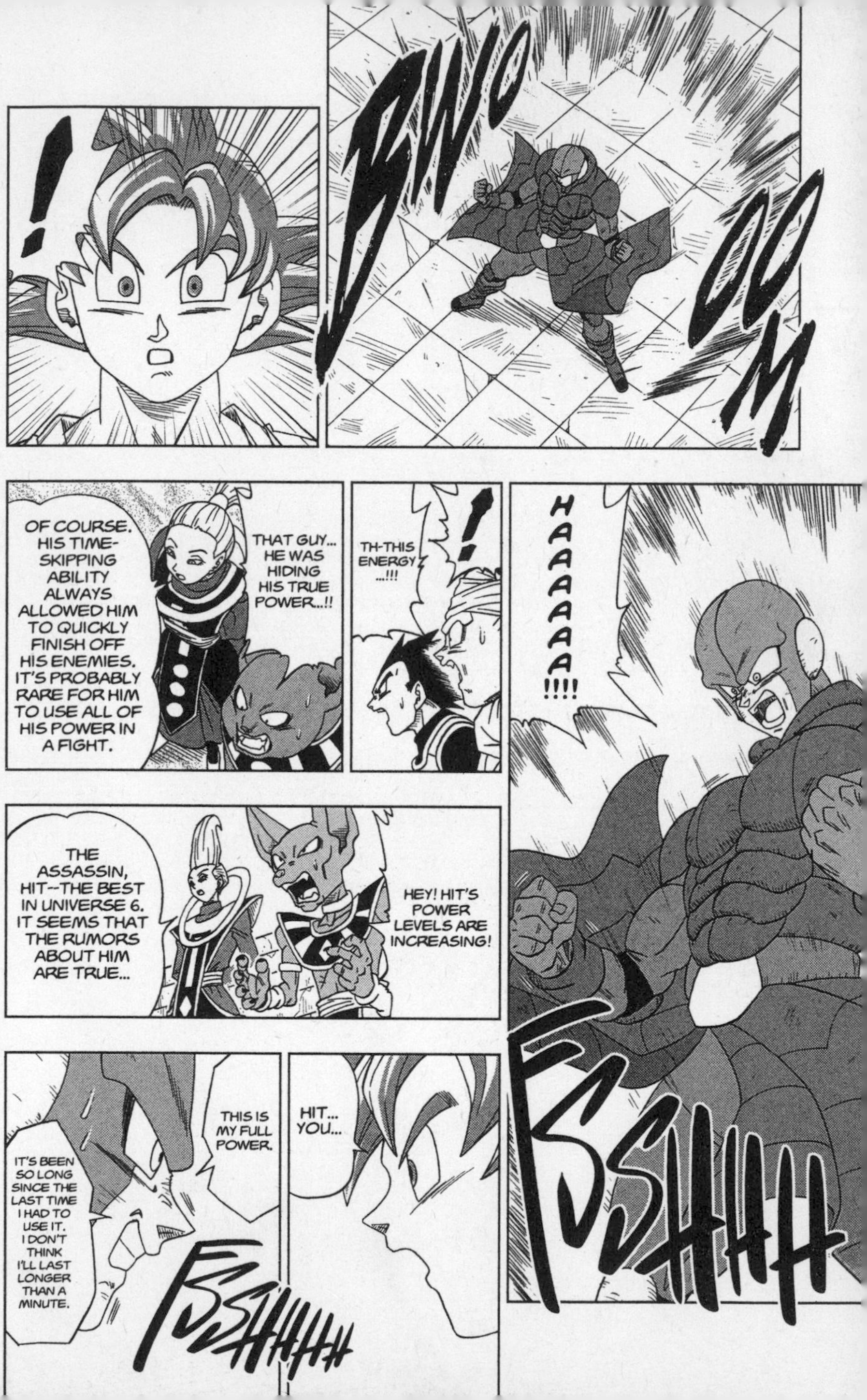
BWOOOM
!
HAAAAAAAA!!!!
FSSHHHH
TH-THIS ENERGY ...!!!
!
THAT GUY... HE WAS HIDING HIS TRUE POWER...!!
OF COURSE. HIS TIME-SKIPPING ABILITY ALWAYS ALLOWED HIM TO QUICKLY FINISH OFF HIS ENEMIES. IT'S PROBABLY RARE FOR HIM TO USE ALL OF HIS POWER IN A FIGHT.
HEY! HIT'S POWER LEVELS ARE INCREASING!
THE ASSASSIN, HIT--THE BEST IN UNIVERSE 6. IT SEEMS THAT THE RUMORS ABOUT HIM ARE TRUE...
HIT... YOU...
THIS IS MY FULL POWER.
IT'S BEEN SO LONG SINCE THE LAST TIME I HAD TO USE IT. I DON'T THINK I'LL LAST LONGER THAN A MINUTE.
FSSHHHHH

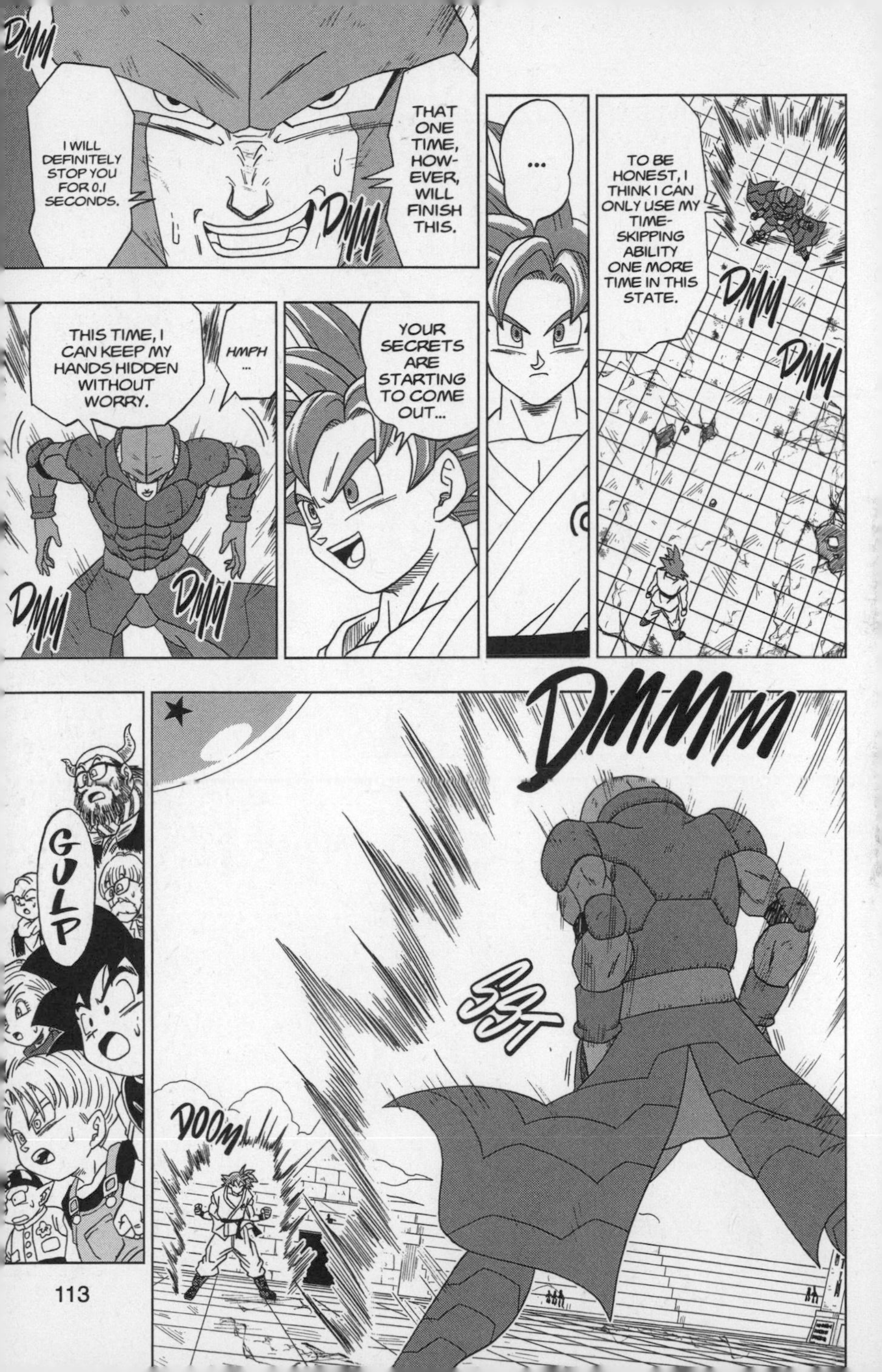
TO BE HONEST, I THINK I CAN ONLY USE MY TIME-SKIPPING ABILITY ONE MORE TIME IN THIS STATE.
DMM
DMM
...
THAT ONE TIME, HOWEVER, WILL FINISH THIS.
I WILL DEFINITELY STOP YOU FOR 0.1 SECONDS.
DMM
DMM
YOUR SECRETS ARE STARTING TO COME OUT...
HMPH ...
THIS TIME, I CAN KEEP MY HANDS HIDDEN WITHOUT WORRY.
DMM
DMM
DMMM
SST
DOOM
GULP

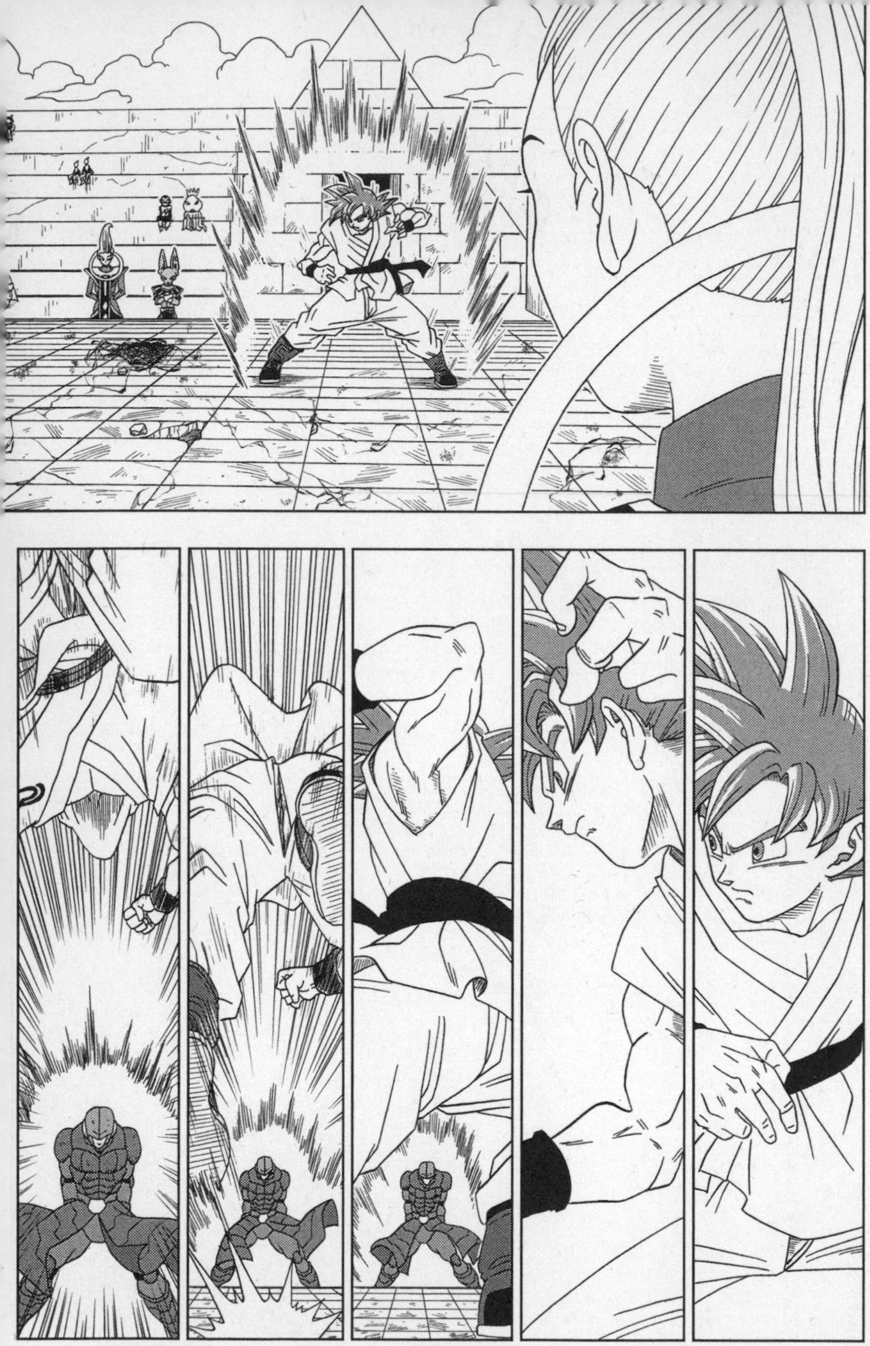

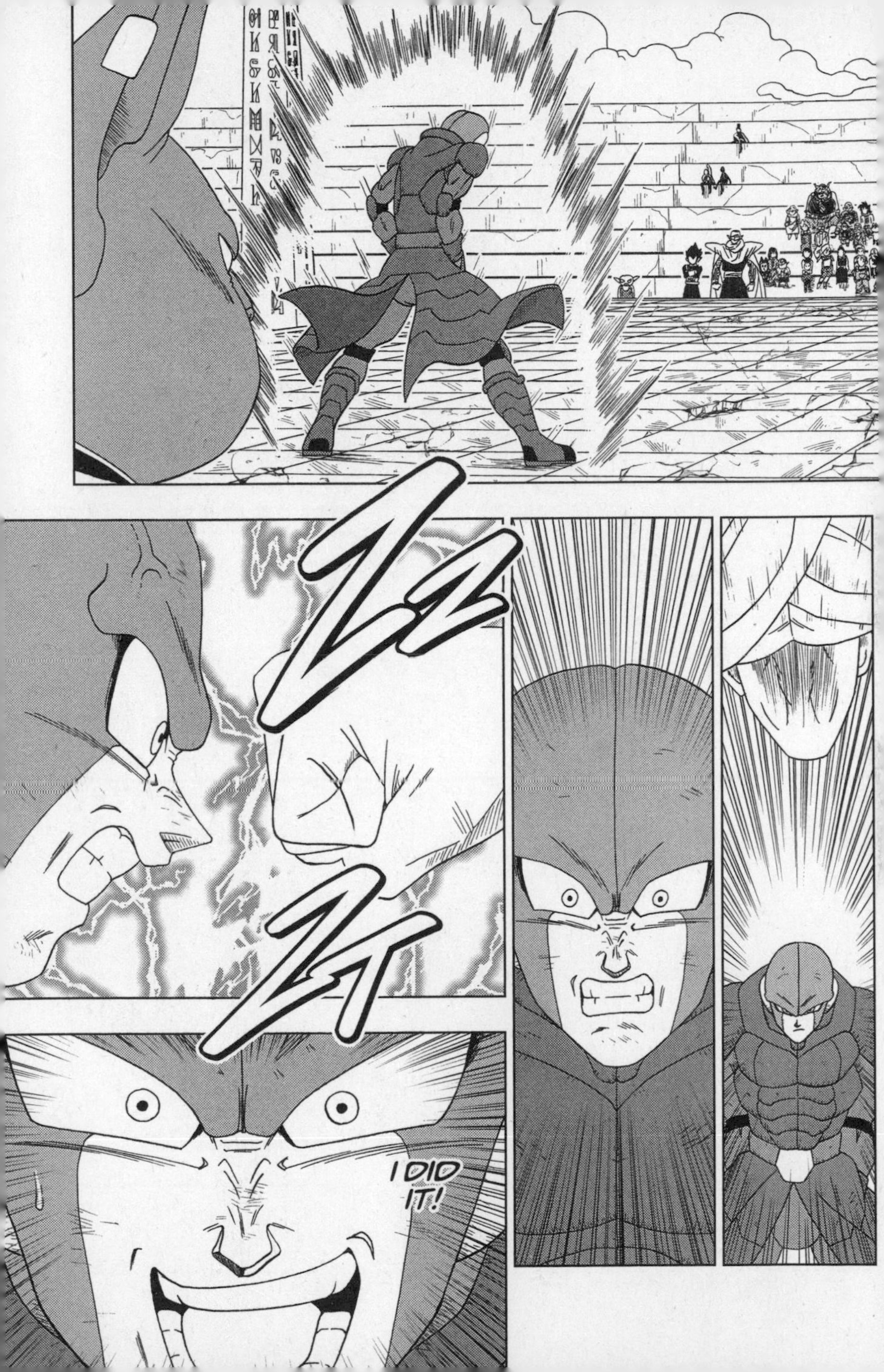
I DID IT!

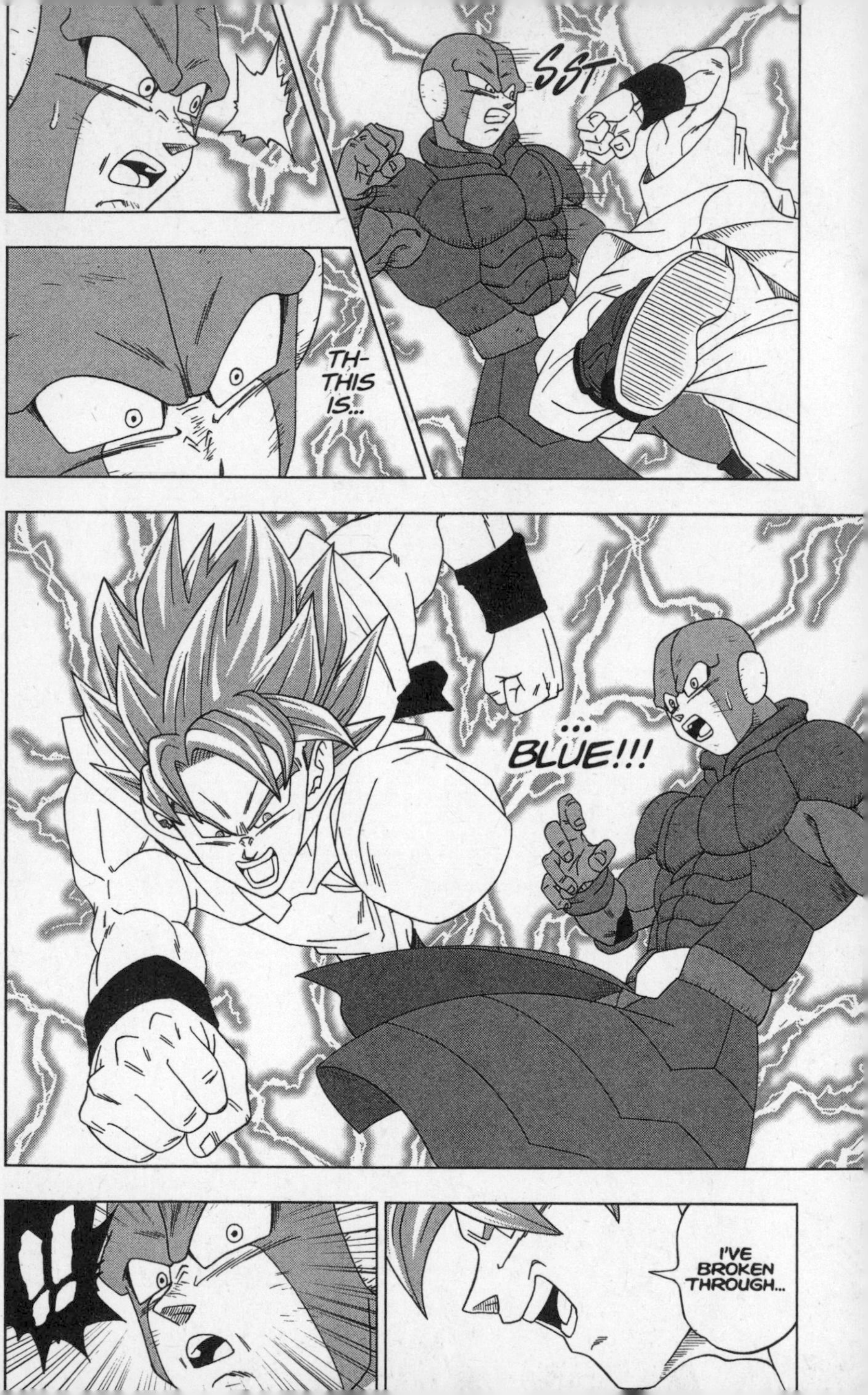
SST
TH- THIS IS...
...BLUE!!!
I'VE BROKEN THROUGH...

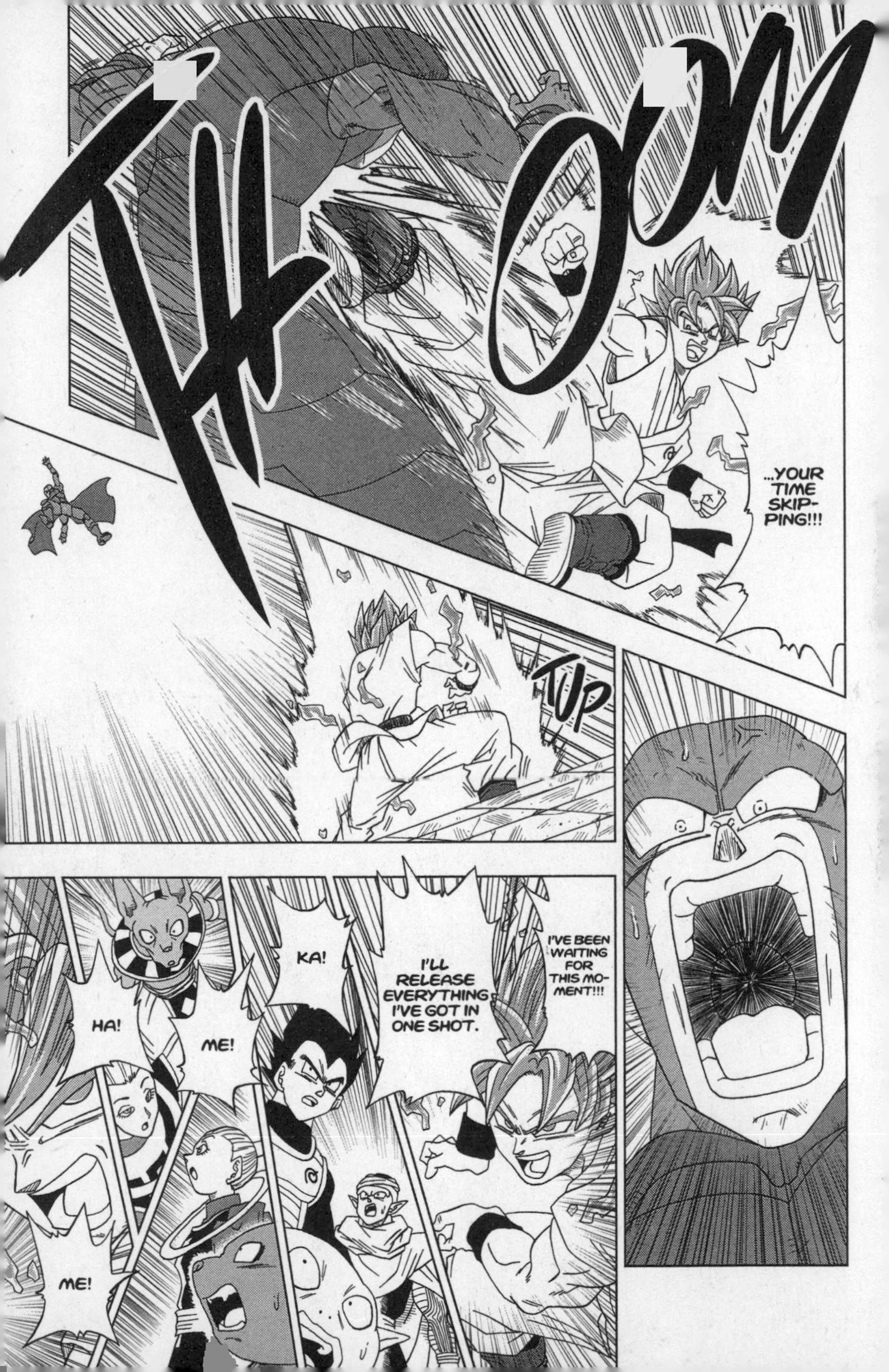

THOOM
...YOUR TIME SKIP-PING!!!
TUP
I'VE BEEN WAITING FOR THIS MO-MENT!!!
I'LL RELEASE EVERYTHING I'VE GOT IN ONE SHOT.
KA!
ME!
HA!
ME!

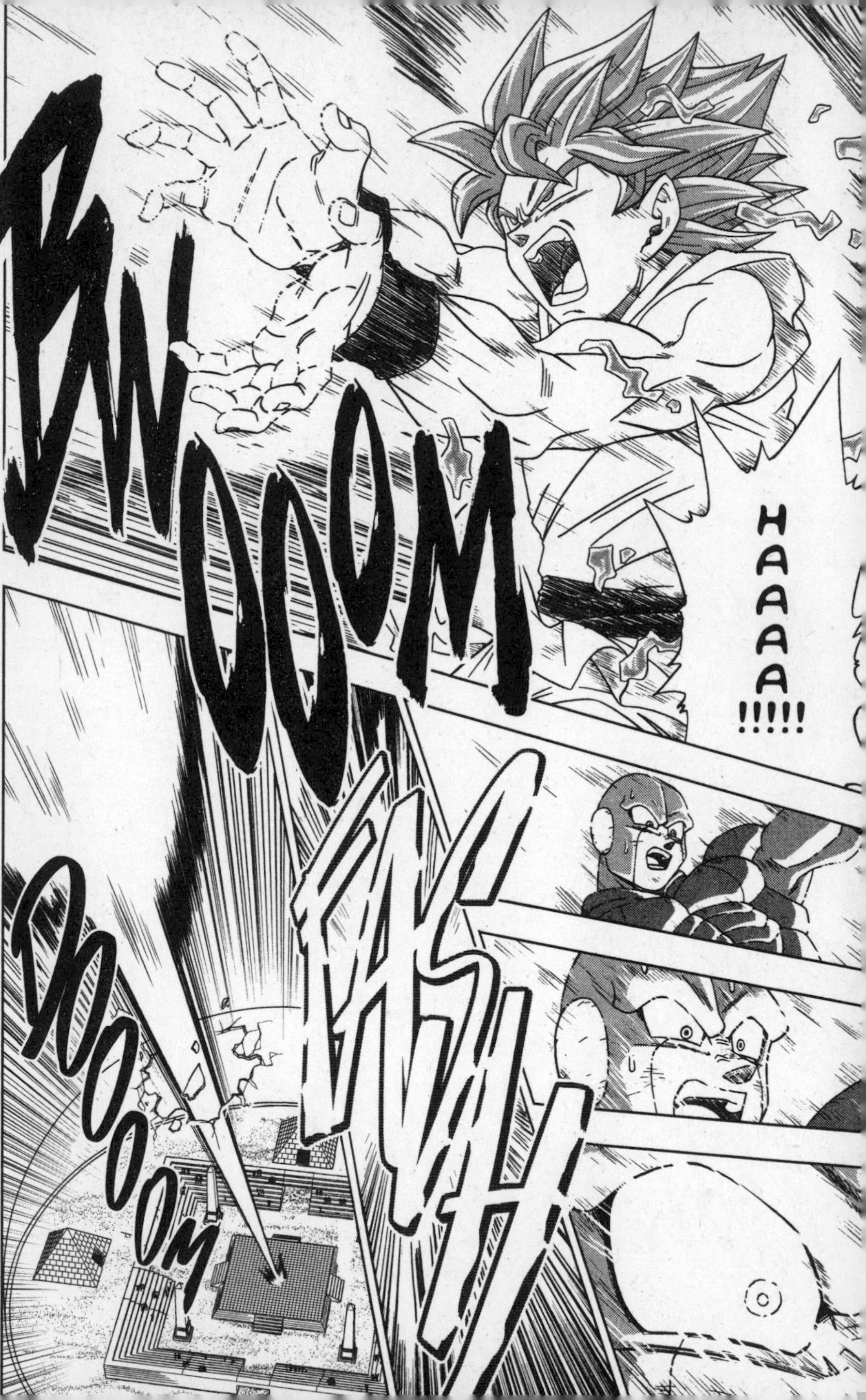
HAAAAA!!!!!
BWOOOM
BOOOOOOM

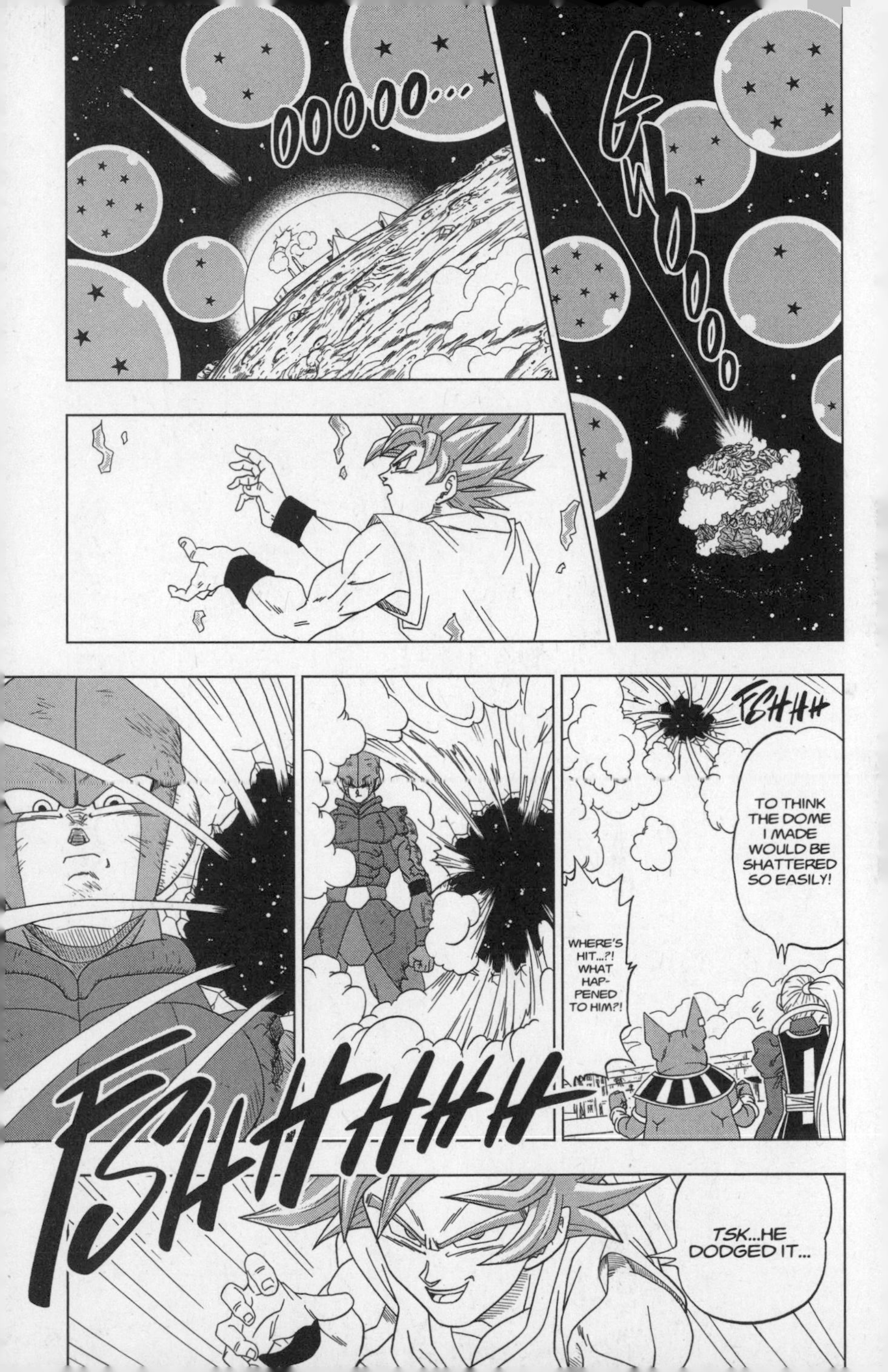
GWOOOOOOO
OOOOO...
FSHHH
TO THINK THE DOME I MADE WOULD BE SHATTERED SO EASILY!
WHERE'S HIT...?! WHAT HAP-PENED TO HIM?!
FSHHHHHH
TSK...HE DODGED IT...

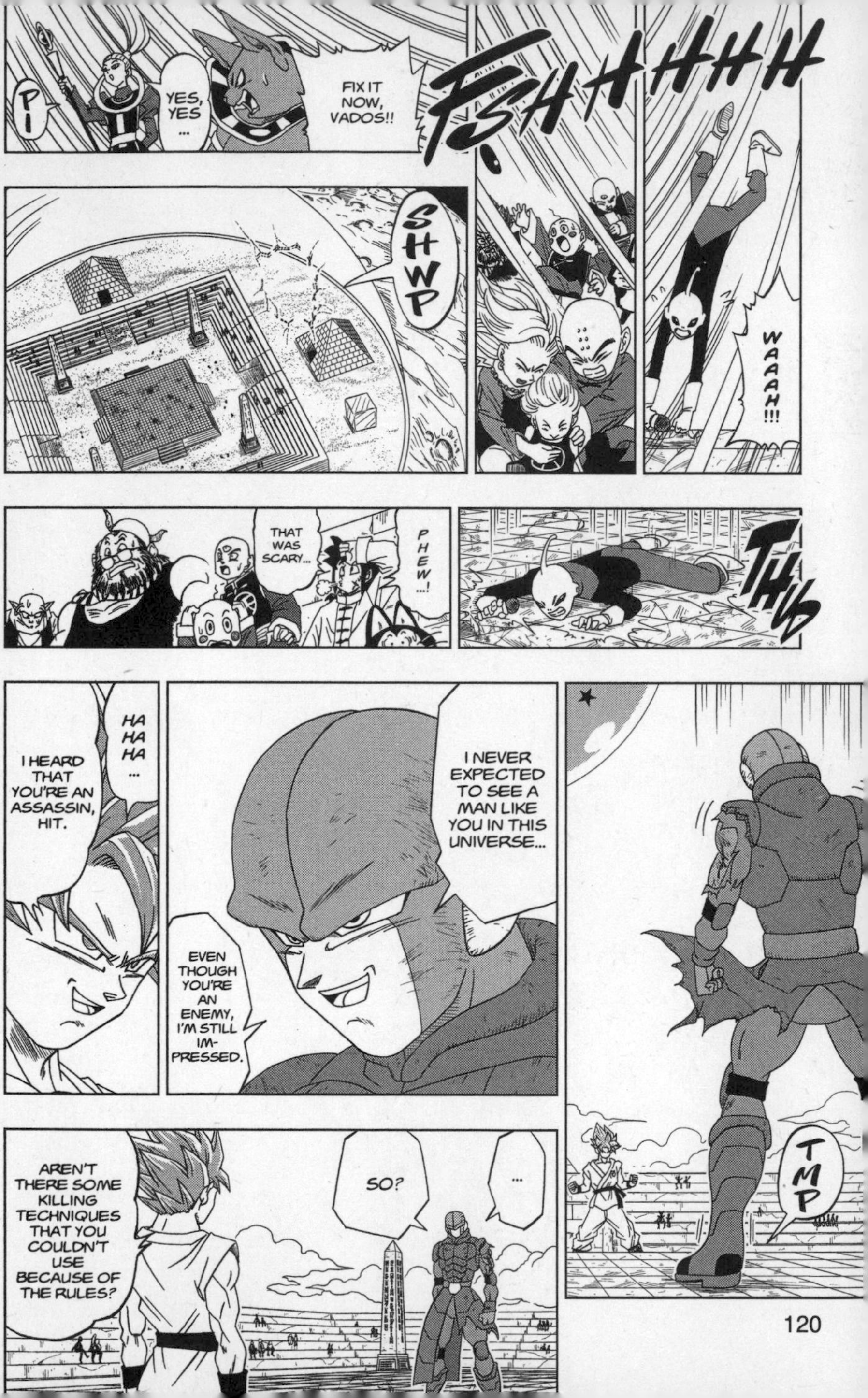
FSHHHHHH
WAAAH!!!
FIX IT NOW, VADOS!!
YES, YES...
PI
SHWP
THUD
PHEW...!
THAT WAS SCARY...
TMP
I NEVER EXPECTED TO SEE A MAN LIKE YOU IN THIS UNIVERSE...
EVEN THOUGH YOU'RE AN ENEMY, I'M STILL IM-PRESSED.
HA HA HA...
I HEARD THAT YOU'RE AN ASSASSIN, HIT.
...
SO?
AREN'T THERE SOME KILLING TECHNIQUES THAT YOU COULDN'T USE BECAUSE OF THE RULES?

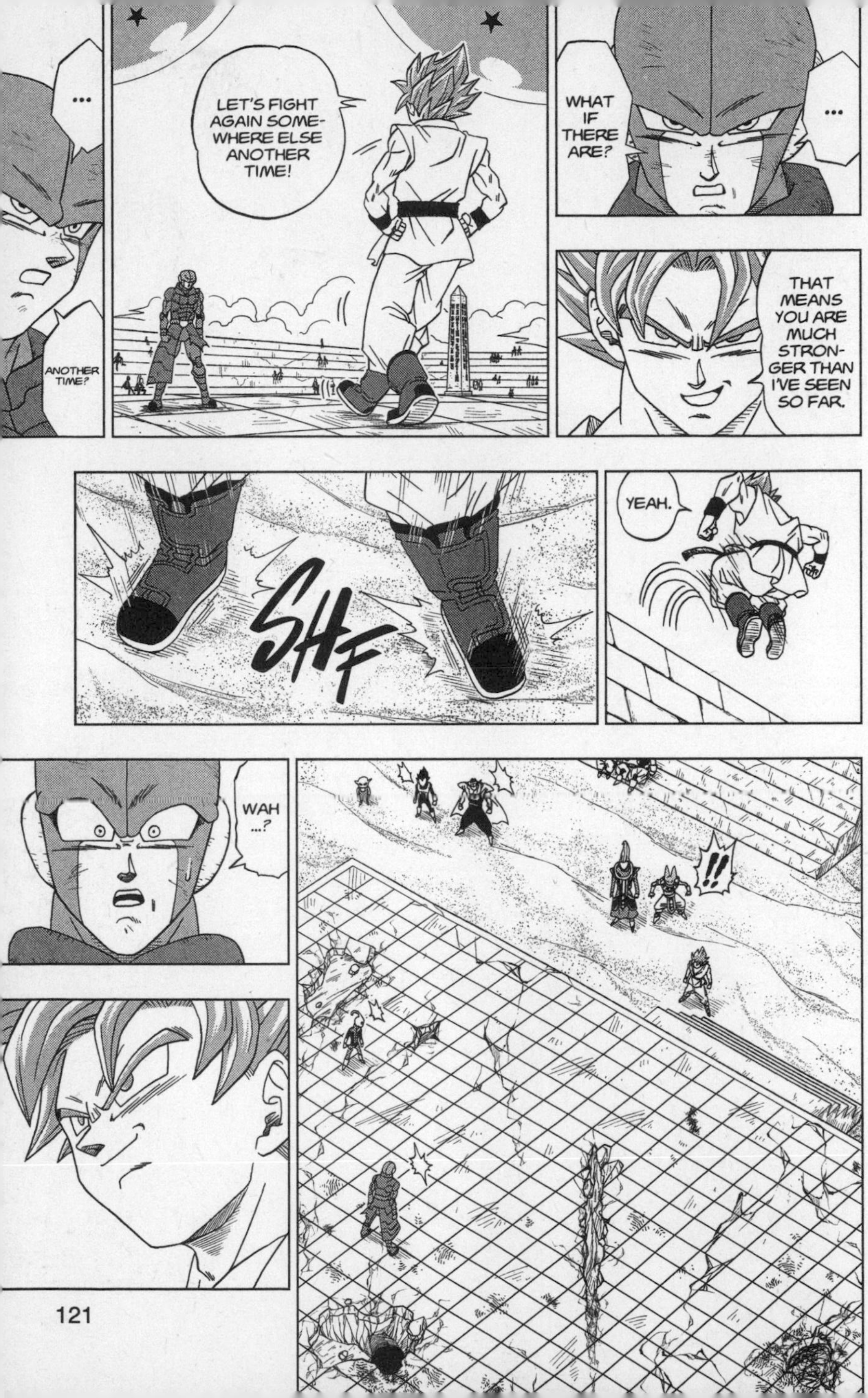
...
WHAT IF THERE ARE?
THAT MEANS YOU ARE MUCH STRONGER THAN I'VE SEEN SO FAR.
LET'S FIGHT AGAIN SOMEWHERE ELSE ANOTHER TIME!
...
ANOTHER TIME?
YEAH.
SHF
!!
WAH ...?

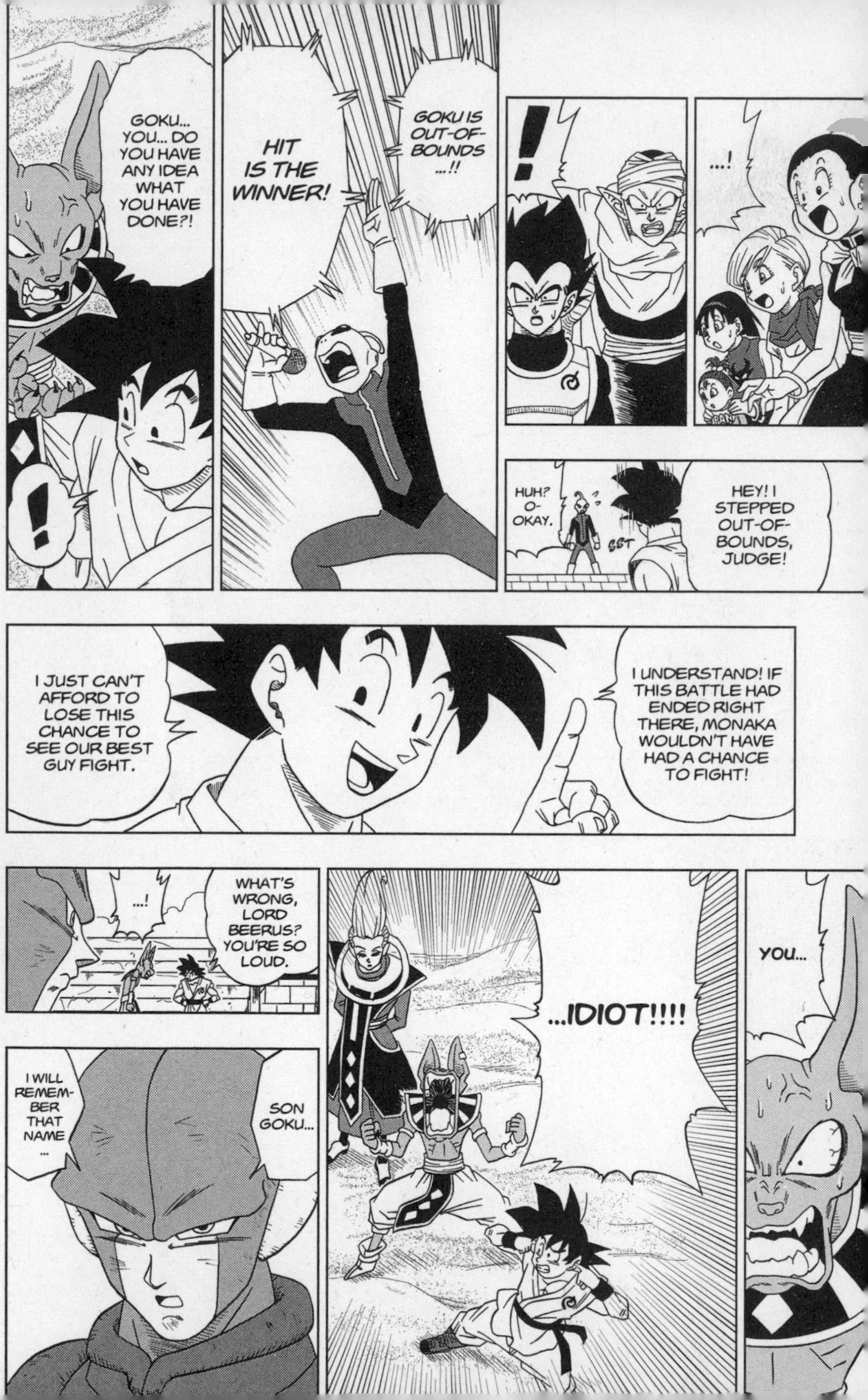
...!
!
HEY! I STEPPED OUT-OF-BOUNDS, JUDGE!
SBT
HUH? O-OKAY.
GOKU IS OUT-OF-BOUNDS ...!!
HIT IS THE WINNER!
GOKU... YOU... DO YOU HAVE ANY IDEA WHAT YOU HAVE DONE?!
!
I UNDERSTAND! IF THIS BATTLE HAD ENDED RIGHT THERE, MONAKA WOULDN'T HAVE HAD A CHANCE TO FIGHT!
I JUST CAN'T AFFORD TO LOSE THIS CHANCE TO SEE OUR BEST GUY FIGHT.
YOU...
...IDIOT!!!!
WHAT'S WRONG, LORD BEERUS? YOU'RE SO LOUD.
...!
SON GOKU...
I WILL REMEMBER THAT NAME ...

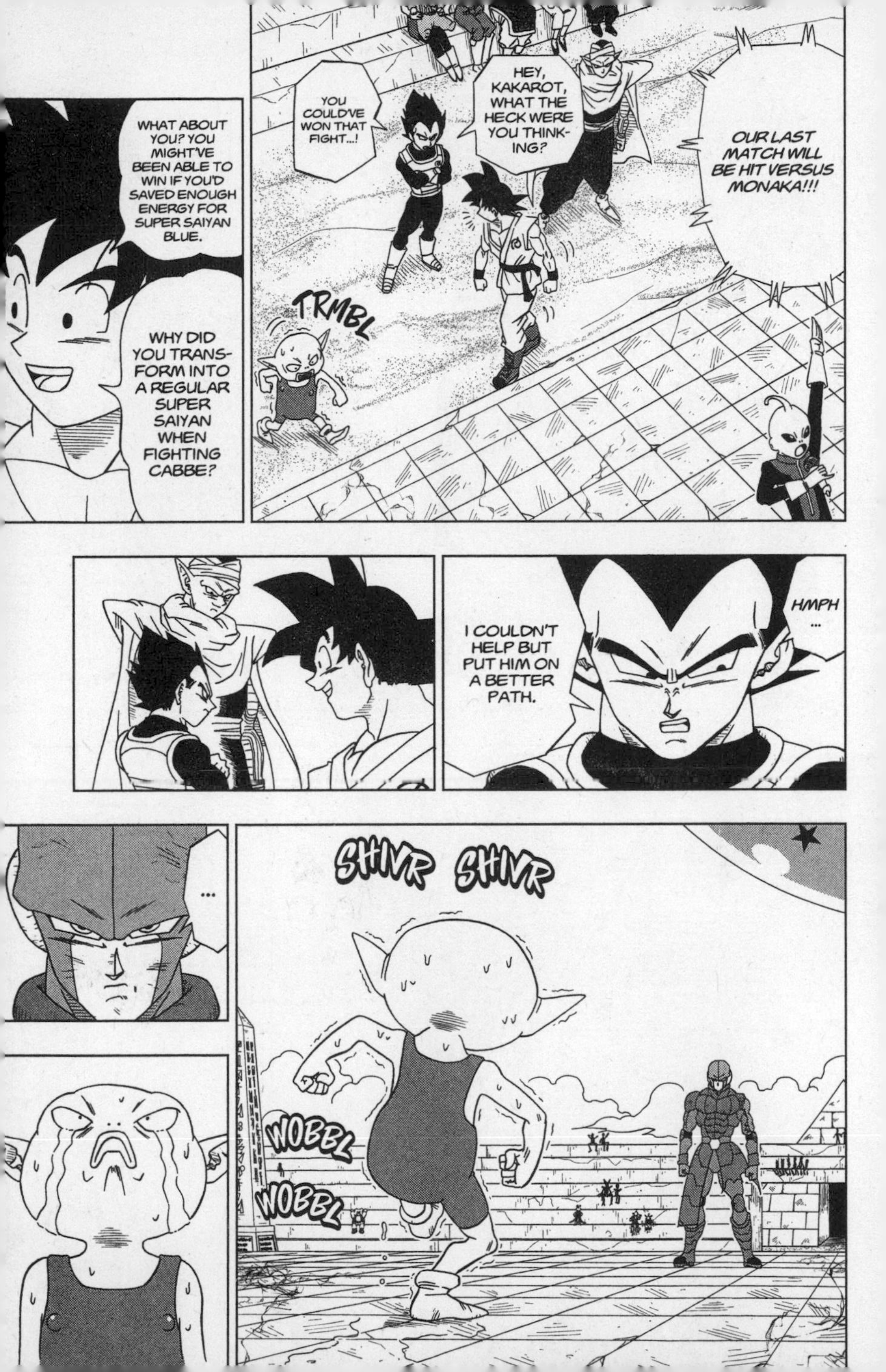
OUR LAST MATCH WILL BE HIT VERSUS MONAKA!!!
HEY, KAKAROT, WHAT THE HECK WERE YOU THINKING?
YOU COULD'VE WON THAT FIGHT...!
TRMBL
WHAT ABOUT YOU? YOU MIGHT'VE BEEN ABLE TO WIN IF YOU'D SAVED ENOUGH ENERGY FOR SUPER SAIYAN BLUE.
WHY DID YOU TRANSFORM INTO A REGULAR SUPER SAIYAN WHEN FIGHTING CABBE?
HMPH ...
I COULDN'T HELP BUT PUT HIM ON A BETTER PATH.
SHIVR SHIVR
WOBBL
WOBBL
...

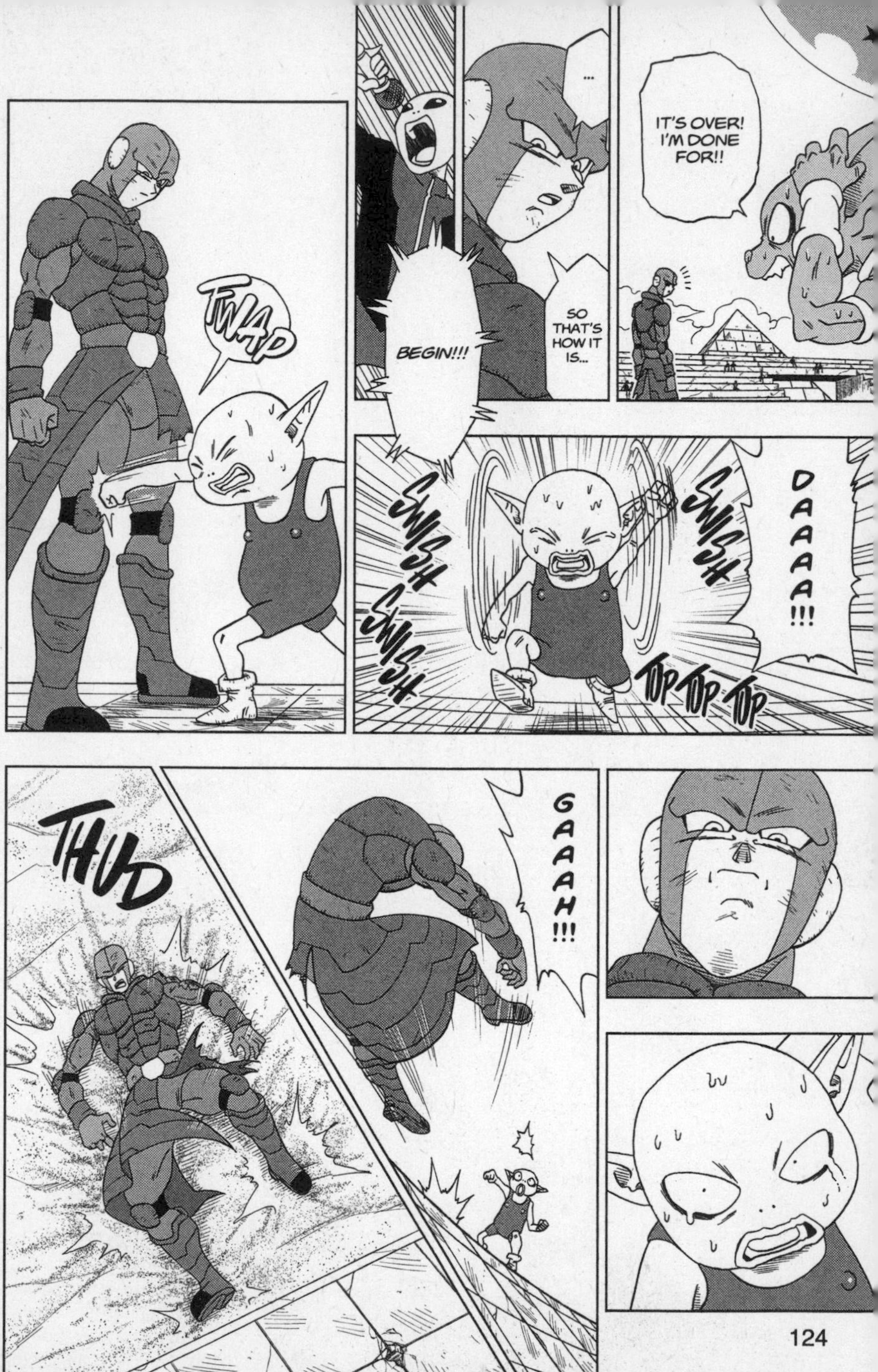

IT'S OVER! I'M DONE FOR!!
...
SO THAT'S HOW IT IS...
BEGIN!!!
DAAAAA!!!
SWISH
SWISH SWISH
TOP TOP TOP
FWAP
GAAAAH!!!
THUD

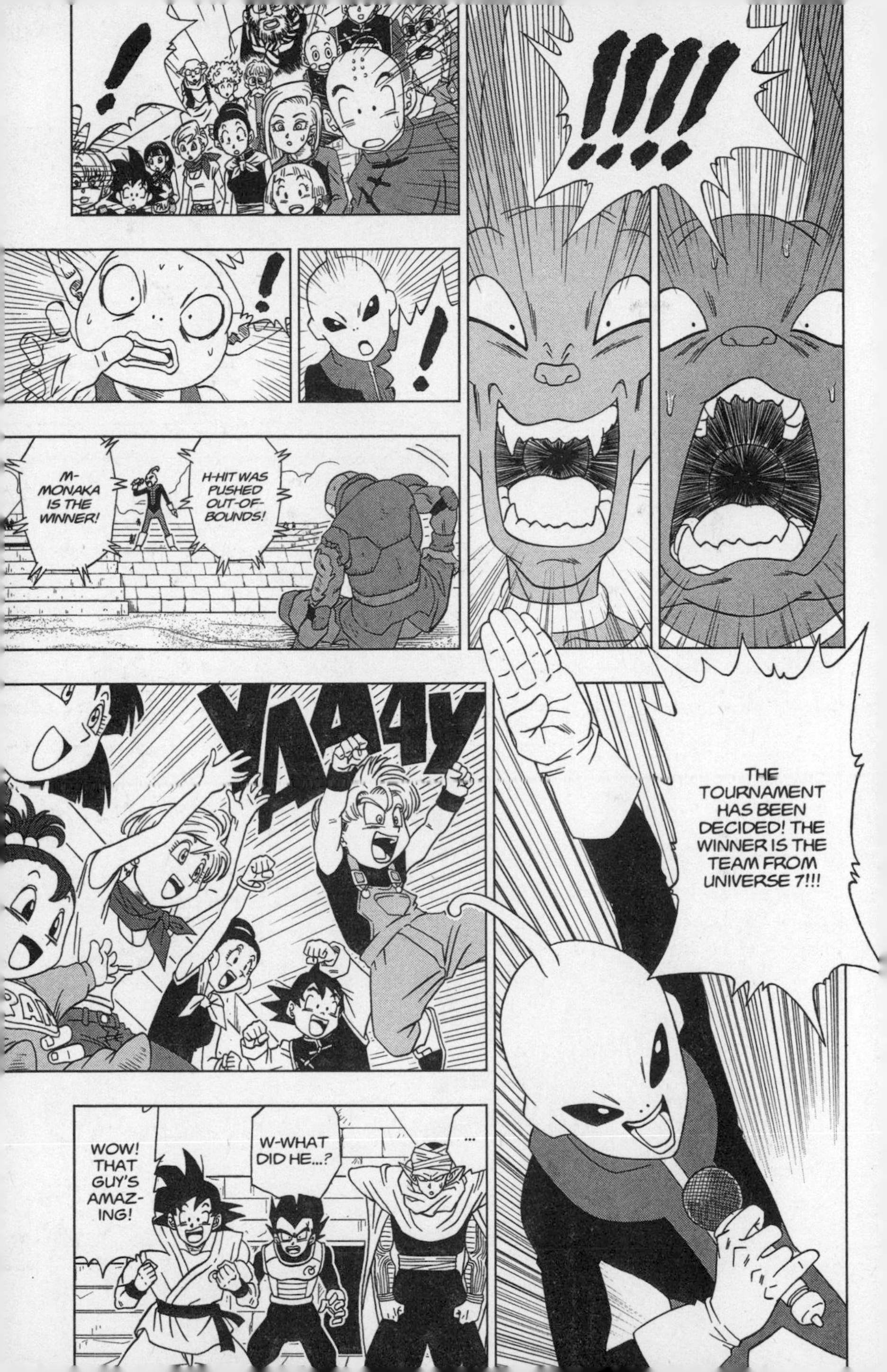
!!!!
!
!
!
H-HIT WAS PUSHED OUT-OF-BOUNDS!
M-MONAKA IS THE WINNER!
THE TOURNAMENT HAS BEEN DECIDED! THE WINNER IS THE TEAM FROM UNIVERSE 7!!!
YAAY
...
W-WHAT DID HE...?
WOW! THAT GUY'S AMAZ-ING!

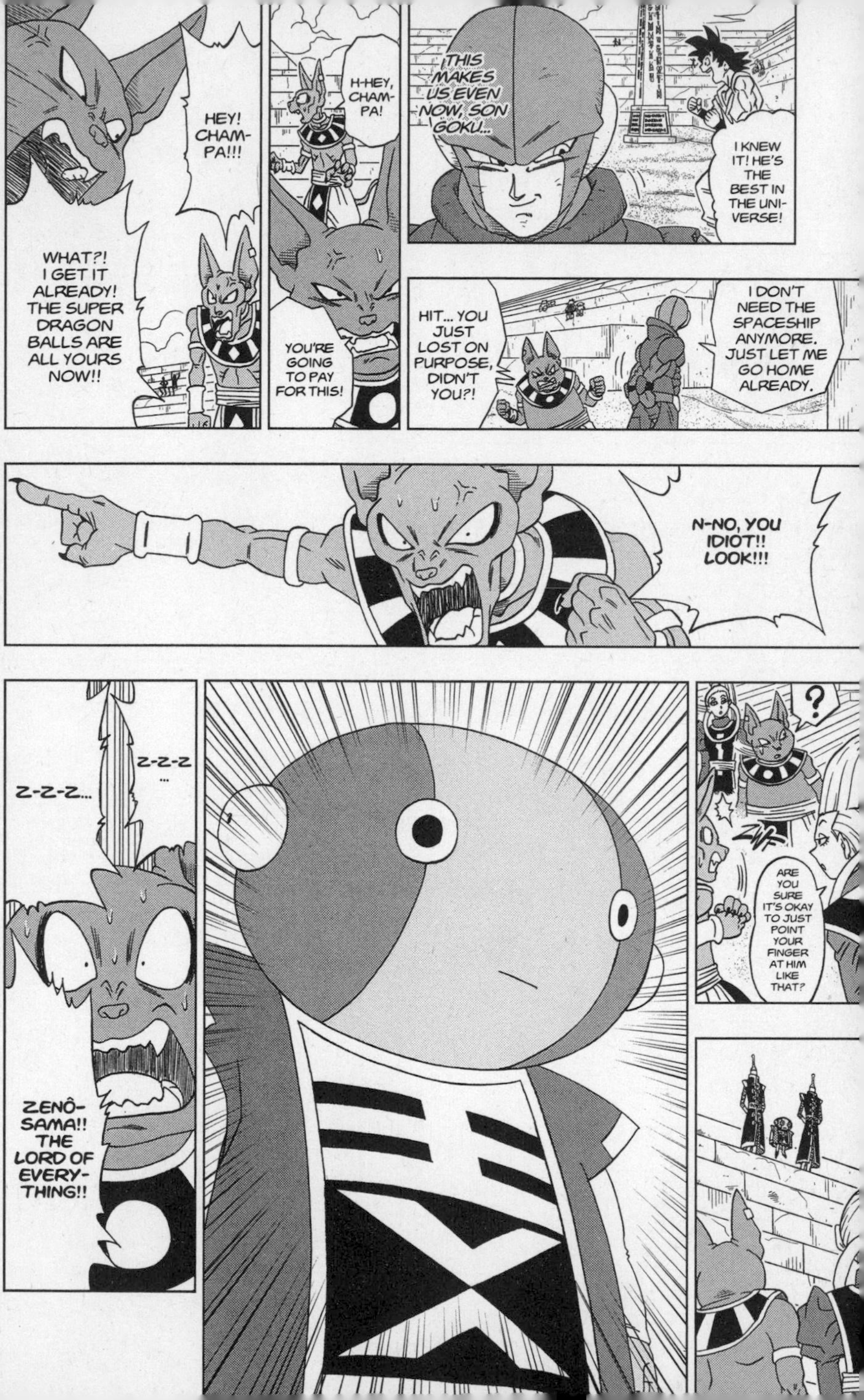
THIS MAKES US EVEN NOW, SON GOKU...
I KNEW IT! HE'S THE BEST IN THE UNIVERSE!
I DON'T NEED THE SPACESHIP ANYMORE. JUST LET ME GO HOME ALREADY.
HIT... YOU JUST LOST ON PURPOSE, DIDN'T YOU?!
H-HEY, CHAMPA!
YOU'RE GOING TO PAY FOR THIS!
HEY! CHAMPA!!!
WHAT?! I GET IT ALREADY! THE SUPER DRAGON BALLS ARE ALL YOURS NOW!!
N-NO, YOU IDIOT!! LOOK!!!
?
ARE YOU SURE IT'S OKAY TO JUST POINT YOUR FINGER AT HIM LIKE THAT?
Z-Z-Z...
Z-Z-Z...
ZENÔ-SAMA!! THE LORD OF EVERYTHING!!

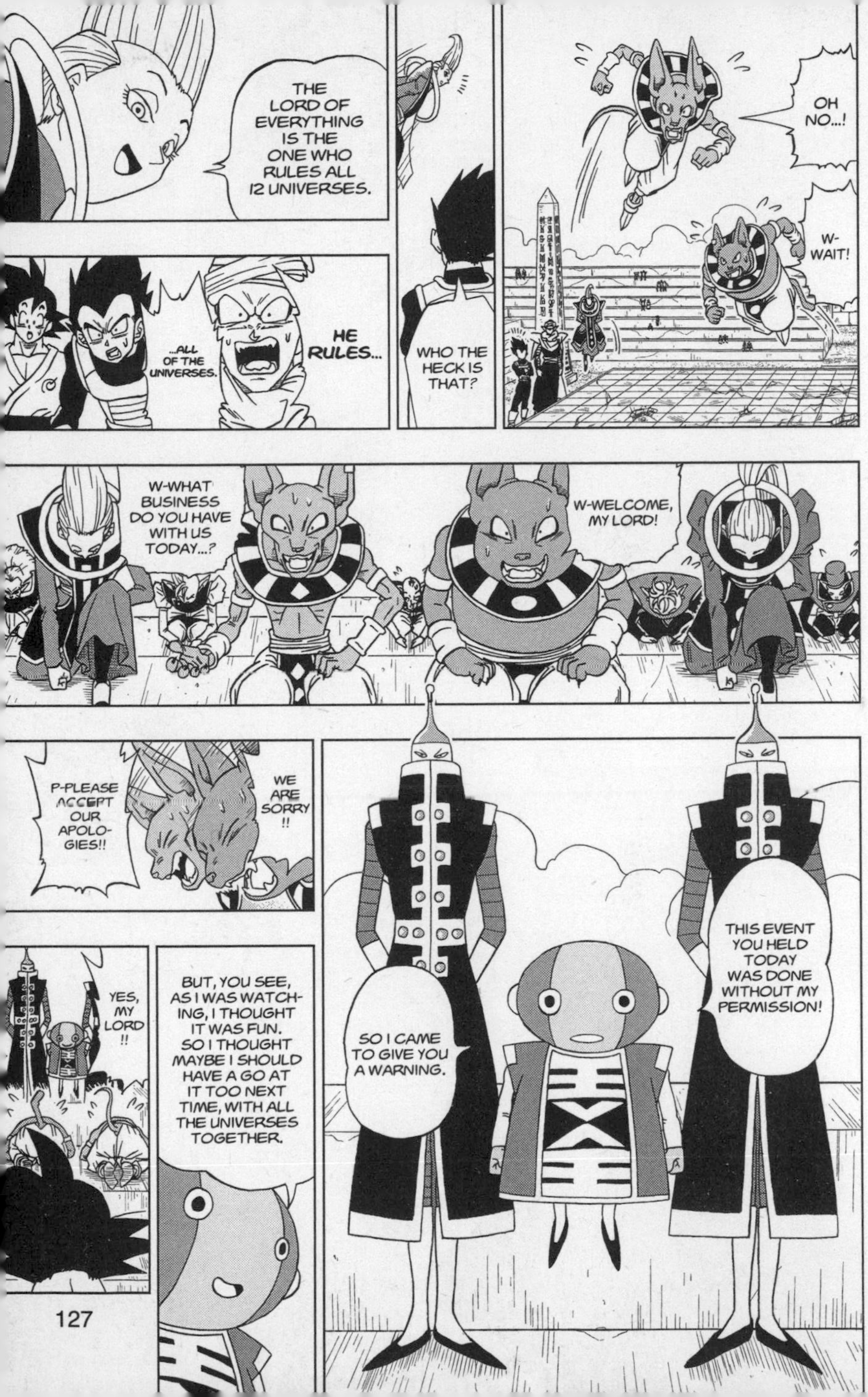
OH NO...!
W-WAIT!
WHO THE HECK IS THAT?
THE LORD OF EVERYTHING IS THE ONE WHO RULES ALL 12 UNIVERSES.
HE RULES...
...ALL OF THE UNIVERSES.
W-WELCOME, MY LORD!
W-WHAT BUSINESS DO YOU HAVE WITH US TODAY...?
THIS EVENT YOU HELD TODAY WAS DONE WITHOUT MY PERMISSION!
SO I CAME TO GIVE YOU A WARNING.
WE ARE SORRY!!
P-PLEASE ACCEPT OUR APOLOGIES!!
BUT, YOU SEE, AS I WAS WATCHING, I THOUGHT IT WAS FUN. SO I THOUGHT MAYBE I SHOULD HAVE A GO AT IT TOO NEXT TIME, WITH ALL THE UNIVERSES TOGETHER.
YES, MY LORD!!

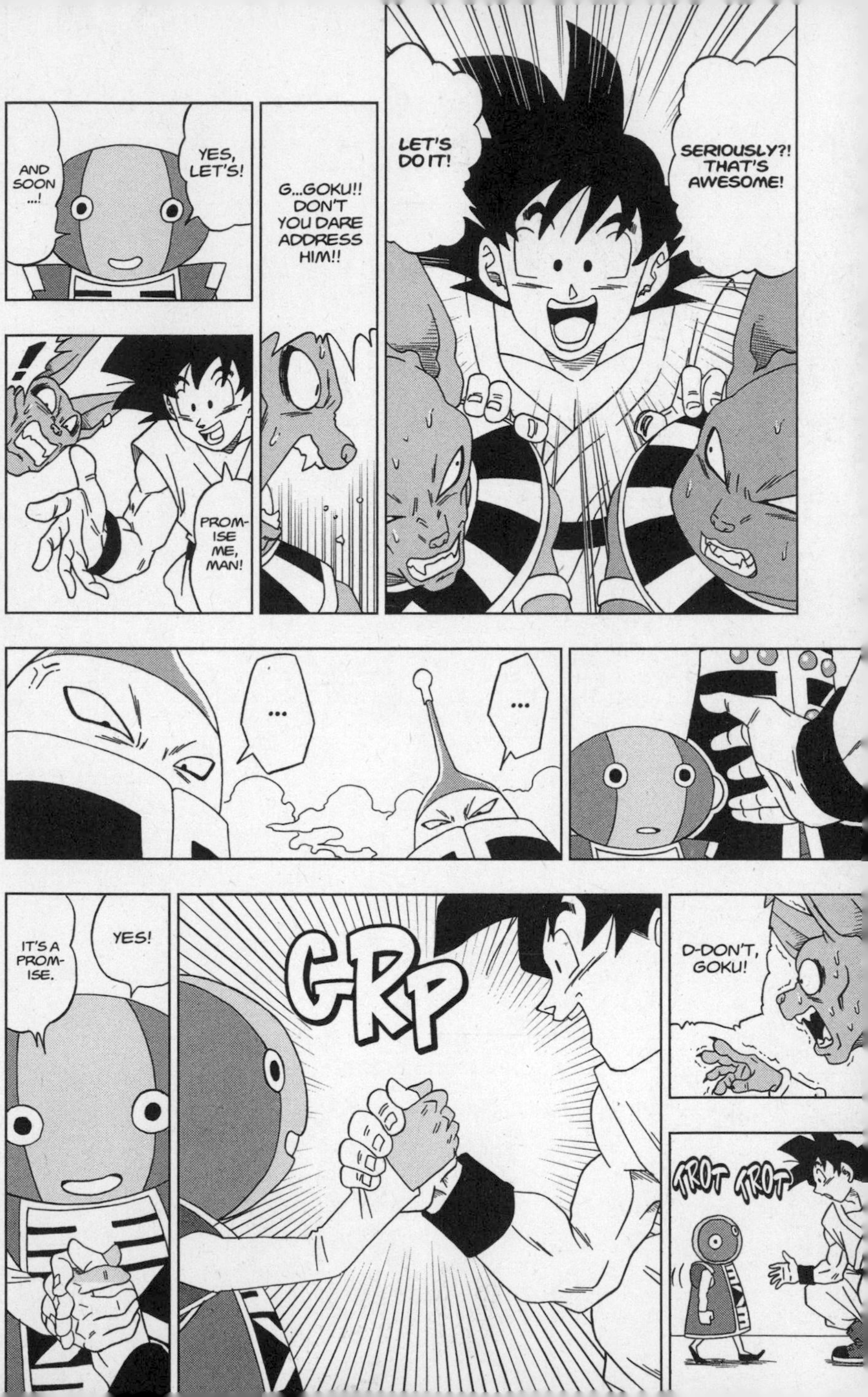
SERIOUSLY?! THAT'S AWESOME!
LET'S DO IT!
G...GOKU!! DON'T YOU DARE ADDRESS HIM!!
YES, LET'S!
AND SOON ...!
PROMISE ME, MAN!
...
...
D-DON'T, GOKU!
TROT TROT
GRP
YES!
IT'S A PROMISE.

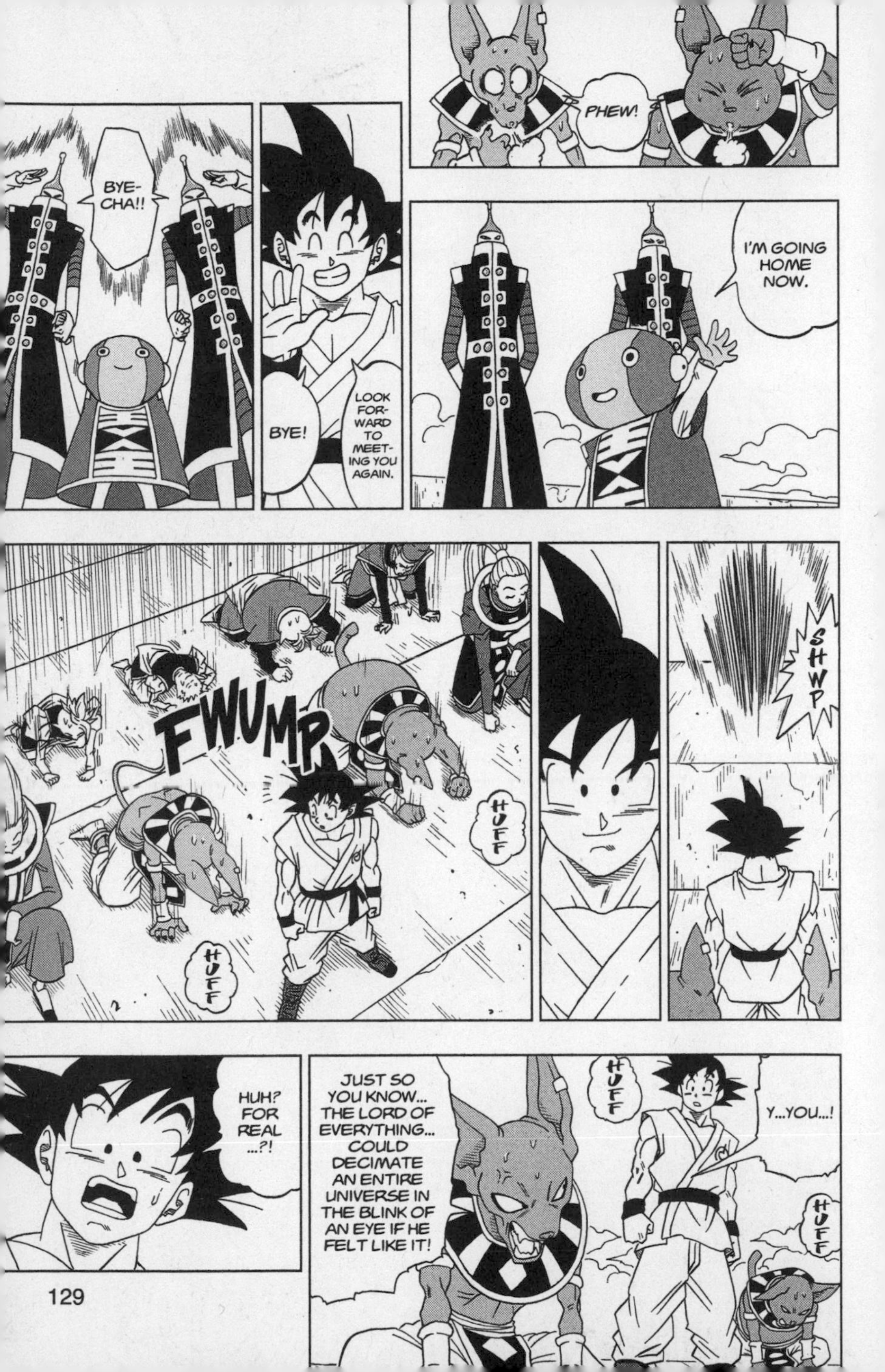
PHEW!
I'M GOING HOME NOW.
LOOK FORWARD TO MEETING YOU AGAIN.
BYE!
BYE-CHA!!
SHWP
FWUMP
HUFF
HUFF
Y...YOU...!
HUFF
HUFF
JUST SO YOU KNOW... THE LORD OF EVERYTHING... COULD DECIMATE AN ENTIRE UNIVERSE IN THE BLINK OF AN EYE IF HE FELT LIKE IT!
HUH? FOR REAL ...?!

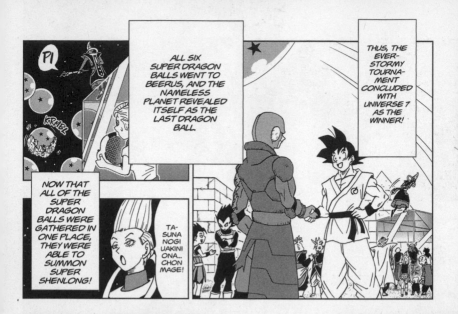

THUS, THE EVER-STORMY TOURNAMENT CONCLUDED WITH UNIVERSE 7 AS THE WINNER!
ALL SIX SUPER DRAGON BALLS WENT TO BEERUS, AND THE NAMELESS PLANET REVEALED ITSELF AS THE LAST DRAGON BALL.
PI
KRMBL
NOW THAT ALL OF THE SUPER DRAGON BALLS WERE GATHERED IN ONE PLACE, THEY WERE ABLE TO SUMMON SUPER SHENLONG!
TA-SUNA NOGI UAKINI ONA... CHON MAGE!
THE SIZE OF SUPER SHENLONG WAS INCOMPARABLY LARGER THAN THE SHENLONG OF EARTH.
ONCE IT GRANTED BEERUS'S WISH, ALL OF THE SUPER DRAGON BALLS SCATTERED ACROSS UNIVERSES 6 AND 7 AND DISAPPEARED.
SO BIG!!
JI UWAKE ERU YOEHA...
SO WHAT DID YOU WISH FOR?
IT'S A SECRET...
CHAMPA'S CUBE SHIP...

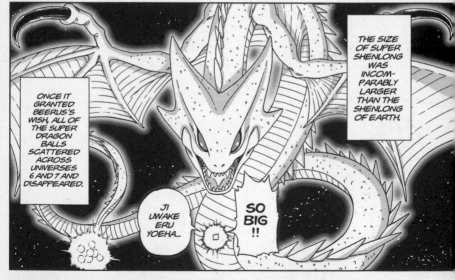

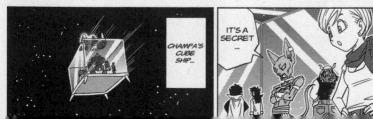

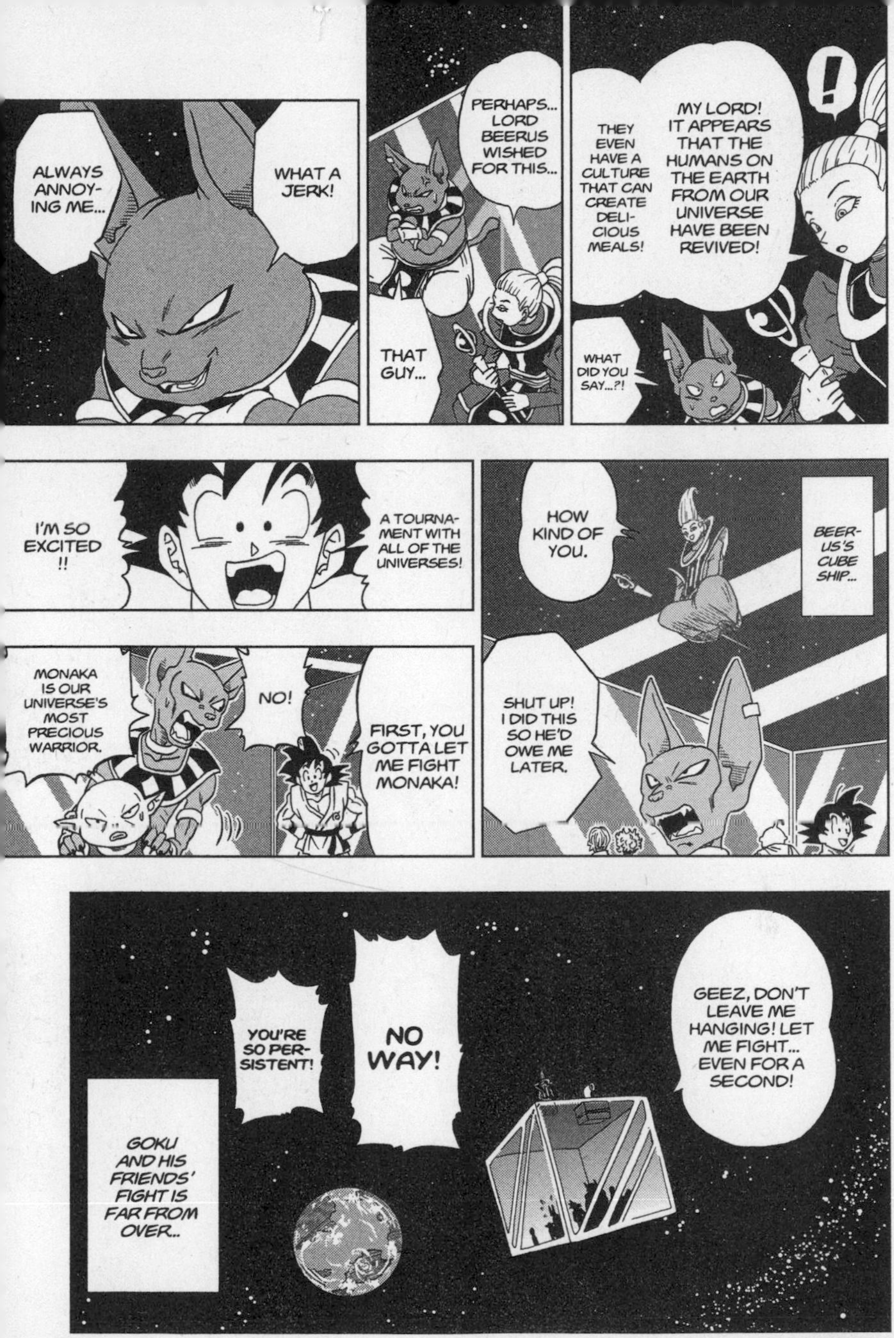
!
MY LORD! IT APPEARS THAT THE HUMANS ON THE EARTH FROM OUR UNIVERSE HAVE BEEN REVIVED!
THEY EVEN HAVE A CULTURE THAT CAN CREATE DELI-CIOUS MEALS!
WHAT DID YOU SAY...?!
PERHAPS... LORD BEERUS WISHED FOR THIS...
THAT GUY...
WHAT A JERK!
ALWAYS ANNOY-ING ME...
BEER-US'S CUBE SHIP...
HOW KIND OF YOU.
SHUT UP! I DID THIS SO HE'D OWE ME LATER.
A TOURNA-MENT WITH ALL OF THE UNIVERSES!
I'M SO EXCITED !!
FIRST, YOU GOTTA LET ME FIGHT MONAKA!
NO!
MONAKA IS OUR UNIVERSE'S MOST PRECIOUS WARRIOR.
GEEZ, DON'T LEAVE ME HANGING! LET ME FIGHT... EVEN FOR A SECOND!
NO WAY!
YOU'RE SO PER-SISTENT!
GOKU AND HIS FRIENDS' FIGHT IS FAR FROM OVER...

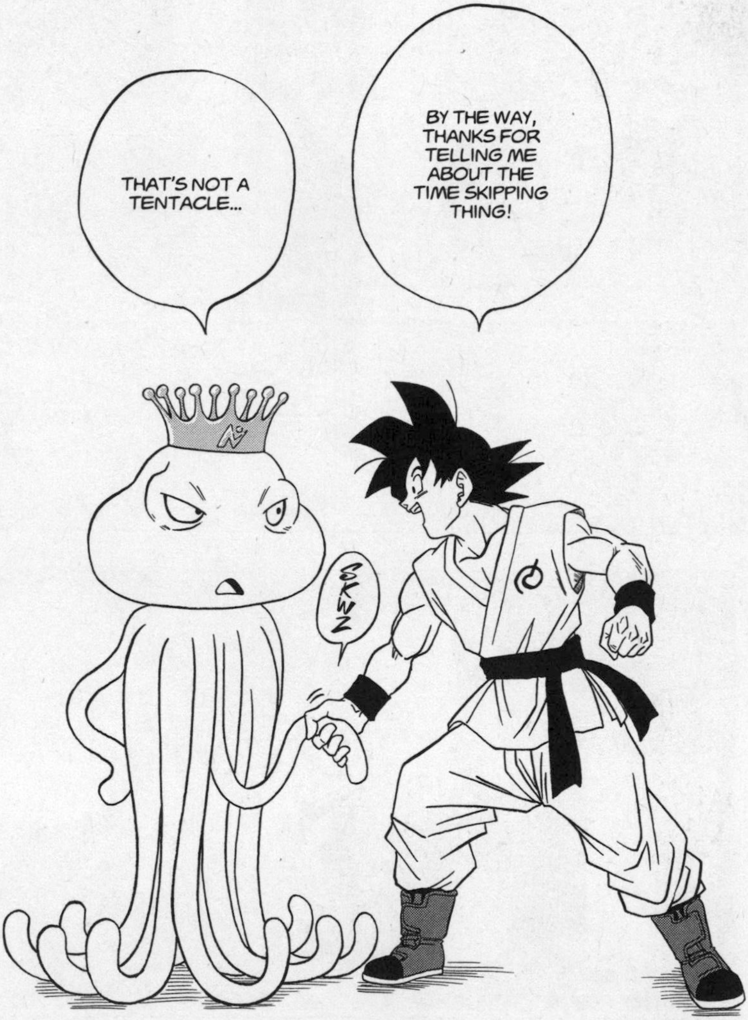
BY THE WAY, THANKS FOR TELLING ME ABOUT THE TIME SKIPPING THING!
THAT'S NOT A TENTACLE...
SKWZ

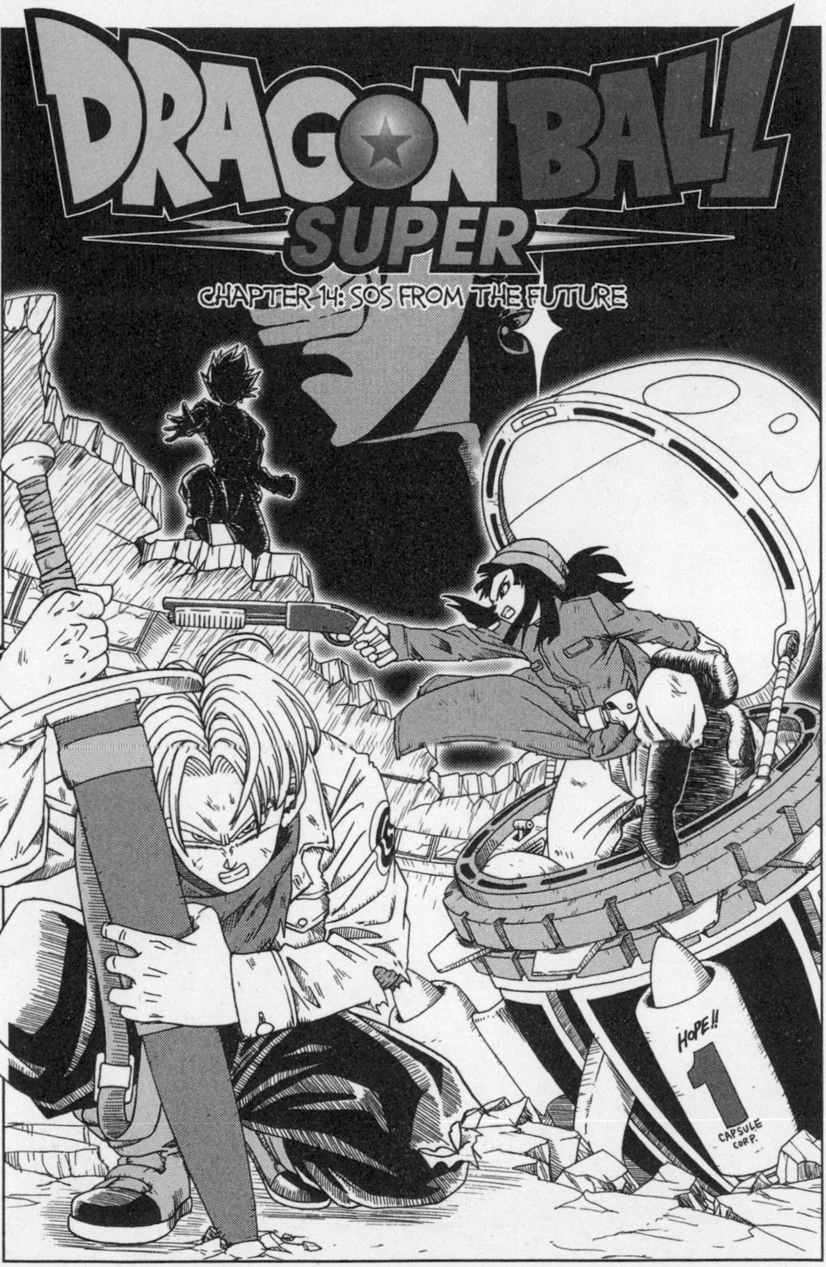

DRAGON BALL SUPER
CHAPTER 14: SOS FROM THE FUTURE
HOPE!!
1
CAPSULE CORP.

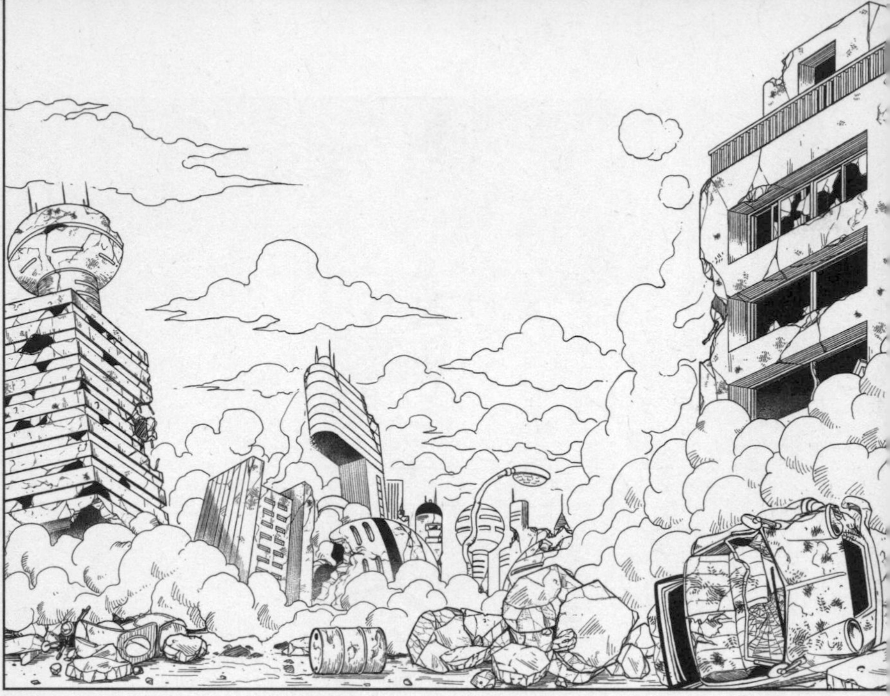

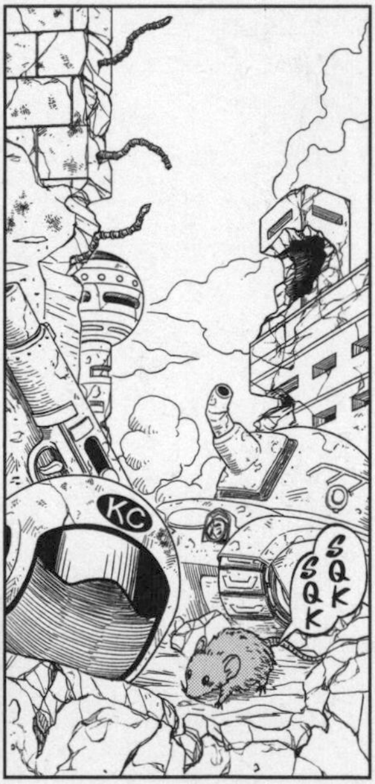
KC
SQK SQK

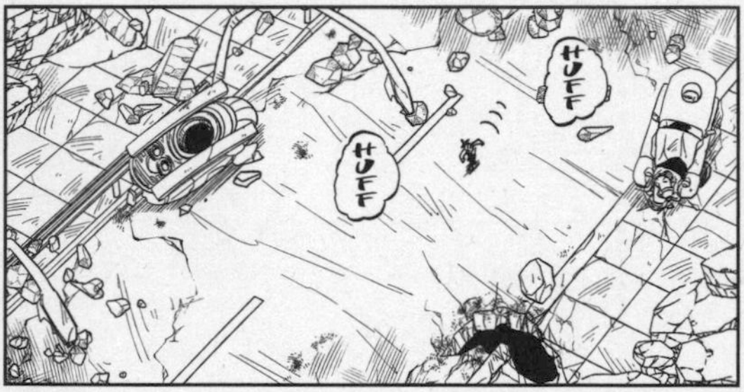
HUFF
HUFF

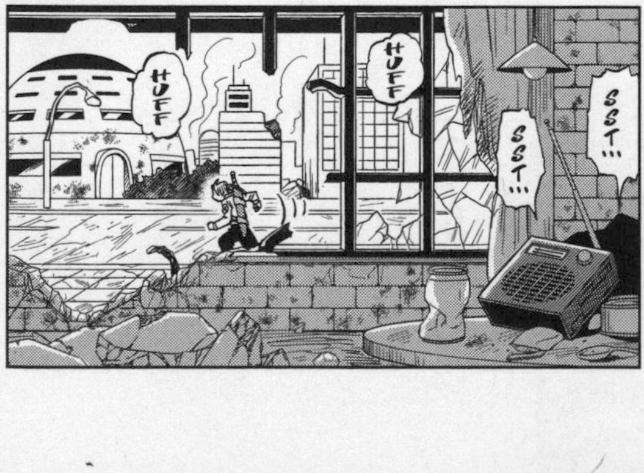
HUFF
HUFF
SST...
SST...

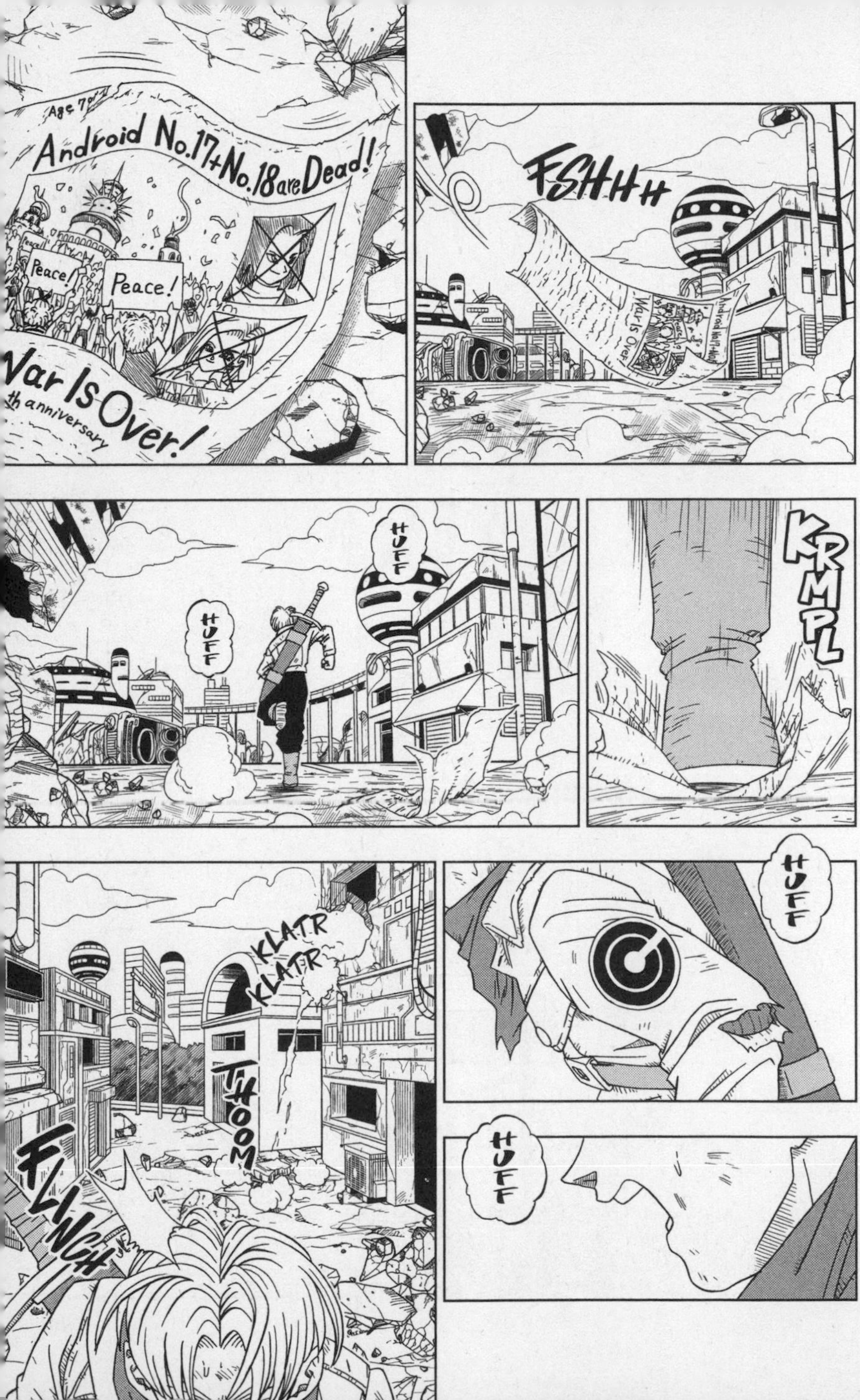
FSHHH
Android No.17+No.18 are Dead!
Peace!
Peace!
Peace!
War Is Over!
th anniversary
KRMPL
HUFF
HUFF
HUFF
HUFF
KLATR
KLATR
THOOM
FLINCH

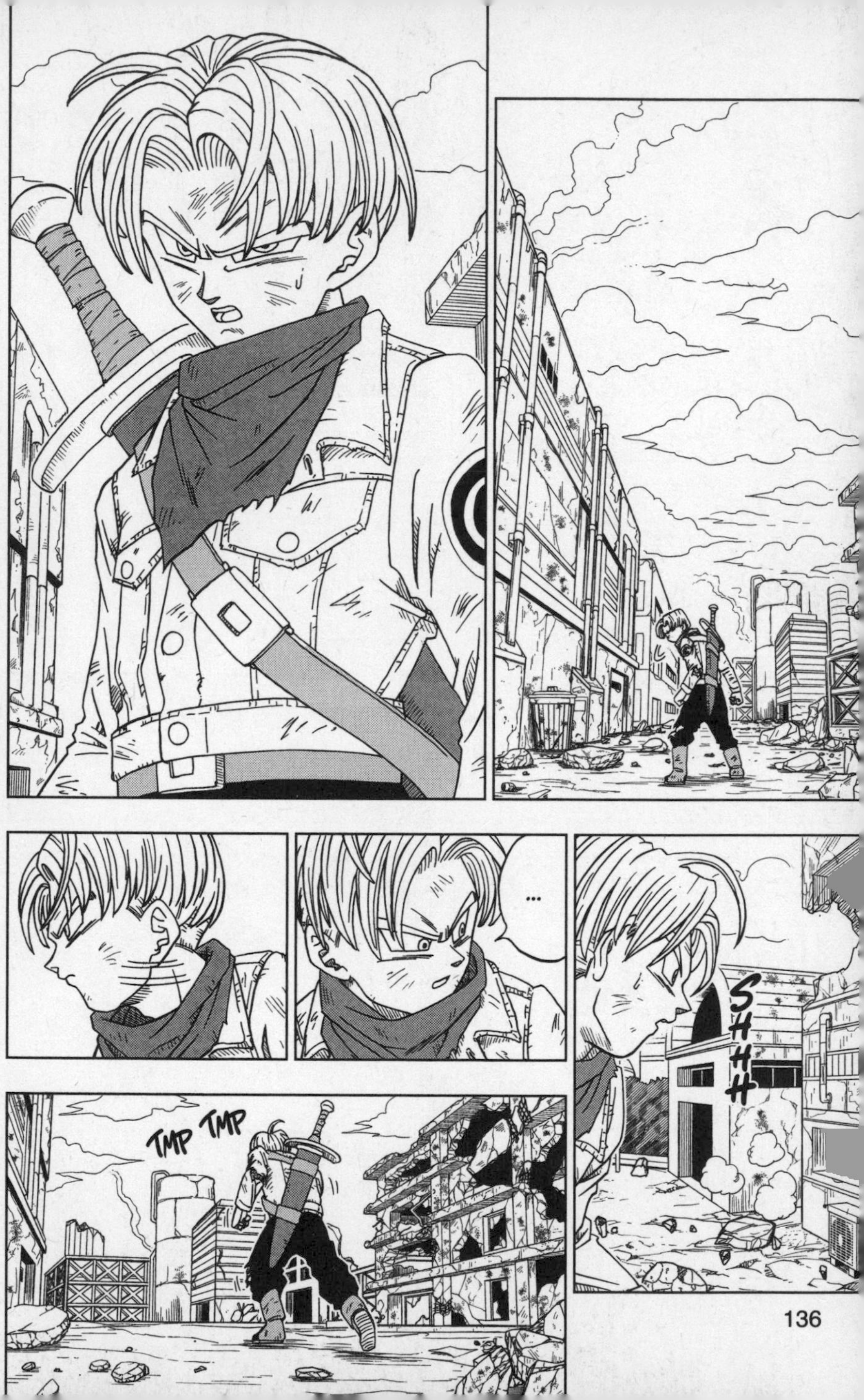
SHHH
...
TMP TMP

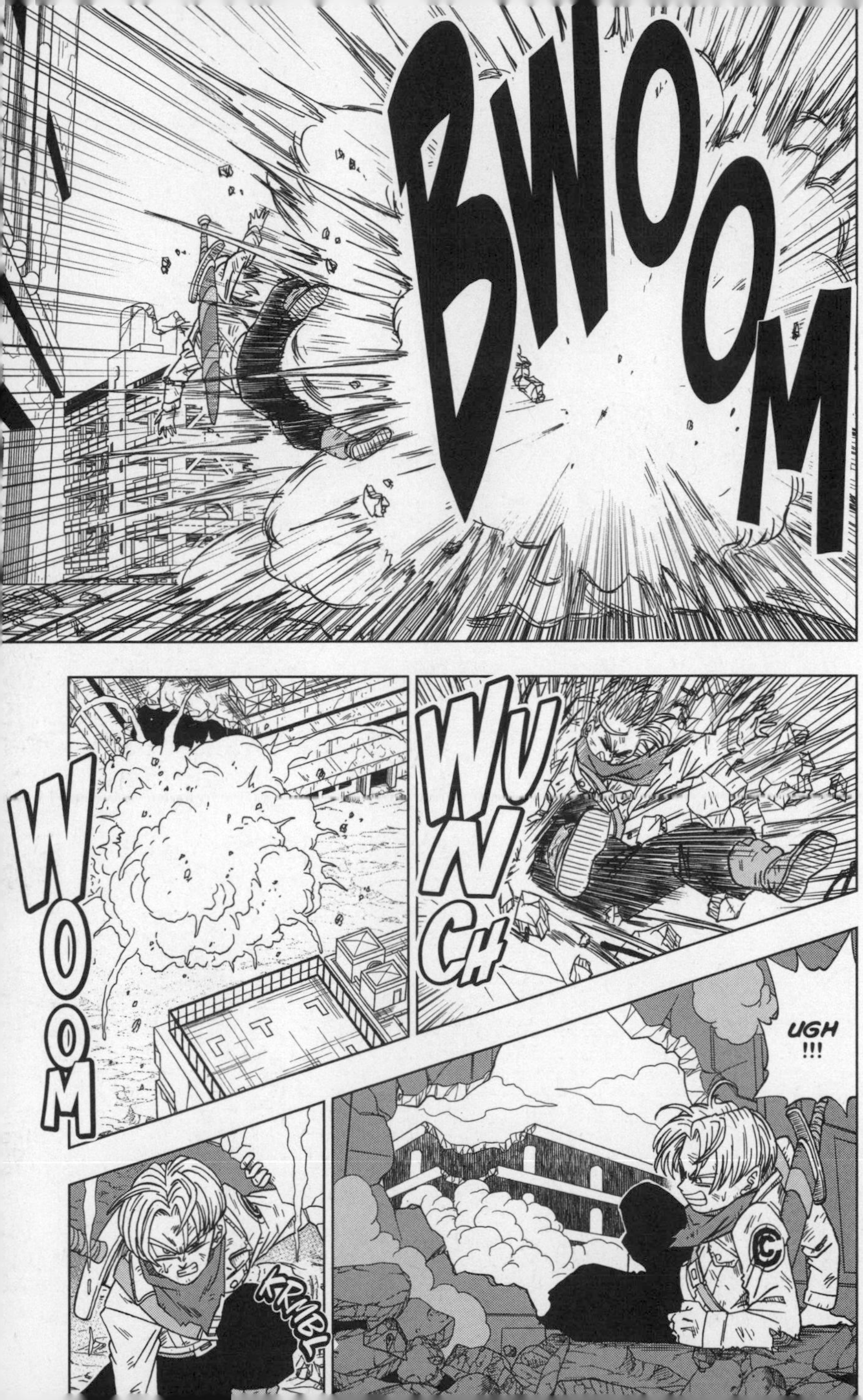
BWOOM
WUNCH
WOOOM
UGH!!!
KRMBL

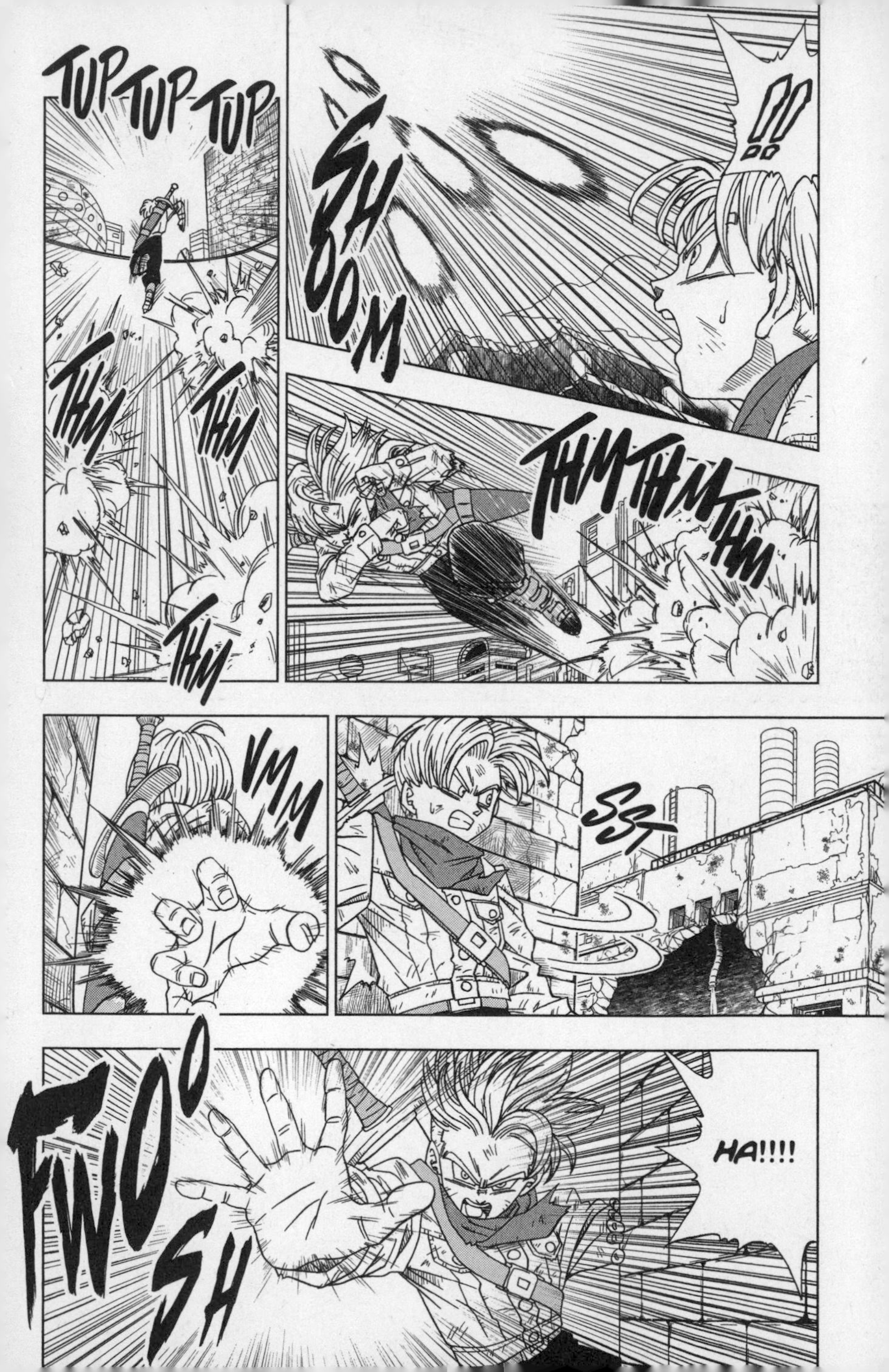

!!
SHOOOM
THM THM THM THM
TUP-TUP-TUP
THM
THM
THM
SST
VMM
HA!!!!
FWOOOSH

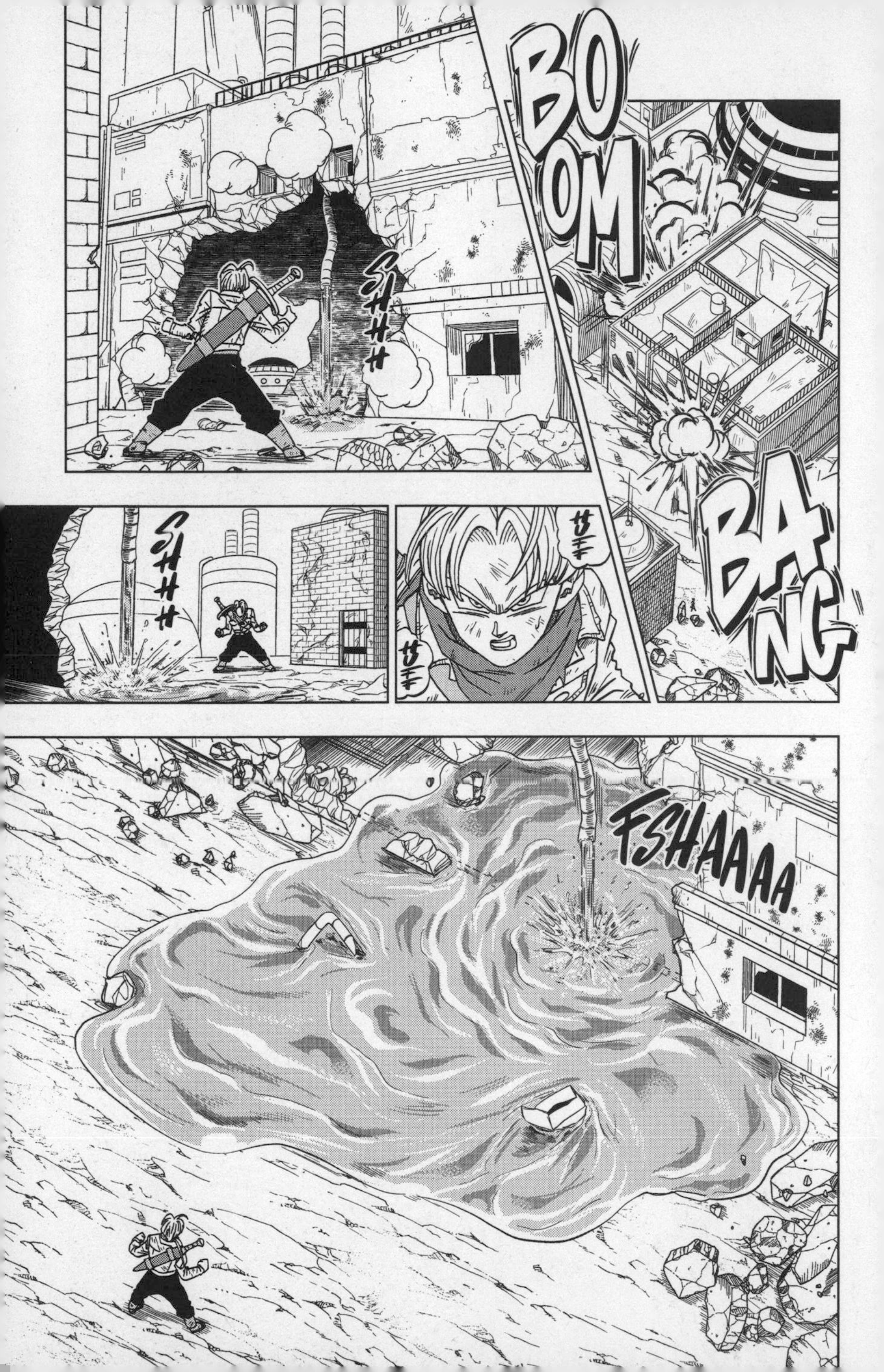
BOOM
BANG
SHHHH
HUFF
HUFF
SHHHH
FSHAAAAA

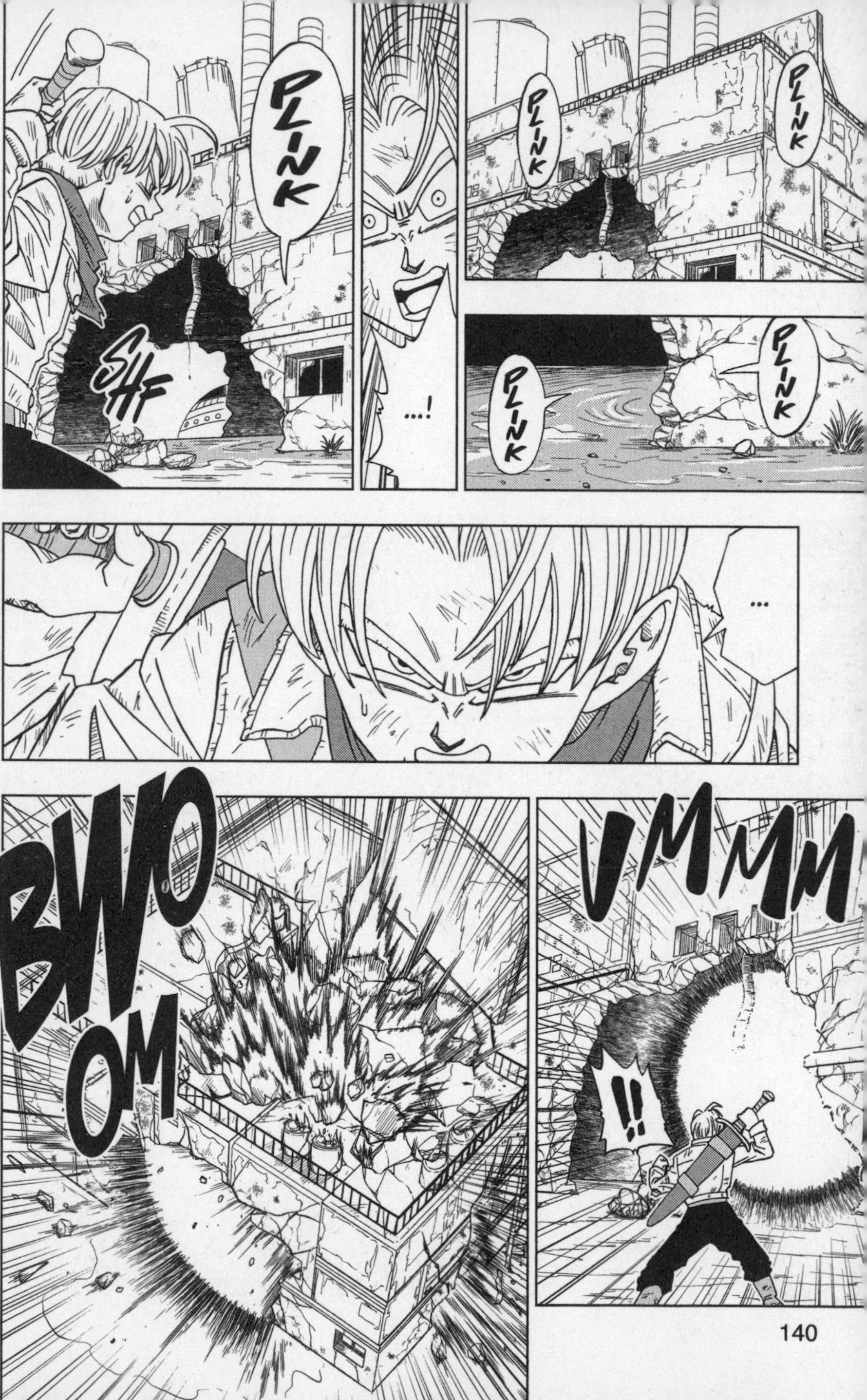

PLINK
PLINK
PLINK
PLINK
...!
PLINK
SHF
...
VMMM
!!
BWOOM

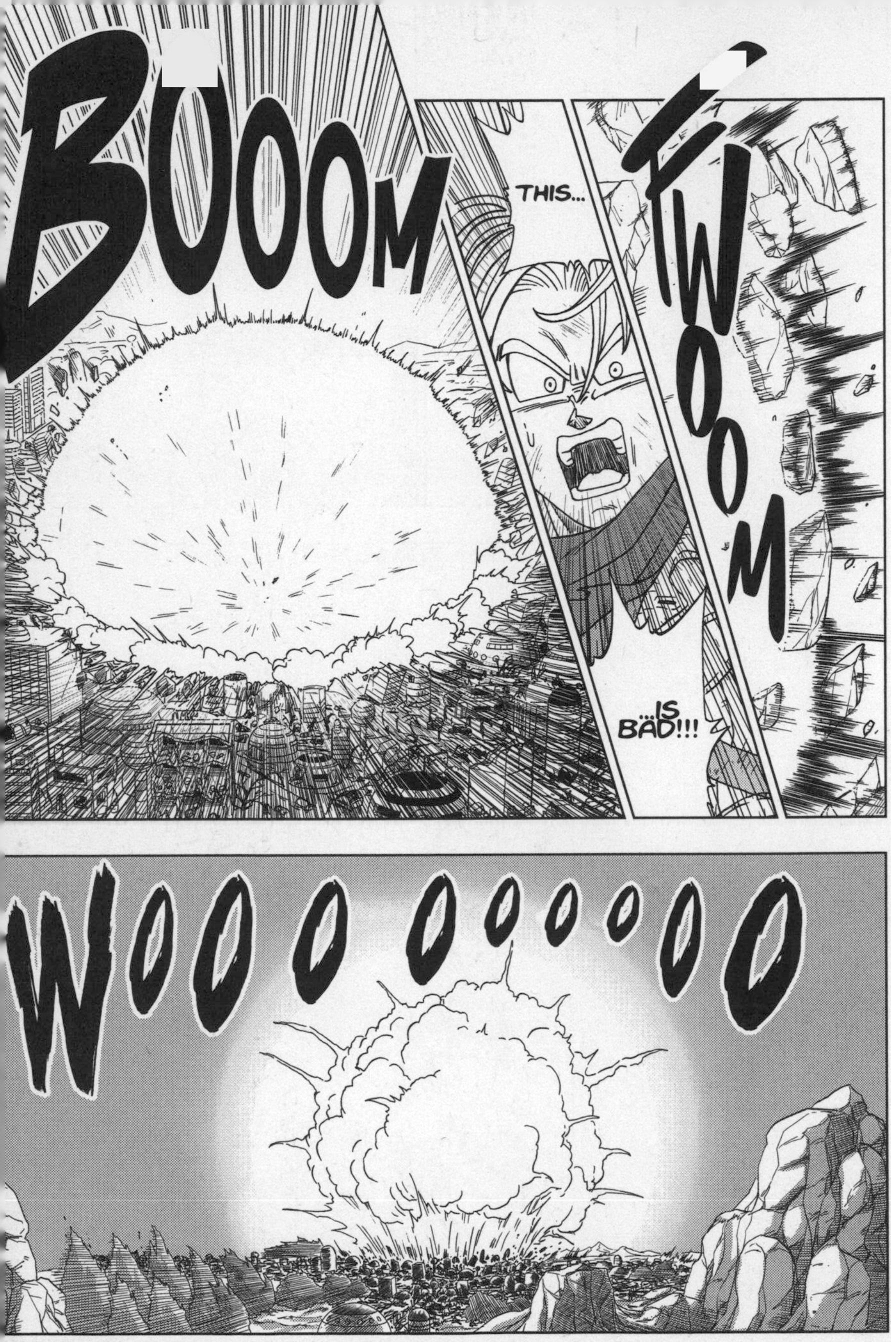
FWOOOM
THIS...
...IS BAD!!!
BOOOM
WOOOOOOO

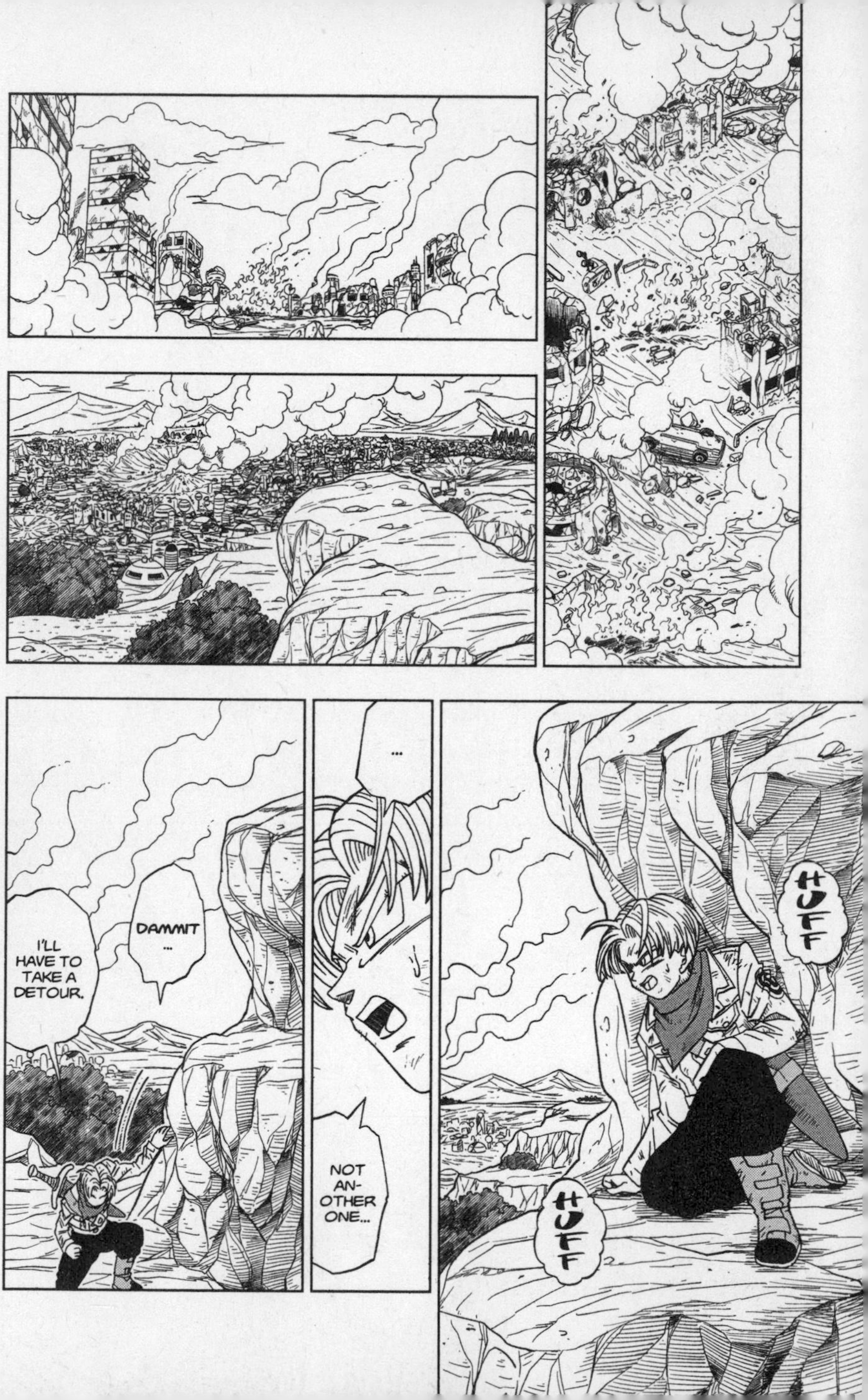
HUFF
HUFF
...
NOT AN-OTHER ONE...
DAMMIT ...
I'LL HAVE TO TAKE A DETOUR.

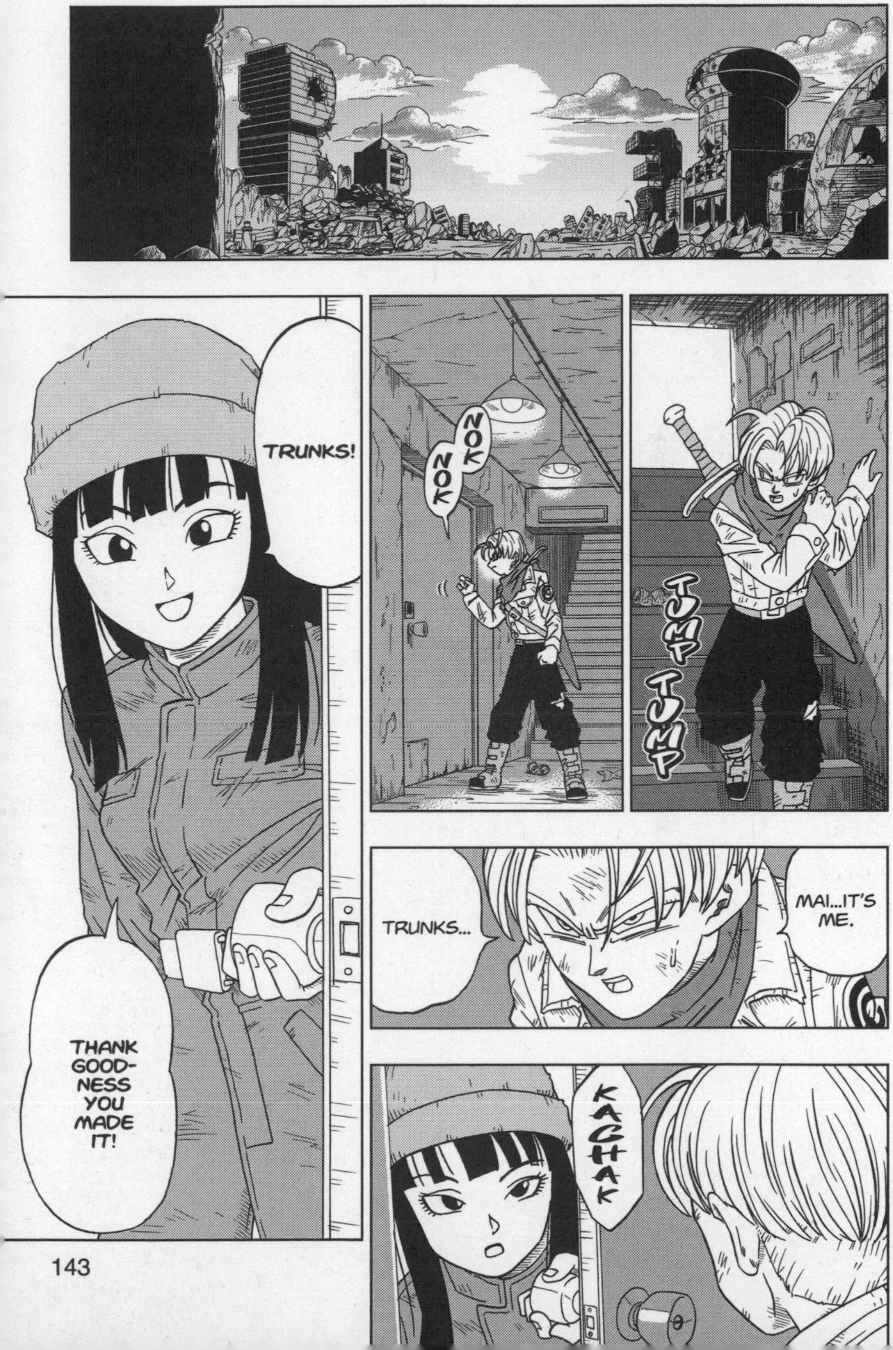
JUMP JUMP
NOK NOK
MAI...IT'S ME.
TRUNKS...
KACHAK
TRUNKS!
THANK GOODNESS YOU MADE IT!

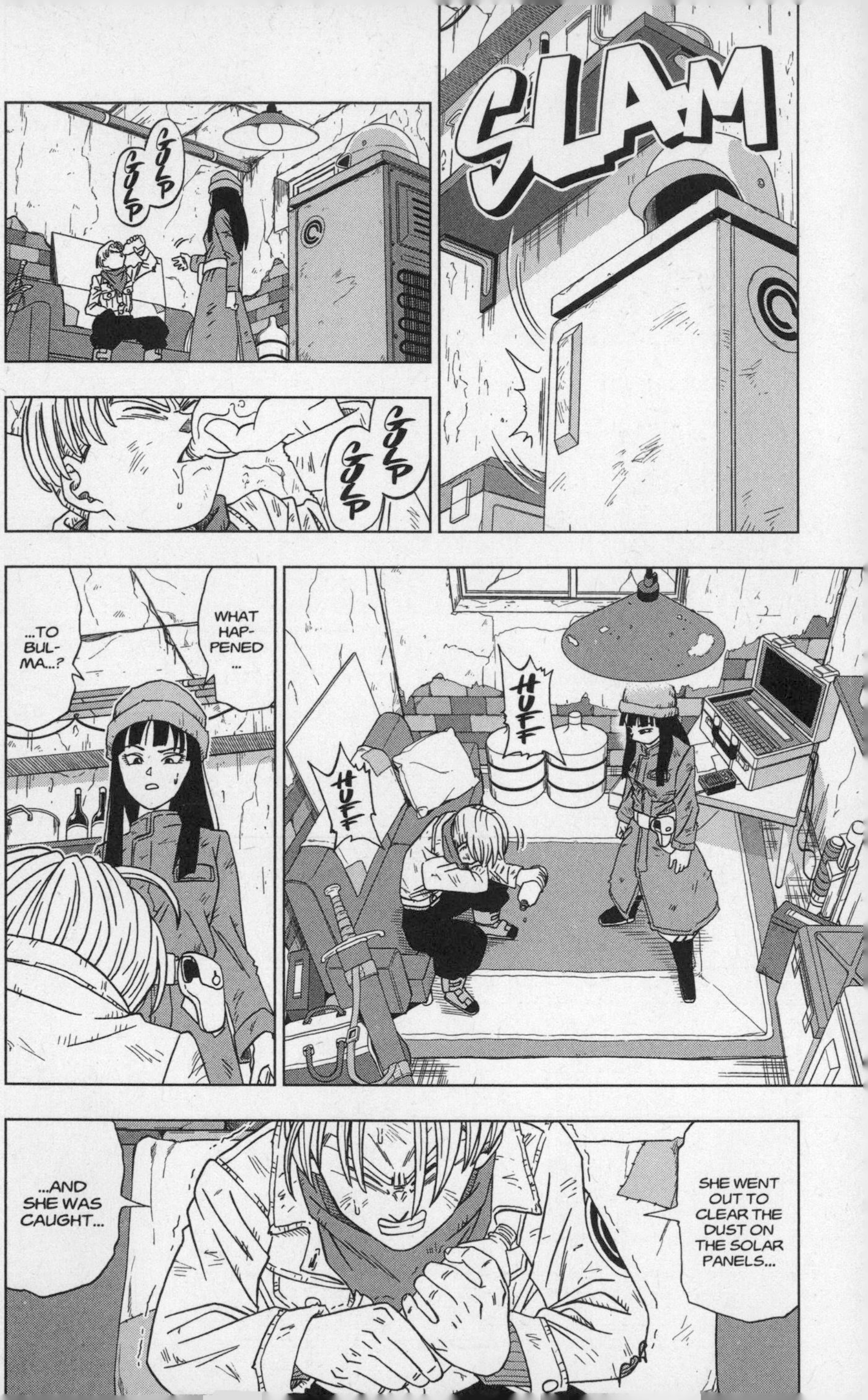
SLAM
GULP GULP
GULP GULP
HUFF
HUFF
WHAT HAPPENED...
...TO BULMA...?
SHE WENT OUT TO CLEAR THE DUST ON THE SOLAR PANELS...
...AND SHE WAS CAUGHT...

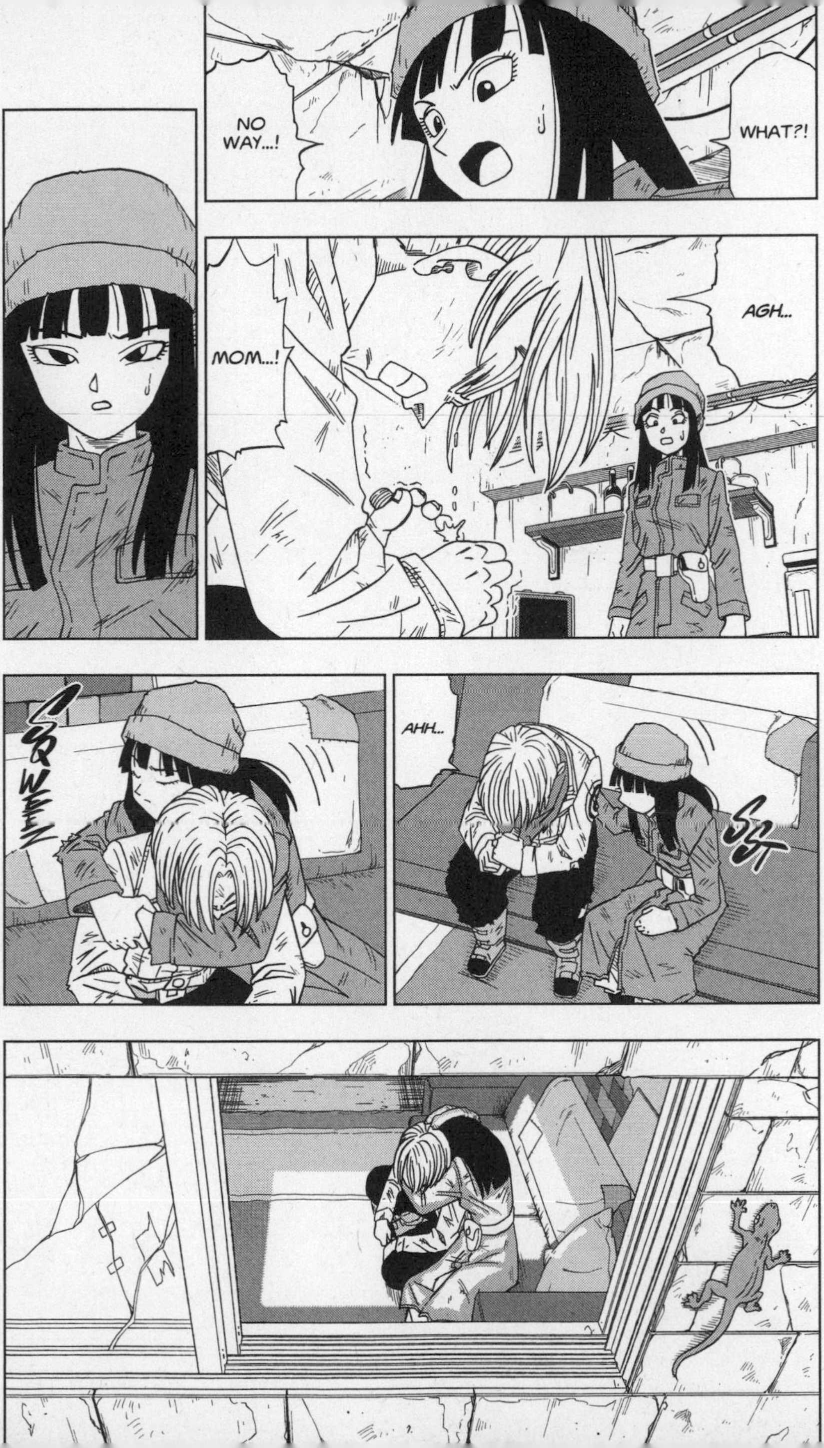
WHAT?!
NO WAY...!
AGH...
MOM...!
AHH...
SST
SQWEEZ

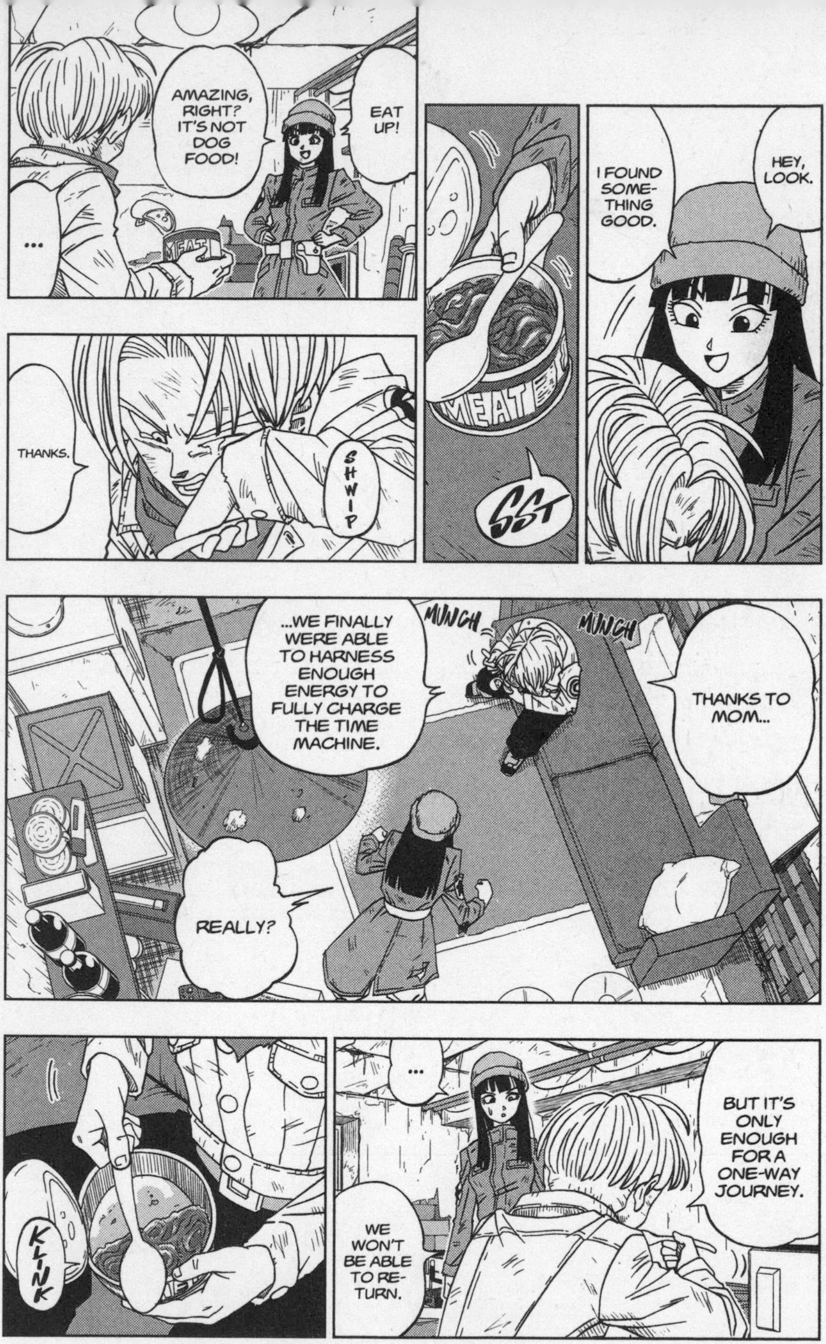
HEY, LOOK.
I FOUND SOME-THING GOOD.
SST
EAT UP!
AMAZING, RIGHT? IT'S NOT DOG FOOD!
...
SHWIP
THANKS.
THANKS TO MOM...
MUNCH
MUNCH
...WE FINALLY WERE ABLE TO HARNESS ENOUGH ENERGY TO FULLY CHARGE THE TIME MACHINE.
REALLY?
BUT IT'S ONLY ENOUGH FOR A ONE-WAY JOURNEY.
...
WE WON'T BE ABLE TO RE-TURN.
KLINK

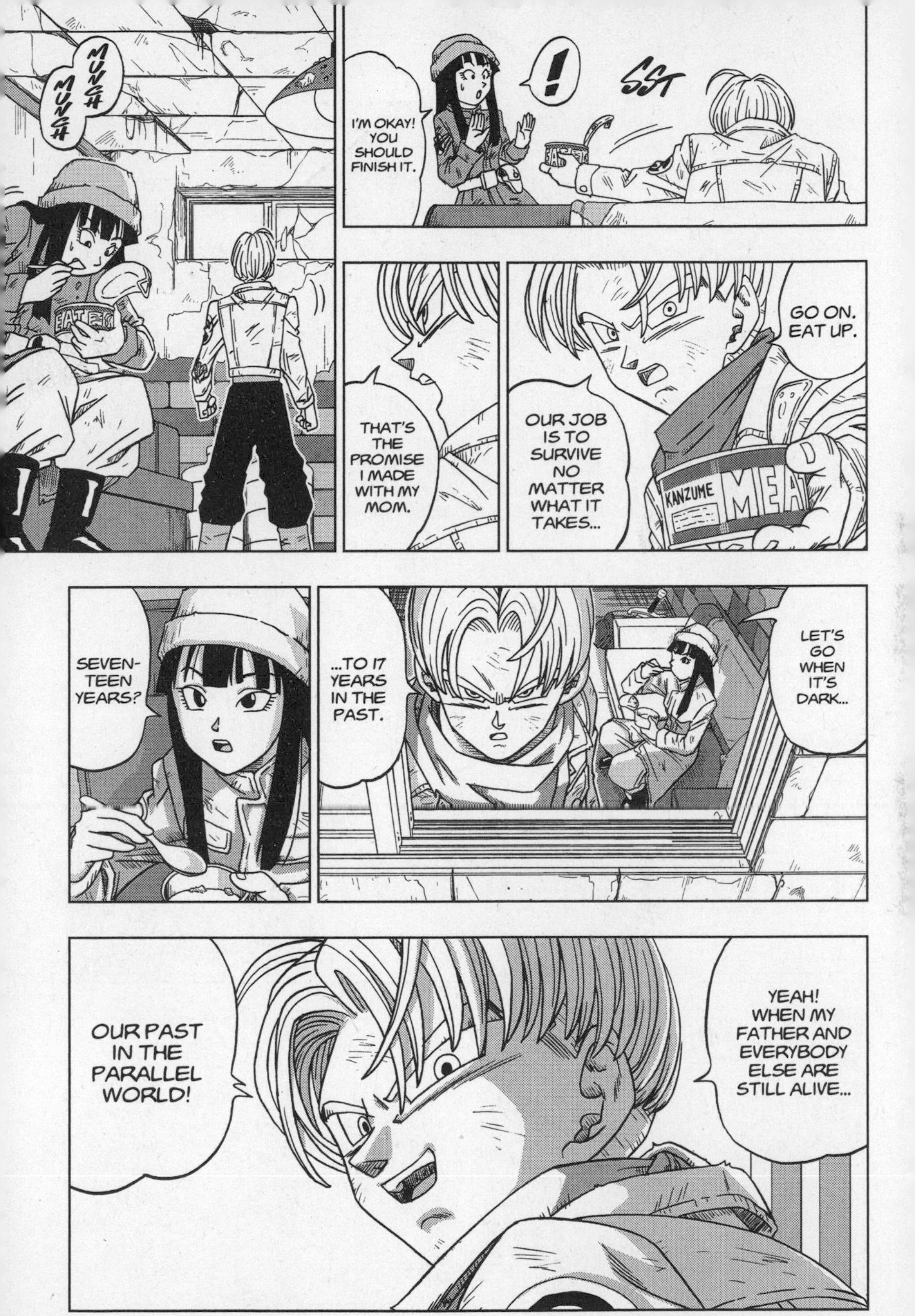
SST
!
I'M OKAY! YOU SHOULD FINISH IT.
GO ON. EAT UP.
OUR JOB IS TO SURVIVE NO MATTER WHAT IT TAKES...
KANZUME MEAT
THAT'S THE PROMISE I MADE WITH MY MOM.
MUNCH MUNCH
LET'S GO WHEN IT'S DARK...
...TO 17 YEARS IN THE PAST.
SEVEN-TEEN YEARS?
YEAH! WHEN MY FATHER AND EVERYBODY ELSE ARE STILL ALIVE...
OUR PAST IN THE PARALLEL WORLD!

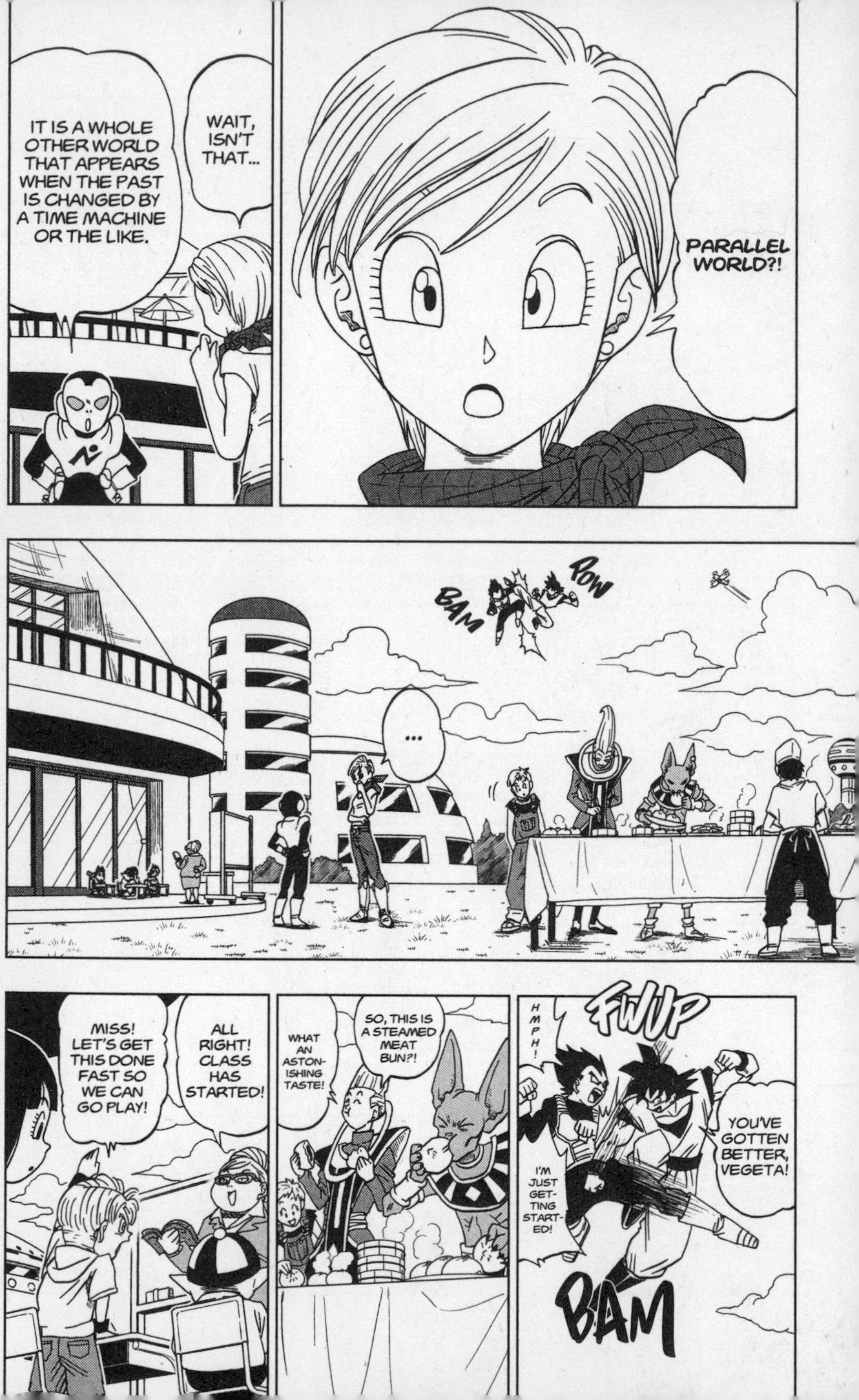
PARALLEL WORLD?!
WAIT, ISN'T THAT...
IT IS A WHOLE OTHER WORLD THAT APPEARS WHEN THE PAST IS CHANGED BY A TIME MACHINE OR THE LIKE.
POW
BAM
...
FWUP
HMPH!
YOU'VE GOTTEN BETTER, VEGETA!
I'M JUST GETTING STARTED!
BAM
SO, THIS IS A STEAMED MEAT BUN?!
WHAT AN ASTONISHING TASTE!
ALL RIGHT! CLASS HAS STARTED!
MISS! LET'S GET THIS DONE FAST SO WE CAN GO PLAY!

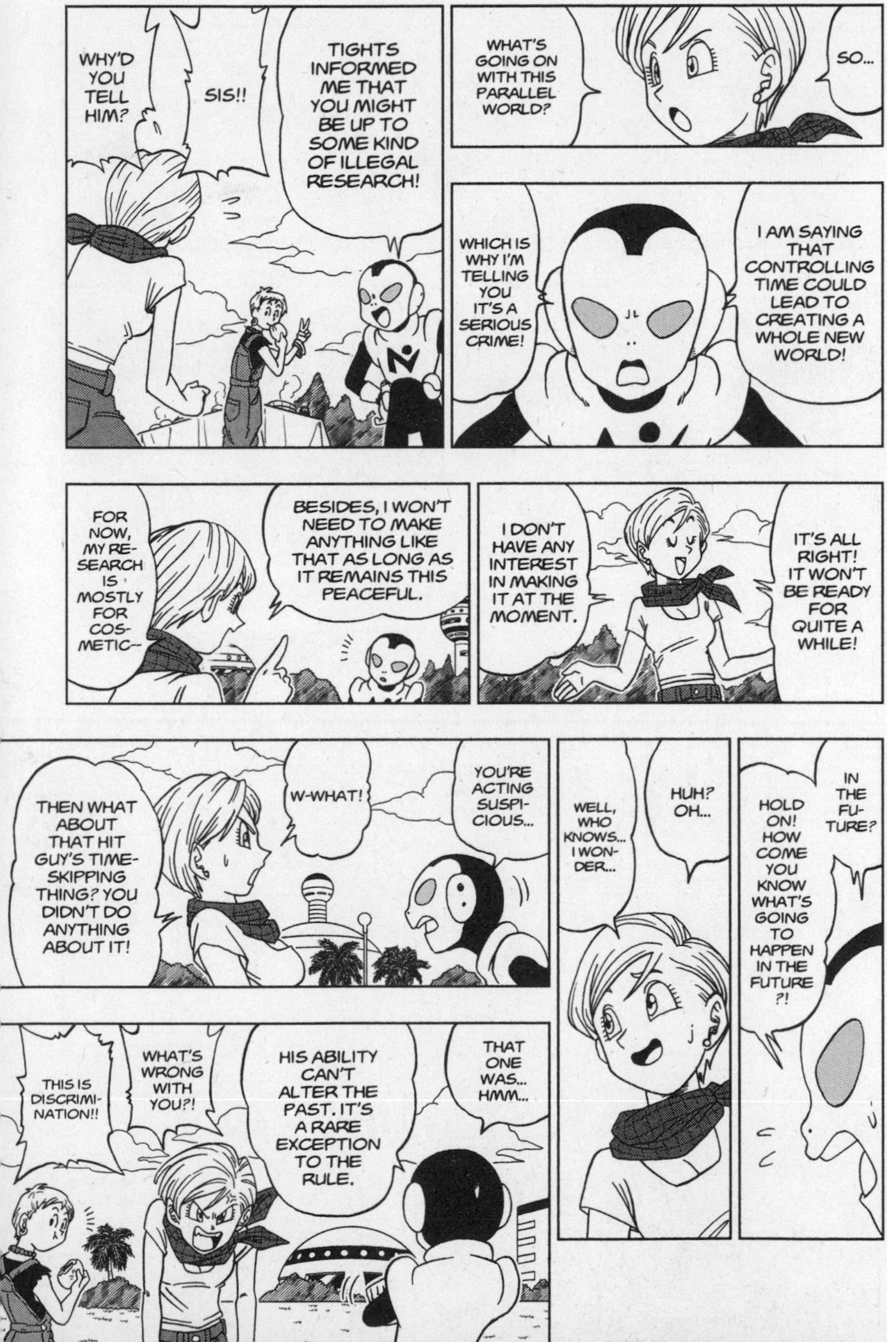
SO...
WHAT'S GOING ON WITH THIS PARALLEL WORLD?
I AM SAYING THAT CONTROLLING TIME COULD LEAD TO CREATING A WHOLE NEW WORLD!
WHICH IS WHY I'M TELLING YOU IT'S A SERIOUS CRIME!
TIGHTS INFORMED ME THAT YOU MIGHT BE UP TO SOME KIND OF ILLEGAL RESEARCH!
SIS!!
WHY'D YOU TELL HIM?
IT'S ALL RIGHT! IT WON'T BE READY FOR QUITE A WHILE!
I DON'T HAVE ANY INTEREST IN MAKING IT AT THE MOMENT.
BESIDES, I WON'T NEED TO MAKE ANYTHING LIKE THAT AS LONG AS IT REMAINS THIS PEACEFUL.
FOR NOW, MY RE-SEARCH IS MOSTLY FOR COS-METIC--
IN THE FU-TURE?
HOLD ON! HOW COME YOU KNOW WHAT'S GOING TO HAPPEN IN THE FUTURE?!
HUH? OH...
WELL, WHO KNOWS... I WON-DER...
YOU'RE ACTING SUSPI-CIOUS...
W-WHAT!
THEN WHAT ABOUT THAT HIT GUY'S TIME-SKIPPING THING? YOU DIDN'T DO ANYTHING ABOUT IT!
THAT ONE WAS... HMM...
HIS ABILITY CAN'T ALTER THE PAST. IT'S A RARE EXCEPTION TO THE RULE.
WHAT'S WRONG WITH YOU?!
THIS IS DISCRIMI-NATION!!

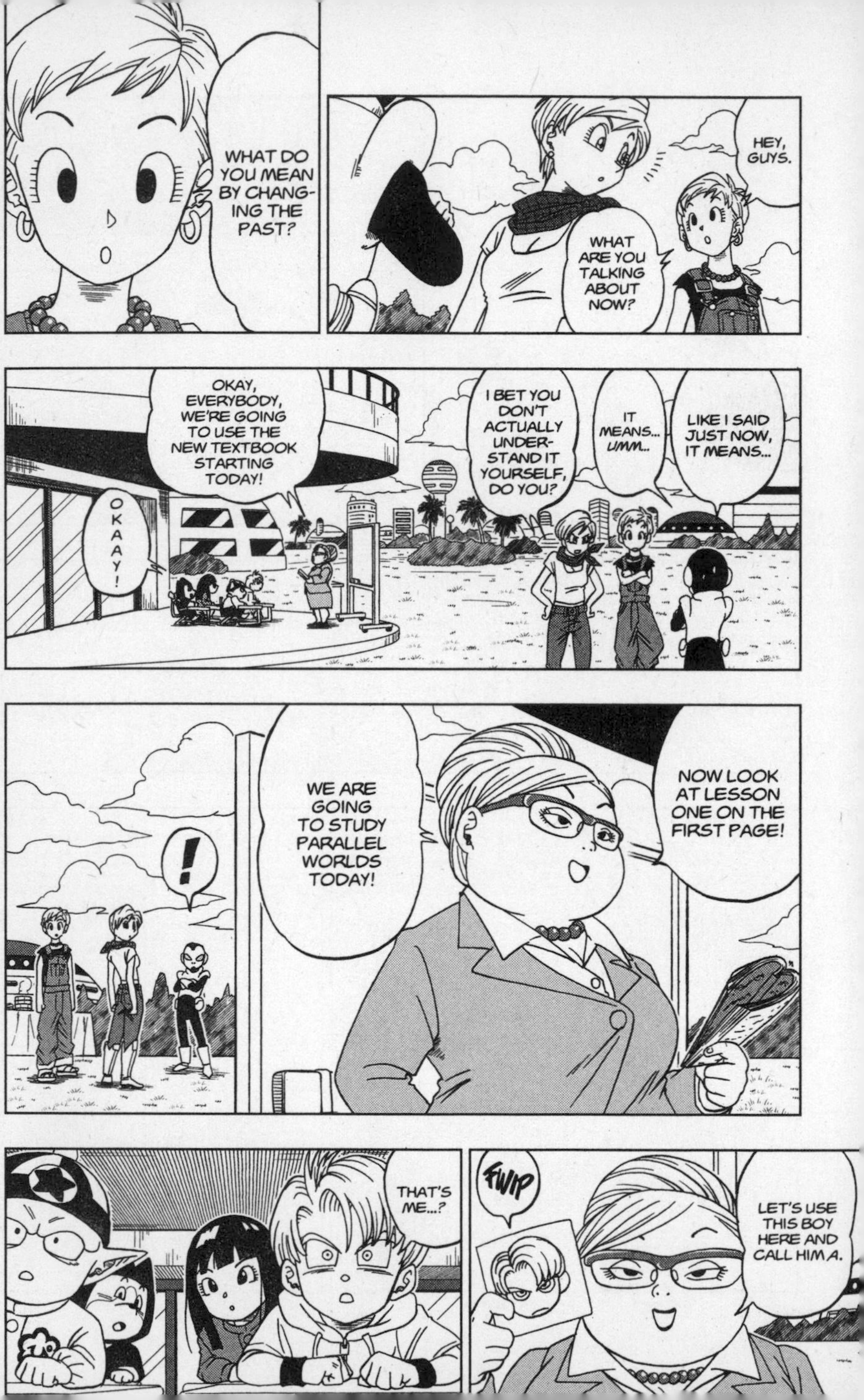
HEY, GUYS.
WHAT ARE YOU TALKING ABOUT NOW?
WHAT DO YOU MEAN BY CHANGING THE PAST?
LIKE I SAID JUST NOW, IT MEANS...
IT MEANS... UMM...
I BET YOU DON'T ACTUALLY UNDERSTAND IT YOURSELF, DO YOU?
OKAY, EVERYBODY, WE'RE GOING TO USE THE NEW TEXTBOOK STARTING TODAY!
OKAAY!
NOW LOOK AT LESSON ONE ON THE FIRST PAGE!
WE ARE GOING TO STUDY PARALLEL WORLDS TODAY!
!
FWIP
LET'S USE THIS BOY HERE AND CALL HIM A.
THAT'S ME...?

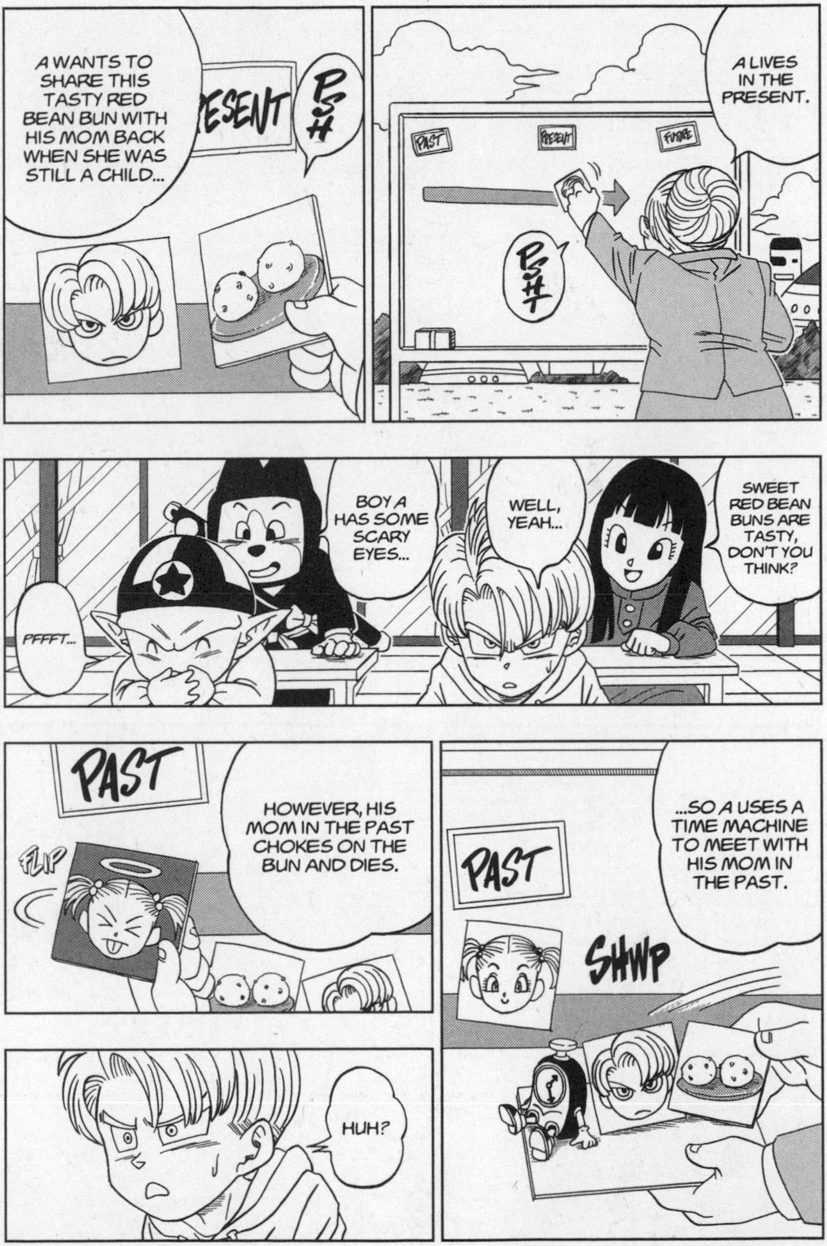
A LIVES IN THE PRESENT.
PAST
PRESENT
FUTURE
PSH
A WANTS TO SHARE THIS TASTY RED BEAN BUN WITH HIS MOM BACK WHEN SHE WAS STILL A CHILD...
PSH
PRESENT
SWEET RED BEAN BUNS ARE TASTY, DON'T YOU THINK?
WELL, YEAH...
BOY A HAS SOME SCARY EYES...
PFFFT...
...SO A USES A TIME MACHINE TO MEET WITH HIS MOM IN THE PAST.
PAST
SHWP
PAST
HOWEVER, HIS MOM IN THE PAST CHOKES ON THE BUN AND DIES.
FLIP
HUH?

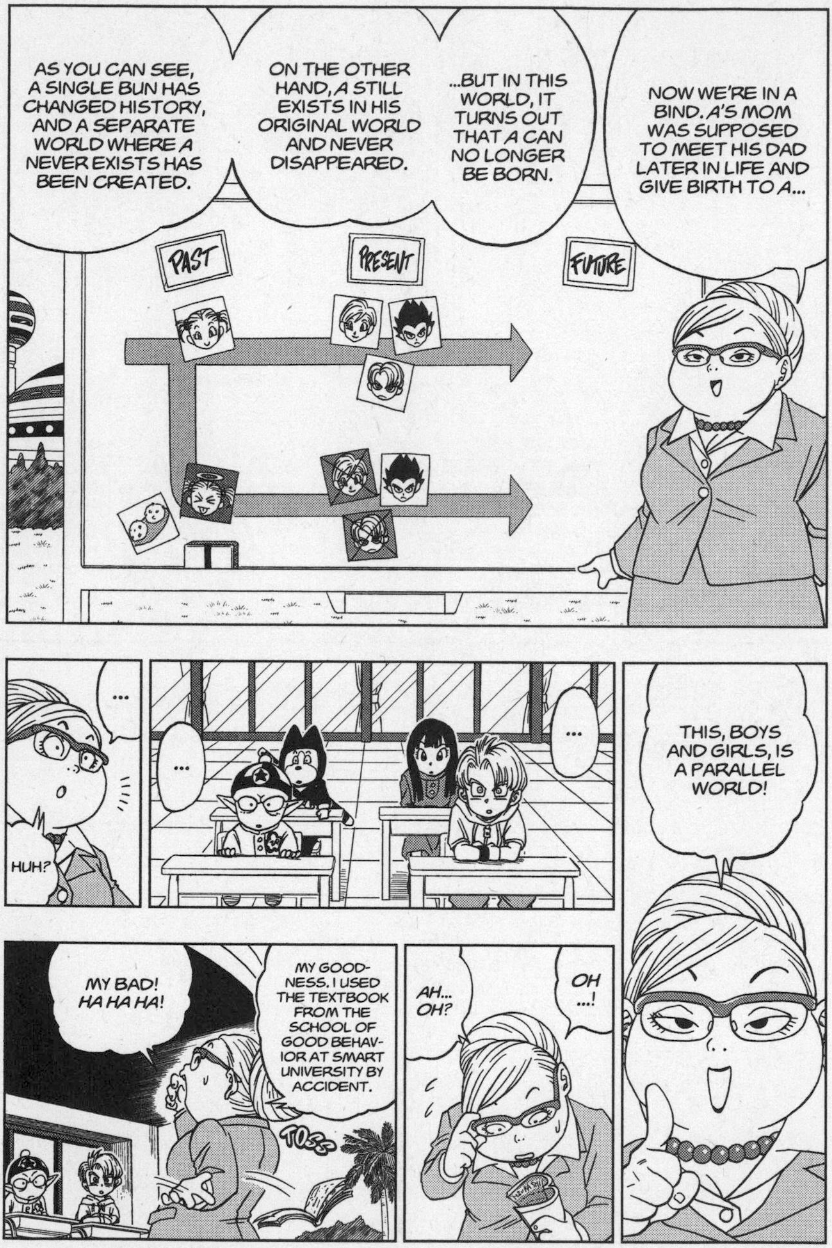
AS YOU CAN SEE, A SINGLE BUN HAS CHANGED HISTORY, AND A SEPARATE WORLD WHERE A NEVER EXISTS HAS BEEN CREATED.
ON THE OTHER HAND, A STILL EXISTS IN HIS ORIGINAL WORLD AND NEVER DISAPPEARED.
...BUT IN THIS WORLD, IT TURNS OUT THAT A CAN NO LONGER BE BORN.
NOW WE'RE IN A BIND. A'S MOM WAS SUPPOSED TO MEET HIS DAD LATER IN LIFE AND GIVE BIRTH TO A...
PAST
PRESENT
FUTURE
THIS, BOYS AND GIRLS, IS A PARALLEL WORLD!
...
...
...
HUH?
OH ...!
AH... OH?
MY GOODNESS. I USED THE TEXTBOOK FROM THE SCHOOL OF GOOD BEHAVIOR AT SMART UNIVERSITY BY ACCIDENT.
MY BAD! HA HA HA!
TOSS

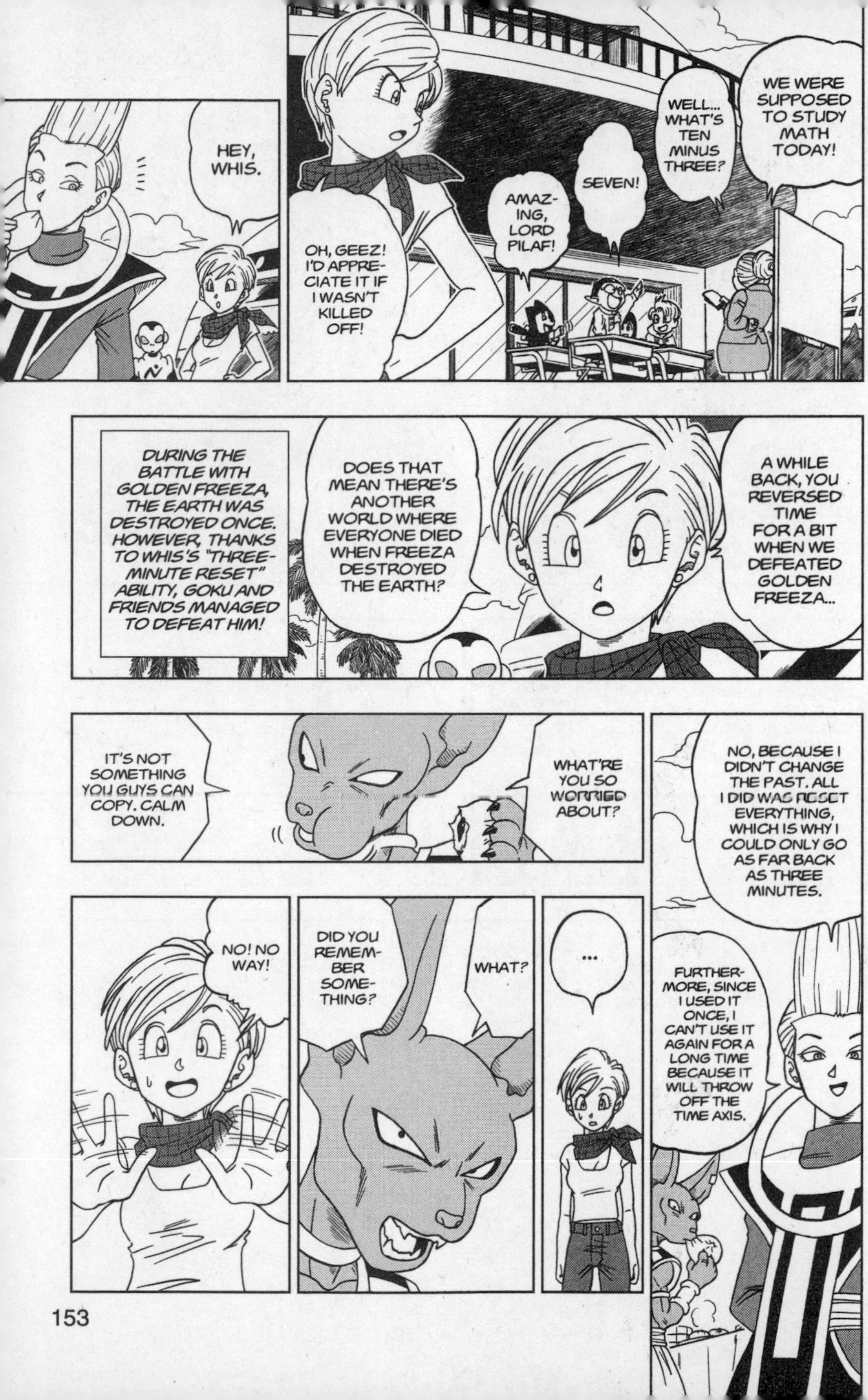
WE WERE SUPPOSED TO STUDY MATH TODAY!
WELL... WHAT'S TEN MINUS THREE?
SEVEN!
AMAZING, LORD PILAF!
OH, GEEZ! I'D APPRECIATE IT IF I WASN'T KILLED OFF!
HEY, WHIS.
A WHILE BACK, YOU REVERSED TIME FOR A BIT WHEN WE DEFEATED GOLDEN FREEZA...
DOES THAT MEAN THERE'S ANOTHER WORLD WHERE EVERYONE DIED WHEN FREEZA DESTROYED THE EARTH?
DURING THE BATTLE WITH GOLDEN FREEZA, THE EARTH WAS DESTROYED ONCE. HOWEVER, THANKS TO WHIS'S "THREE-MINUTE RESET" ABILITY, GOKU AND FRIENDS MANAGED TO DEFEAT HIM!
NO, BECAUSE I DIDN'T CHANGE THE PAST. ALL I DID WAS RESET EVERYTHING, WHICH IS WHY I COULD ONLY GO AS FAR BACK AS THREE MINUTES.
FURTHERMORE, SINCE I USED IT ONCE, I CAN'T USE IT AGAIN FOR A LONG TIME BECAUSE IT WILL THROW OFF THE TIME AXIS.
WHAT'RE YOU SO WORRIED ABOUT?
IT'S NOT SOMETHING YOU GUYS CAN COPY. CALM DOWN.
...
WHAT?
DID YOU REMEMBER SOMETHING?
NO! NO WAY!

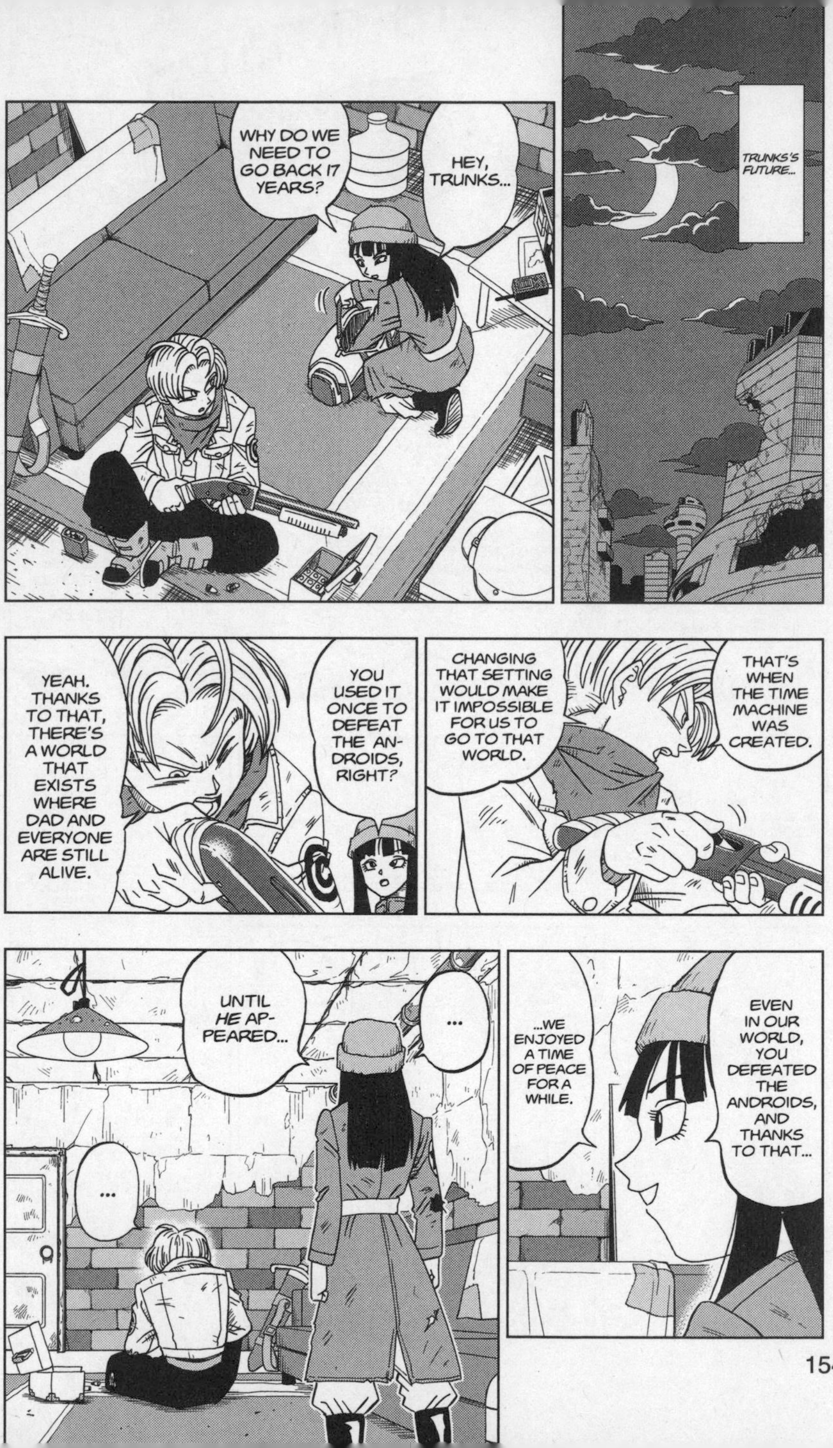
TRUNKS'S FUTURE...
HEY, TRUNKS...
WHY DO WE NEED TO GO BACK 17 YEARS?
THAT'S WHEN THE TIME MACHINE WAS CREATED.
CHANGING THAT SETTING WOULD MAKE IT IMPOSSIBLE FOR US TO GO TO THAT WORLD.
YOU USED IT ONCE TO DEFEAT THE ANDROIDS, RIGHT?
YEAH. THANKS TO THAT, THERE'S A WORLD THAT EXISTS WHERE DAD AND EVERYONE ARE STILL ALIVE.
EVEN IN OUR WORLD, YOU DEFEATED THE ANDROIDS, AND THANKS TO THAT...
...WE ENJOYED A TIME OF PEACE FOR A WHILE.
...
UNTIL *HE* APPEARED...
...

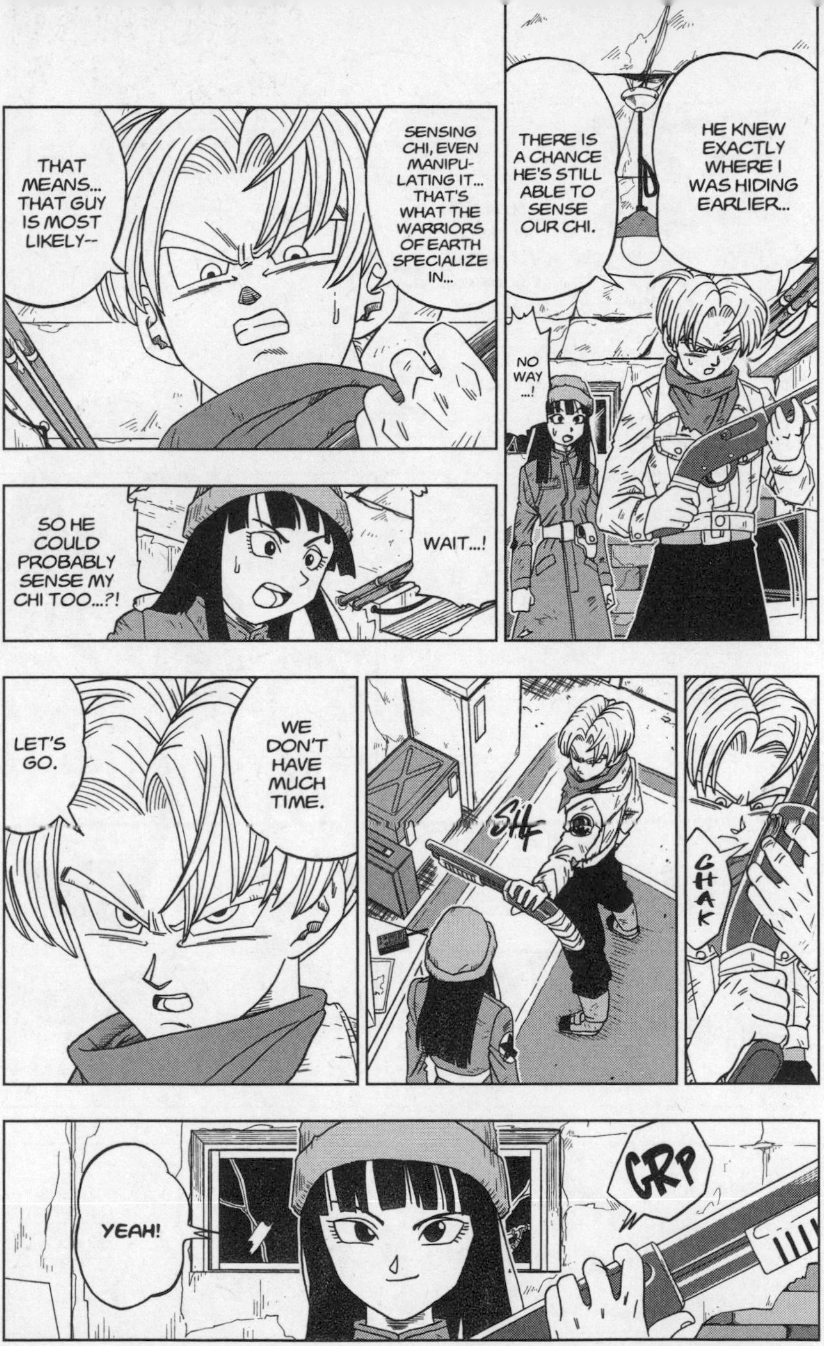
HE KNEW EXACTLY WHERE I WAS HIDING EARLIER...
THERE IS A CHANCE HE'S STILL ABLE TO SENSE OUR CHI.
NO WAY ...!
SENSING CHI, EVEN MANIPU-LATING IT... THAT'S WHAT THE WARRIORS OF EARTH SPECIALIZE IN...
THAT MEANS... THAT GUY IS MOST LIKELY--
WAIT...!
SO HE COULD PROBABLY SENSE MY CHI TOO...?!
CHAK
WE DON'T HAVE MUCH TIME.
LET'S GO.
GRP
YEAH!

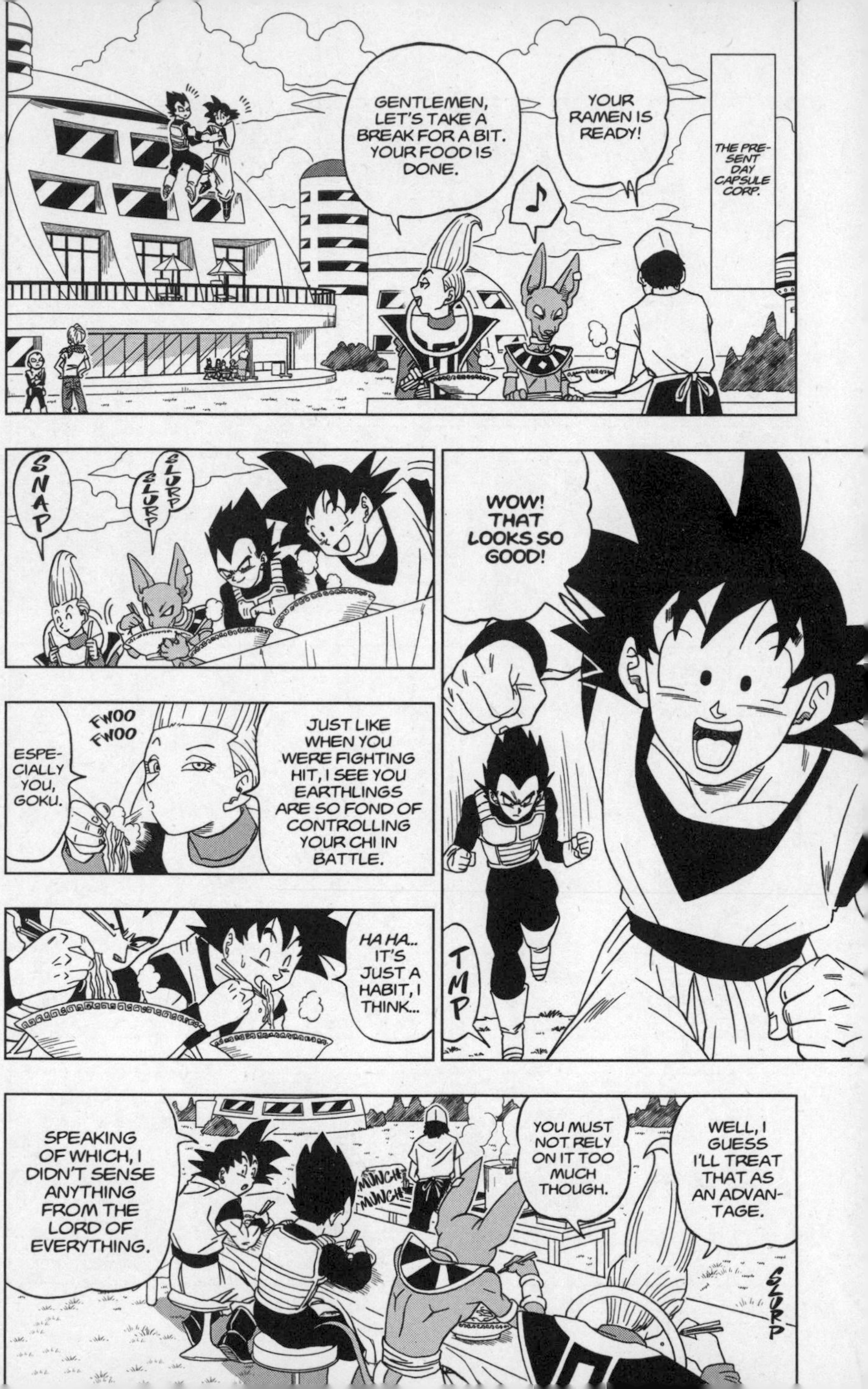
THE PRESENT DAY CAPSULE CORP.
YOUR RAMEN IS READY!
♪
GENTLEMEN, LET'S TAKE A BREAK FOR A BIT. YOUR FOOD IS DONE.
WOW! THAT LOOKS SO GOOD!
TMP
SLURP SLURP
SNAP
JUST LIKE WHEN YOU WERE FIGHTING HIT, I SEE YOU EARTHLINGS ARE SO FOND OF CONTROLLING YOUR CHI IN BATTLE.
FWOO FWOO
ESPECIALLY YOU, GOKU.
HA HA.. IT'S JUST A HABIT, I THINK...
WELL, I GUESS I'LL TREAT THAT AS AN ADVANTAGE.
SLURP
YOU MUST NOT RELY ON IT TOO MUCH THOUGH.
MUNCH MUNCH
SPEAKING OF WHICH, I DIDN'T SENSE ANYTHING FROM THE LORD OF EVERYTHING.

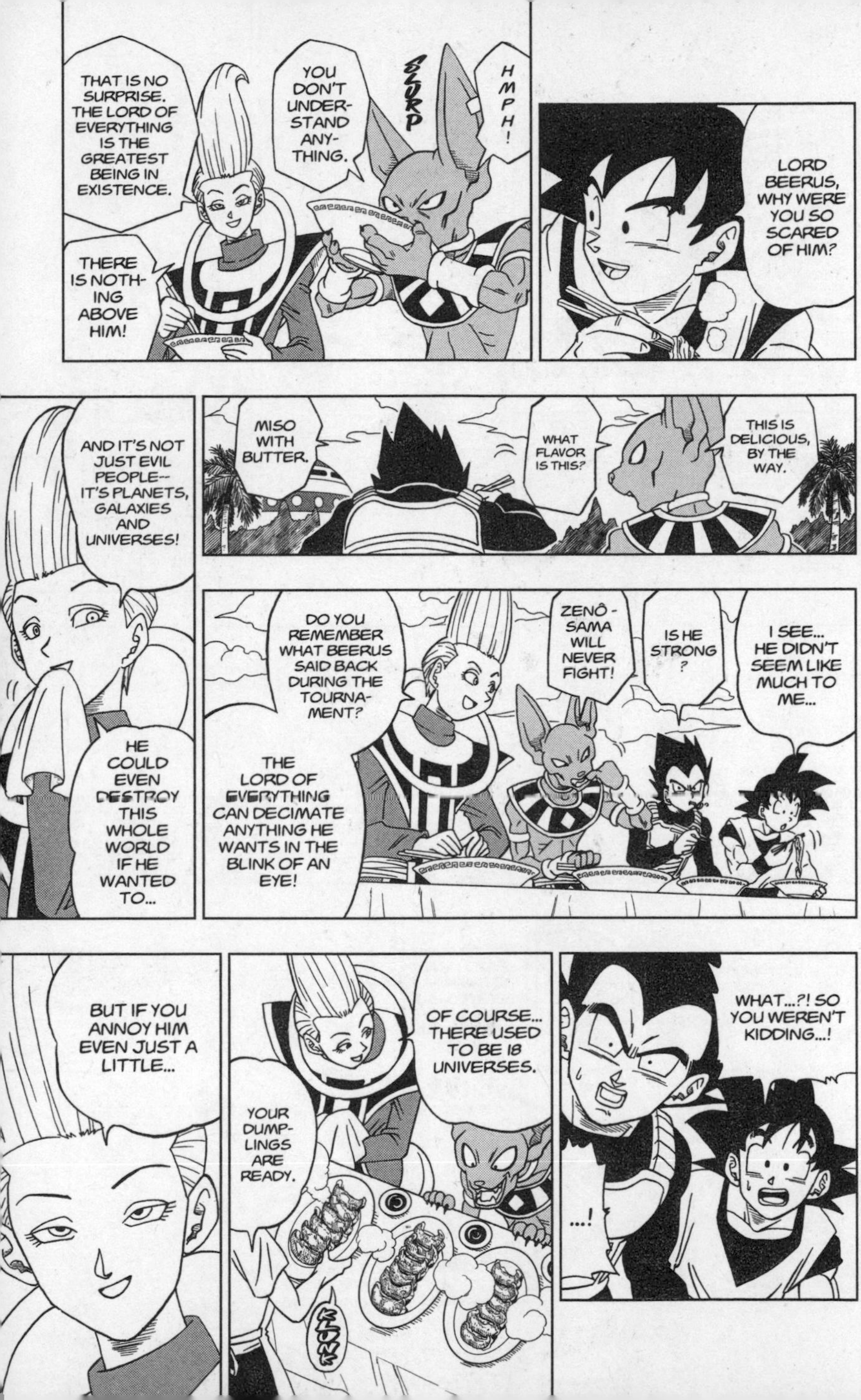

LORD BEERUS, WHY WERE YOU SO SCARED OF HIM?
HMPH!
SLURP
YOU DON'T UNDERSTAND ANYTHING.
THAT IS NO SURPRISE. THE LORD OF EVERYTHING IS THE GREATEST BEING IN EXISTENCE.
THERE IS NOTHING ABOVE HIM!
THIS IS DELICIOUS, BY THE WAY.
WHAT FLAVOR IS THIS?
MISO WITH BUTTER.
I SEE... HE DIDN'T SEEM LIKE MUCH TO ME...
IS HE STRONG?
ZENÔ-SAMA WILL NEVER FIGHT!
DO YOU REMEMBER WHAT BEERUS SAID BACK DURING THE TOURNAMENT?
THE LORD OF EVERYTHING CAN DECIMATE ANYTHING HE WANTS IN THE BLINK OF AN EYE!
AND IT'S NOT JUST EVIL PEOPLE-- IT'S PLANETS, GALAXIES AND UNIVERSES!
HE COULD EVEN DESTROY THIS WHOLE WORLD IF HE WANTED TO...
WHAT...?! SO YOU WEREN'T KIDDING...!
...!
OF COURSE... THERE USED TO BE 18 UNIVERSES.
YOUR DUMPLINGS ARE READY.
KLUNK
BUT IF YOU ANNOY HIM EVEN JUST A LITTLE...

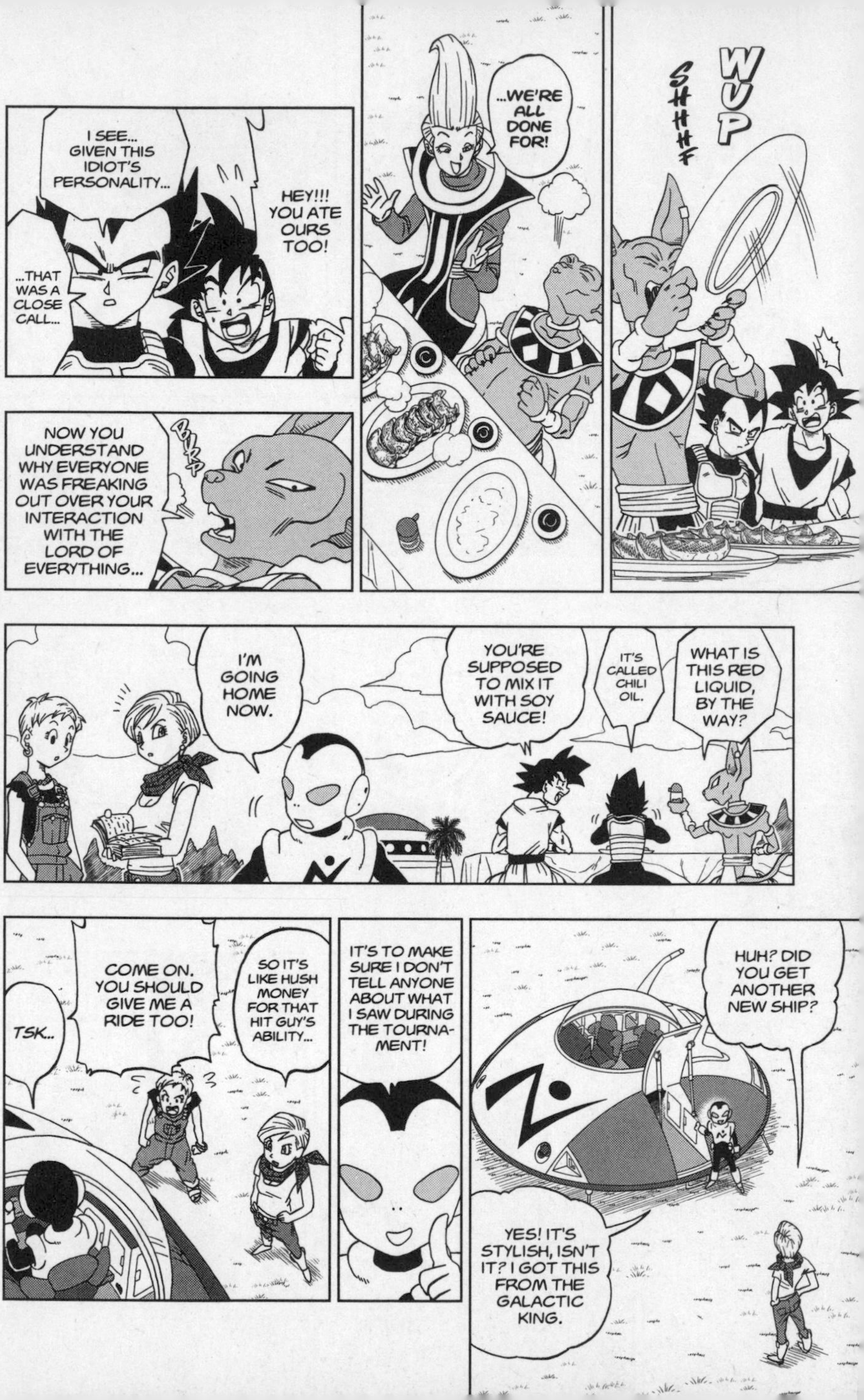
WUP
SHHHF
...WE'RE ALL DONE FOR!
I SEE... GIVEN THIS IDIOT'S PERSONALITY...
HEY!!! YOU ATE OURS TOO!
...THAT WAS A CLOSE CALL...
NOW YOU UNDERSTAND WHY EVERYONE WAS FREAKING OUT OVER YOUR INTERACTION WITH THE LORD OF EVERYTHING...
WHAT IS THIS RED LIQUID, BY THE WAY?
IT'S CALLED CHILI OIL.
YOU'RE SUPPOSED TO MIX IT WITH SOY SAUCE!
I'M GOING HOME NOW.
HUH? DID YOU GET ANOTHER NEW SHIP?
YES! IT'S STYLISH, ISN'T IT? I GOT THIS FROM THE GALACTIC KING.
IT'S TO MAKE SURE I DON'T TELL ANYONE ABOUT WHAT I SAW DURING THE TOURNA-MENT!
SO IT'S LIKE HUSH MONEY FOR THAT HIT GUY'S ABILITY...
COME ON. YOU SHOULD GIVE ME A RIDE TOO!
TSK...

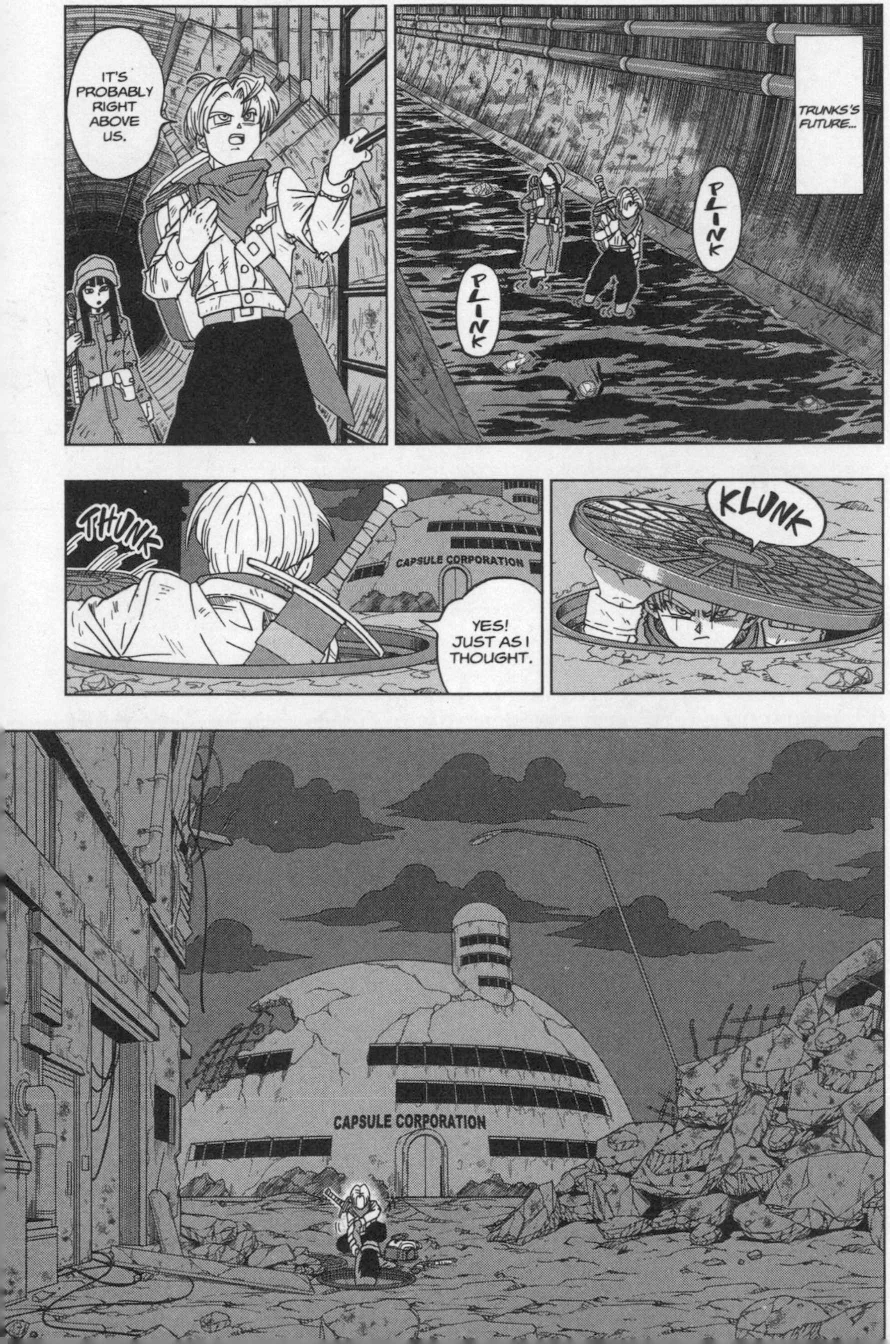
TRUNKS'S FUTURE...
PLINK
PLINK
IT'S PROBABLY RIGHT ABOVE US.
KLUNK
THUNK
CAPSULE CORPORATION
YES! JUST AS I THOUGHT.
CAPSULE CORPORATION

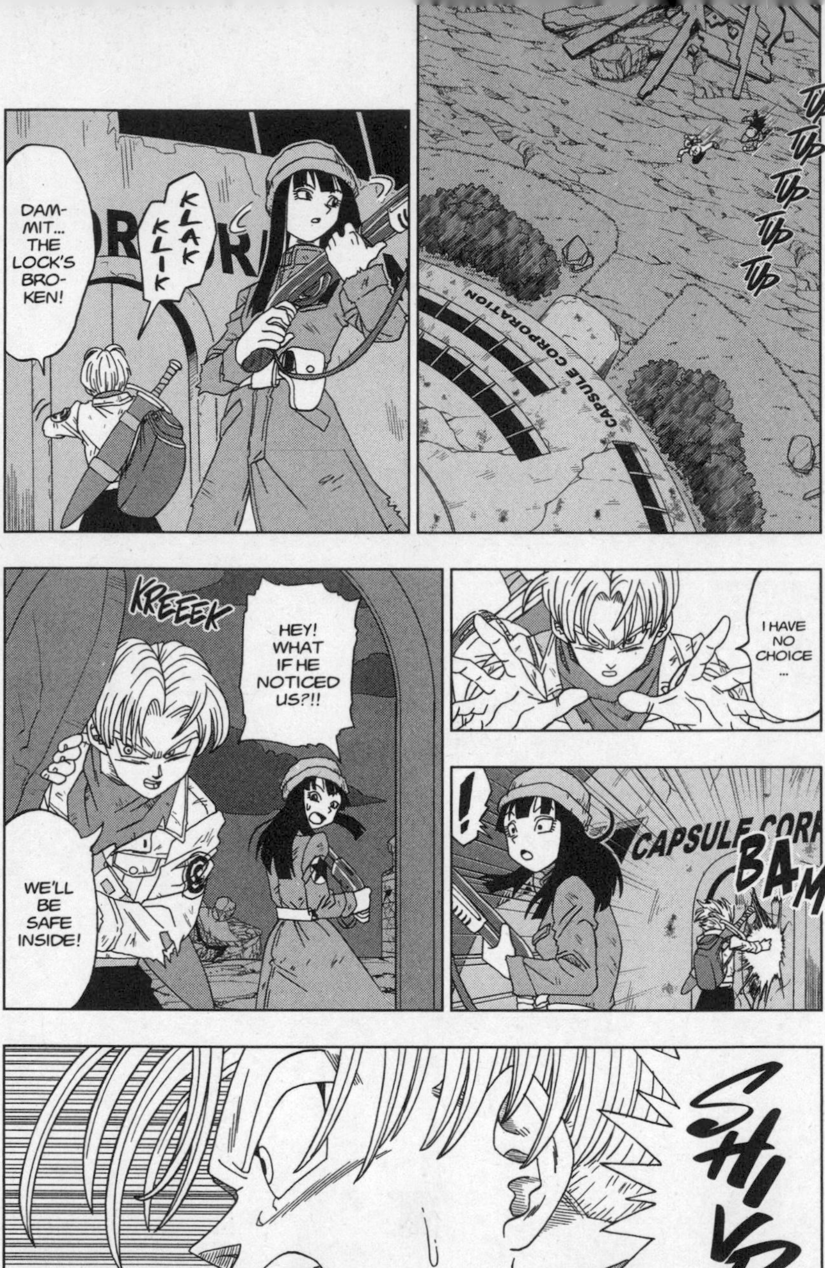
TUP TUP TUP TUP TUP
CAPSULE CORPORATION
KLIK KLAK
DAM-MIT... THE LOCK'S BRO-KEN!
I HAVE NO CHOICE ...
!
CAPSULE CORP
BAM
KREEEK
HEY! WHAT IF HE NOTICED US?!!
WE'LL BE SAFE INSIDE!
SHIVR

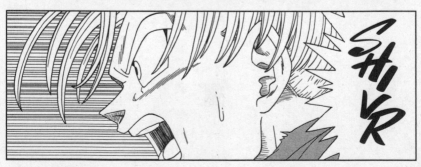

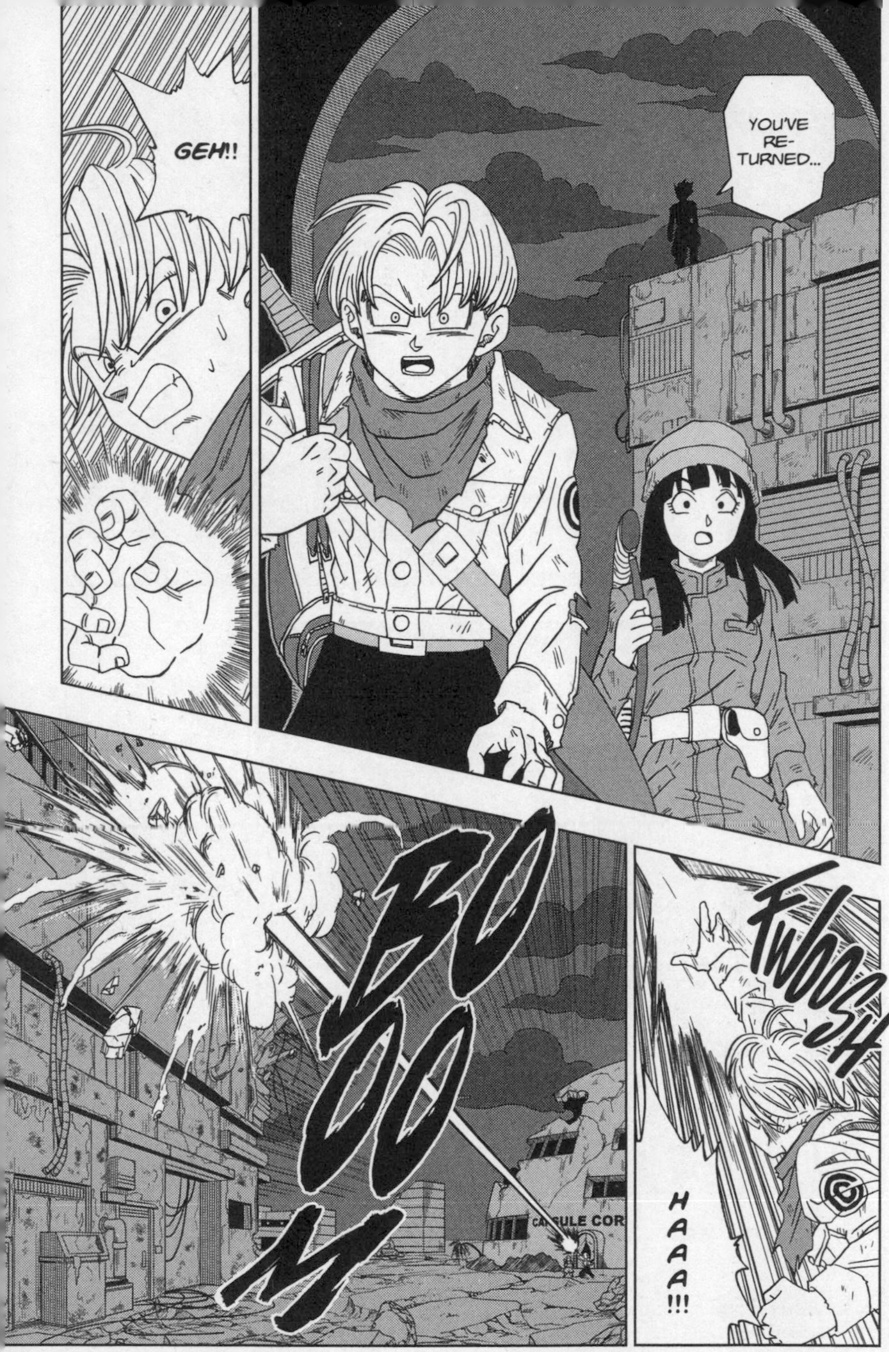
YOU'VE RE-TURNED...
GEH!!
FWOOSH
HAAAA!!!
BOOOM
CAPSULE COR

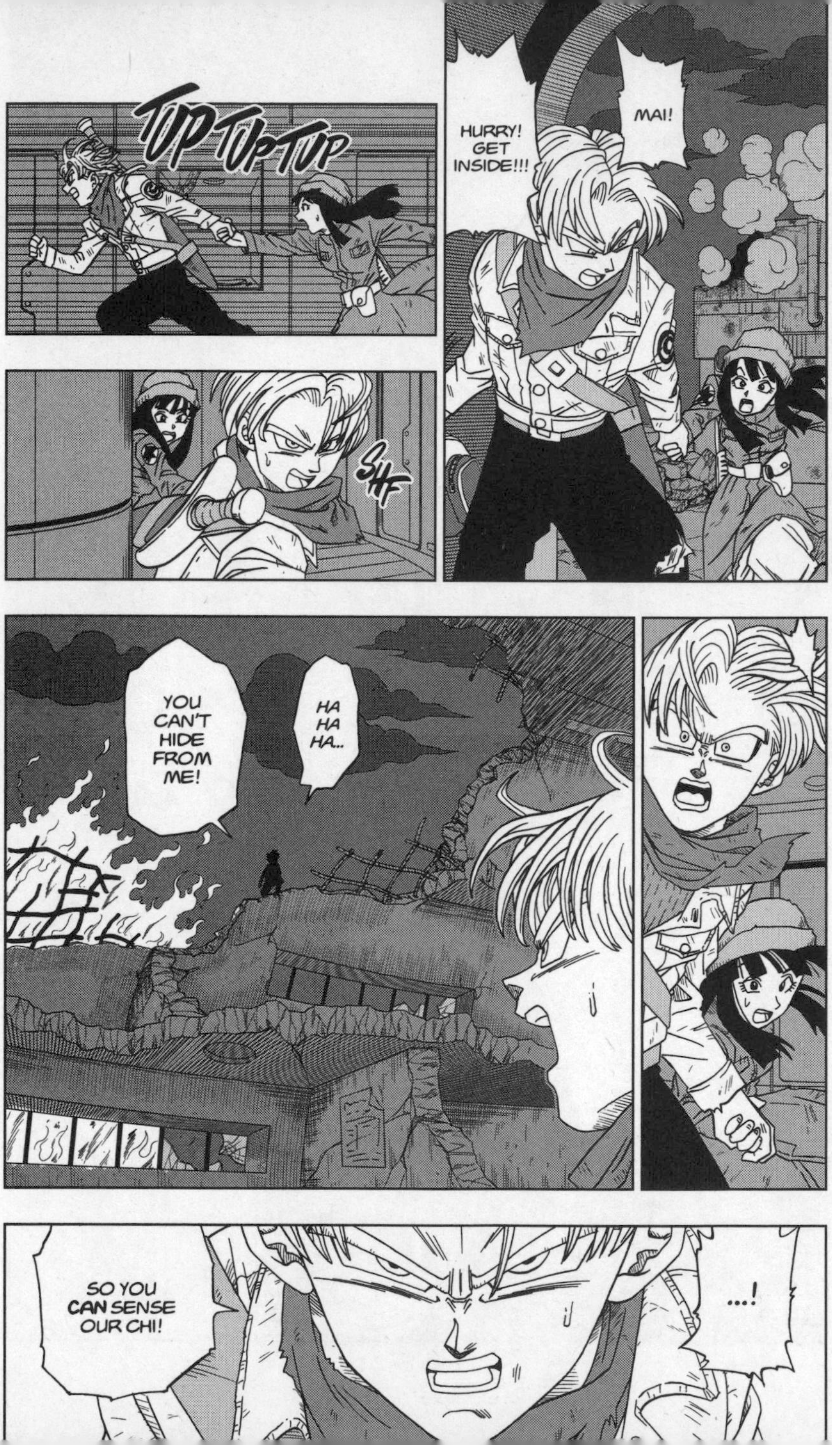
MAI!
HURRY! GET INSIDE!!!
TUP TUP TUP TUP
SHF
HA HA HA...
YOU CAN'T HIDE FROM ME!
...!
SO YOU CAN SENSE OUR CHI!

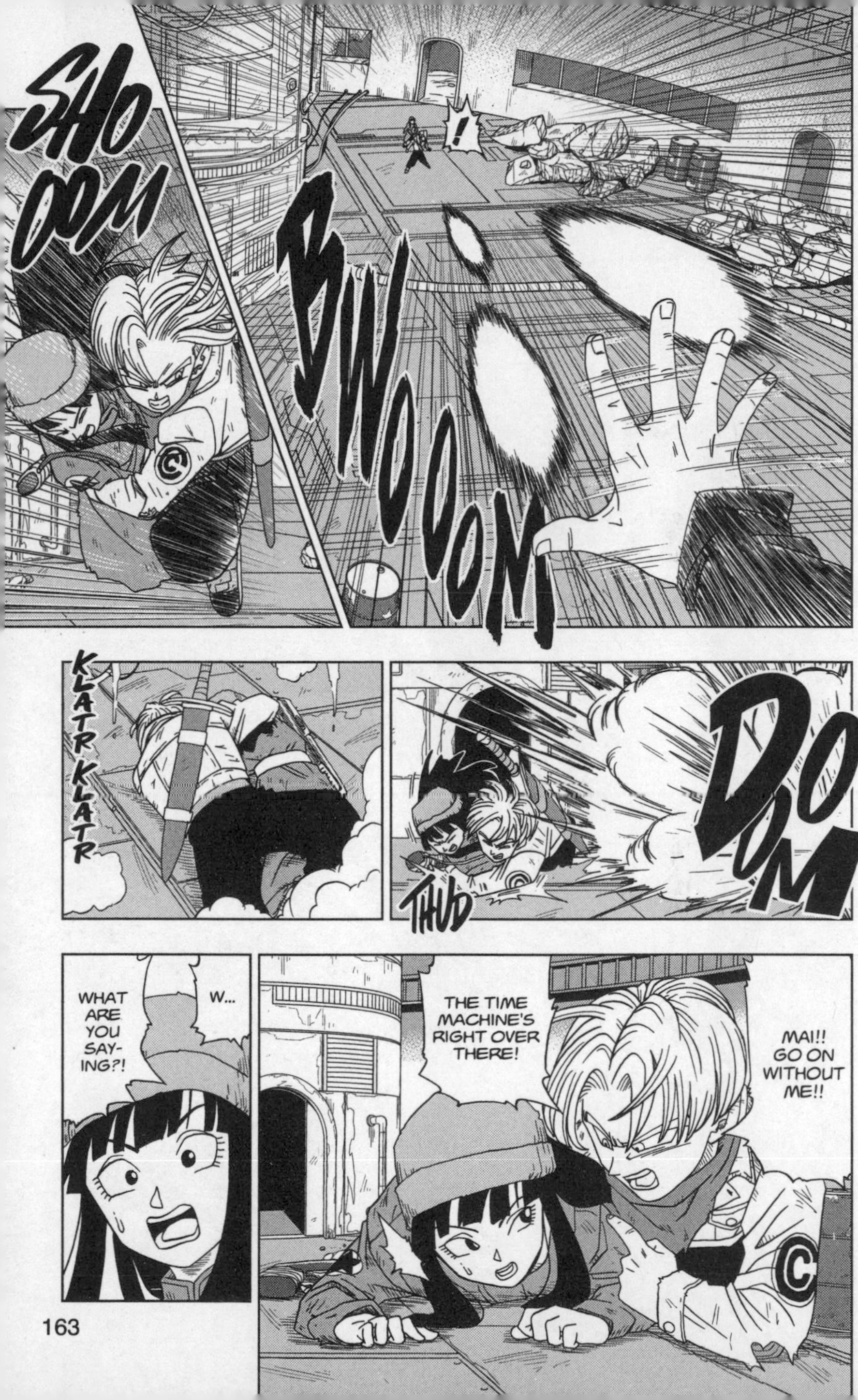
!
SWOOOM
SHOOOM
DOOM
THUD
KLATR KLATR
MAI!! GO ON WITHOUT ME!!
THE TIME MACHINE'S RIGHT OVER THERE!
W...
WHAT ARE YOU SAYING?!

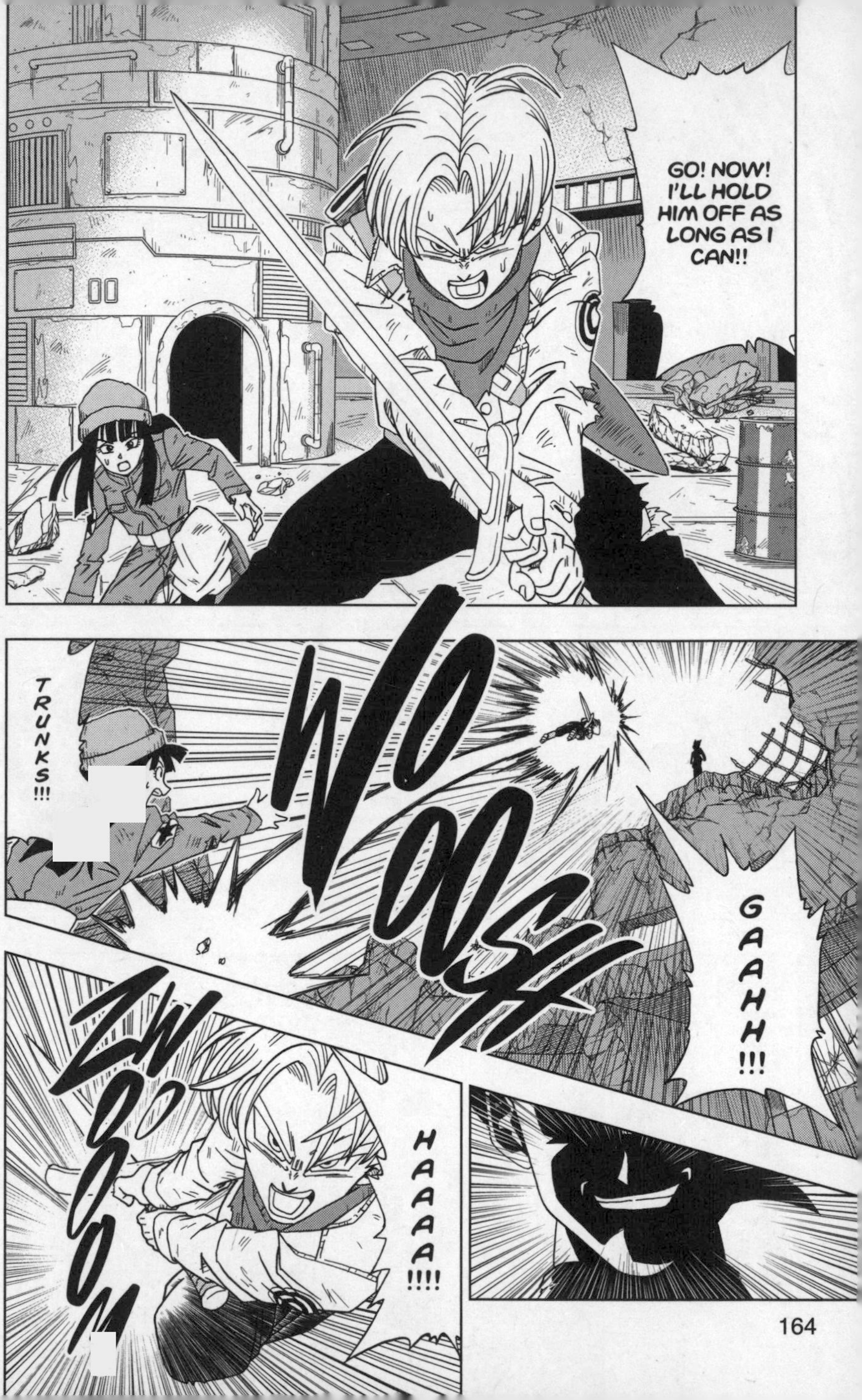
GO! NOW! I'LL HOLD HIM OFF AS LONG AS I CAN!!
GAAHH!!!
WOOSH
TRUNKS!!!
HAAAAA!!!!
ZWOOOOM

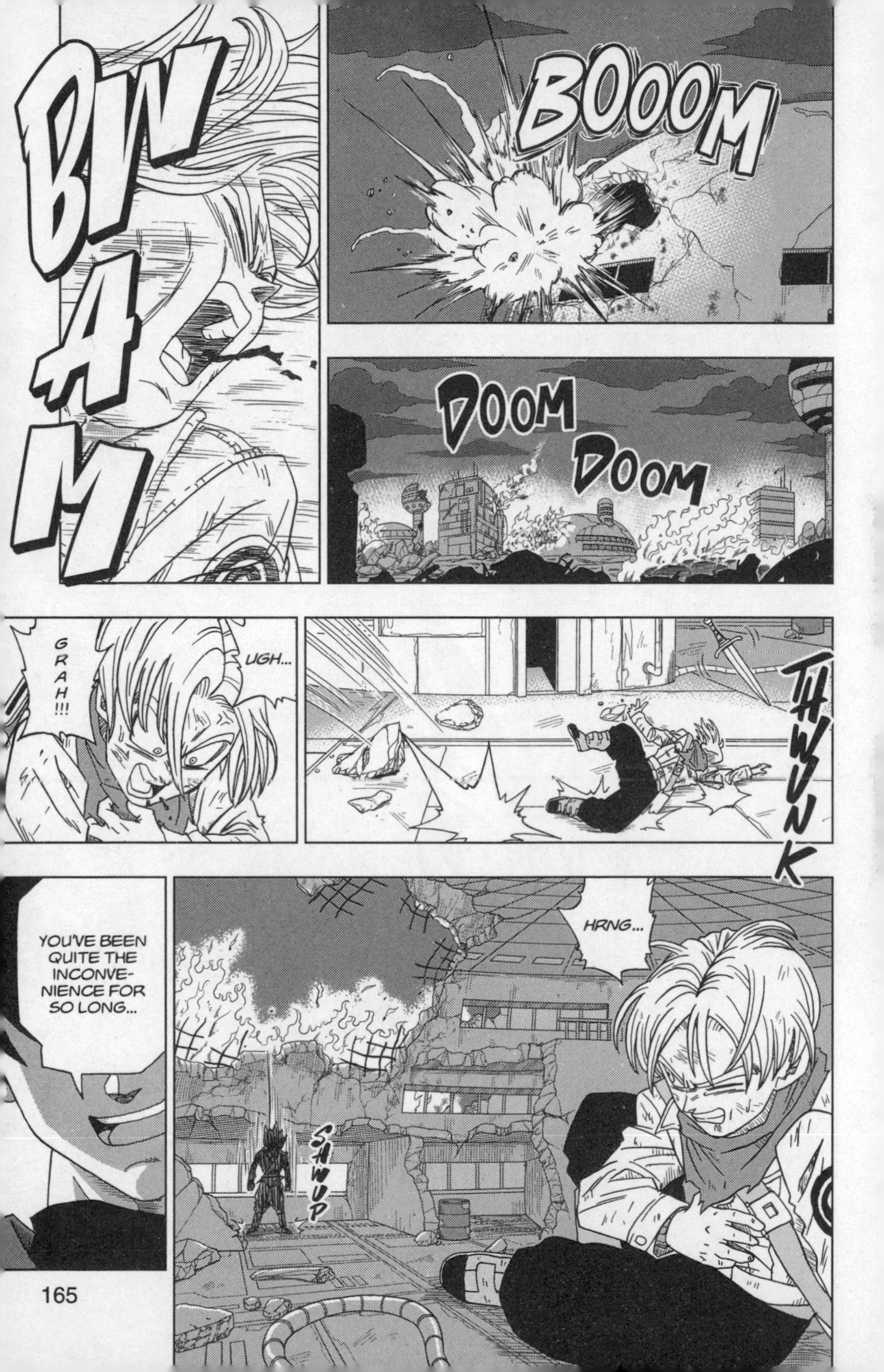
BOOOM
DOOM
DOOM
BAM
THWUNK
UGH...
GRAH!!!
HRNG...
SHWUP
YOU'VE BEEN QUITE THE INCONVE-NIENCE FOR SO LONG...

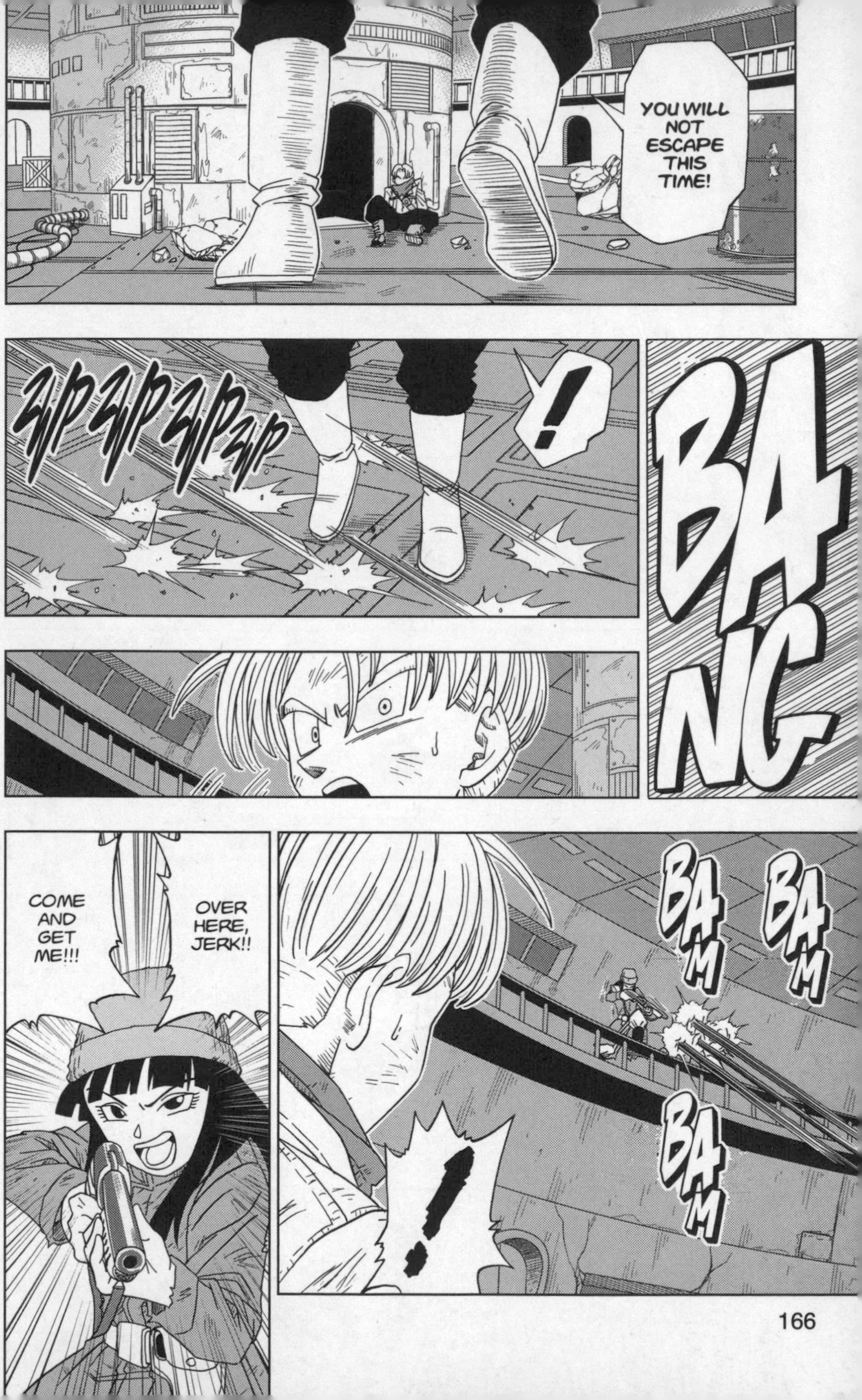
YOU WILL NOT ESCAPE THIS TIME!
BANG
!
ZIP ZIP ZIP ZIP
BAM
BAM
BAM
!
OVER HERE, JERK!!
COME AND GET ME!!!

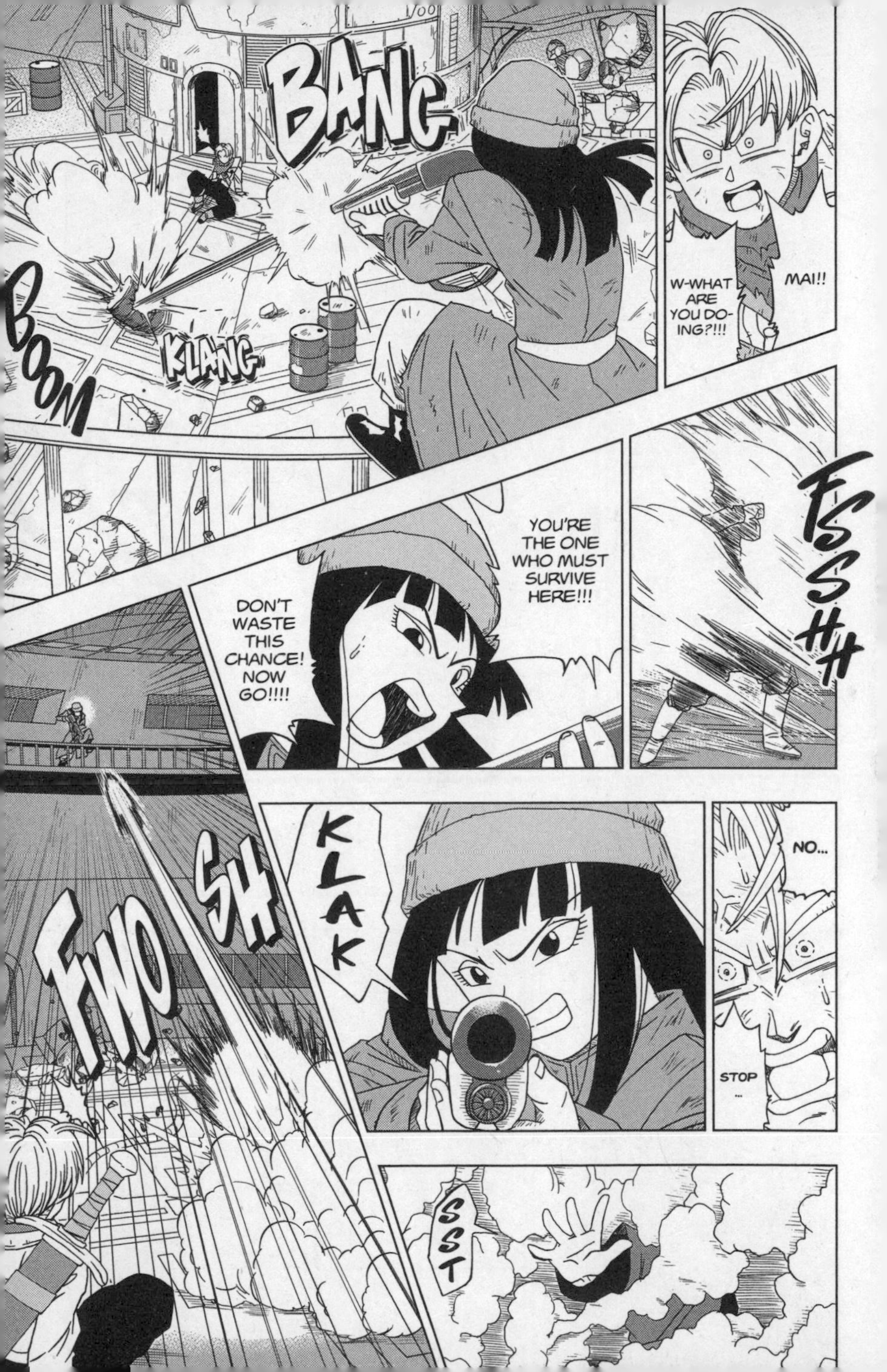
MAI!!
W-WHAT ARE YOU DOING?!!!
BANG
BOOM
KLANG
FSSHH
YOU'RE THE ONE WHO MUST SURVIVE HERE!!!
DON'T WASTE THIS CHANCE! NOW GO!!!!
NO...
STOP ...
KLAK
FWOSH
SST

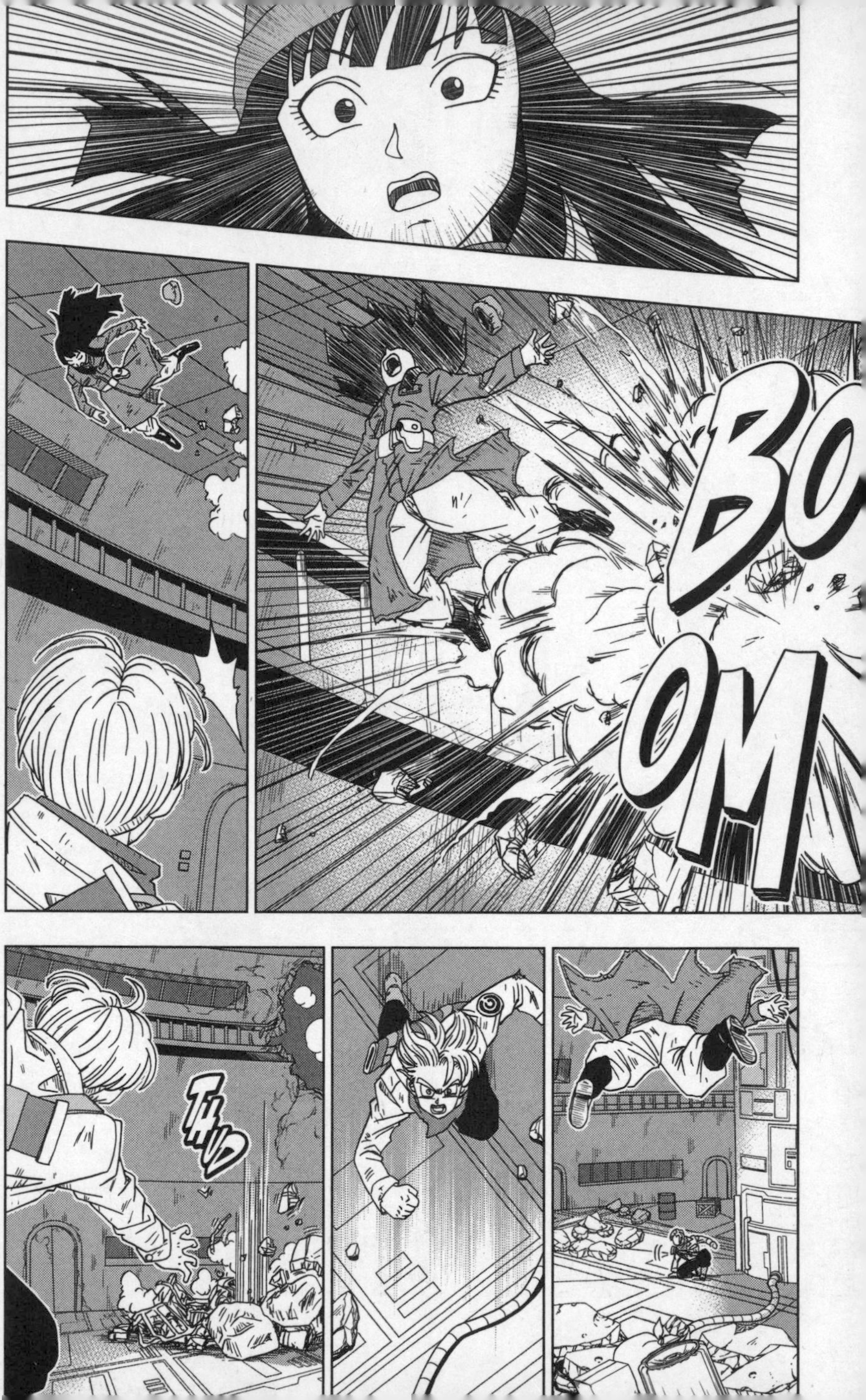
BOOM
THUD

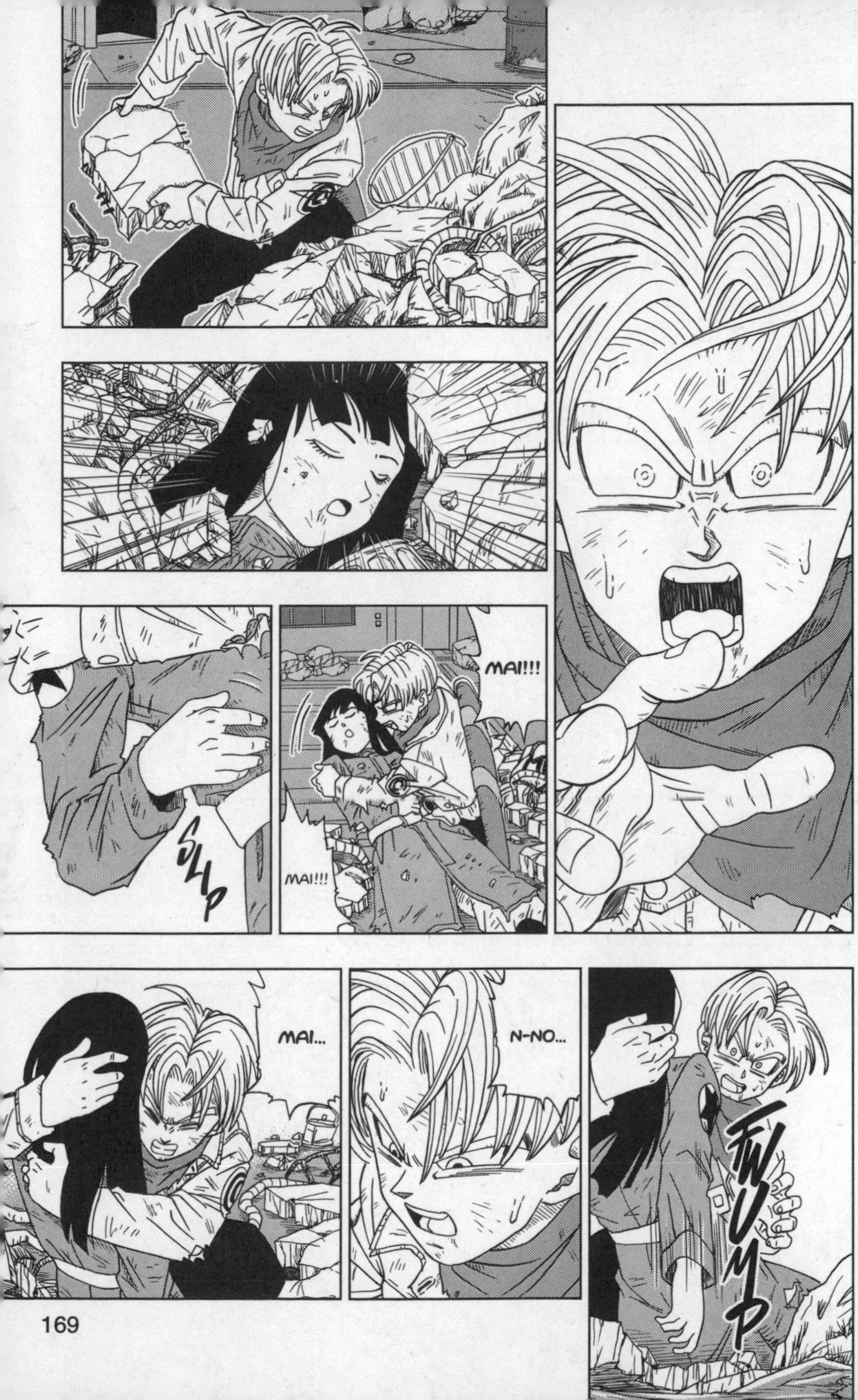
MAI!!!
MAI!!!
SLIP
FWUMP
N-NO...
MAI...

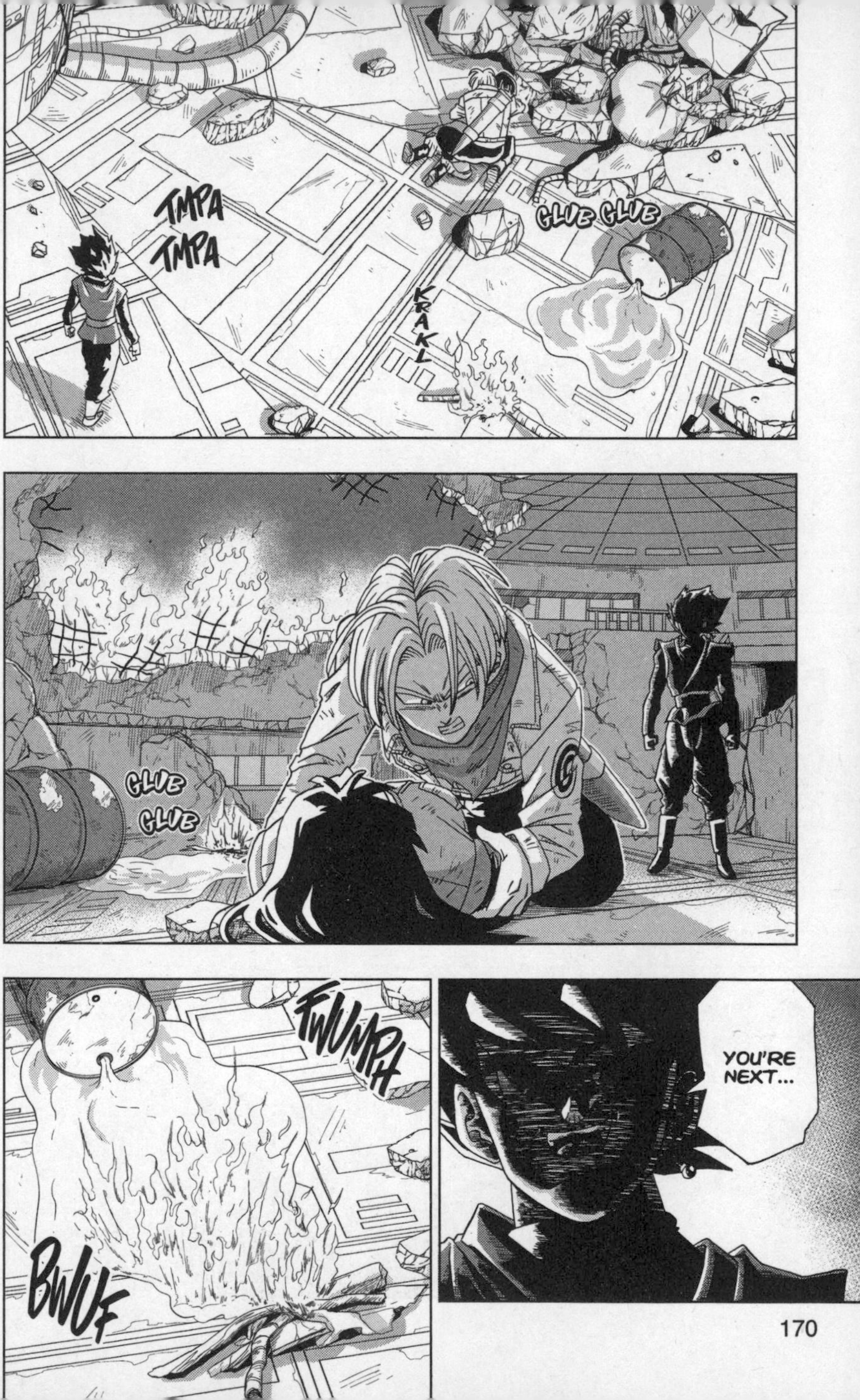
GLUB GLUB
TMPA TMPA
KRAKL
GLUB GLUB
YOU'RE NEXT...
FWUMPH
BWUF

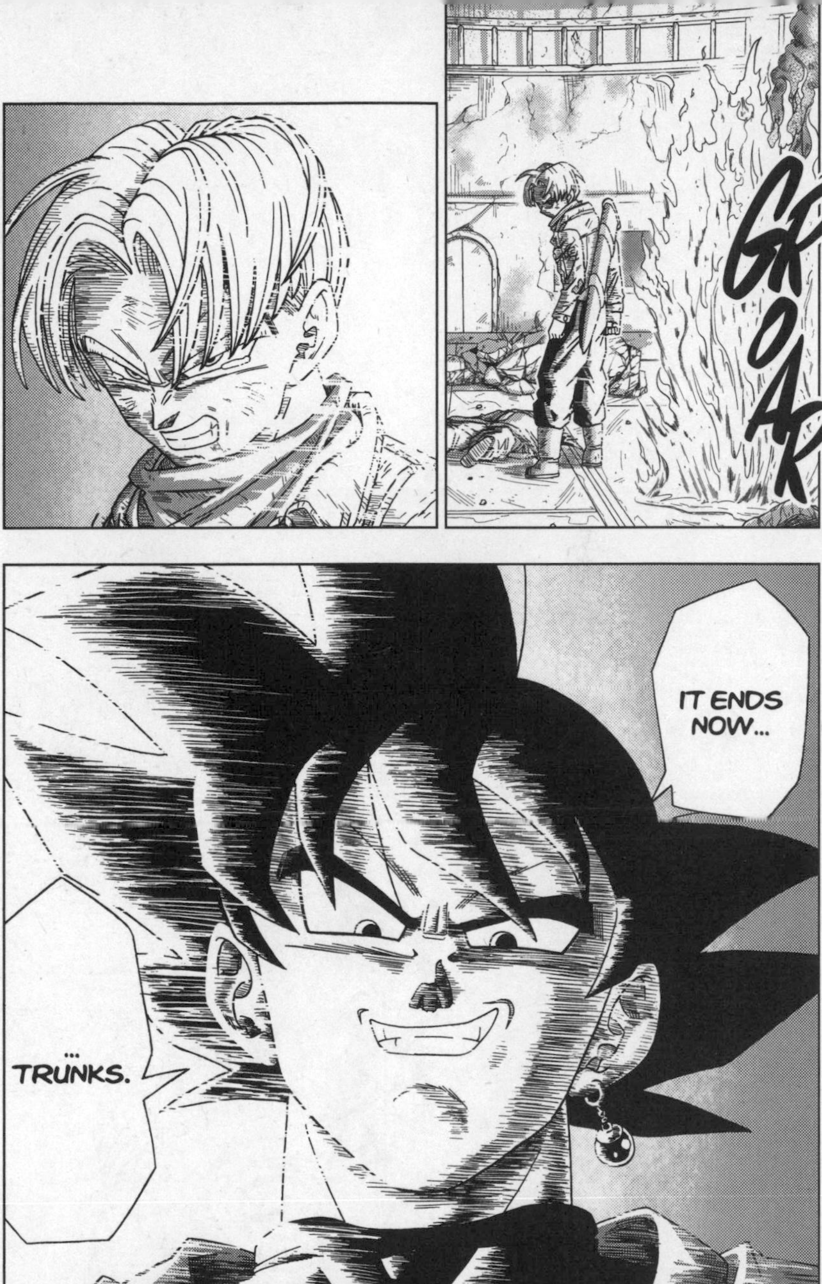
GROOAR
IT ENDS NOW...
... TRUNKS.

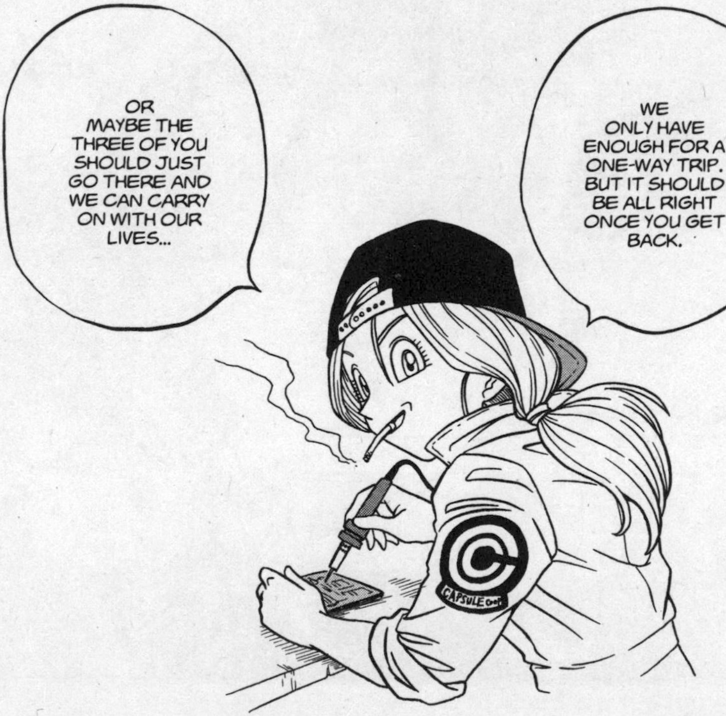
WE ONLY HAVE ENOUGH FOR A ONE-WAY TRIP. BUT IT SHOULD BE ALL RIGHT ONCE YOU GET BACK.
OR MAYBE THE THREE OF YOU SHOULD JUST GO THERE AND WE CAN CARRY ON WITH OUR LIVES...

DRAGON BALL SUPER

CHAPTER 15: HOPE!! ONCE AGAIN

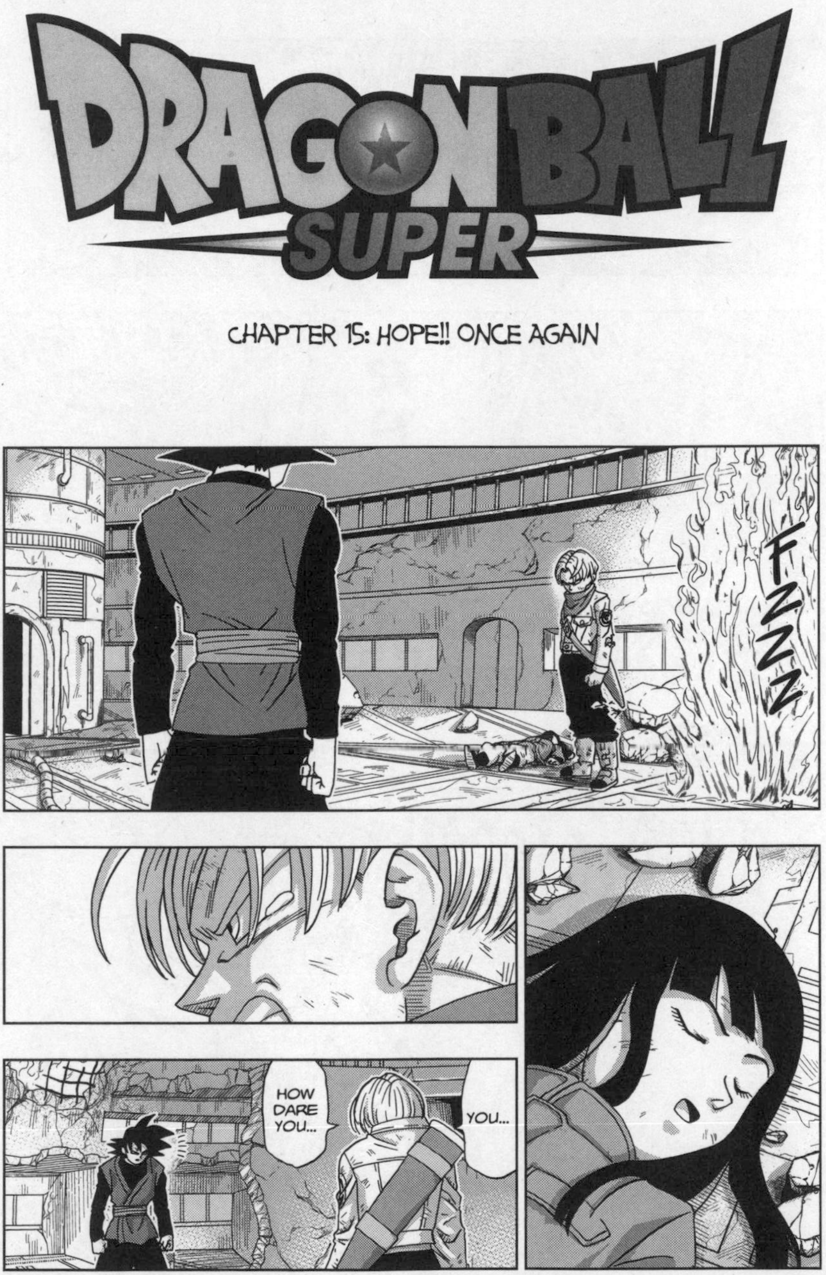
FZZZ
HOW DARE YOU...
YOU...

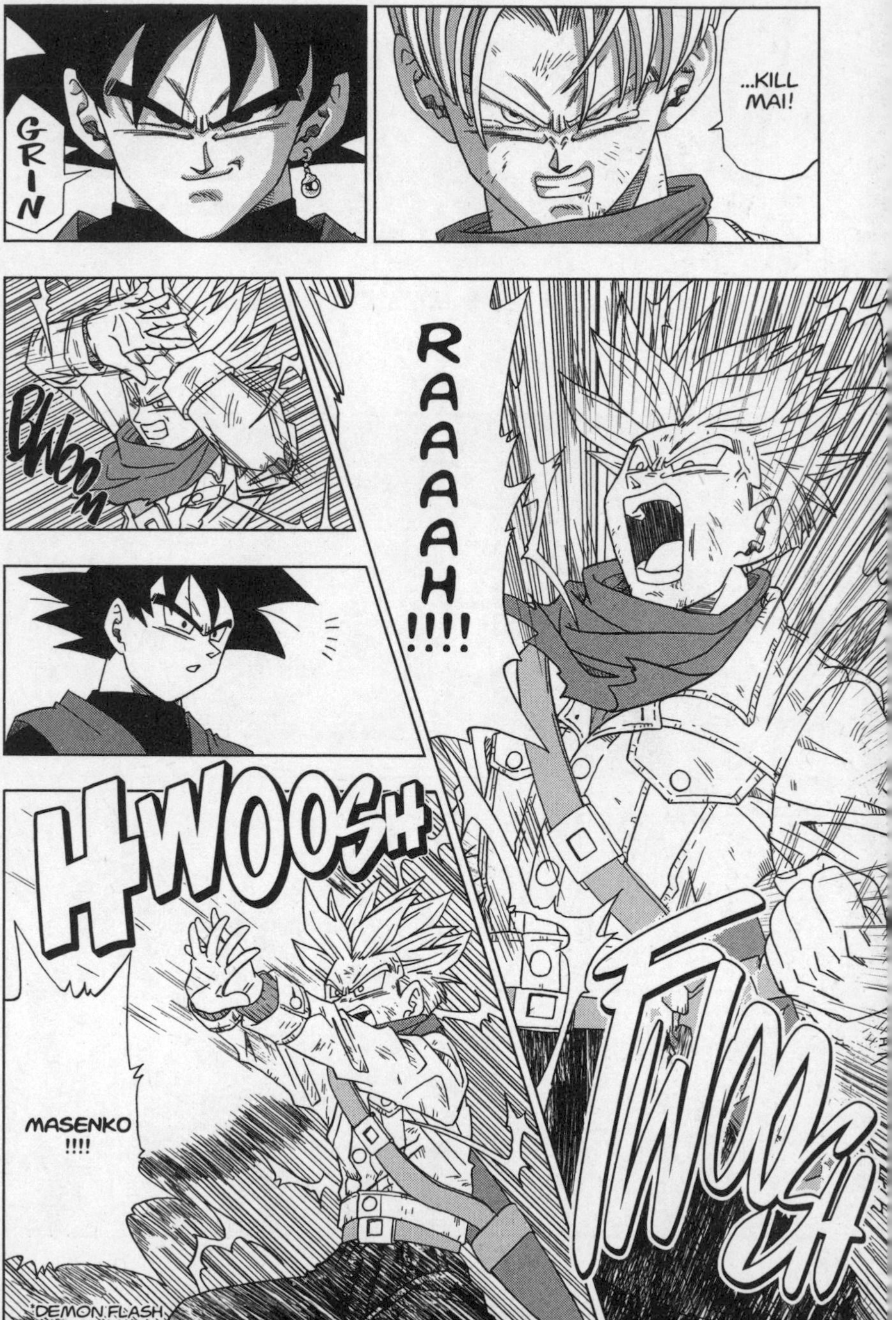
...KILL MAI!
GRIN
RAAAAAH!!!!
BWOOOM
HWOOSH
MASENKO!!!!
*DEMON FLASH

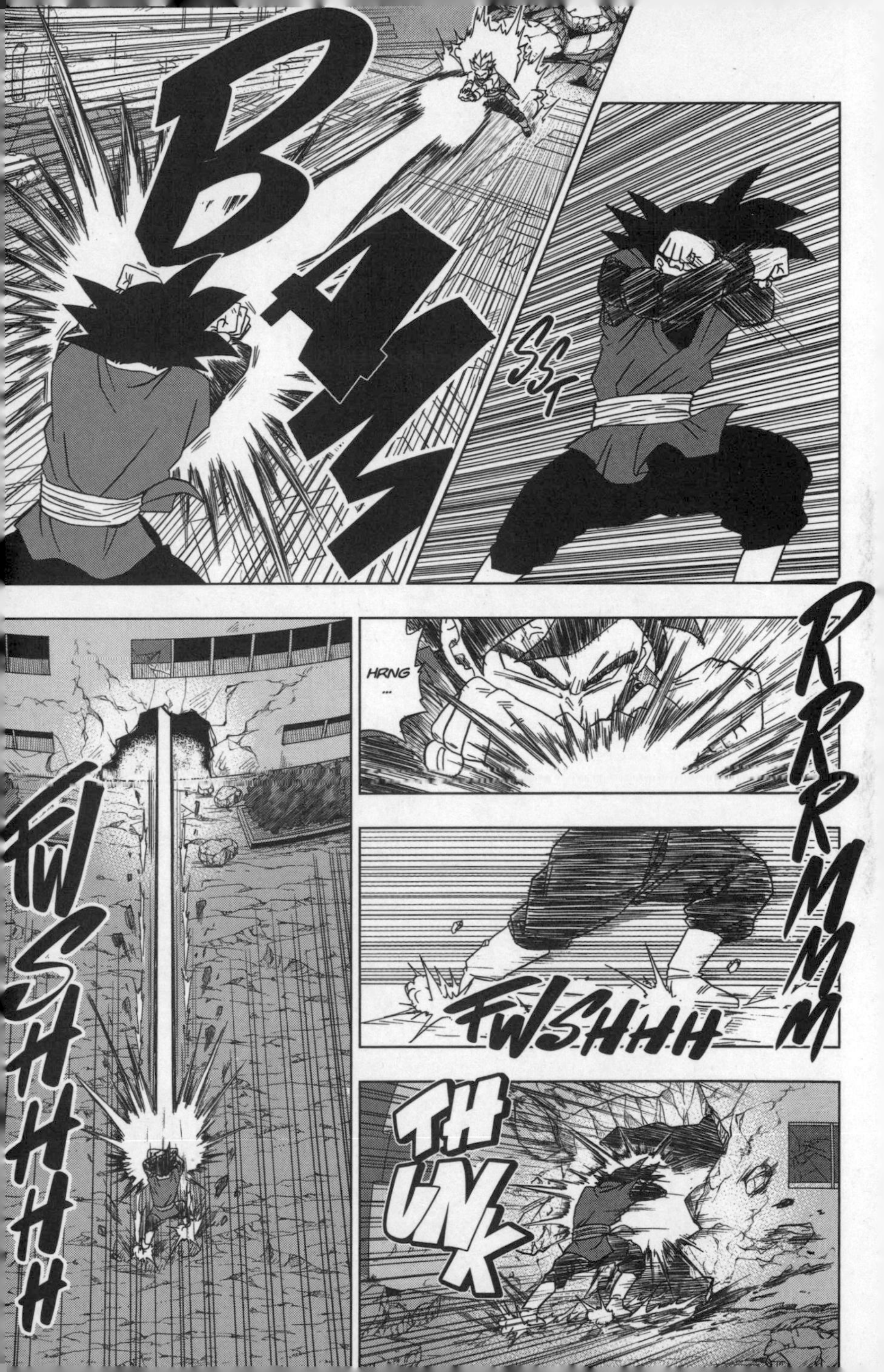
SST
BAM
HRNG...
RRRMMM
FWSHHH
THUNK
FWSHHHHH

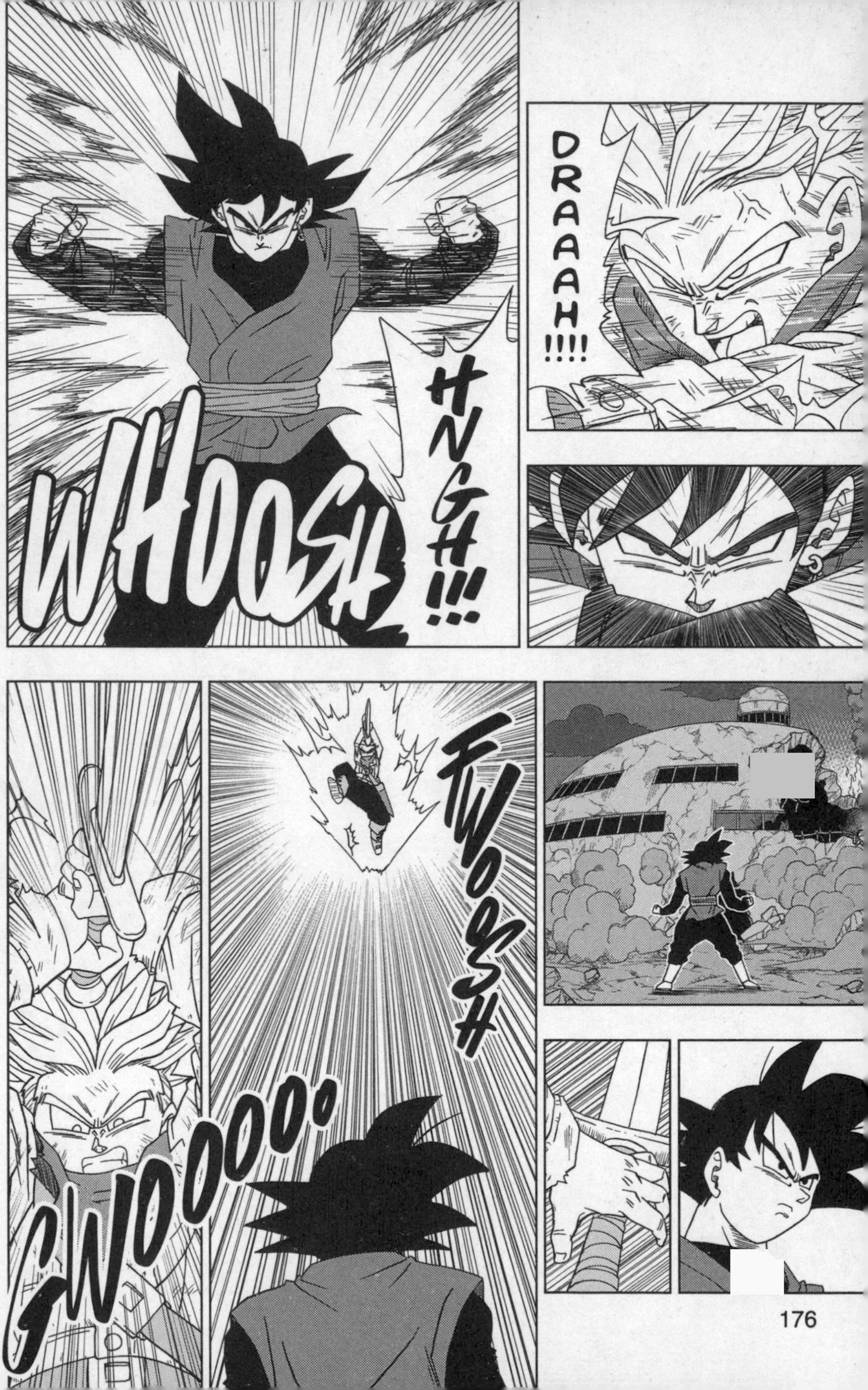
DRAAAAH!!!!
HNGH!!!
WHOOSH
FWOOSH
GWOOOOO

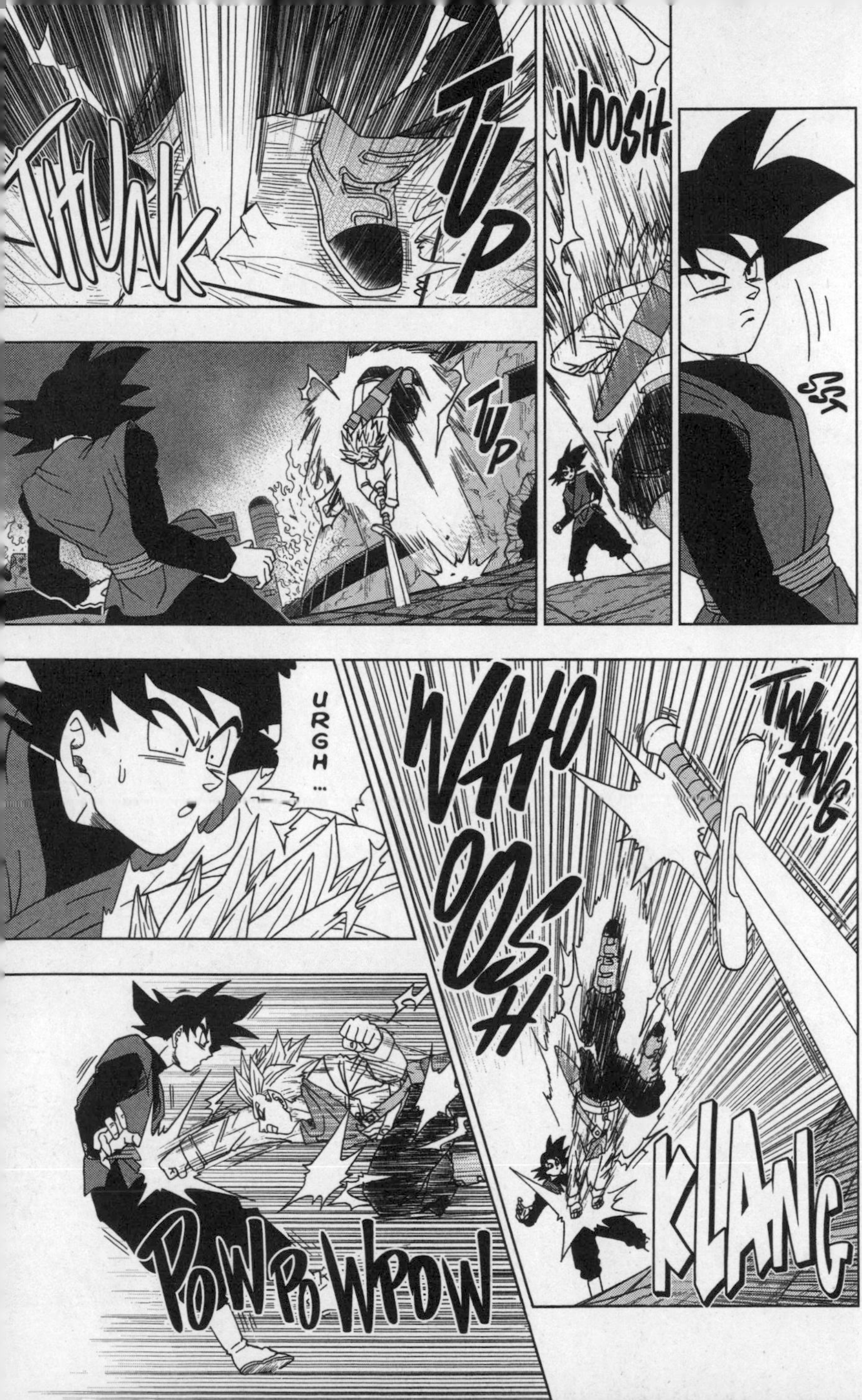

SSK
WOOSH
TUP
THUNK
TUP
TWANG
WHOOOSH
KLANG
URGH...
POW POW POW

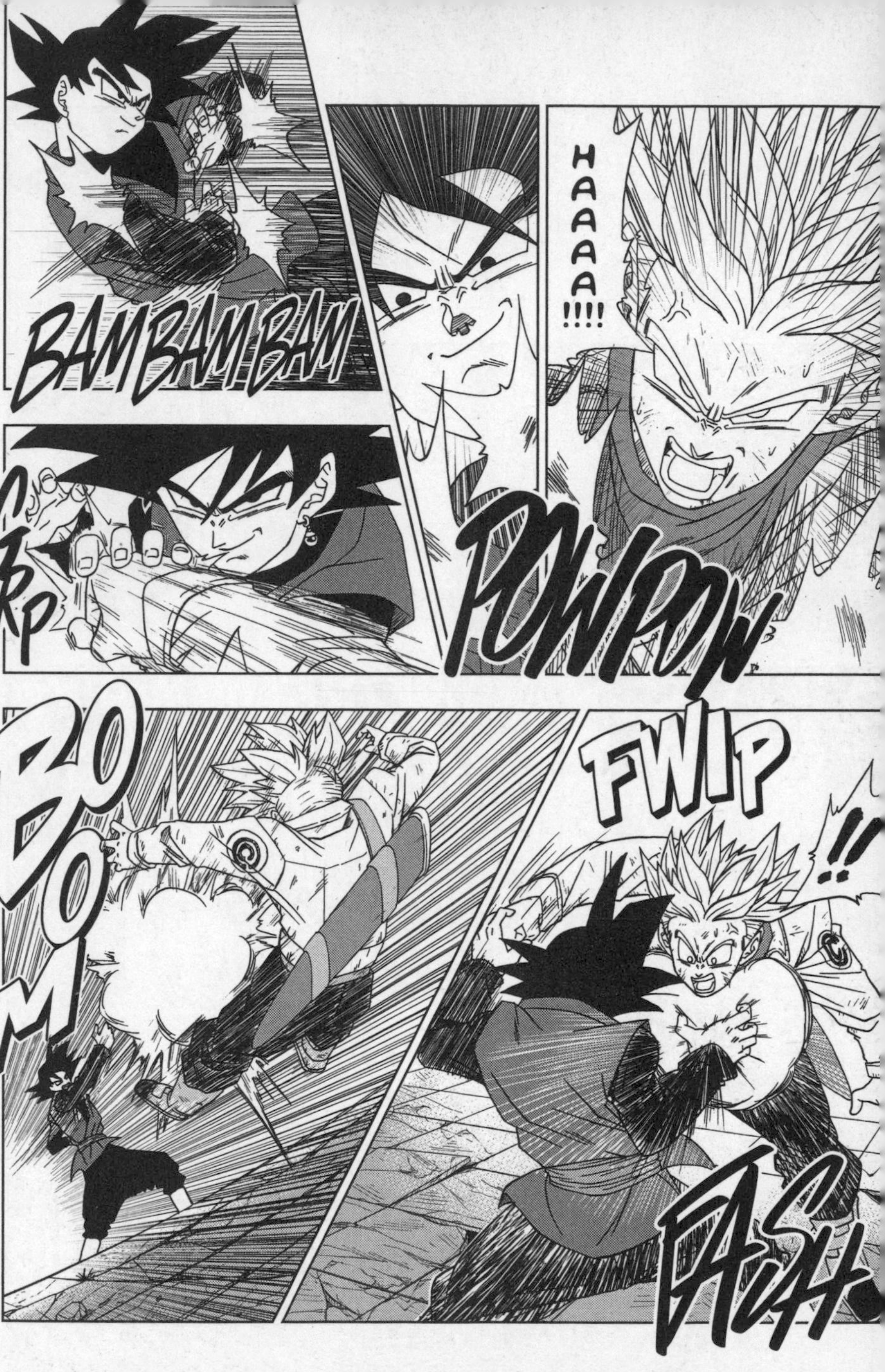
HAAAAA!!!!
BAM BAM BAM
POW POW
GRP
FWIP
!!
DASH
BOOM

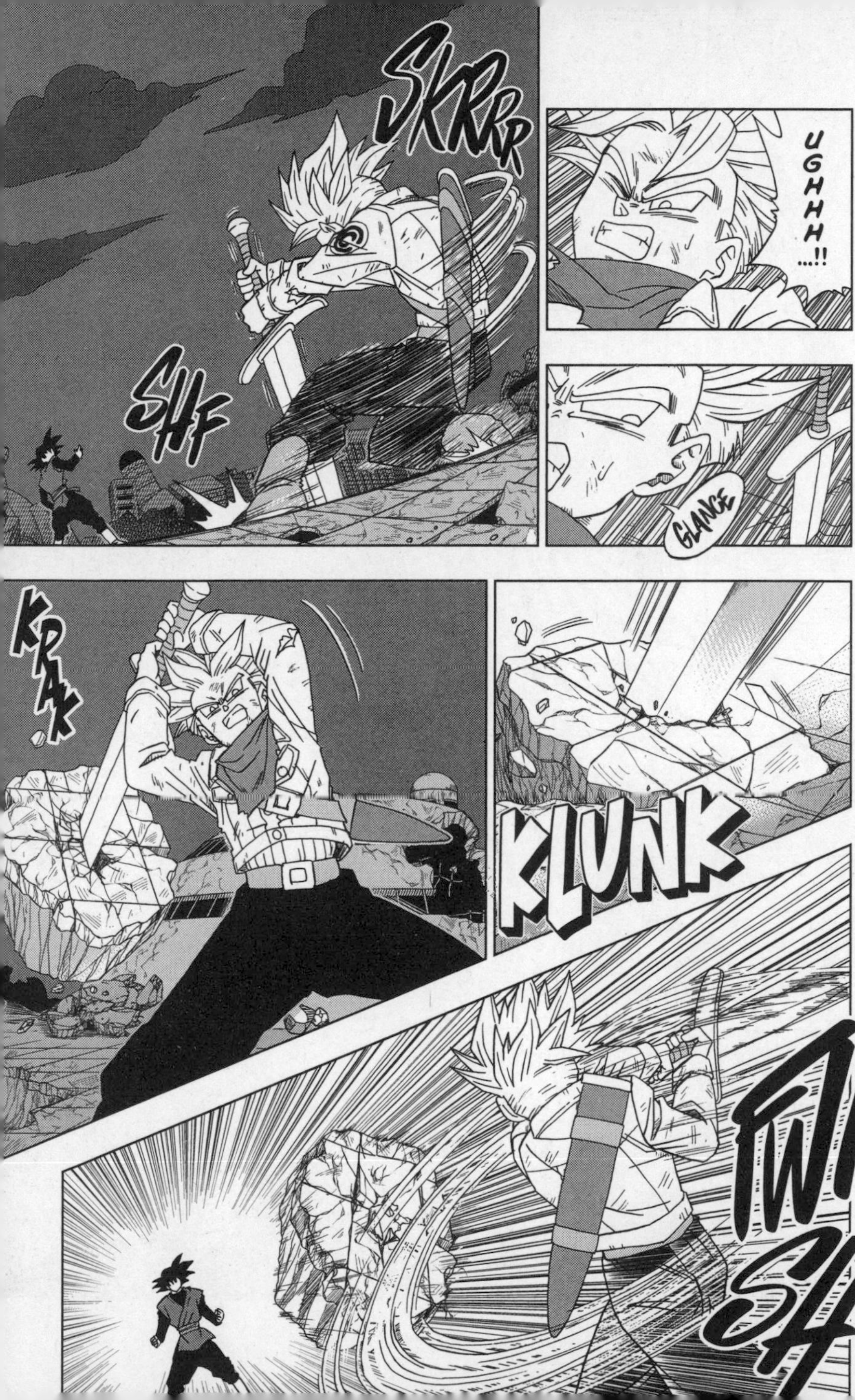
UGHHH...!!
GLANCE
SKRRRR
SHF
KLUNK
KRAK
FWISH

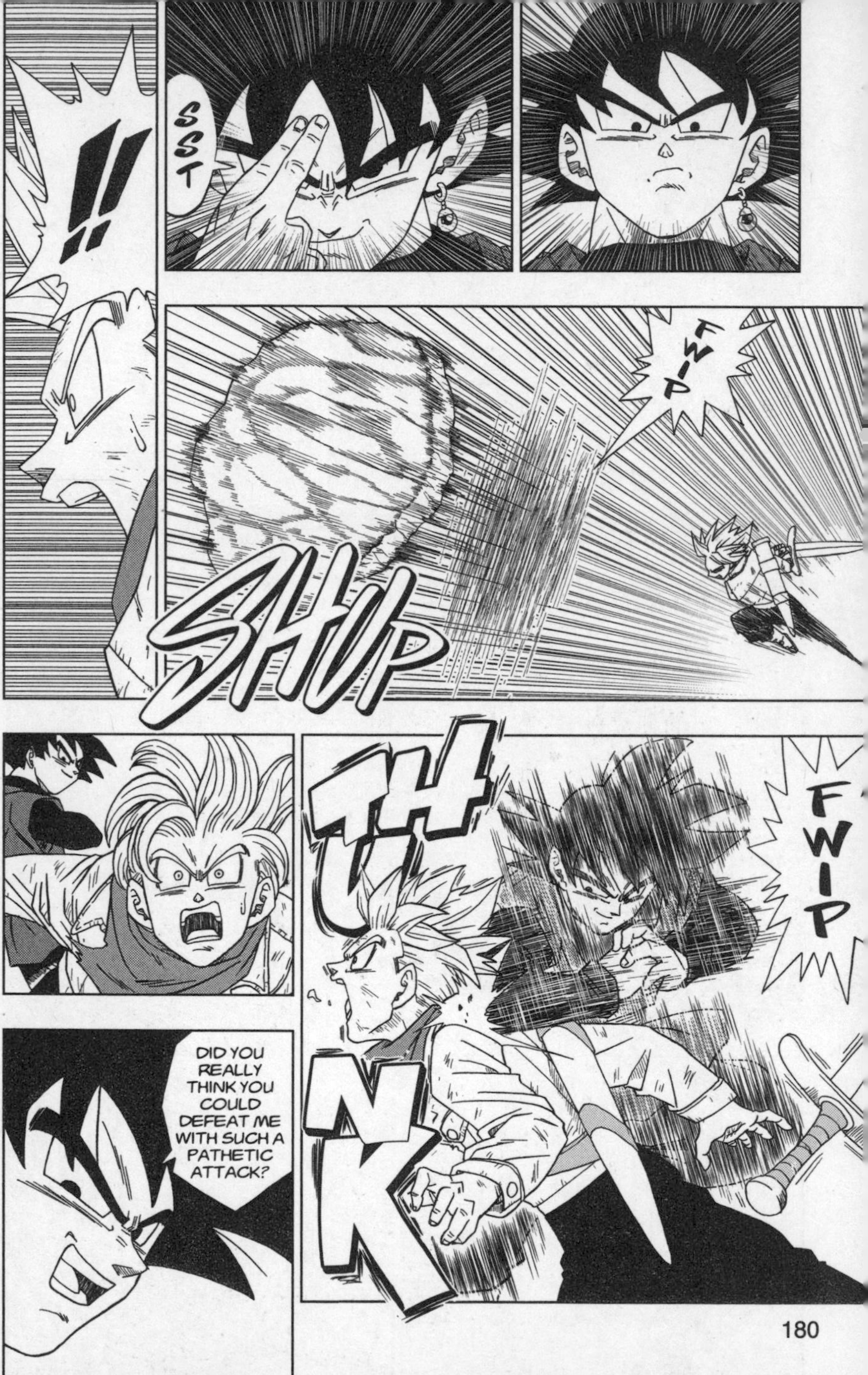
SSST
FWIP
SHUP
!!
FWIP
THUNK
DID YOU REALLY THINK YOU COULD DEFEAT ME WITH SUCH A PATHETIC ATTACK?

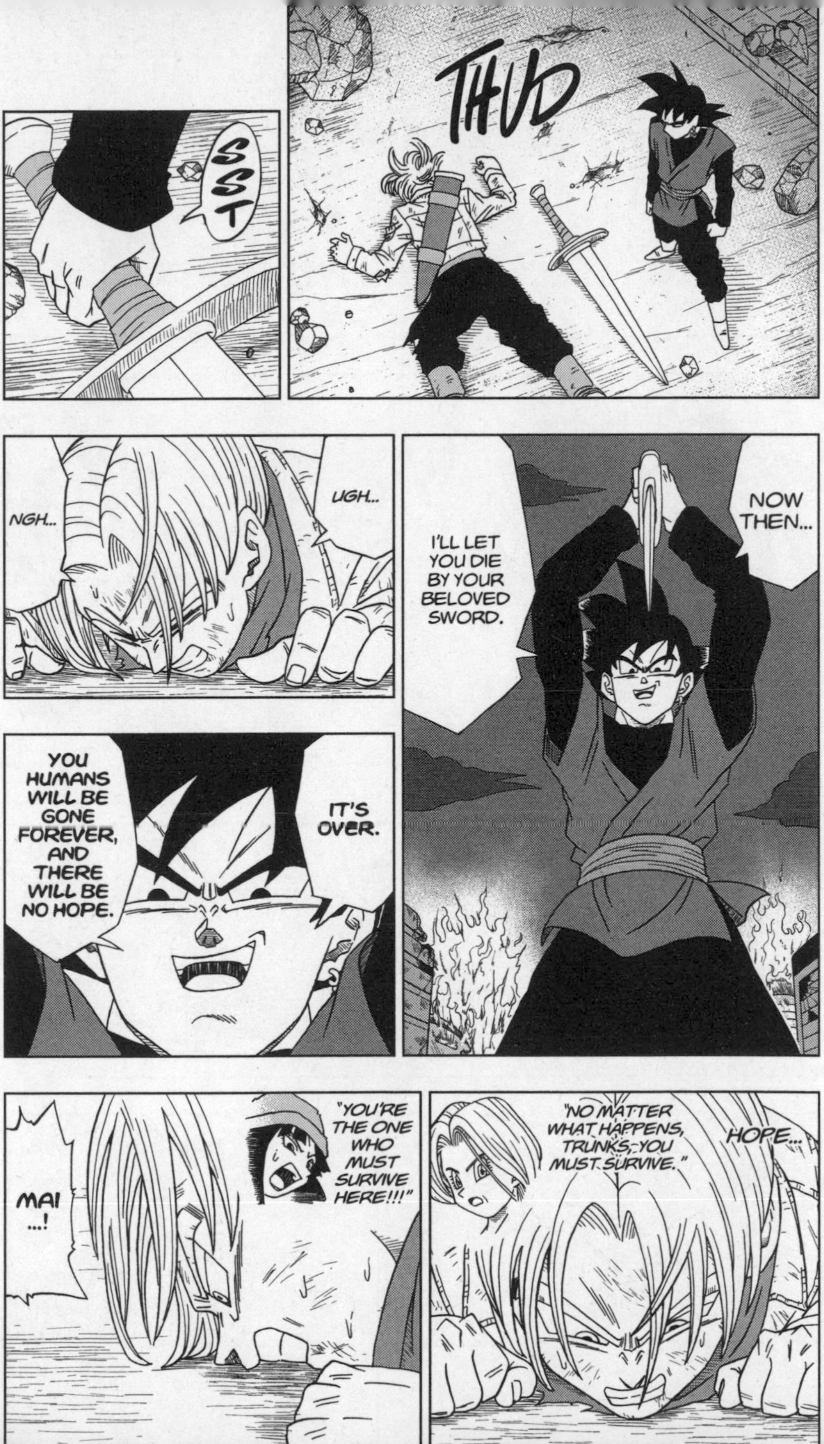
THUD
SST
NOW THEN...
I'LL LET YOU DIE BY YOUR BELOVED SWORD.
UGH...
NGH...
IT'S OVER.
YOU HUMANS WILL BE GONE FOREVER, AND THERE WILL BE NO HOPE.
HOPE...
"NO MATTER WHAT HAPPENS, TRUNKS, YOU MUST SURVIVE."
"YOU'RE THE ONE WHO MUST SURVIVE HERE!!!"
MAI ...!

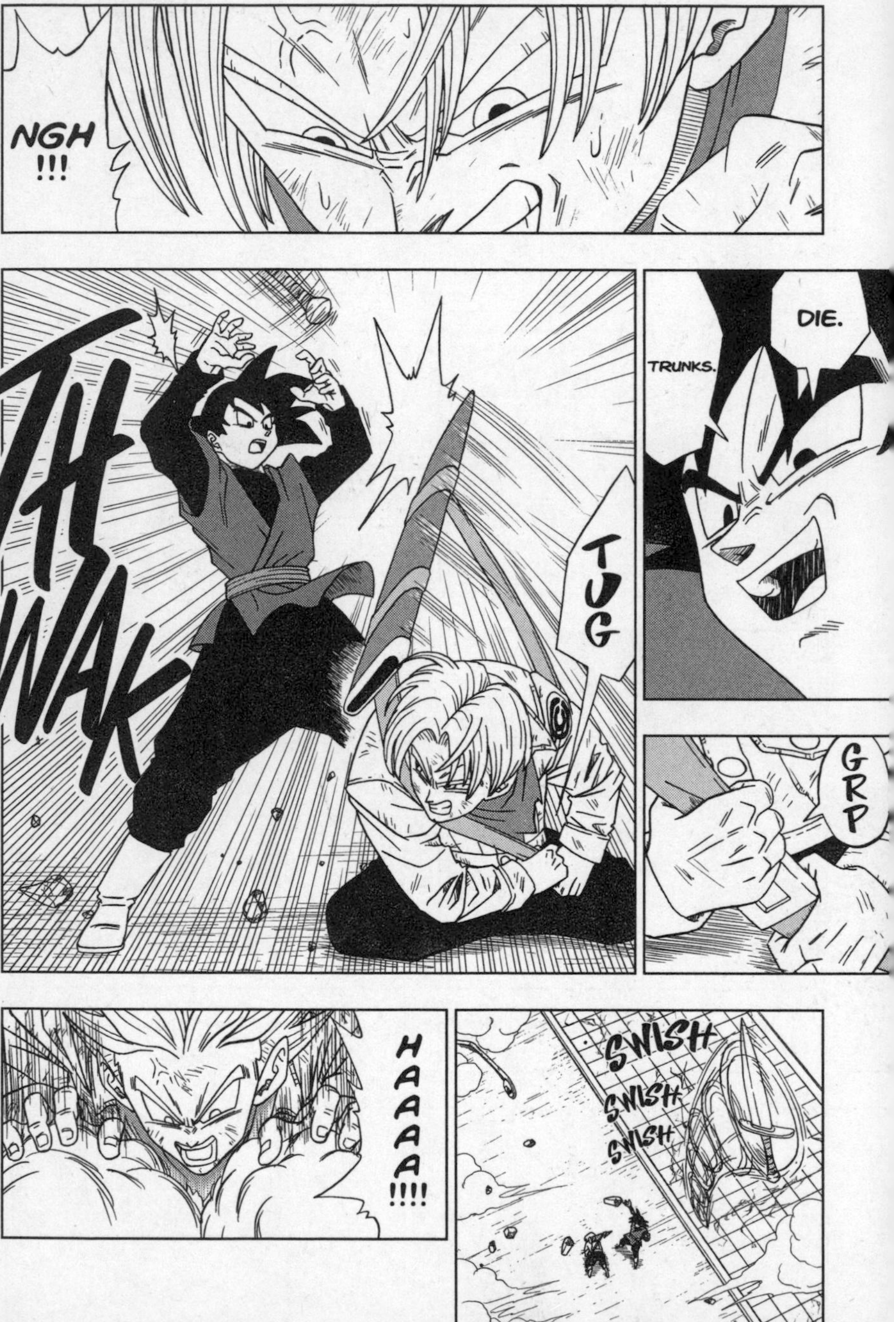
NGH!!!
DIE.
TRUNKS.
GRP
TUG
THWAK
SWISH
SWISH
SWISH
HAAAAA!!!!

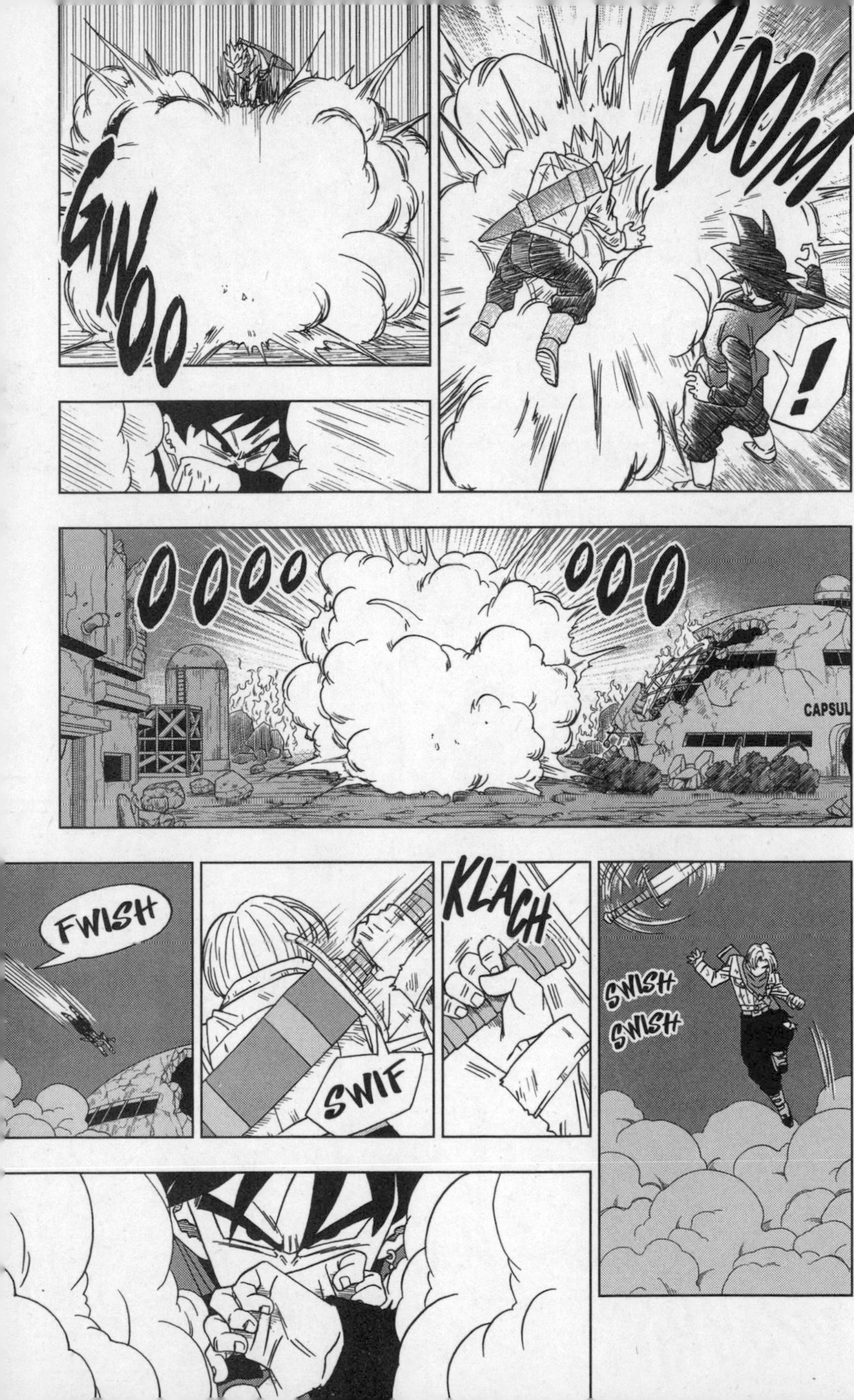
BOOM
!
GWOOO
OOOO OOO
CAPSUL
SWISH SWISH
KLACH
SWIF
FWISH

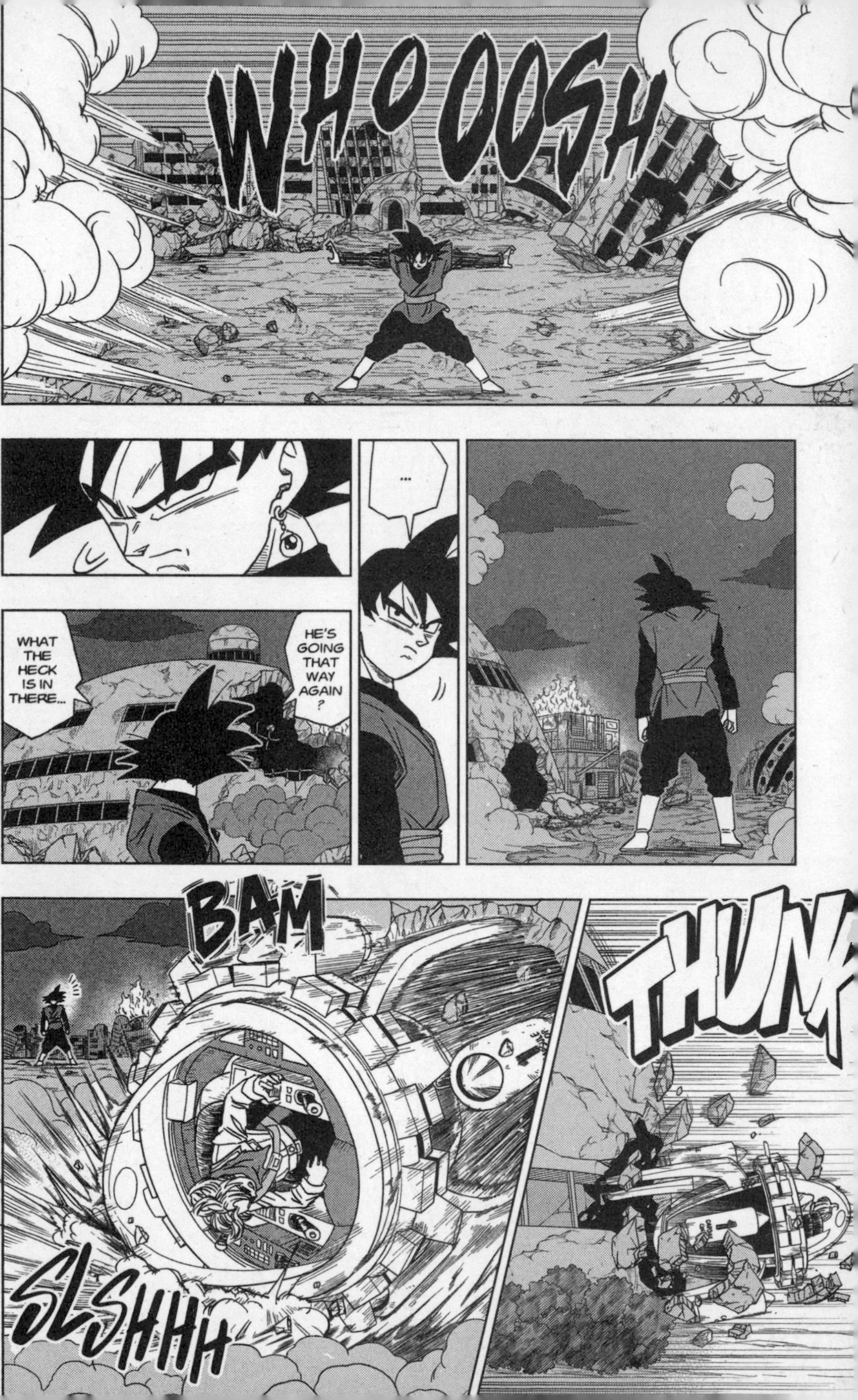
WHOOOSH
...
HE'S GOING THAT WAY AGAIN?
WHAT THE HECK IS IN THERE...
THUNK
BAM
SLSHHH

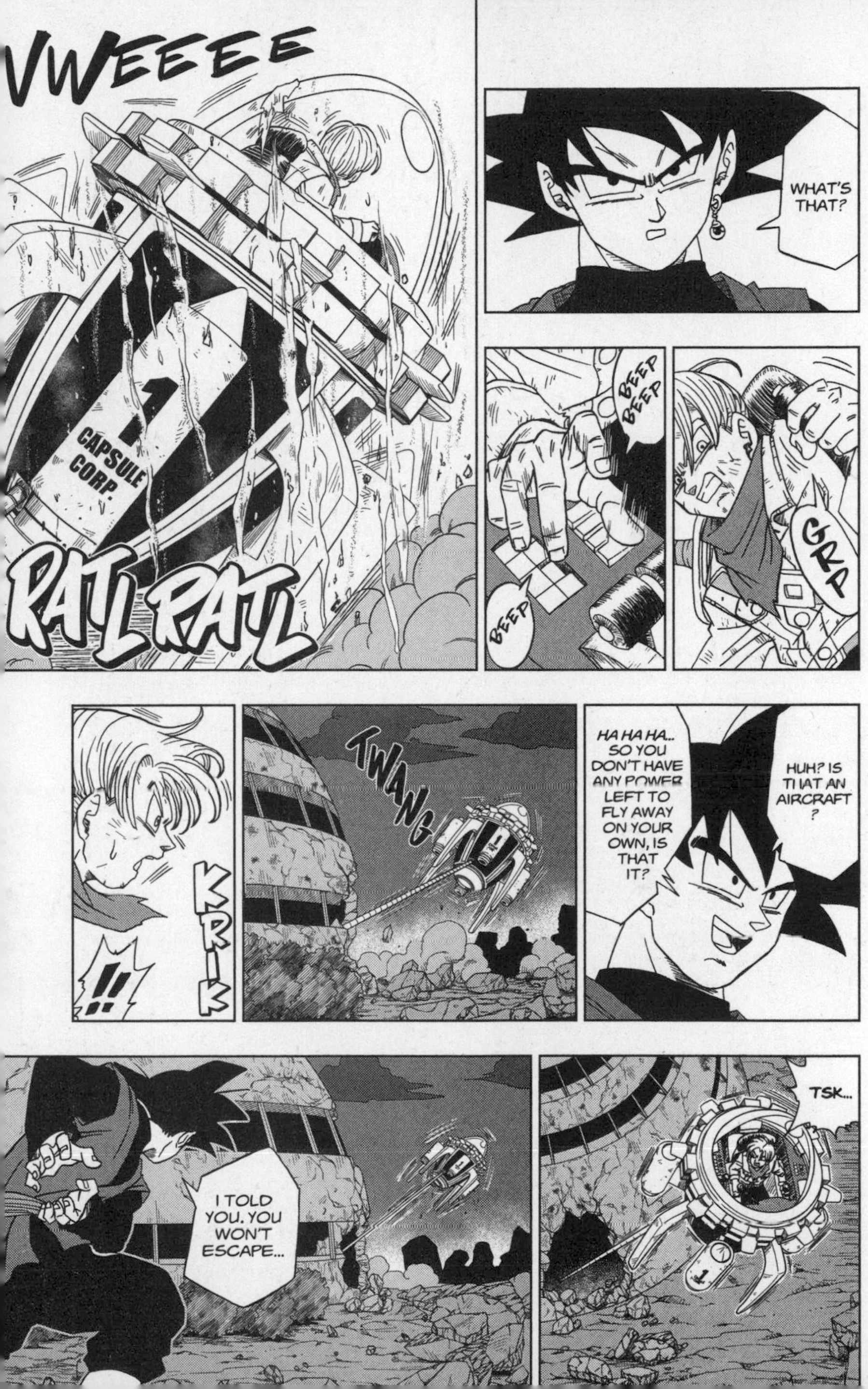
WHAT'S THAT?
GRP
BEEP BEEP
BEEP
VWEEEE
1
CAPSULE CORP.
RATL RATL
HUH? IS THAT AN AIRCRAFT?
HA HA HA... SO YOU DON'T HAVE ANY POWER LEFT TO FLY AWAY ON YOUR OWN, IS THAT IT?
TWANG
KRIK
!!
TSK...
I TOLD YOU. YOU WON'T ESCAPE...

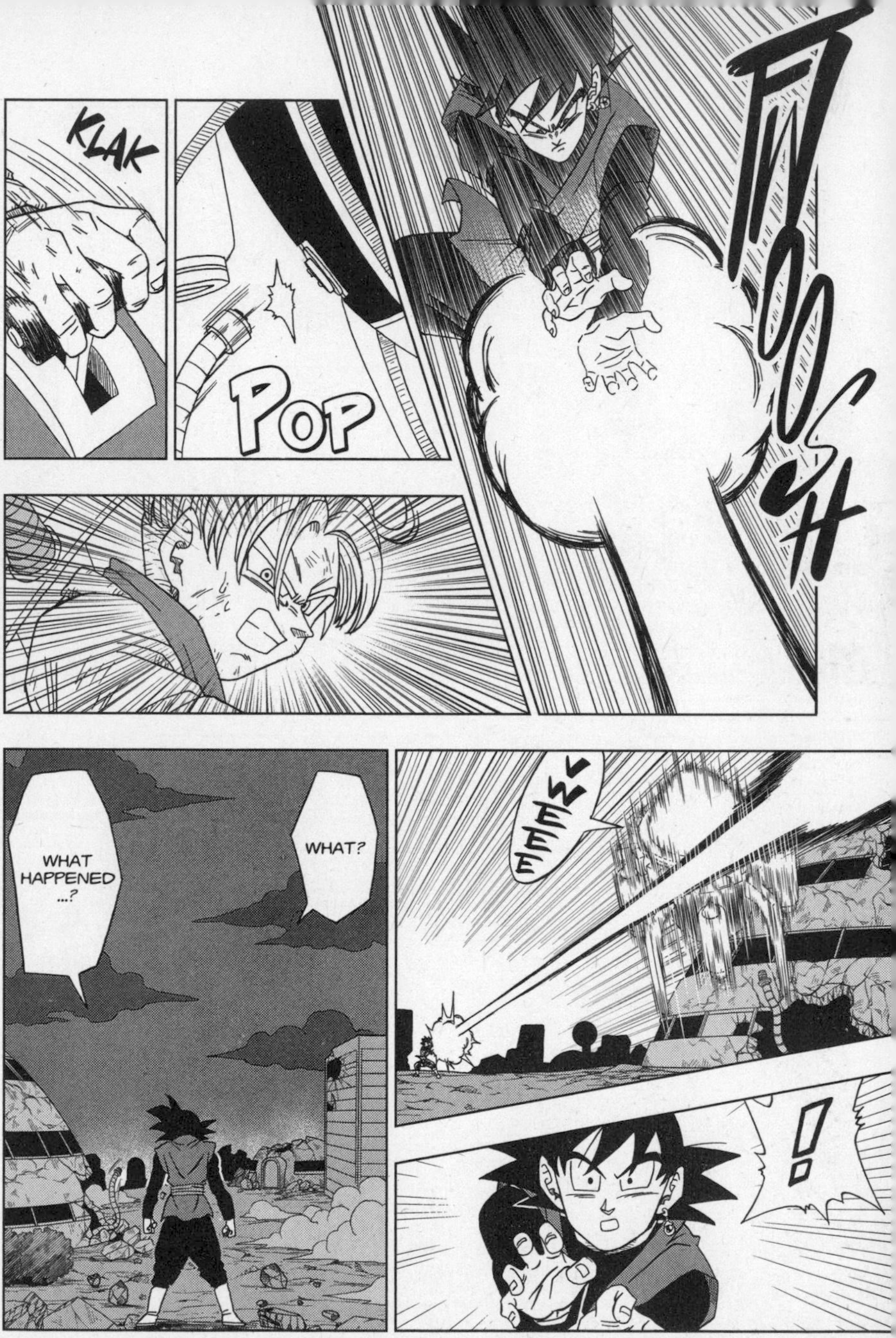
FWOOSH
POP
KLAK
WEEE
!
WHAT?
WHAT HAPPENED ...?

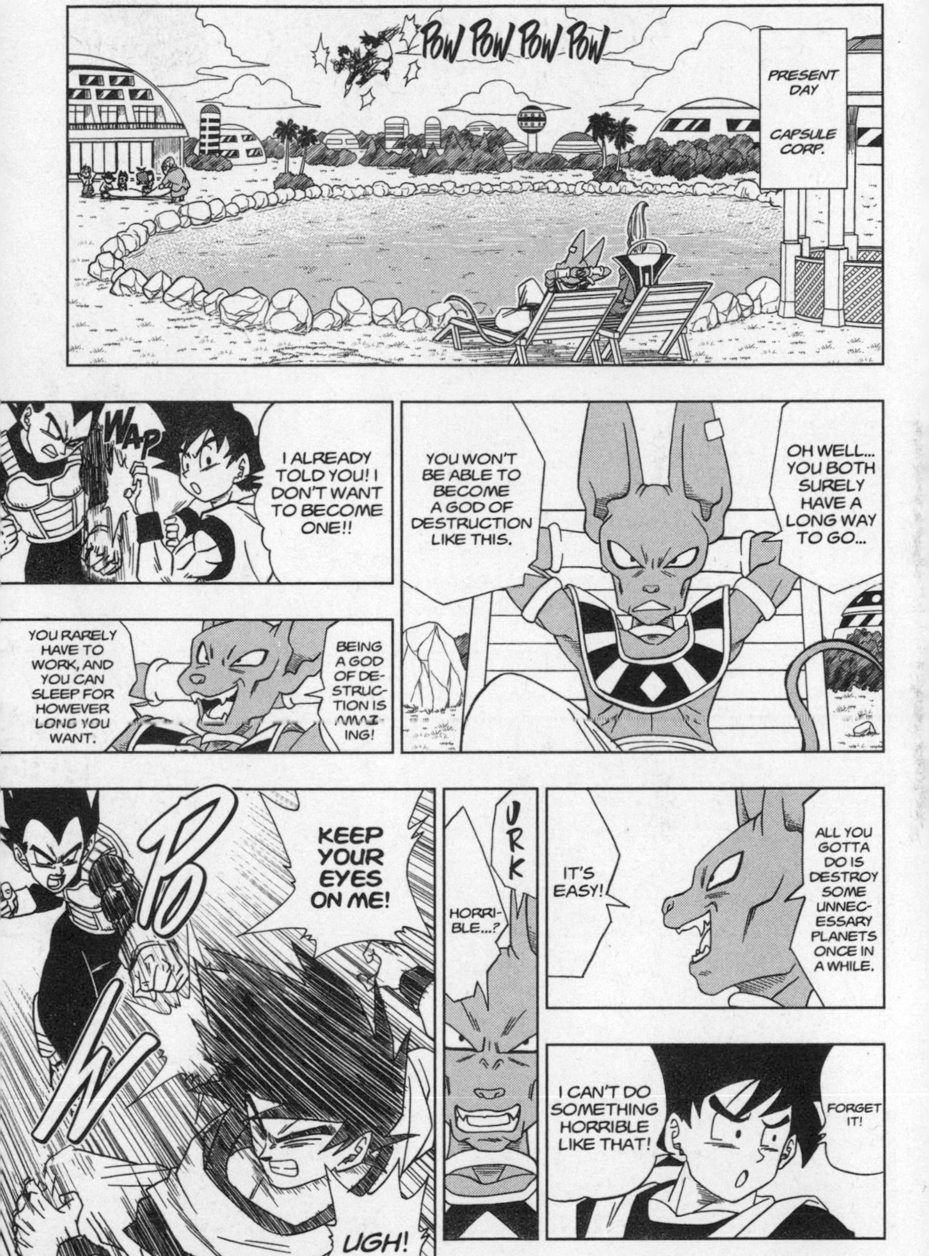
PRESENT DAY
CAPSULE CORP.
POW POW POW POW
OH WELL... YOU BOTH SURELY HAVE A LONG WAY TO GO...
YOU WON'T BE ABLE TO BECOME A GOD OF DESTRUCTION LIKE THIS.
I ALREADY TOLD YOU! I DON'T WANT TO BECOME ONE!!
WAP
BEING A GOD OF DESTRUCTION IS AMAZING!
YOU RARELY HAVE TO WORK, AND YOU CAN SLEEP FOR HOWEVER LONG YOU WANT.
ALL YOU GOTTA DO IS DESTROY SOME UNNECESSARY PLANETS ONCE IN A WHILE.
IT'S EASY!
FORGET IT!
I CAN'T DO SOMETHING HORRIBLE LIKE THAT!
URK
HORRIBLE...?
KEEP YOUR EYES ON ME!
POW
UGH!

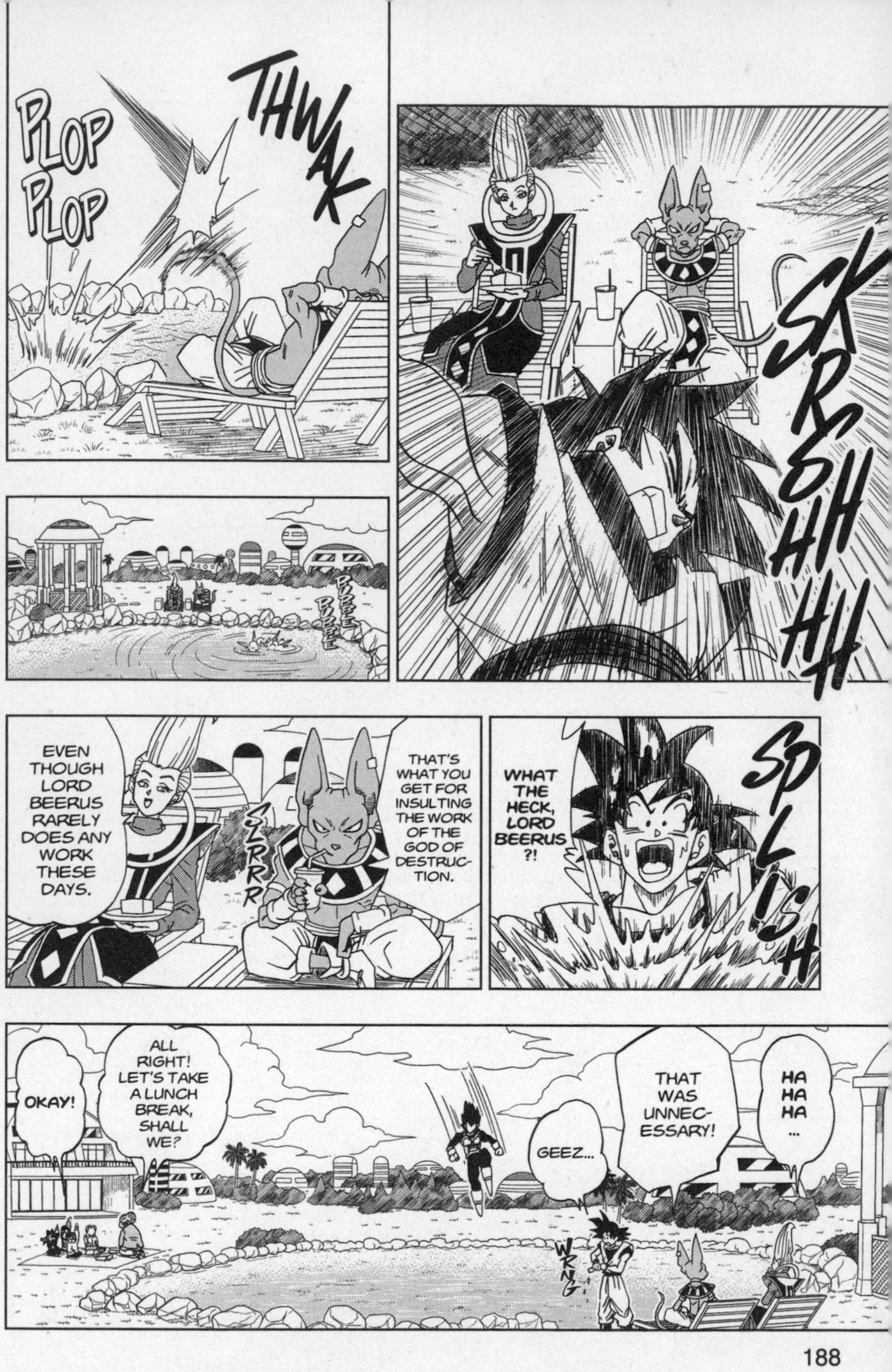
SKRSHHHHH
THWAK
PLOP PLOP
BUBBLE BUBBLE
SPLISH
WHAT THE HECK, LORD BEERUS?!
THAT'S WHAT YOU GET FOR INSULTING THE WORK OF THE GOD OF DESTRUCTION.
SLRRR
EVEN THOUGH LORD BEERUS RARELY DOES ANY WORK THESE DAYS.
HA HA HA...
THAT WAS UNNECESSARY!
GEEZ...
WRNG
ALL RIGHT! LET'S TAKE A LUNCH BREAK, SHALL WE?
OKAY!

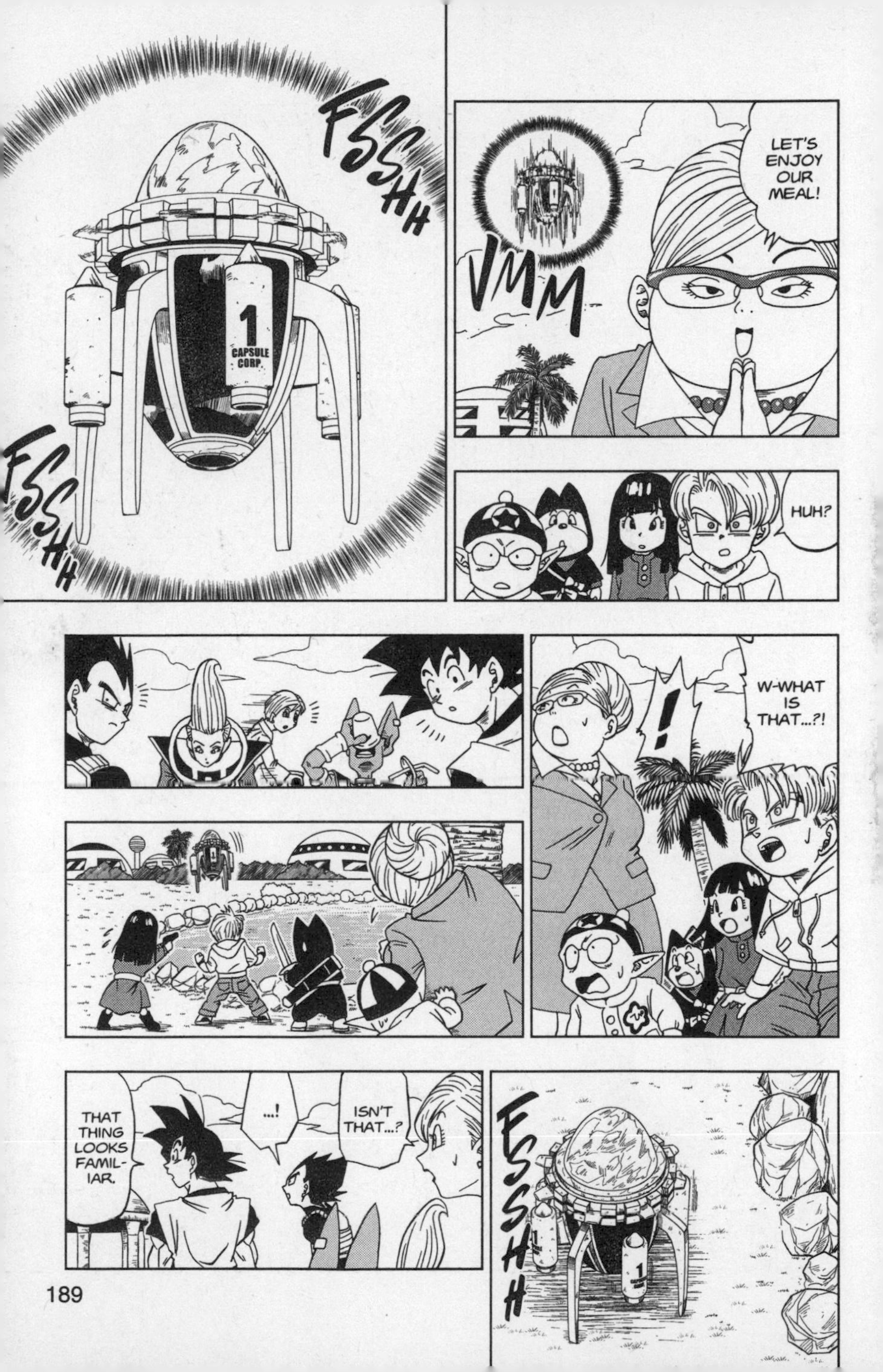
LET'S ENJOY OUR MEAL!
VMM
HUH?
FSSHH
FSSHH
W-WHAT IS THAT...?!
!
FSSHH
ISN'T THAT...?
...!
THAT THING LOOKS FAMIL-IAR.
CAPSULE CORP

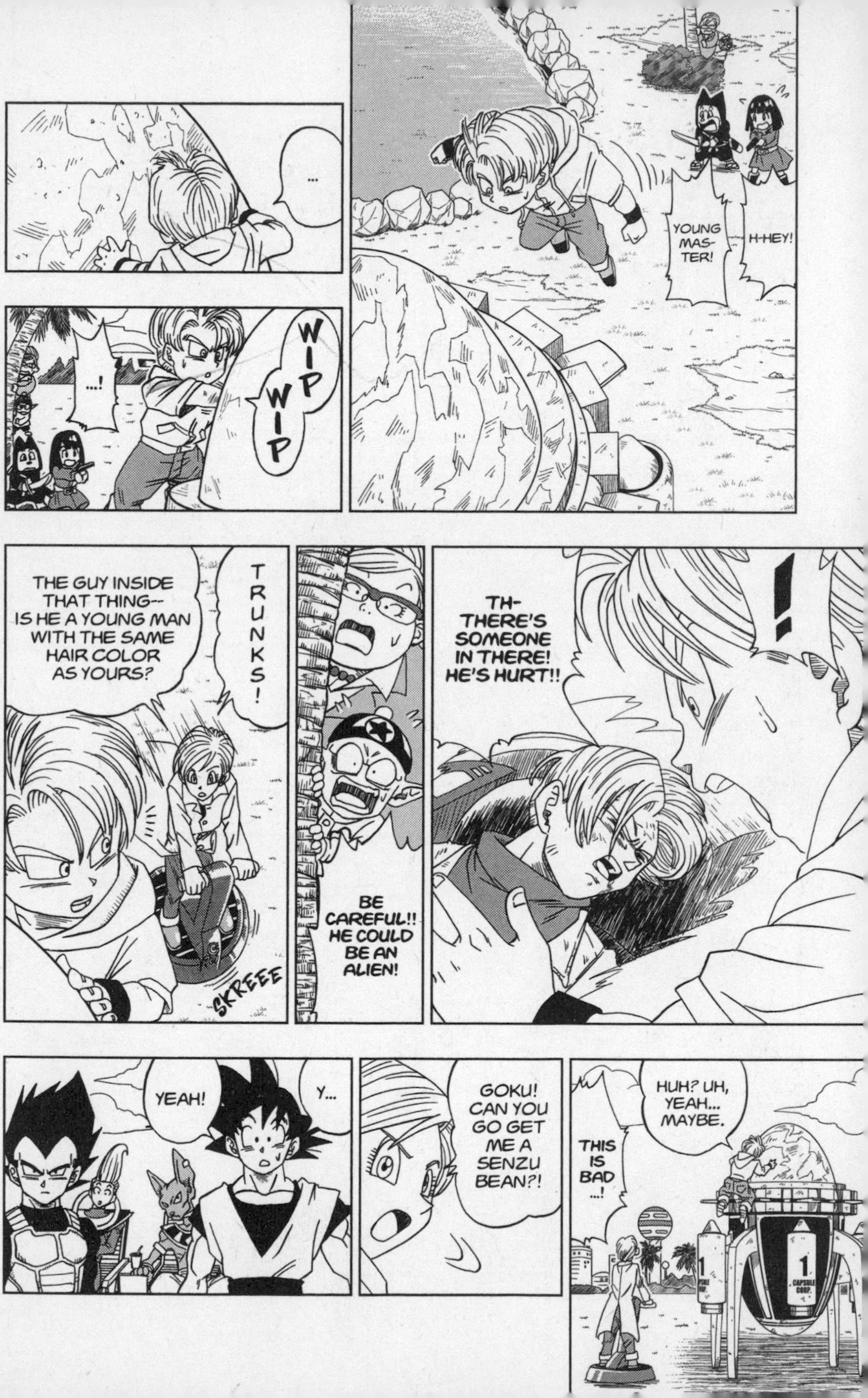
H-HEY!
YOUNG MASTER!
...
WIP WIP WIP
...!
!
TH- THERE'S SOMEONE IN THERE! HE'S HURT!!
BE CAREFUL!! HE COULD BE AN ALIEN!
TRUNKS!
THE GUY INSIDE THAT THING-- IS HE A YOUNG MAN WITH THE SAME HAIR COLOR AS YOURS?
SKREEE
HUH? UH, YEAH... MAYBE.
THIS IS BAD ...!
GOKU! CAN YOU GO GET ME A SENZU BEAN?!
Y...
YEAH!

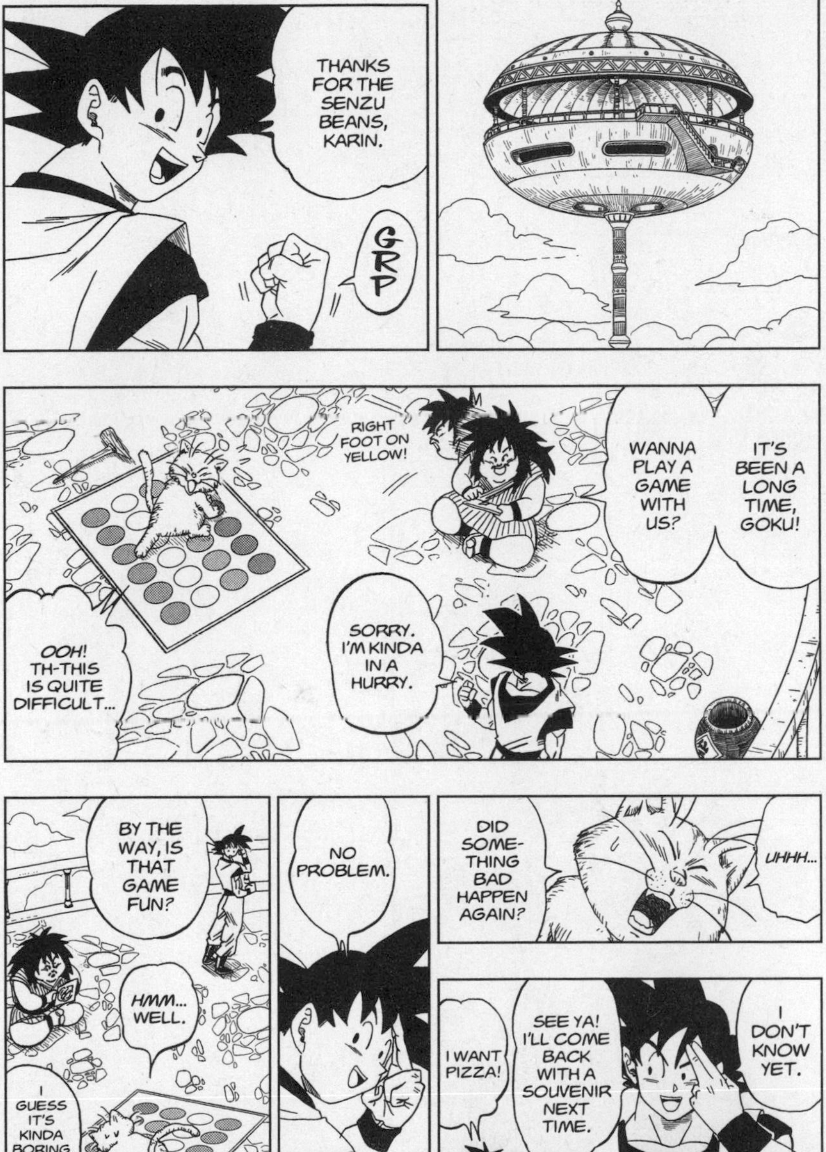
THANKS FOR THE SENZU BEANS, KARIN.
GRP
IT'S BEEN A LONG TIME, GOKU!
WANNA PLAY A GAME WITH US?
RIGHT FOOT ON YELLOW!
SORRY. I'M KINDA IN A HURRY.
OOH! TH-THIS IS QUITE DIFFICULT...
UHHH...
DID SOMETHING BAD HAPPEN AGAIN?
I DON'T KNOW YET.
SEE YA! I'LL COME BACK WITH A SOUVENIR NEXT TIME.
I WANT PIZZA!
NO PROBLEM.
BY THE WAY, IS THAT GAME FUN?
HMM... WELL.
I GUESS IT'S KINDA BORING WITH ONLY TWO GUYS.

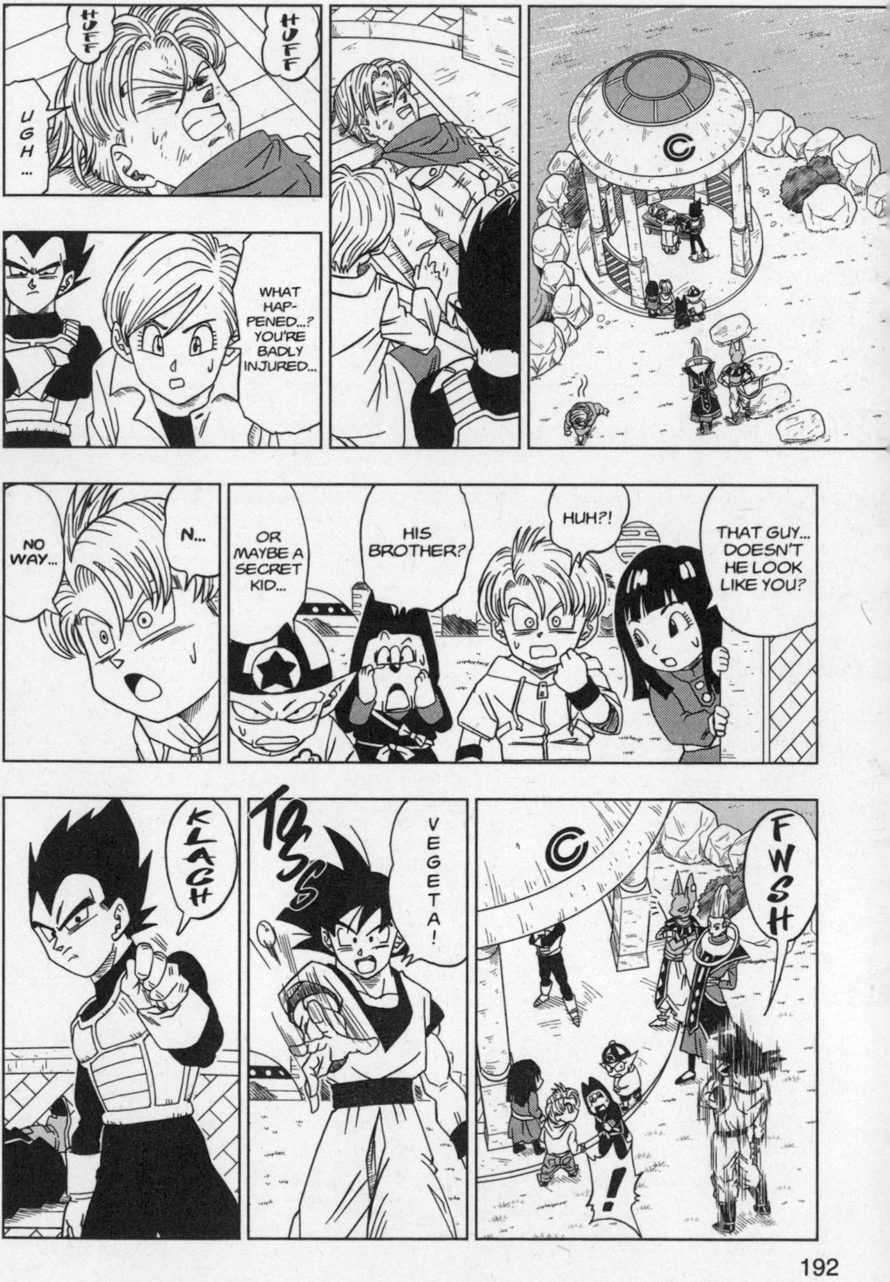

HUFF
HUFF
UGH...
WHAT HAPPENED...? YOU'RE BADLY INJURED...
THAT GUY... DOESN'T HE LOOK LIKE YOU?
HUH?!
HIS BROTHER?
OR MAYBE A SECRET KID...
N...
NO WAY...
FWSH
!
TOSS
VEGETA!
KLACH

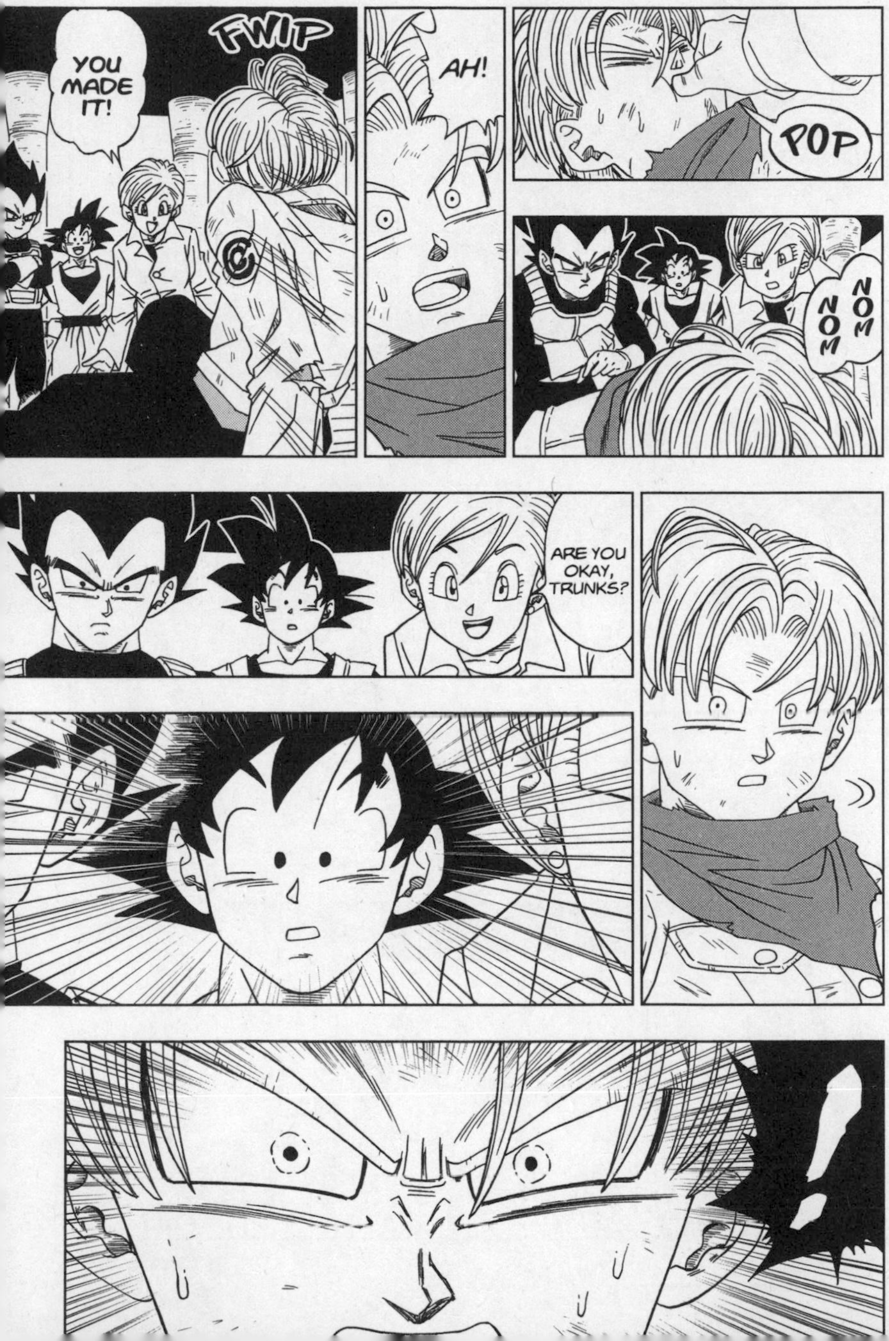
POP
NOM NOM
AH!
FWIP
YOU MADE IT!
ARE YOU OKAY, TRUNKS?
!

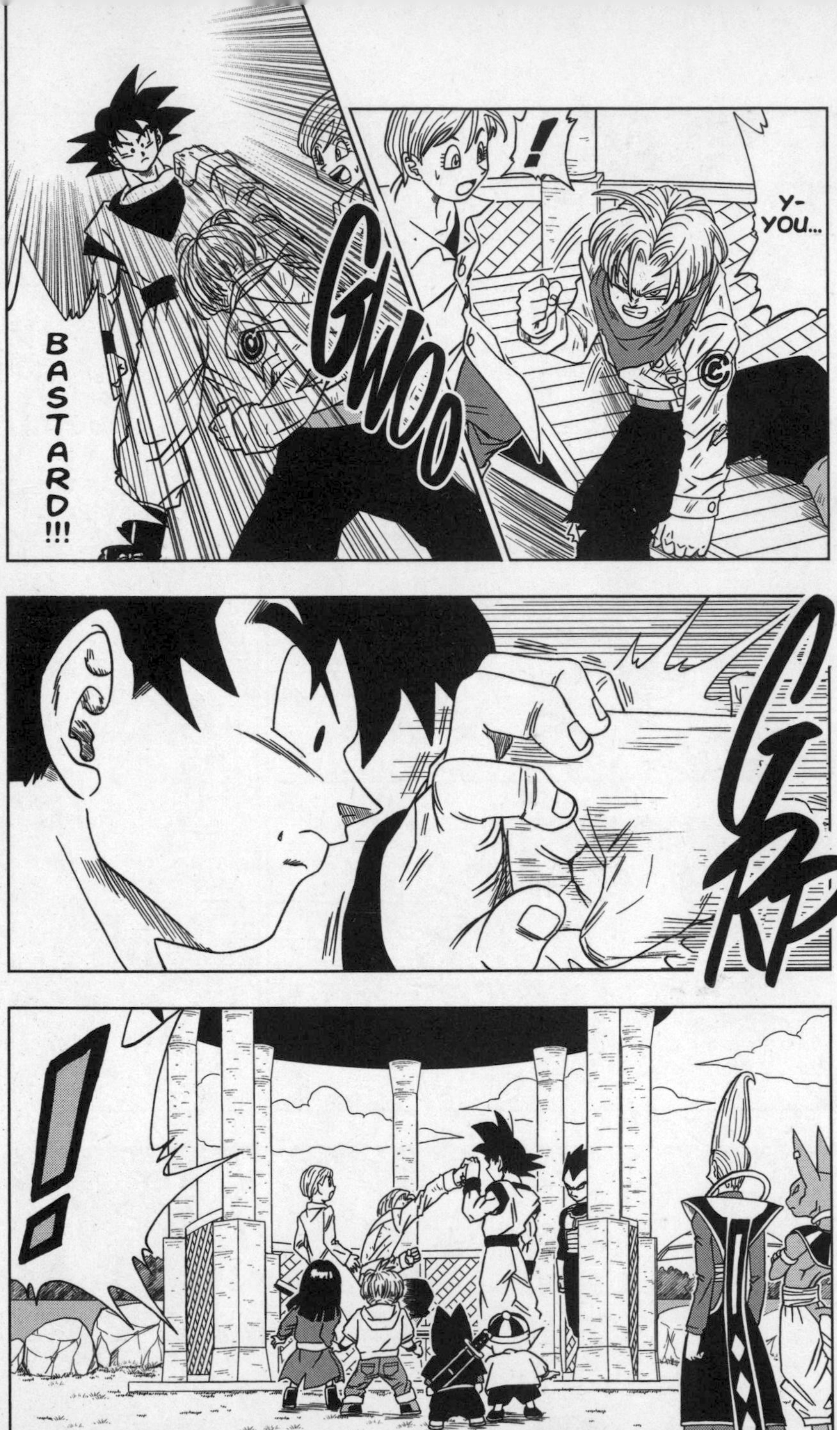
Y-YOU...
!
GWOO
BASTARD!!!
!!

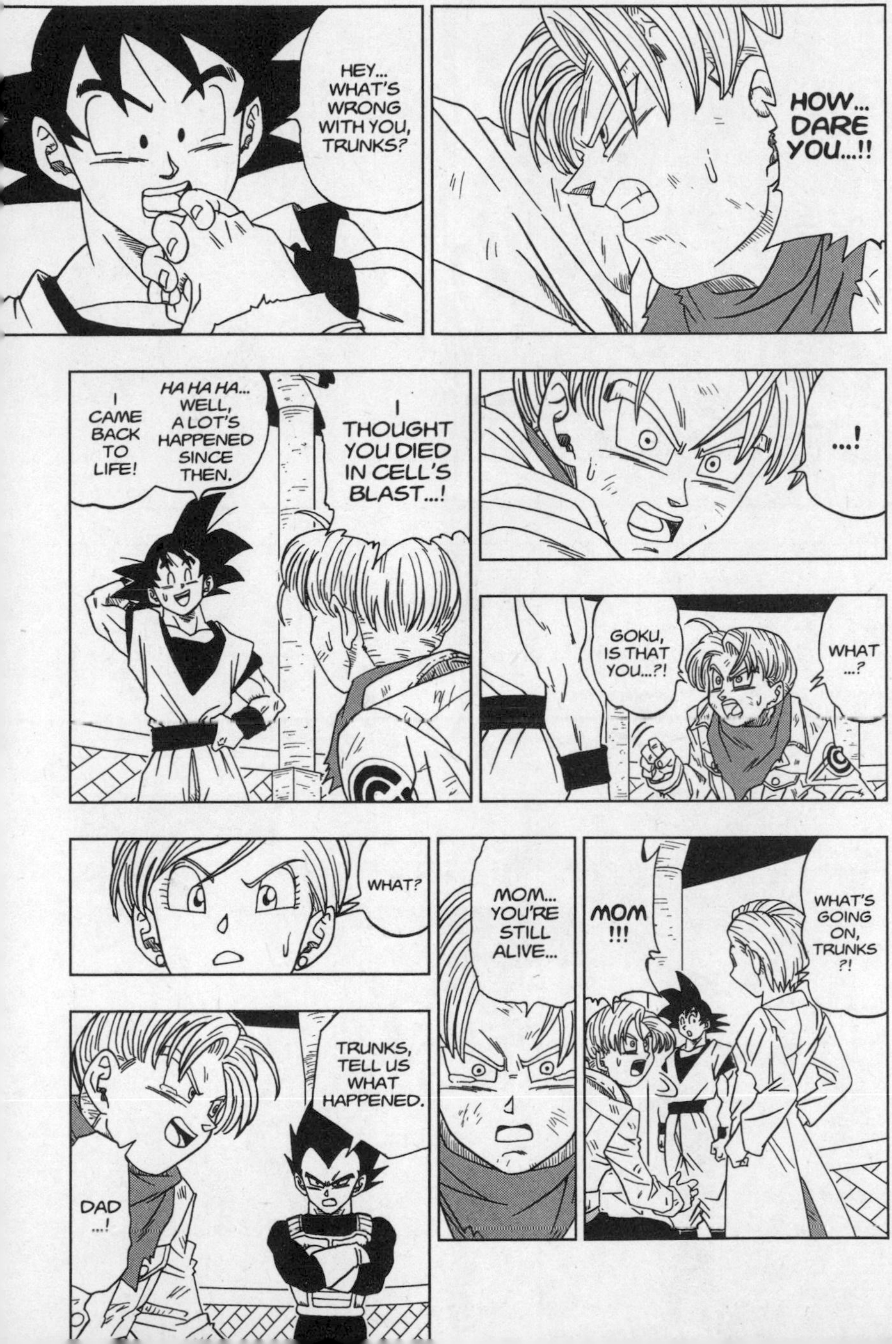
HOW... DARE YOU...!!
HEY... WHAT'S WRONG WITH YOU, TRUNKS?
...!
WHAT ...?
GOKU, IS THAT YOU...?!
I THOUGHT YOU DIED IN CELL'S BLAST...!
HA HA HA... WELL, A LOT'S HAPPENED SINCE THEN.
I CAME BACK TO LIFE!
WHAT'S GOING ON, TRUNKS ?!
MOM !!!
MOM... YOU'RE STILL ALIVE...
WHAT?
TRUNKS, TELL US WHAT HAPPENED.
DAD ...!

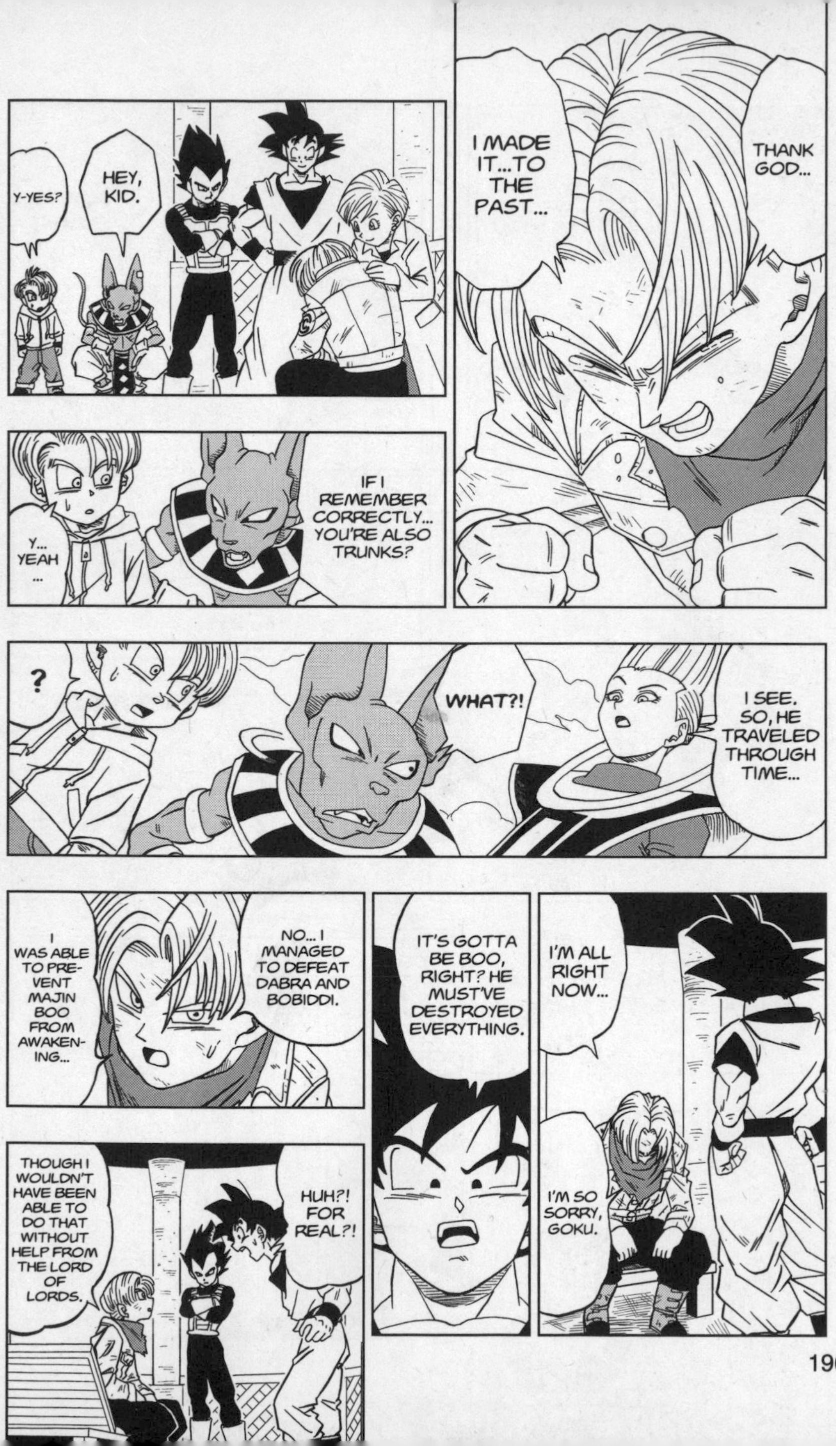
THANK GOD...
I MADE IT...TO THE PAST...
HEY, KID.
Y-YES?
IF I REMEMBER CORRECTLY... YOU'RE ALSO TRUNKS?
Y... YEAH ...
I SEE. SO, HE TRAVELED THROUGH TIME...
WHAT?!
?
I'M ALL RIGHT NOW...
I'M SO SORRY, GOKU.
IT'S GOTTA BE BOO, RIGHT? HE MUST'VE DESTROYED EVERYTHING.
NO... I MANAGED TO DEFEAT DABRA AND BOBIDDI.
I WAS ABLE TO PREVENT MAJIN BOO FROM AWAKENING...
HUH?! FOR REAL?!
THOUGH I WOULDN'T HAVE BEEN ABLE TO DO THAT WITHOUT HELP FROM THE LORD OF LORDS.

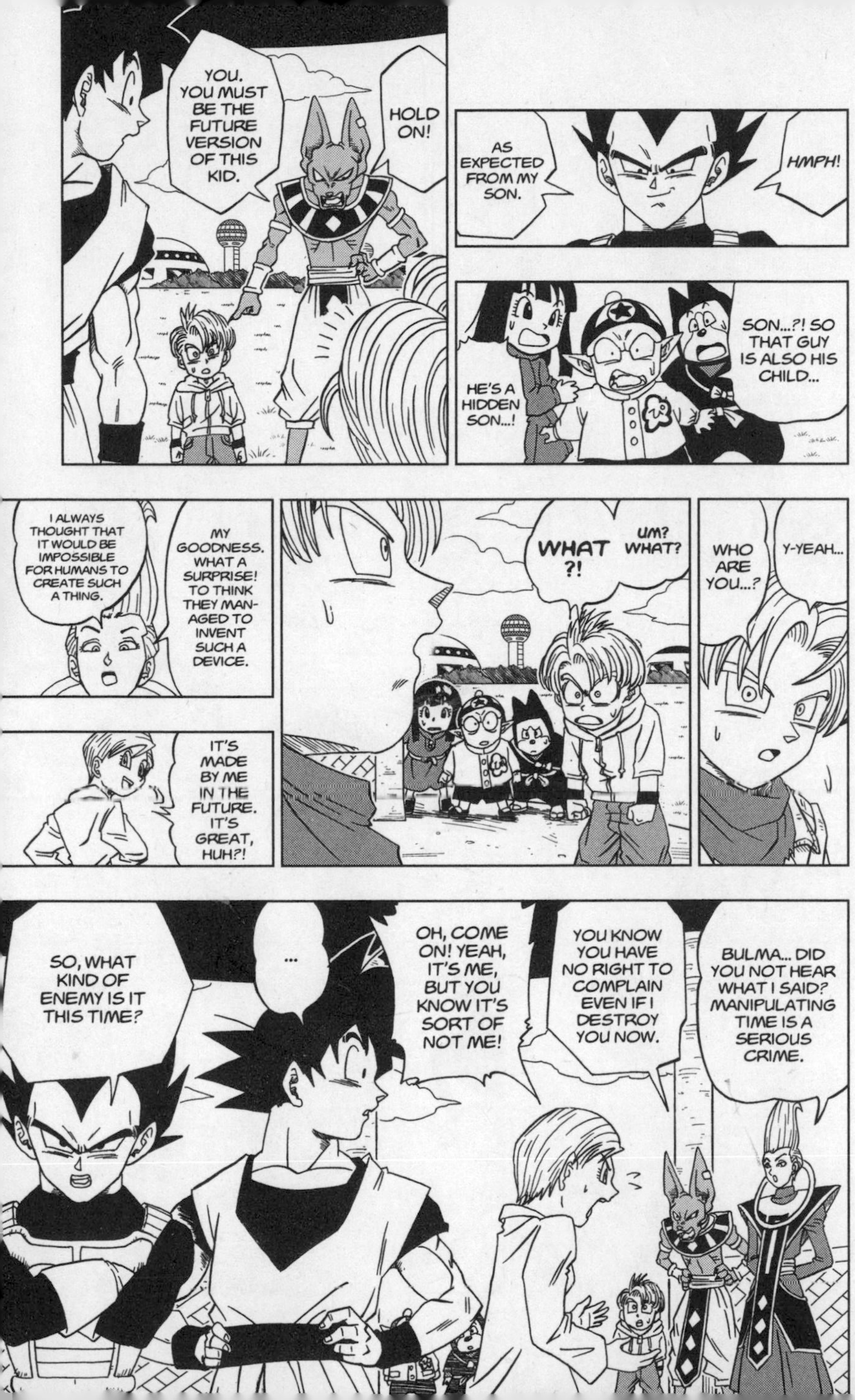
HMPH!
AS EXPECTED FROM MY SON.
SON...?! SO THAT GUY IS ALSO HIS CHILD...
HE'S A HIDDEN SON...!
HOLD ON!
YOU. YOU MUST BE THE FUTURE VERSION OF THIS KID.
Y-YEAH...
WHO ARE YOU...?
UM? WHAT?
WHAT ?!
MY GOODNESS. WHAT A SURPRISE! TO THINK THEY MANAGED TO INVENT SUCH A DEVICE.
I ALWAYS THOUGHT THAT IT WOULD BE IMPOSSIBLE FOR HUMANS TO CREATE SUCH A THING.
IT'S MADE BY ME IN THE FUTURE. IT'S GREAT, HUH?!
BULMA... DID YOU NOT HEAR WHAT I SAID? MANIPULATING TIME IS A SERIOUS CRIME.
YOU KNOW YOU HAVE NO RIGHT TO COMPLAIN EVEN IF I DESTROY YOU NOW.
OH, COME ON! YEAH, IT'S ME, BUT YOU KNOW IT'S SORT OF NOT ME!
...
SO, WHAT KIND OF ENEMY IS IT THIS TIME?

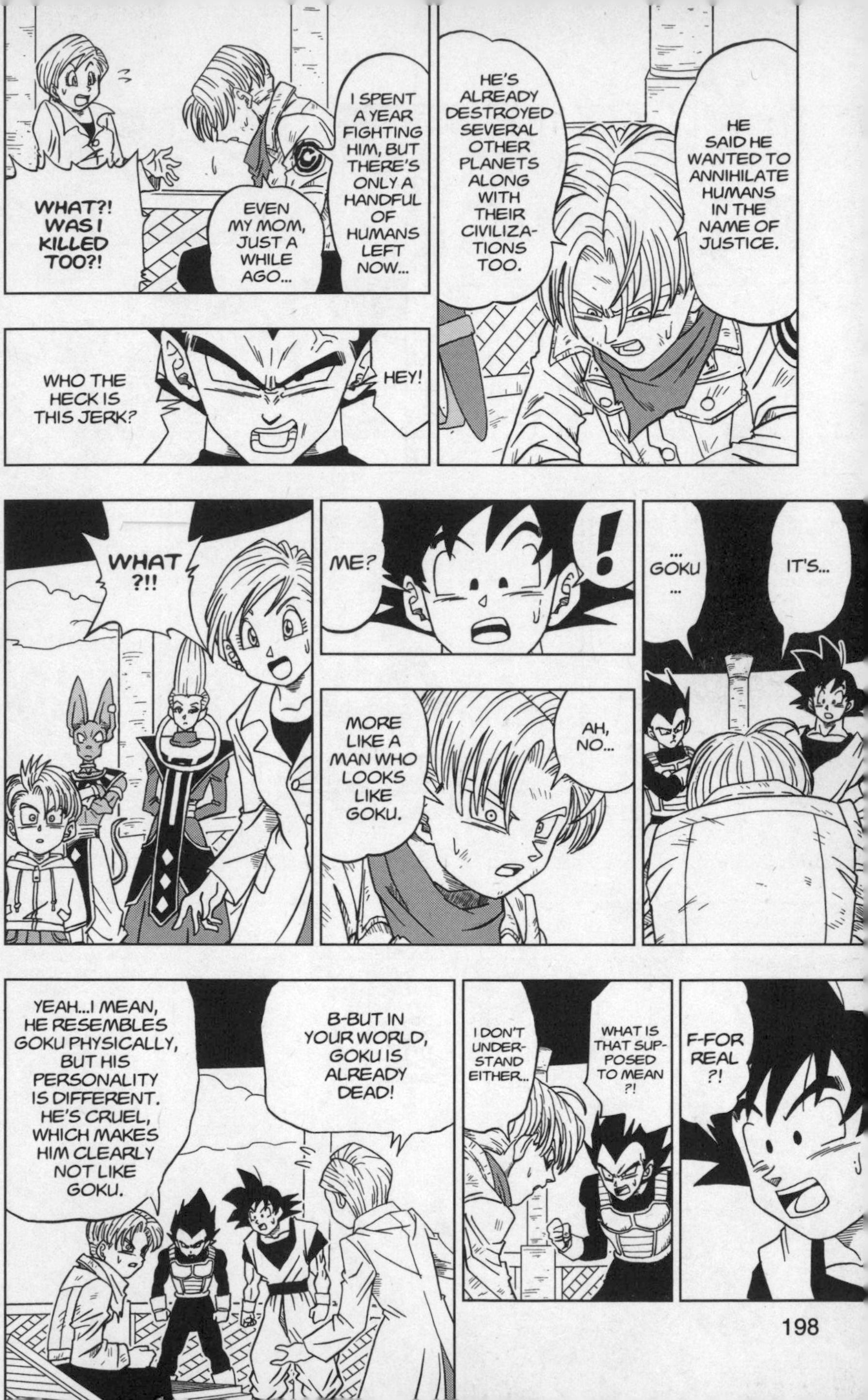
HE SAID HE WANTED TO ANNIHILATE HUMANS IN THE NAME OF JUSTICE.
HE'S ALREADY DESTROYED SEVERAL OTHER PLANETS ALONG WITH THEIR CIVILIZATIONS TOO.
I SPENT A YEAR FIGHTING HIM, BUT THERE'S ONLY A HANDFUL OF HUMANS LEFT NOW...
EVEN MY MOM, JUST A WHILE AGO...
WHAT?! WAS I KILLED TOO?!
HEY!
WHO THE HECK IS THIS JERK?
IT'S...
... GOKU ...
!
ME?
AH, NO...
MORE LIKE A MAN WHO LOOKS LIKE GOKU.
WHAT ?!!
F-FOR REAL ?!
WHAT IS THAT SUPPOSED TO MEAN ?!
I DON'T UNDERSTAND EITHER...
B-BUT IN YOUR WORLD, GOKU IS ALREADY DEAD!
YEAH...I MEAN, HE RESEMBLES GOKU PHYSICALLY, BUT HIS PERSONALITY IS DIFFERENT. HE'S CRUEL, WHICH MAKES HIM CLEARLY NOT LIKE GOKU.

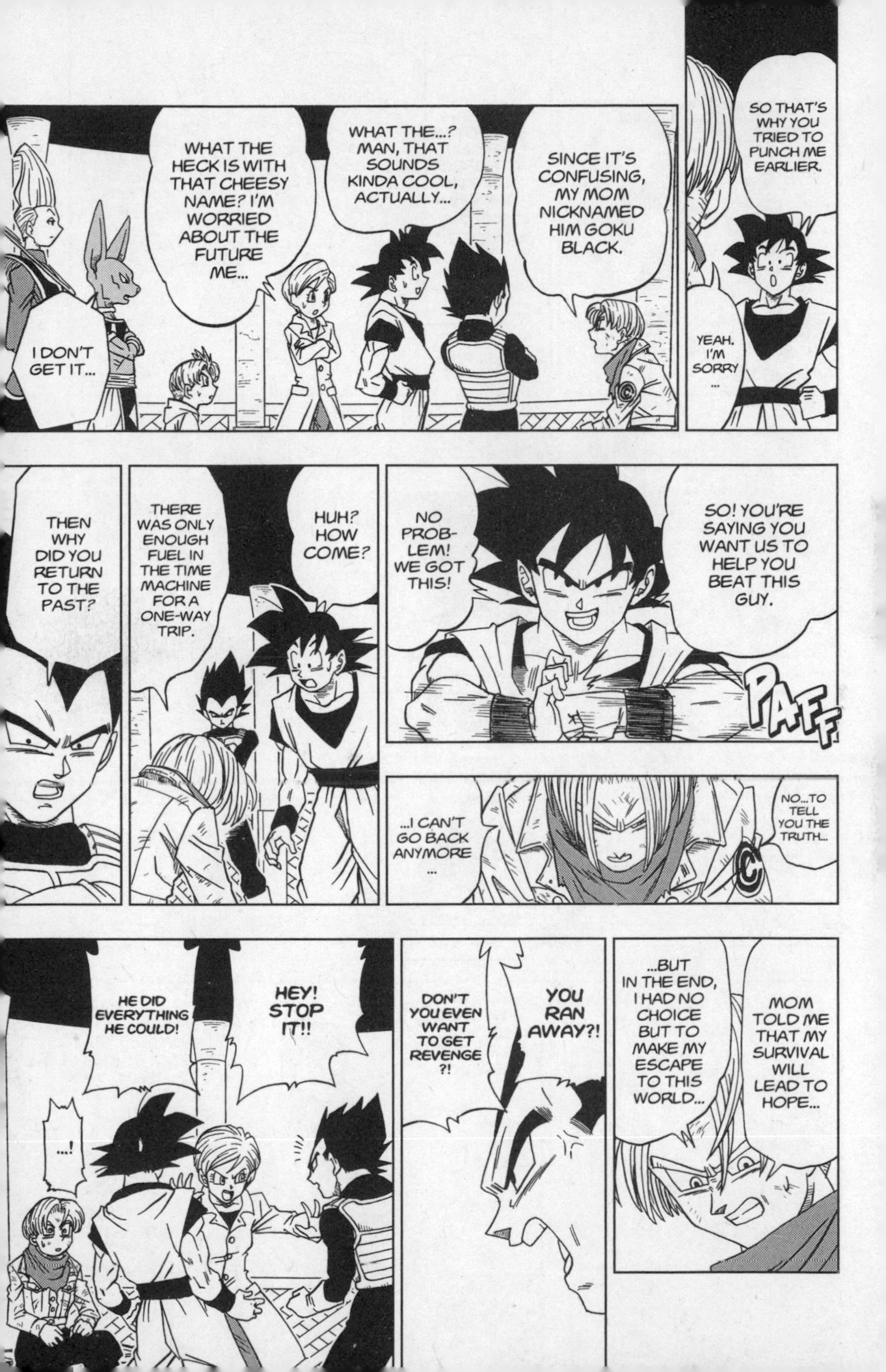
SO THAT'S WHY YOU TRIED TO PUNCH ME EARLIER.
YEAH. I'M SORRY...
SINCE IT'S CONFUSING, MY MOM NICKNAMED HIM GOKU BLACK.
WHAT THE...? MAN, THAT SOUNDS KINDA COOL, ACTUALLY...
WHAT THE HECK IS WITH THAT CHEESY NAME? I'M WORRIED ABOUT THE FUTURE ME...
I DON'T GET IT...
SO! YOU'RE SAYING YOU WANT US TO HELP YOU BEAT THIS GUY.
PAFF
NO PROBLEM! WE GOT THIS!
NO...TO TELL YOU THE TRUTH...
...I CAN'T GO BACK ANYMORE...
HUH? HOW COME?
THERE WAS ONLY ENOUGH FUEL IN THE TIME MACHINE FOR A ONE-WAY TRIP.
THEN WHY DID YOU RETURN TO THE PAST?
MOM TOLD ME THAT MY SURVIVAL WILL LEAD TO HOPE...
...BUT IN THE END, I HAD NO CHOICE BUT TO MAKE MY ESCAPE TO THIS WORLD...
YOU RAN AWAY?!
DON'T YOU EVEN WANT TO GET REVENGE?!
HEY! STOP IT!!
HE DID EVERYTHING HE COULD!
...!

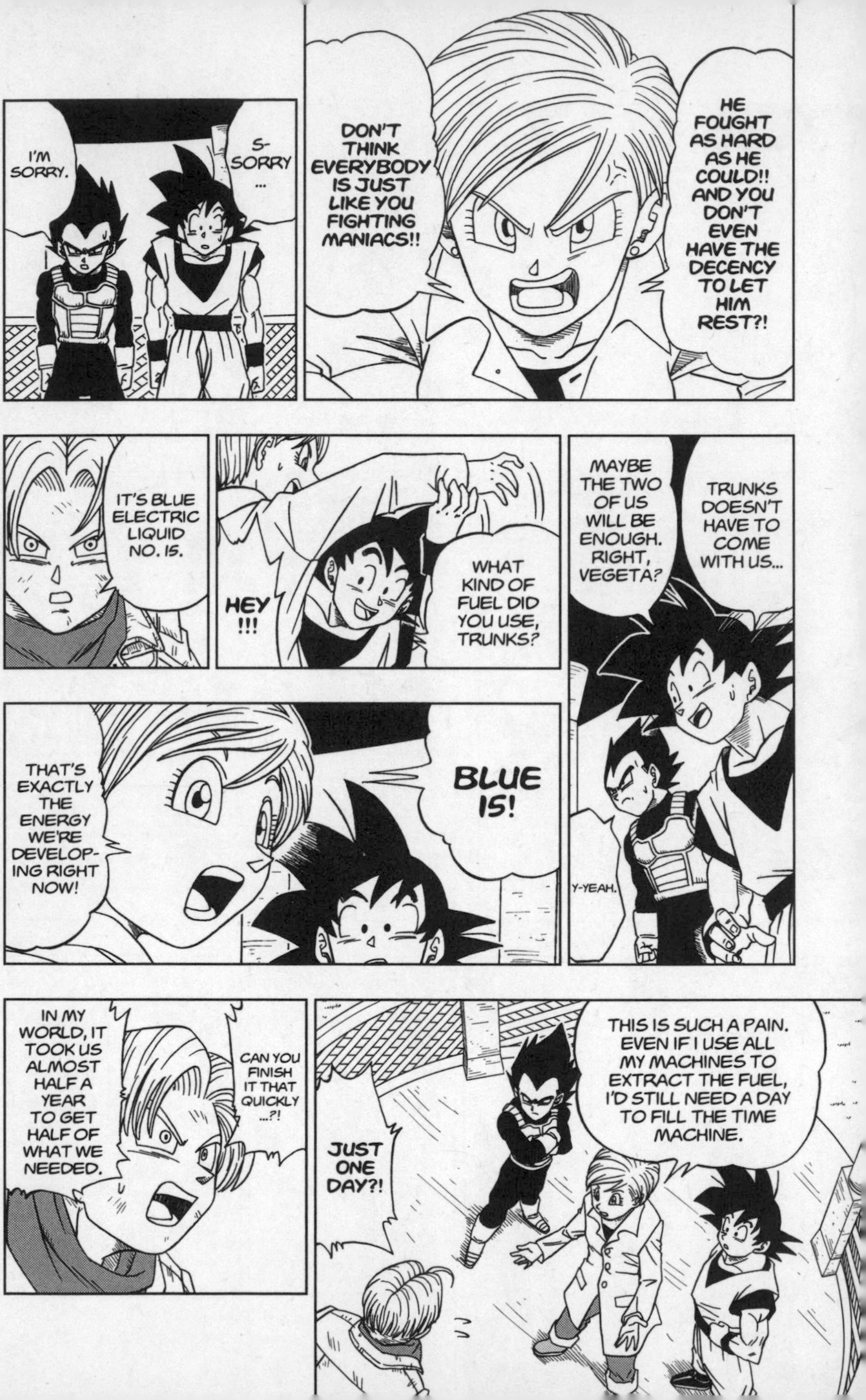
HE FOUGHT AS HARD AS HE COULD!! AND YOU DON'T EVEN HAVE THE DECENCY TO LET HIM REST?!
DON'T THINK EVERYBODY IS JUST LIKE YOU FIGHTING MANIACS!!
S-SORRY ...
I'M SORRY.
TRUNKS DOESN'T HAVE TO COME WITH US...
MAYBE THE TWO OF US WILL BE ENOUGH. RIGHT, VEGETA?
Y-YEAH.
WHAT KIND OF FUEL DID YOU USE, TRUNKS?
HEY !!!
IT'S BLUE ELECTRIC LIQUID NO. 15.
BLUE 15!
THAT'S EXACTLY THE ENERGY WE'RE DEVELOPING RIGHT NOW!
THIS IS SUCH A PAIN. EVEN IF I USE ALL MY MACHINES TO EXTRACT THE FUEL, I'D STILL NEED A DAY TO FILL THE TIME MACHINE.
JUST ONE DAY?!
IN MY WORLD, IT TOOK US ALMOST HALF A YEAR TO GET HALF OF WHAT WE NEEDED.
CAN YOU FINISH IT THAT QUICKLY ...?!

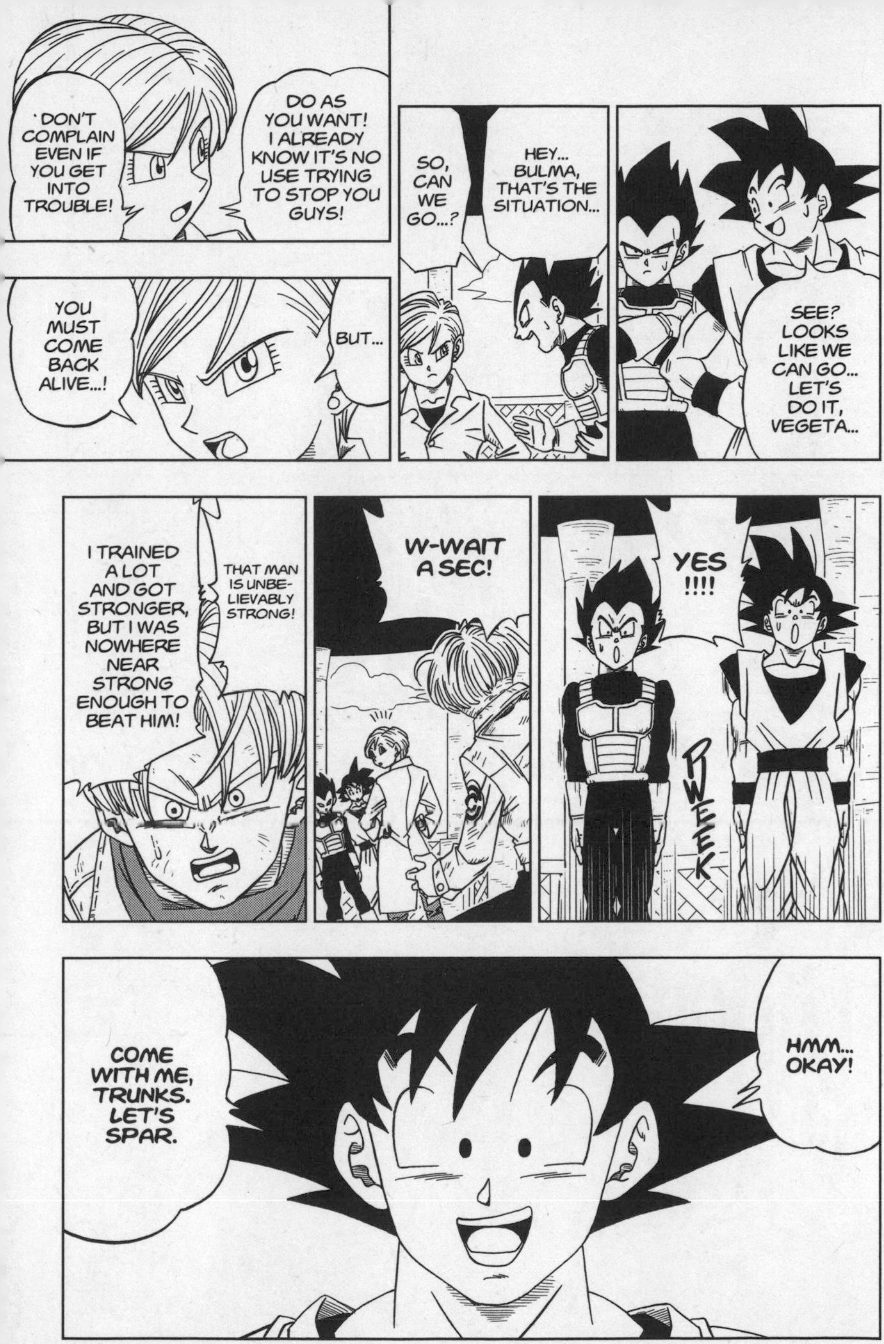
SEE? LOOKS LIKE WE CAN GO... LET'S DO IT, VEGETA...
HEY... BULMA, THAT'S THE SITUATION...
SO, CAN WE GO...?
DO AS YOU WANT! I ALREADY KNOW IT'S NO USE TRYING TO STOP YOU GUYS!
DON'T COMPLAIN EVEN IF YOU GET INTO TROUBLE!
BUT...
YOU MUST COME BACK ALIVE...!
YES !!!!
PWEEK
W-WAIT A SEC!
THAT MAN IS UNBE-LIEVABLY STRONG!
I TRAINED A LOT AND GOT STRONGER, BUT I WAS NOWHERE NEAR STRONG ENOUGH TO BEAT HIM!
HMM... OKAY!
COME WITH ME, TRUNKS. LET'S SPAR.

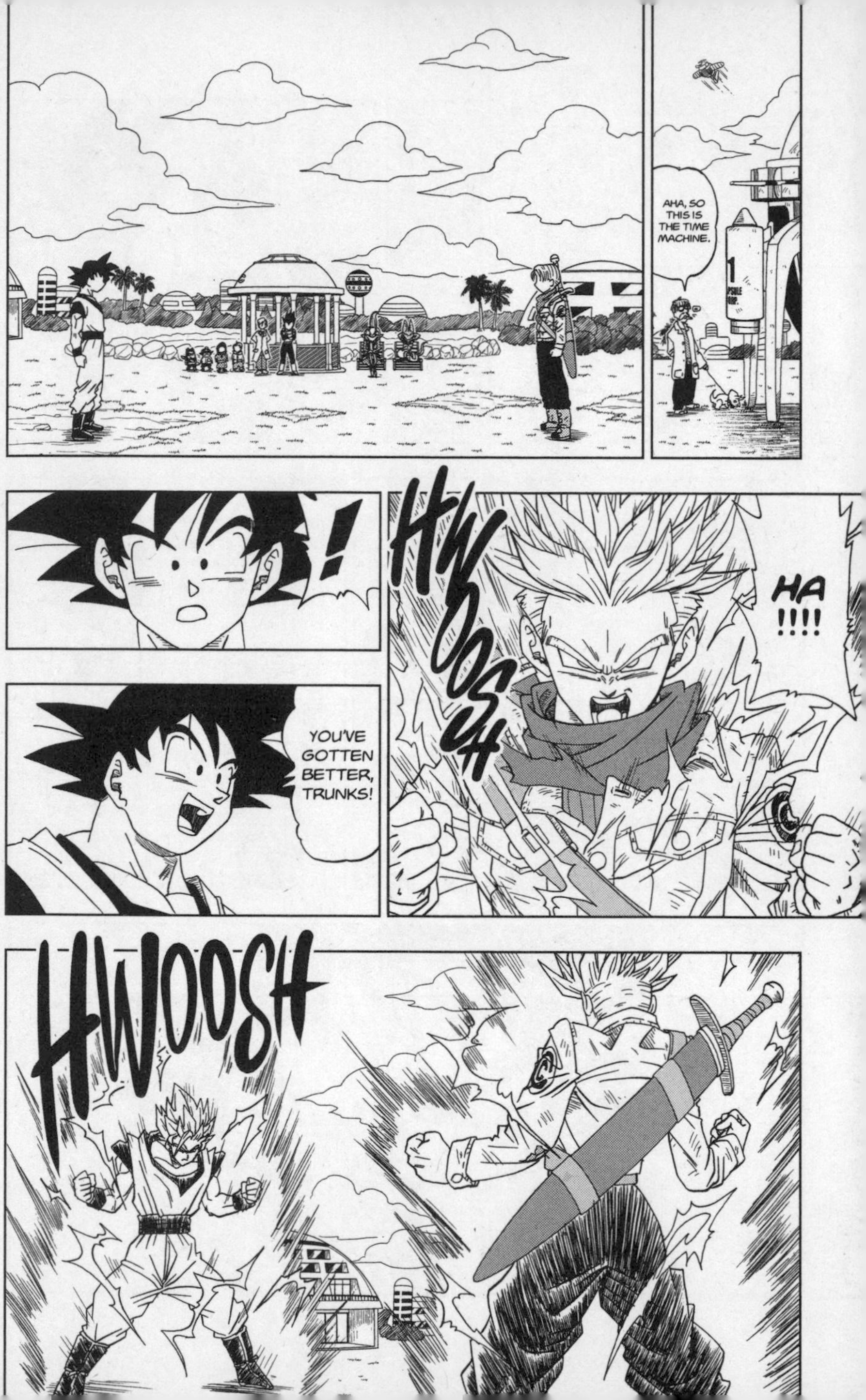
AHA, SO THIS IS THE TIME MACHINE.
HWOOSH
HA!!!!
!
YOU'VE GOTTEN BETTER, TRUNKS!
HWOOSH

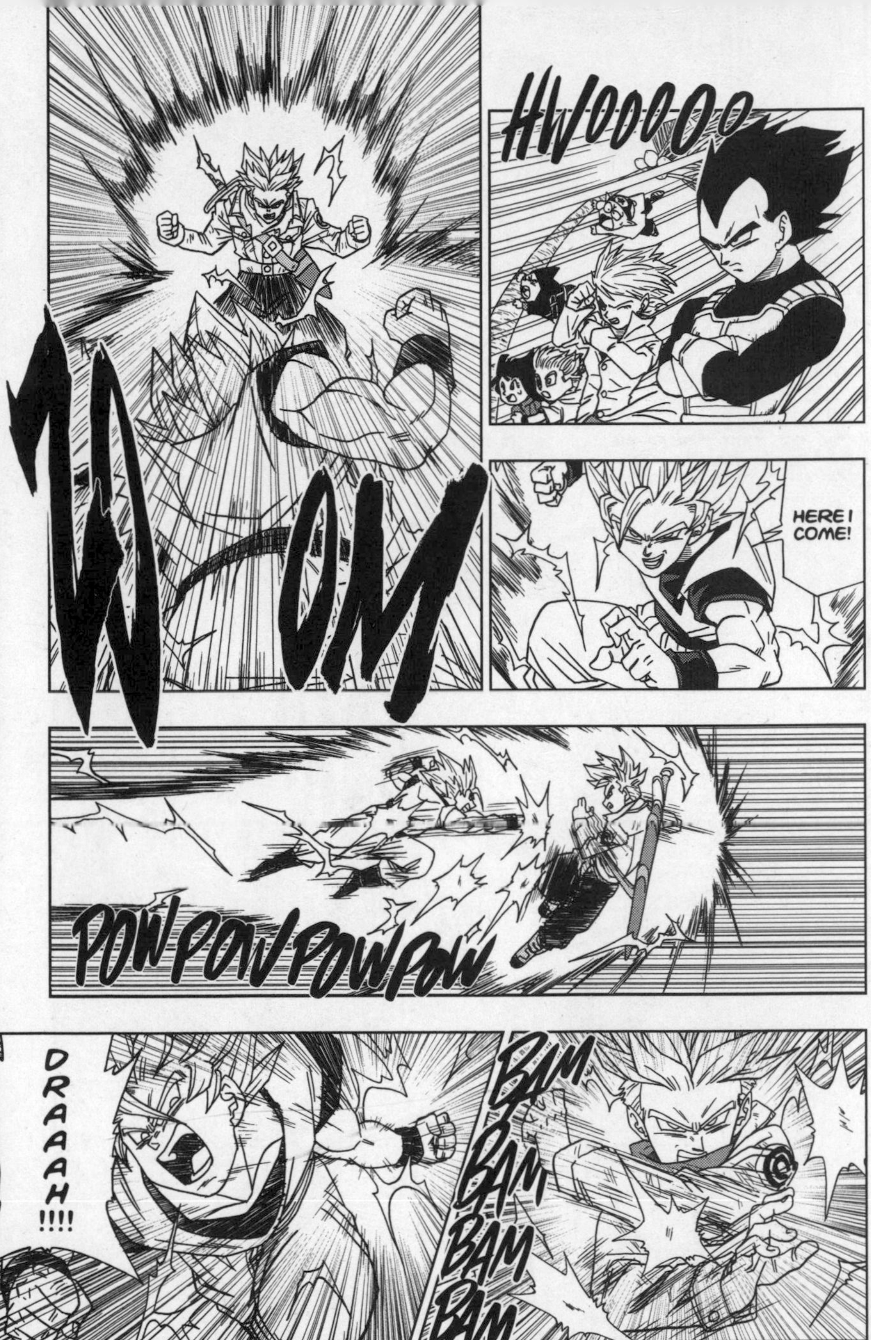
HWOOOOO
HERE I COME!
WOM
POWPOWPOWPOW
BAM BAM BAM BAM BAM
DRAAAAH!!!!

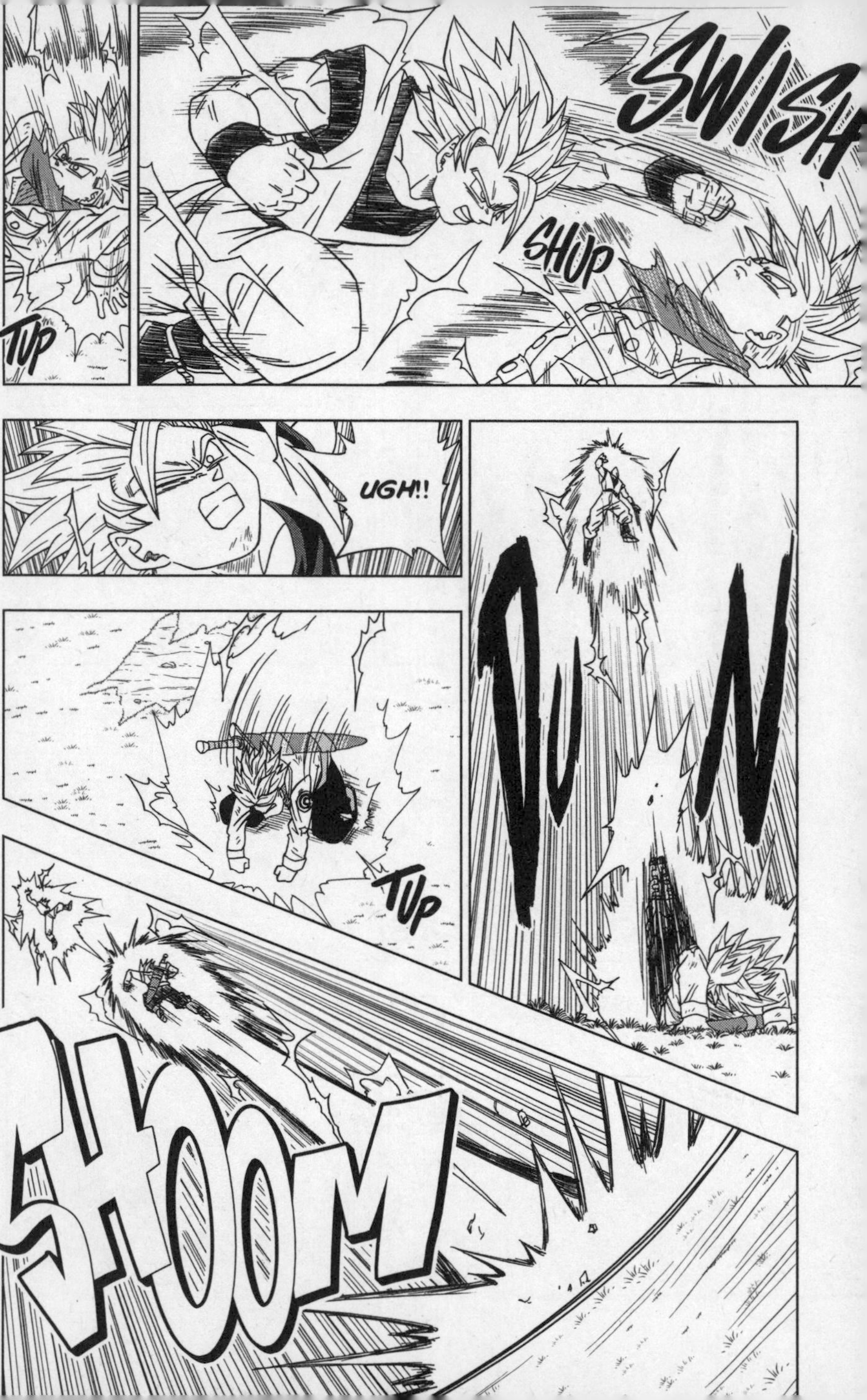
SWISH
SHUP
TUP
DUN
UGH!!
TUP
SHOOM

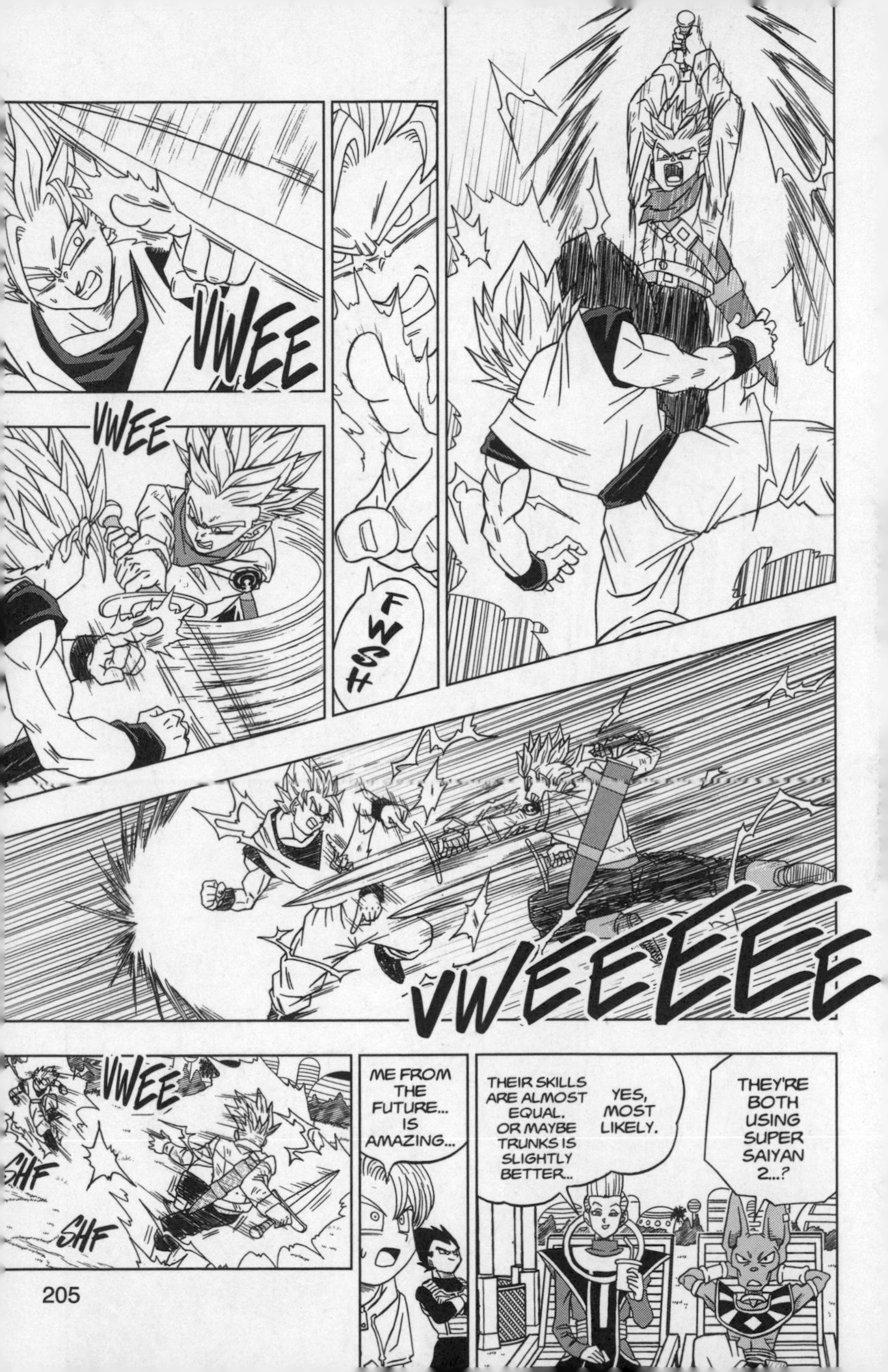
FWSH
VWEE
VWEE
VWEEEEE
THEY'RE BOTH USING SUPER SAIYAN 2...?
YES, MOST LIKELY.
THEIR SKILLS ARE ALMOST EQUAL. OR MAYBE TRUNKS IS SLIGHTLY BETTER...
ME FROM THE FUTURE... IS AMAZING...
VWEE
SHF
SHF

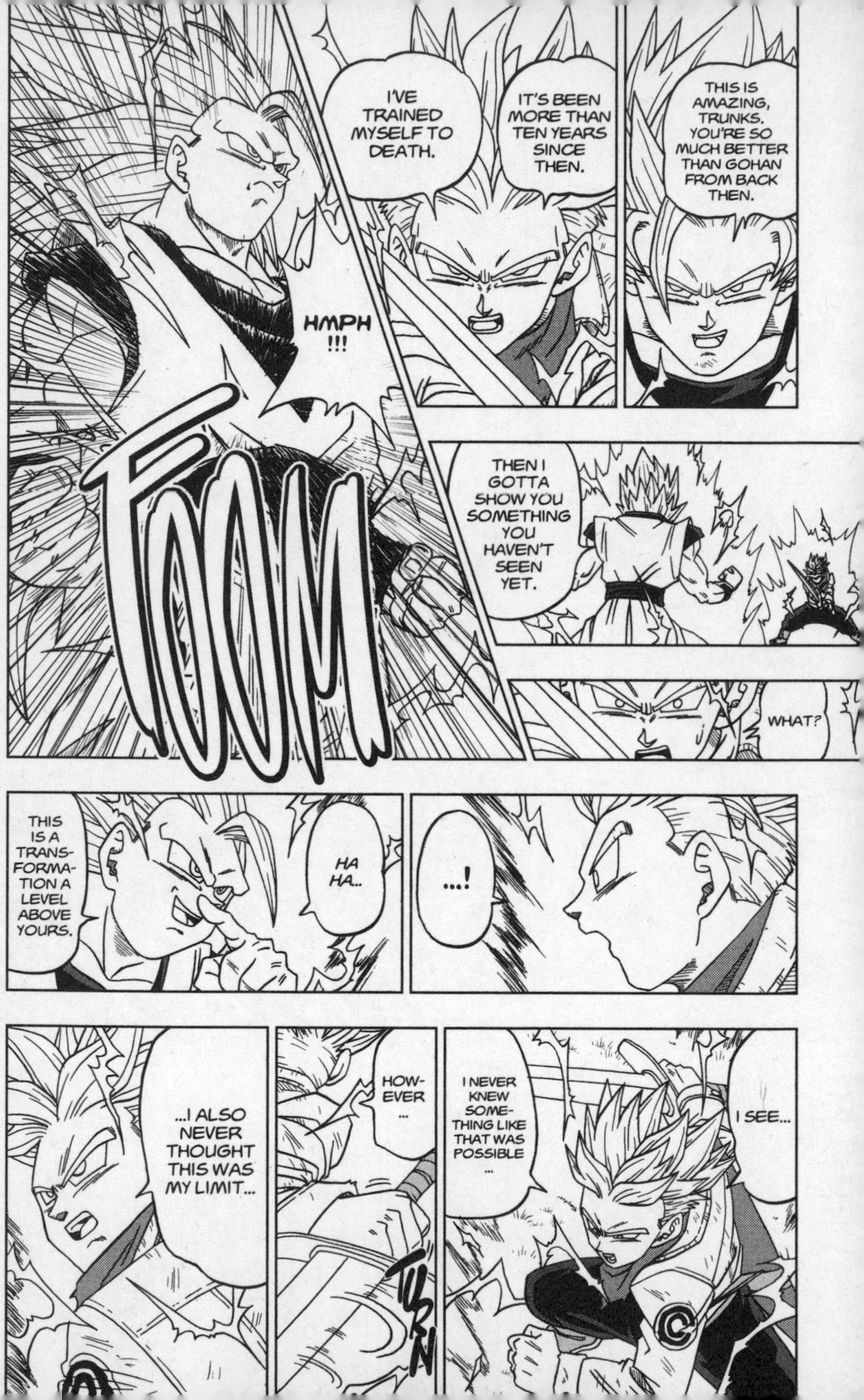
THIS IS AMAZING, TRUNKS. YOU'RE SO MUCH BETTER THAN GOHAN FROM BACK THEN.
IT'S BEEN MORE THAN TEN YEARS SINCE THEN.
I'VE TRAINED MYSELF TO DEATH.
THEN I GOTTA SHOW YOU SOMETHING YOU HAVEN'T SEEN YET.
WHAT?
HMPH !!!
FOOM
...!
HA HA...
THIS IS A TRANSFORMATION A LEVEL ABOVE YOURS.
I SEE...
I NEVER KNEW SOMETHING LIKE THAT WAS POSSIBLE...
HOWEVER...
TURN
...I ALSO NEVER THOUGHT THIS WAS MY LIMIT...

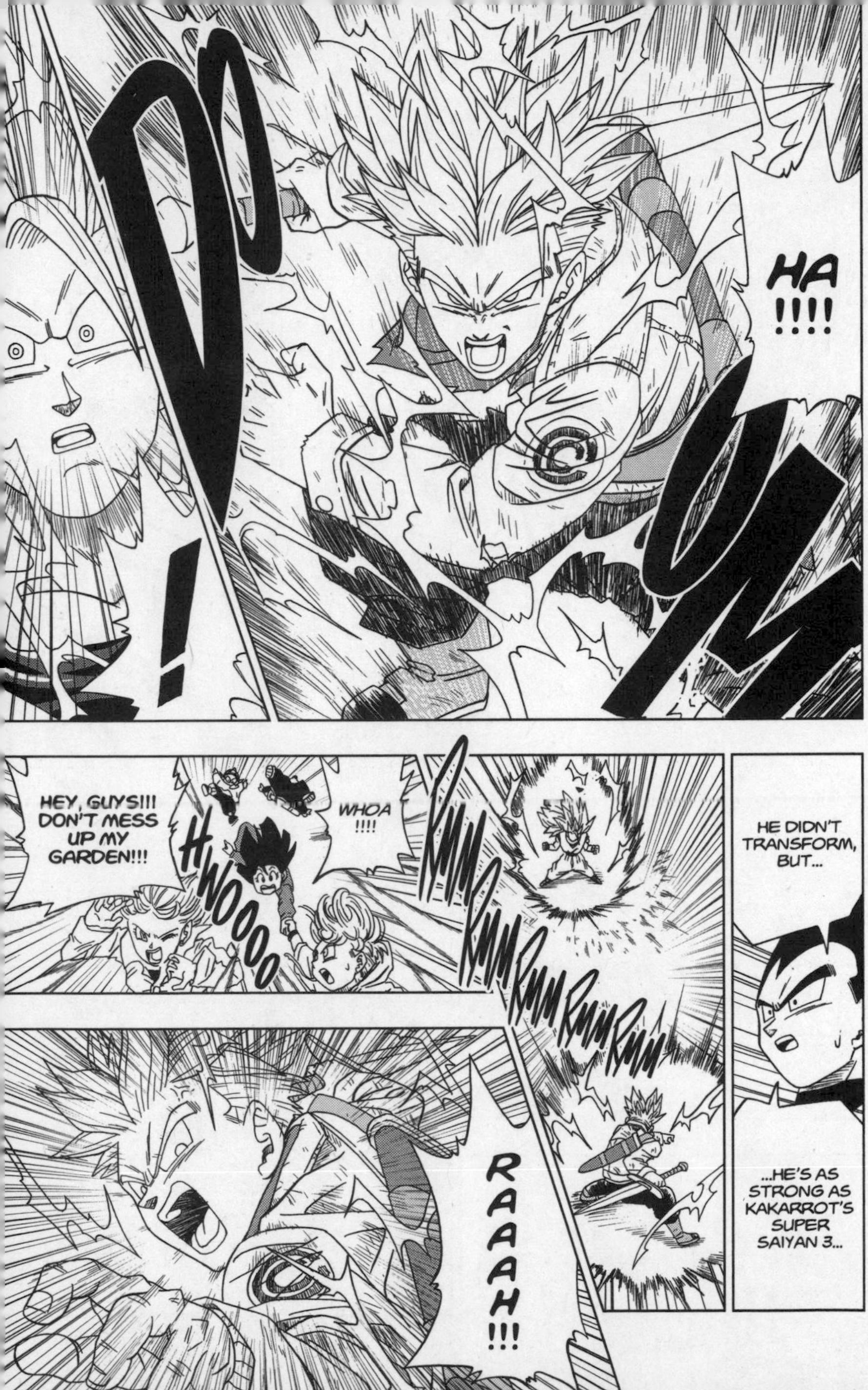
HA !!!!
HE DIDN'T TRANSFORM, BUT...
...HE'S AS STRONG AS KAKARROT'S SUPER SAIYAN 3...
WHOA !!!!
HEY, GUYS!!! DON'T MESS UP MY GARDEN!!!
HWOOOOO
RAAAAH!!!

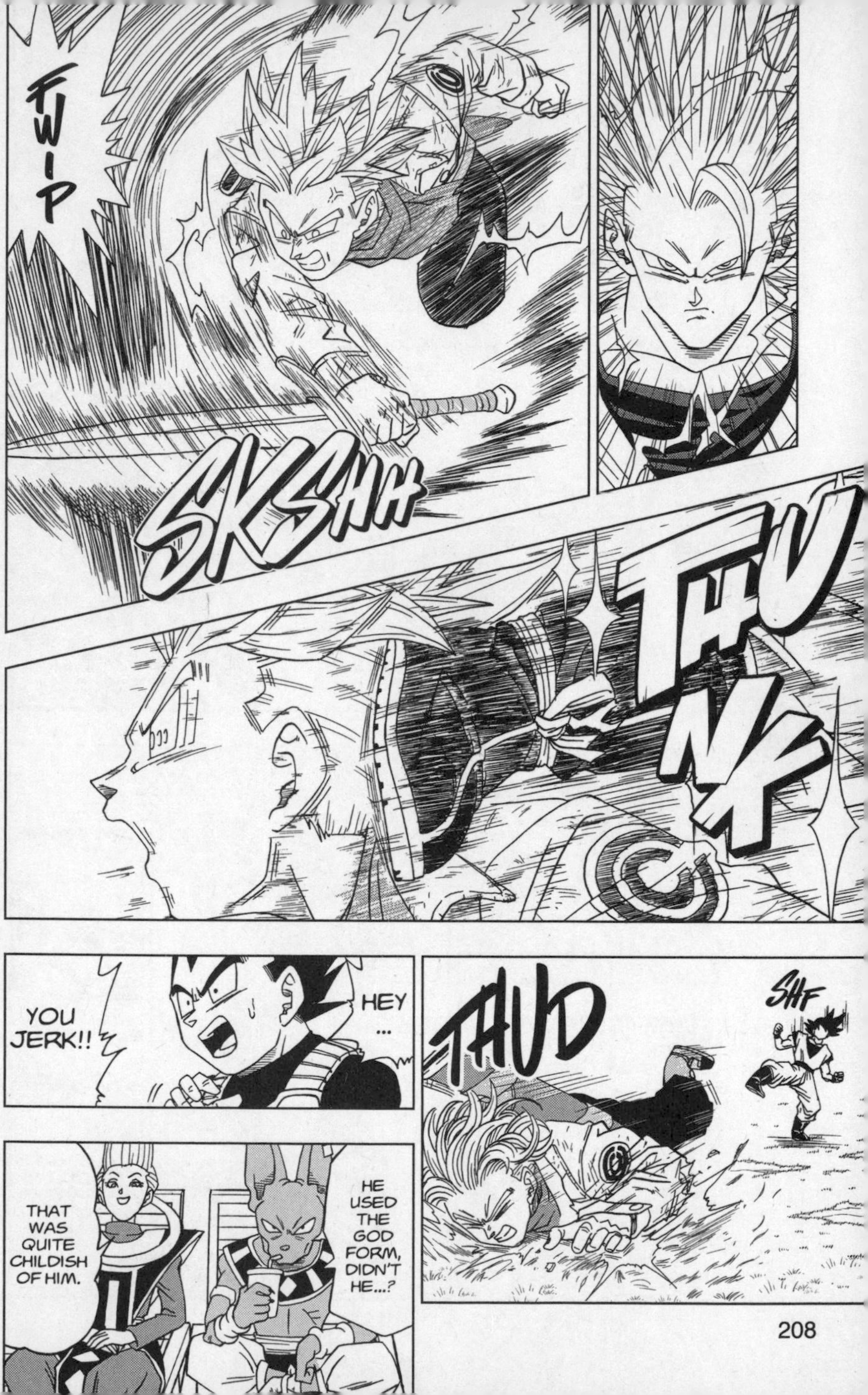
FWIP
SKSHH
THUNK
THUD
SHF
HEY ...
YOU JERK!!
HE USED THE GOD FORM, DIDN'T HE...?
THAT WAS QUITE CHILDISH OF HIM.

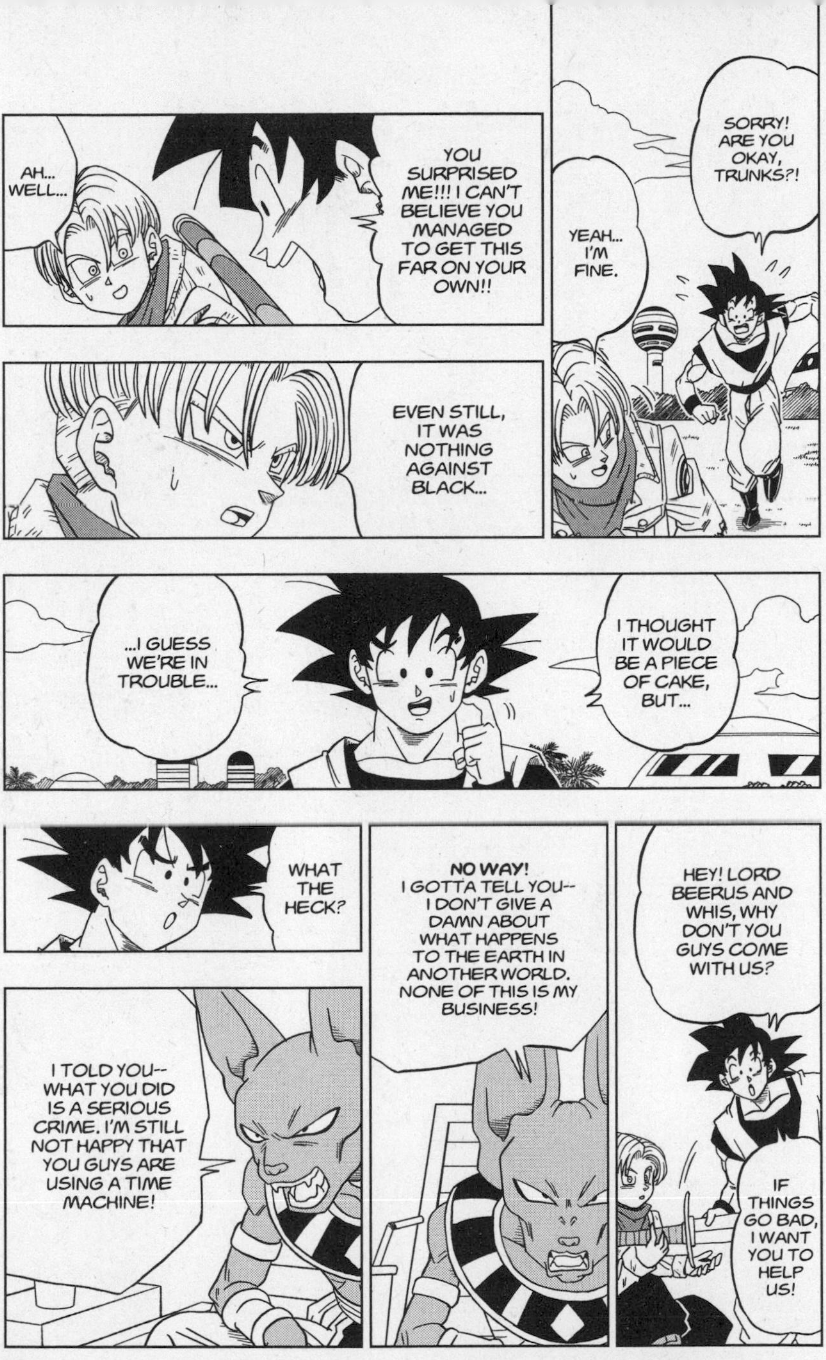
SORRY! ARE YOU OKAY, TRUNKS?!
YEAH... I'M FINE.
YOU SURPRISED ME!!! I CAN'T BELIEVE YOU MANAGED TO GET THIS FAR ON YOUR OWN!!
AH... WELL...
EVEN STILL, IT WAS NOTHING AGAINST BLACK...
I THOUGHT IT WOULD BE A PIECE OF CAKE, BUT...
...I GUESS WE'RE IN TROUBLE...
HEY! LORD BEERUS AND WHIS, WHY DON'T YOU GUYS COME WITH US?
IF THINGS GO BAD, I WANT YOU TO HELP US!
NO WAY! I GOTTA TELL YOU-- I DON'T GIVE A DAMN ABOUT WHAT HAPPENS TO THE EARTH IN ANOTHER WORLD. NONE OF THIS IS MY BUSINESS!
WHAT THE HECK?
I TOLD YOU-- WHAT YOU DID IS A SERIOUS CRIME. I'M STILL NOT HAPPY THAT YOU GUYS ARE USING A TIME MACHINE!

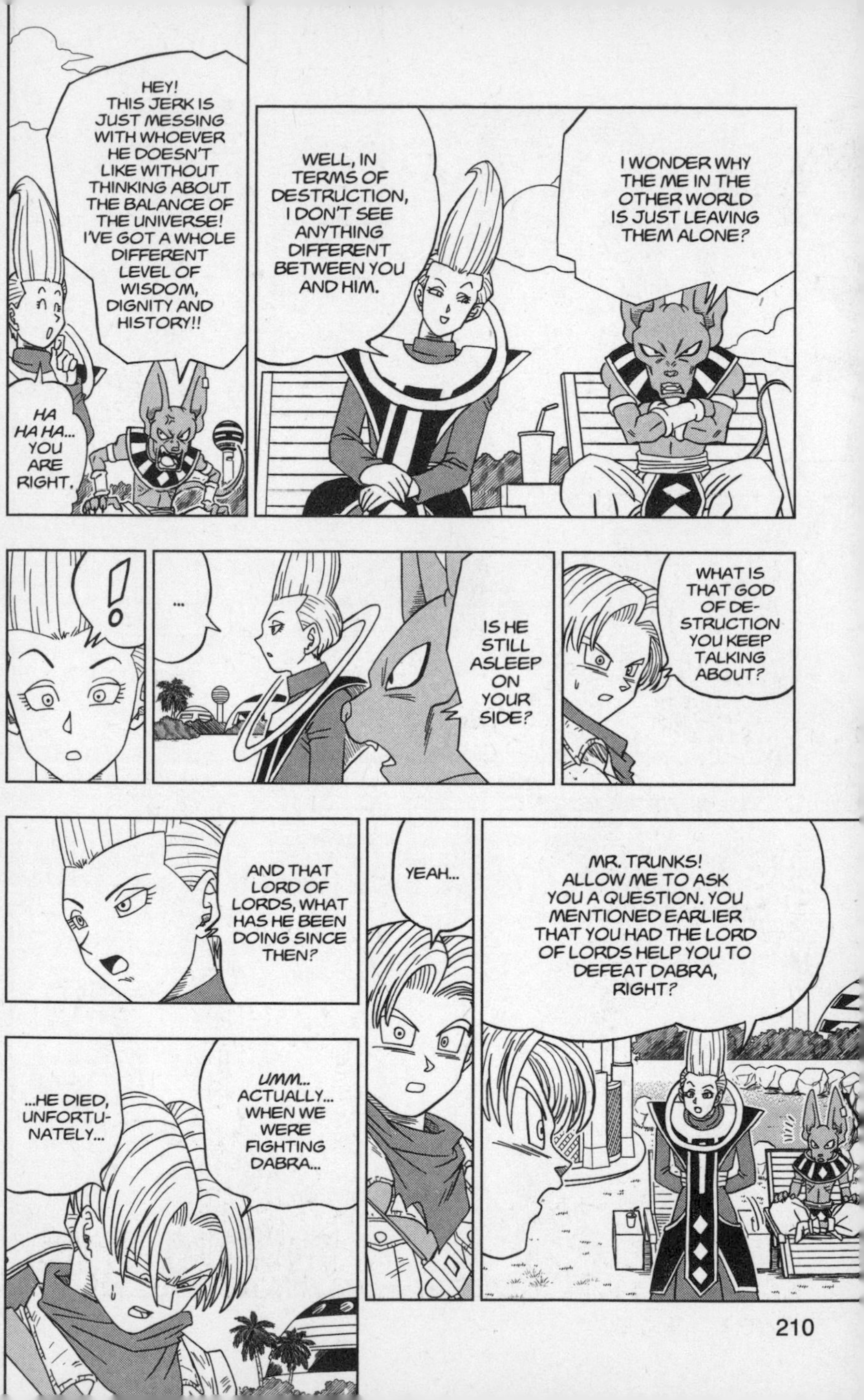
I WONDER WHY THE ME IN THE OTHER WORLD IS JUST LEAVING THEM ALONE?
WELL, IN TERMS OF DESTRUCTION, I DON'T SEE ANYTHING DIFFERENT BETWEEN YOU AND HIM.
HEY! THIS JERK IS JUST MESSING WITH WHOEVER HE DOESN'T LIKE WITHOUT THINKING ABOUT THE BALANCE OF THE UNIVERSE! I'VE GOT A WHOLE DIFFERENT LEVEL OF WISDOM, DIGNITY AND HISTORY!!
HA HA HA... YOU ARE RIGHT.
WHAT IS THAT GOD OF DE-STRUCTION YOU KEEP TALKING ABOUT?
IS HE STILL ASLEEP ON YOUR SIDE?
...
!
MR. TRUNKS! ALLOW ME TO ASK YOU A QUESTION. YOU MENTIONED EARLIER THAT YOU HAD THE LORD OF LORDS HELP YOU TO DEFEAT DABRA, RIGHT?
YEAH...
AND THAT LORD OF LORDS, WHAT HAS HE BEEN DOING SINCE THEN?
UMM... ACTUALLY... WHEN WE WERE FIGHTING DABRA...
...HE DIED, UNFORTU-NATELY...

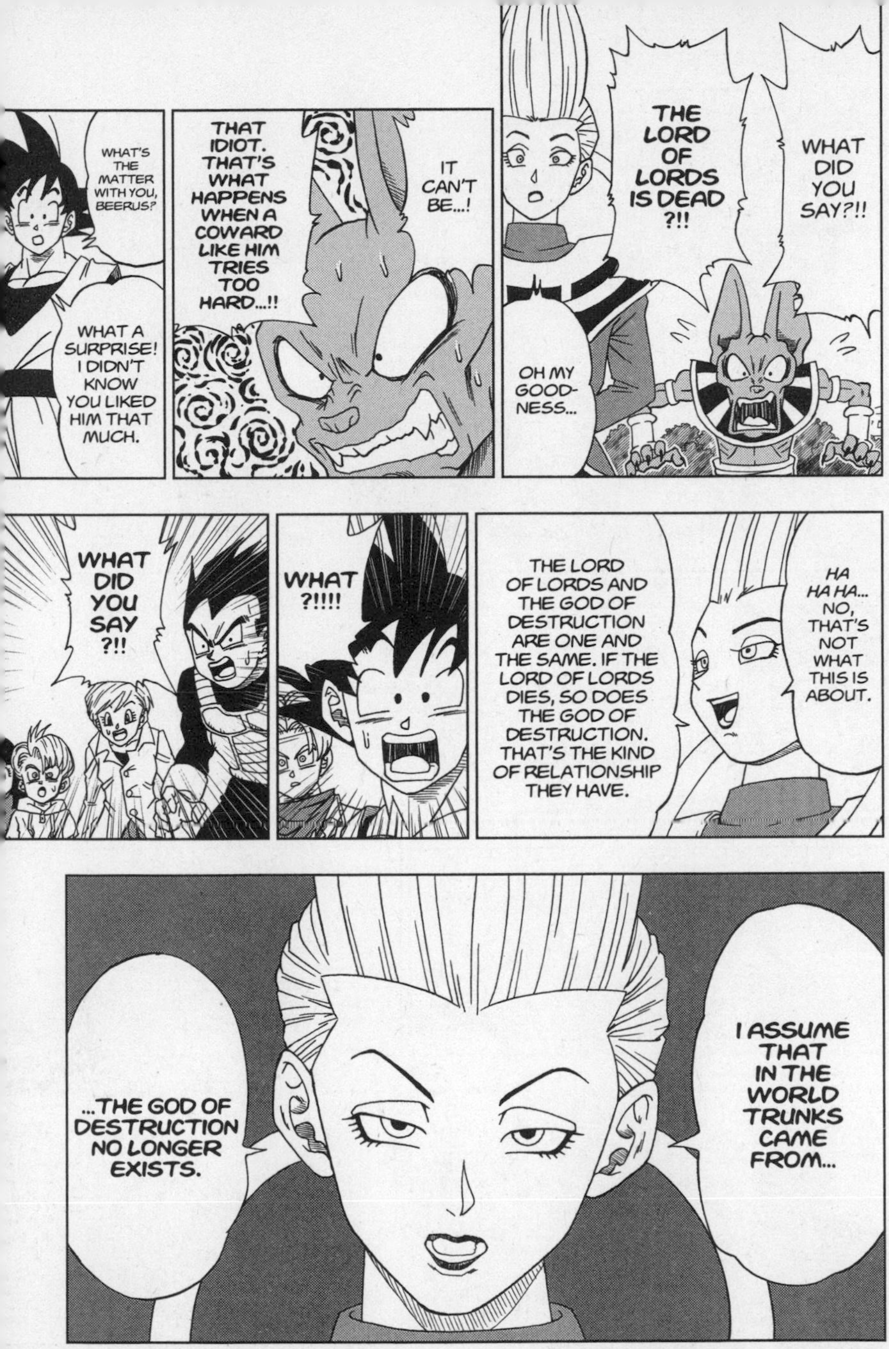
WHAT DID YOU SAY?!!
THE LORD OF LORDS IS DEAD ?!!
OH MY GOODNESS...
IT CAN'T BE...!
THAT IDIOT. THAT'S WHAT HAPPENS WHEN A COWARD LIKE HIM TRIES TOO HARD...!!
WHAT'S THE MATTER WITH YOU, BEERUS?
WHAT A SURPRISE! I DIDN'T KNOW YOU LIKED HIM THAT MUCH.
HA HA HA... NO, THAT'S NOT WHAT THIS IS ABOUT.
THE LORD OF LORDS AND THE GOD OF DESTRUCTION ARE ONE AND THE SAME. IF THE LORD OF LORDS DIES, SO DOES THE GOD OF DESTRUCTION. THAT'S THE KIND OF RELATIONSHIP THEY HAVE.
WHAT ?!!!!
WHAT DID YOU SAY ?!!
I ASSUME THAT IN THE WORLD TRUNKS CAME FROM...
...THE GOD OF DESTRUCTION NO LONGER EXISTS.

TO BE CONTINUED!

BONUS STORY

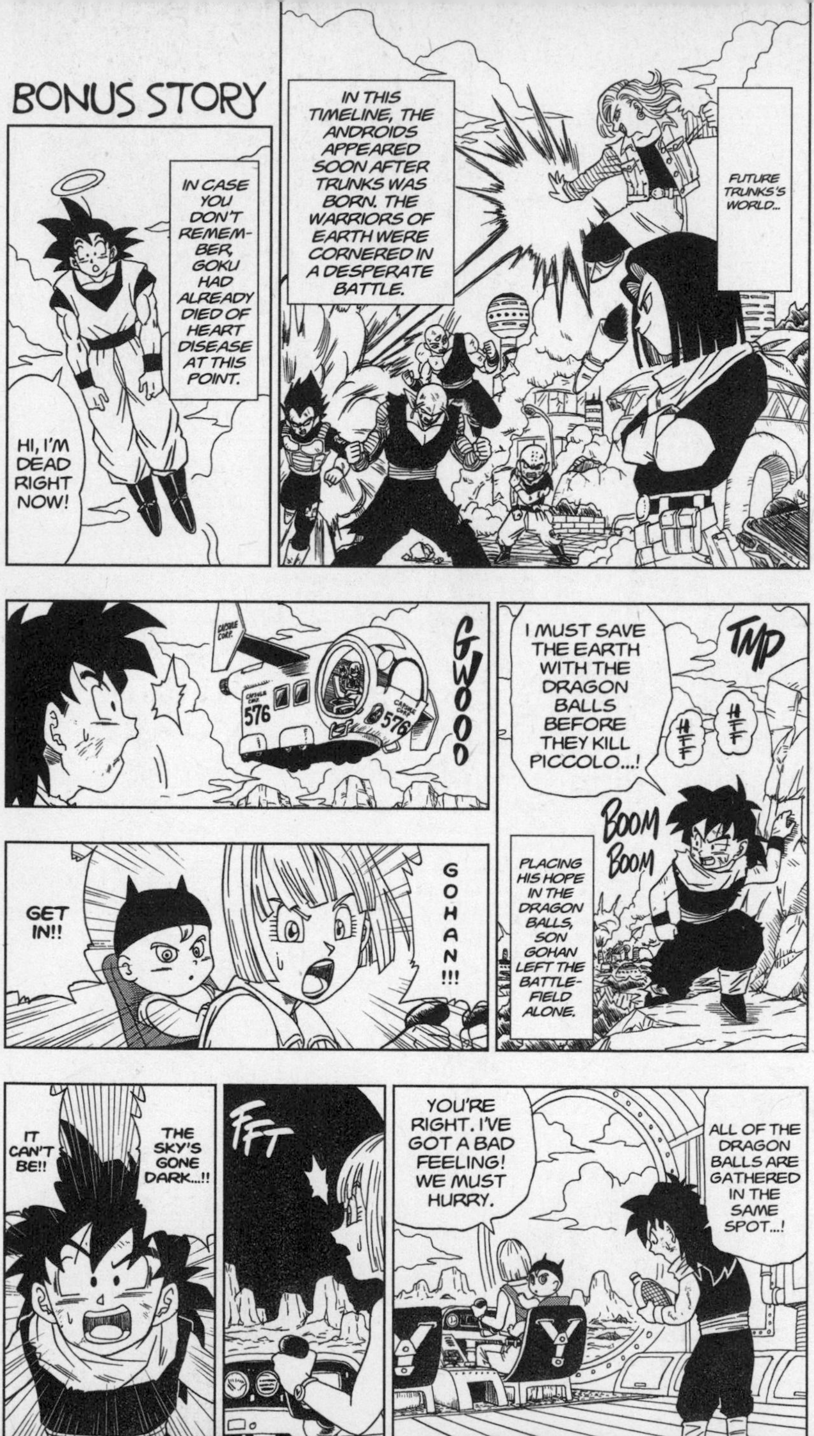
FUTURE TRUNKS'S WORLD...
IN THIS TIMELINE, THE ANDROIDS APPEARED SOON AFTER TRUNKS WAS BORN. THE WARRIORS OF EARTH WERE CORNERED IN A DESPERATE BATTLE.
IN CASE YOU DON'T REMEMBER, GOKU HAD ALREADY DIED OF HEART DISEASE AT THIS POINT.
HI, I'M DEAD RIGHT NOW!
TMP
I MUST SAVE THE EARTH WITH THE DRAGON BALLS BEFORE THEY KILL PICCOLO...!
HFF
HFF
BOOM BOOM
PLACING HIS HOPE IN THE DRAGON BALLS, SON GOHAN LEFT THE BATTLEFIELD ALONE.
GWOOOO
576
576
GOHAN!!!
GET IN!!
ALL OF THE DRAGON BALLS ARE GATHERED IN THE SAME SPOT...!
YOU'RE RIGHT. I'VE GOT A BAD FEELING! WE MUST HURRY.
FFT
THE SKY'S GONE DARK...!!
IT CAN'T BE!!

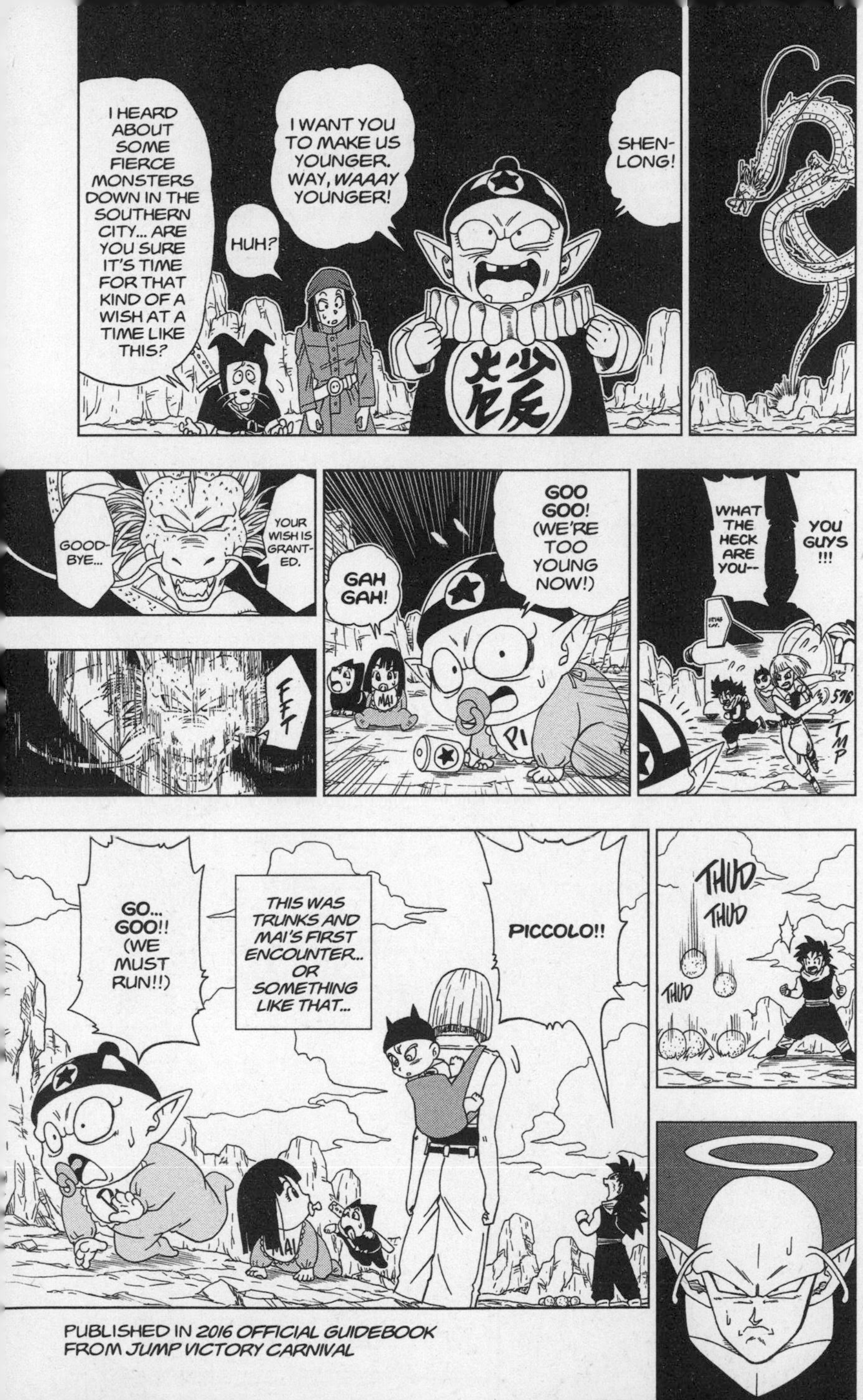
SHEN-LONG!
I WANT YOU TO MAKE US YOUNGER. WAY, WAAAY YOUNGER!
HUH?
I HEARD ABOUT SOME FIERCE MONSTERS DOWN IN THE SOUTHERN CITY... ARE YOU SURE IT'S TIME FOR THAT KIND OF A WISH AT A TIME LIKE THIS?
YOU GUYS!!!
WHAT THE HECK ARE YOU--
TMP
GOO GOO! (WE'RE TOO YOUNG NOW!)
GAH GAH!
PI
MAI
YOUR WISH IS GRANTED.
GOOD-BYE...
FFT
THUD
THUD
THUD
PICCOLO!!
THIS WAS TRUNKS AND MAI'S FIRST ENCOUNTER... OR SOMETHING LIKE THAT...
GO... GOO!! (WE MUST RUN!!)
MAI

PUBLISHED IN 2016 OFFICIAL GUIDEBOOK FROM JUMP VICTORY CARNIVAL

★★★ V JUMP Editorial Team Presents ★★★

TOYOTAROU SENSEI

SUPER DISSECTING THE BOOK!!!

ink

Toyotarou Sensei answers all our questions!!

When did you begin drawing manga?!

Back when I was in elementary school, I would sketch *Dragon Ball* characters in my notebooks without even realizing it. At that point, I was already making up imaginary *Dragon Ball* chapters in my head. The first story I ever came up with was Chaozu's arc.

TOYOTAROU GOES TO NY COMIC CONVENTION!!

NEW YORK COMIC CON

NY Comic Con is an anime comic and media convention held in New York every year. Toyotarou Sensei held autograph sessions. America has so many *Dragon Ball* fans!! Having interacted with many of them, Sensei reaffirmed his determination in what we could only call "a very sobering experience."

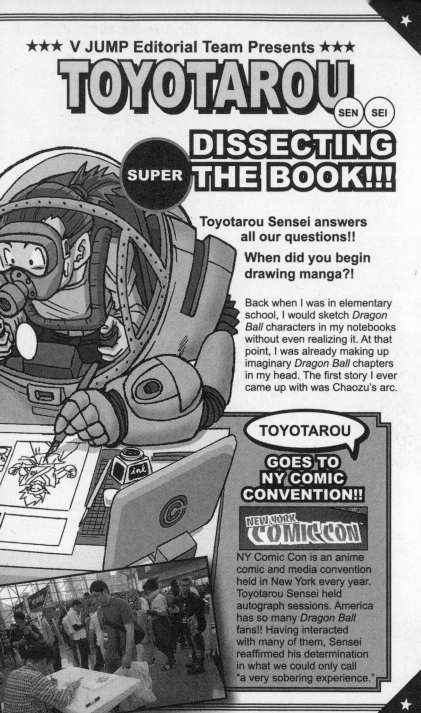

What kind of interactions do you have with Toriyama Sensei?!

I draw a rough draft based on original scripts from Toriyama Sensei. I pass it to the editor and Sensei and they review it. It's an honor to bring Sensei's imagination to life! Sometimes he'll send me a draft he drew instead and that's a big deal for me since it makes me both happy and a little sad.

A rough draft by Toyotarou Sensei. At this stage, the stars were smaller and there was no text.

WE'RE GONNA NEED RESTROOMS.

Who is the most difficult character to draw?!

I would say it's the new characters who first appeared in *Dragon Ball Super* such as Beerus and Whis, since there's no similar characters in the past who I could use for reference. Whis's eyes are especially difficult! It's a struggle. It's a new feature that no other characters in *Dragon Ball* have had before.

IT SEEMS LIKE MY EYES ARE HARD TO DRAW.

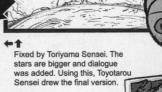

Fixed by Toriyama Sensei. The stars are bigger and dialogue was added. Using this, Toyotarou Sensei drew the final version.

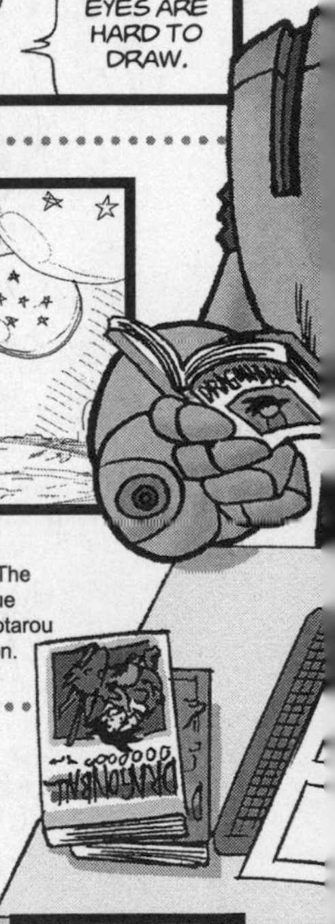

What's in store for the Future Trunks Arc and the story after that?!

HA !!!!

What?! Trunks's outfit is the same as the ones that the masters used to wear?!

The development of the Future Trunks Arc will be slightly different compared to the TV anime. After that... ...Everyone's long awaited promise will be fulfilled! That's Toriyama Sensei for you! He's always one step ahead of us! Stay tuned!!

TOYOTARO

The author picture for this volume has a hidden secret! It will be revealed next volume!!

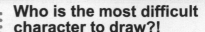

YOU'RE READING
THE WRONG WAY!

Dragon Ball Super reads from right to left, starting in the
upper-right corner. Japanese is read from right to left,
meaning that action, sound effects, and word-balloon
order are completely reversed from English order.